New Frontiers in Translation Studies

Series Editor

Defeng Li, Center for Studies of Translation, Interpreting and Cognition, University of Macau, Macao SAR, China

Translation Studies as a discipline has witnessed the fastest growth in the last 40 years. With translation becoming increasingly more important in today's glocalized world, some have even observed a general translational turn in humanities in recent years. The New Frontiers in Translation Studies aims to capture the newest developments in translation studies, with a focus on:

- Translation Studies research methodology, an area of growing interest amongst translation students and teachers;
- Data-based empirical translation studies, a strong point of growth for the discipline because of the scientific nature of the quantitative and/or qualitative methods adopted in the investigations; and Asian translation thoughts and theories, to complement the current Eurocentric translation studies.

Submission and Peer Review:

The editor welcomes book proposals from experienced scholars as well as young aspiring researchers. Please send a short description of 500 words to the editor Prof. Defeng Li at Springernfits@gmail.com and Springer Senior Publishing Editor Rebecca Zhu: Rebecca.zhu@springernature.com. All proposals will undergo peer review to permit an initial evaluation. If accepted, the final manuscript will be peer reviewed internally by the series editor as well as externally (single blind) by Springer ahead of acceptance and publication.

Yuhong Peng · Huihui Huang · Defeng Li
Editors

New Advances in Translation Technology

Applications and Pedagogy

Springer

Editors
Yuhong Peng
BNU-HKBU
United International College
Zhuhai, China

Huihui Huang
School of Foreign Languages
Henan University of Technology
Zhengzhou, China

Defeng Li
Faculty of Arts and Humanities
University of Macao
Taipa, Macau, China

ISSN 2197-8689 ISSN 2197-8697 (electronic)
New Frontiers in Translation Studies
ISBN 978-981-97-2957-9 ISBN 978-981-97-2958-6 (eBook)
https://doi.org/10.1007/978-981-97-2958-6

This Springer imprint is published by the registered company Springer Nature Singapore Pte Ltd.
The registered company address is: 152 Beach Road, #21-01/04 Gateway East, Singapore 189721, Singapore

Contents

Pedagogy and Students' Feedback on Translation Technology

Introduction: Charting the Future of Translation Technology

Yuhong Peng

Abstract The introductory chapter introduces new advances in translation technologies within the context of artificial intelligence. It divides the contributing chapters into two parts and provides a summary of the main themes of each chapter. Through this structure, readers are given an overview of the diverse perspectives and insights offered by scholars and researchers in the field, setting the stage for further exploration of the evolving landscape of translation technologies.

In recent years, the field of translation has undergone a revolutionary transformation with the advent of new advances in translation technologies. This has been a result of significant breakthroughs in various areas, most notably in the development of generative AI. The rapid progress of technology has paved the way for exciting possibilities that have forever changed the landscape of translation (Eszenyi et al. 2023).

Throughout history, translation has played a crucial role in bridging the linguistic and cultural divide that separates our interconnected world. From ancient scribes meticulously translating texts by hand to the emergence of computer-assisted translation tools, each advancement has brought us closer to the goal of effective cross-cultural communication. It can be said that the recent development in generative AI has truly captured the imagination of both researchers and practitioners alike, and reshaped translation as practice, profession and consequently as training and education.

To capture recent advances in translation technologies and their impact on the practice, profession, and training in diverse social and cultural contexts, we have invited distinguished scholars and researchers from around the world to contribute their latest projects. By bringing together the expertise of these professionals, we aim to present a holistic overview of translation technologies and their implications. This edited volume analyzes the innovative approaches undertaken by the contributors,

Y. Peng (✉)
Shandong University & Beijing Normal University-Hong Kong Baptist University United International College (UIC), China
e-mail: amandayhpeng@uic.edu.cn

Y. Peng et al. (eds.), *New Advances in Translation Technology*, New Frontiers in Translation Studies, https://doi.org/10.1007/978-981-97-2958-6_1

offering valuable insights for both experienced practitioners and newcomers to the field.

The first part of the book focuses on the **rise and application of translation technology**. Each of the seven chapters provides invaluable insights into specific aspects of translation technology. Experts from around the world contribute their perspectives, shared experiences, and groundbreaking research, creating a dynamic tapestry of knowledge that invites readers to deepen their understanding in translation technology. ***Mustafa*** delves into the ideological origins of machine translation, focusing on the 1954 Georgetown experiment, an event often tied more to political showmanship than linguistic accuracy. It critiques the notion that early MT was a failure, suggesting its success lay in fulfilling ideological objectives. The chapter draws parallels with modern military translation technologies post-9/11, arguing they serve as symbols of power and maintain cultural hierarchies. In this way technological advancements in translation is linked to broader themes in translation studies, especially after the so-called cultural turn (Wang 2023).

Siu takes us right to the heart of neural machine translation (NMT) and large language models (LLMs), the twin powerhouses propelling the translation industry and translation technology forward. Grounded in the latest deep learning techniques and the transformative Transformer model, this chapter presents a candid examination of their impressive capabilities and the hurdles yet to be overcome. With an eye towards practical application, the chapter imparts valuable guidance for educators and developers, aimed at maximizing AI's potential for translation.

One noticeable development in translation technology is the integration of cloud-based technologies in media localization. Cloud solutions have transformed collaboration and mobility, enabling distributed work and agile development. ***BOLAÑOS and GARCÍA-ESCRIBANO*** evaluate the transformative role of cloud technology in reshaping translator education, with a focus on practices like subtitling and revoicing; strategies are provided for utilizing these tools in training in order to ensure students are proficient in state-of-the-art platforms. The insightful discussions highlight how cloud technologies are revolutionizing workflows in media localization, offering flexibility and scalability for stakeholders. This chapter examines the wide-reaching influence of cloud technologies in translation studies and education, and stress their potential to revolutionize pedagogical approaches in media localization training.

Along similar lines, ***Sandrelli*** points out that cloud-based tools have transformed localisation workflows, enabling virtual teams to collaborate globally in real-time. Innovations like automatic speech recognition (ASR) and machine translation (MT) are increasingly integrated into audiovisual translation to expedite processes, leading to new professional roles and challenges. This chapter discusses results from the ¡Sub!: Localisation Workflows that Work (2020–2021) and its follow-up ¡Sub!2 (2021–2022) projects by Università degli Studi Internazionali di Roma and Roehampton University. It presents effective cloud subtitling workflows combining human expertise with technology.

Roser also examines the issue of how human translators coexist with advancing tools such as machine translation (MT), artificial intelligence (AI), and cloud-based solutions. She argues that despite a technologically rich landscape, human expertise remains essential, especially for tasks like MT training and data curation. She further points out that human translation and MT post-editing will emerge as top services, even as the market adapts to new tools and methodologies.

Ayvazyan, Torres-Simón and ***Pym*** raise the question we all wonder—what kind of translation literacy will be automation resistant. Employing data from the O*Net database to discern the skills and knowledge within the translation field most susceptible to automation, the authors project which competencies are likely to remain impervious to the encroachment of such technology. In a sense, this chapter may serve as a prospective guide for shaping a future where translators harmonize their unique human language and translation skills with the inexorable march of technological progress.

The magical interplay between language and technology takes center stage in the chapter by ***Lefever*** and ***Terryn*** on computational terminology. Their chapter demystifies the processes behind automatic terminology extraction and the integration of domain-specific vocabulary into neural machine translation, highlighting both their remarkable advancements and current limitations. The chapter concludes with an invaluable resource guide, comprising a curated list of tools for both the seasoned professional and the curious novice.

The second part of the book opens with a call from ***Bowker*** to adopt plain language in both writing and translation in the age of machine translation. She argues that blending the clarity-focused principles of plain language with the advanced capabilities of Neural Machine Translation (NMT) can yield superior outcomes. Through a detailed comparison of plain language and NMT writing guidelines, she made clear the remarkable compatibility, laying the foundation for a unified strategy that fosters content that is both accessible to readers and optimized for machine translation. The chapter underscores the need for translation education to encompass plain language proficiency, preparing the next wave of language professionals to meet and shape the demands of a changing industry.

Pastor and Alcaide-Martínez approach translation technology from another angle: help students acquire Artificial Intelligence (AI) terminology to empower them in their learning of translation in the era of AI. They delve right into the evolving landscape of Artificial Intelligence (AI) and its intricate terminology, which has become a linguistic challenge in the realm of specialized translation. Emphasizing the urgency for translators to competently navigate the AI lexicon, the authors propose an innovative, technology-assisted methodology to equip translation students with the mastery of AI-specific terminology. Through a pioneering corpus-based gamification approach, they detail a structured four-phase protocol aimed at bolstering the learning experience. The efficacy of the methodology is finally scrutinized via a pilot study with translation undergraduates at the University of Malaga, Spain, combining practical translation exercises with insightful quantitative and qualitative feedback mechanisms.

In a landscape dominated by rapid technological advancement, ***Pym, Hao and Ayvazyan*** confront the surge of AI in the translation industry and its pedagogical implications. The emergence of AI text generation tools has dramatically shifted our understanding of stable knowledge and skills within the field. To meet these educational challenges, the authors advocate for student-led discovery activities that prime a critical, comparative lens on translation technologies. Describing 18 group exercises, the authors chart a course for dynamic, exploratory learning. Students are prompted to draw their own inferences from activities that range from analyzing AI-assisted translation and post-editing to exploring literary translation and the broader societal impacts of these advancements. This chapter presents a critical pedagogy aimed at fostering adaptable, resilient translators equipped with a profound grasp of the capabilities and drawbacks of contemporary translation technologies.

Professional translators often express dissatisfaction with translation tools, particularly concerning machine translation (MT) integration. ***Daems*** shares his attempt to address this issue by incorporating Lilt, an adaptive, interactive MT system, into a postgraduate course on machine translation and post-editing starting in 2019. He analyzes student reflections from four academic years, evaluating Lilt's adaptivity, interactivity, and comparing the performance of a generic Lilt model versus one trained on a specific translation memory. The rich insights into the effectiveness and impact of translation technology in educational settings provide practical guidance for educators and administrators seeking to enhance their translation programs.

Amidst the advancements in translation technology, many translation teachers insist on the value of human intuition, particularly in literary translation. ***Hao, Hu and Pym*** take up the issue by examining 141 students engaging with translations of Agatha Christie's texts. The study differentiates between the approaches of post-editing machine translations and translating from scratch. It is found that post-editors were found to lean on machine outputs in uncertain scenarios—a strategy termed 'risk transfer'—while from-scratch translators exhibited a predilection for 'risk-taking.' Such an insightful analysis of the comparative efficacy and the distinct challenges inherent in post-editing versus traditional translation contributes to a critical perspective to the ongoing dialogue on the future landscape of translation practice.

In this volume, we bring together the diverse threads and issues of translation technologies woven therein while trying to offer a glimpse into the future of translation technology, particularly with artificial intelligence such as sophisticated large language models like Chatgpt. By summarizing the key insights and current developments in the area, we paint a comprehensive picture of the imminent opportunities that unfold. Ultimately, this book is to serve as a useful resource for anyone interested in grasping the present state and future potential of translation technology in the era of AI. Practitioners, researchers, educators, and students alike will find valuable insights and practical applications within these pages. We extend our heartfelt gratitude to all the contributors who have shared their expertise and research, making this volume a testament to collective knowledge and collaboration. Let us embark on this journey together, embracing the boundless opportunities that the latest advancements in translation technology present, while also preparing to meet the challenges that lie ahead.

References

Eszenyi, R., K. Bednarova-Gibova, and R. Edina. 2023. Artificial intelligence, machine translation & cyborg translators: a clash of utopian and dystopian visions. *Orbis Linguarum.* 21 (2): 102–113.

Wang, N. 2023. *The cultural turn in translation studies.* UK: Routledge.

Note: Chatgpt has been used to enhance the language.

Rise and Application of Translation Technology

The Rise of Translation Technology and Its Historical and Continued Symbiotic Relationship to the Pursuit of Ideological Power

Burcin Kagan Mustafa

Abstract The evolution and widespread adoption of translation technology, including computer-aided translation (CAT) tools and machine translation (MT), has increased, and diversified cross-border communication and has altered the very idea of what it means to translate. However, the genesis of these digital technologies did not emerge from a desire to improve human communication but was tethered to the political undercurrents of the 1950s and relied on rudimentary conceptualizations of language and translation. In this context, this chapter explores the ideological drivers of the early MT developments in the US and specifically focuses on the 1954 Georgetown experiment, the first working demonstration of MT. It will be argued that the experiment was more about projecting ideological power than revealing the ability of computers of the period to translate. Moreover, by analysing this historical event the chapter emphasizes the symbiotic relationships that exist between translation and ideological ambitions. Furthermore, from this perspective, it will be contended that these early MT developments were not a failure as they are typically described but a success because they produced ideologically conducive results. In addition, parallels will be drawn with more recent technological developments following the global war on terrorism. It will be shown that this period drove translation technologies that not only combated external threats but also infringed on the liberties of American citizens. Also, focus will be given to the development of handheld translation devices used in theatres of war. In this regard, it will be suggested that the representation of these technologies in popular culture not only acts as symbols of power but also represents ingrained cultural hierarchies, which relate to core themes discussed in Translation Studies following its cultural turn.

B. K. Mustafa (✉)
Prince Sultan University, Riyadh, Saudi Arabia
e-mail: bkmustafa@psu.edu.sa

Y. Peng et al. (eds.), *New Advances in Translation Technology*, New Frontiers in Translation Studies, https://doi.org/10.1007/978-981-97-2958-6_2

1 Introduction

The widespread adoption of computer-aided translation (CAT) tools and the increased presence of machine translation (MT) have in many ways altered the landscape of practical translation. On one end of the spectrum, they have allowed the individual freelance translator to compete in the global market and increase their workflow. On the other end, MT has facilitated translation projects of large and powerful political institutions such as the EU and has allowed private companies such as Google to establish new forms of cross-border communication for its users. However, far removed from these apparent uses of translation technology its development has its genealogy inextricably linked to the pursuit of ideological power. Consequently, exploring this aspect of translation technology is relevant to research that emerged from the cultural turn in Translation Studies. This is because research in this area focuses on how extralinguistic forces such as ideological power affect the formulations and usages of translations, and this chapter investigates how ideological power drove technologies that have and are continuing to change the way translations are produced. To this end, technological developments will be investigated in two different historical periods, the Cold War and the Global War on Terrorism (GWoT), which are connected by the notion of the long war a '… sort of zero-sum, global-scale, generational struggle against anti-liberal ideological extremists who want to rule the world' (Buzan, 2006, p. 1101). Firstly, the embryonic developments that occurred during the Cold War will be investigated and it will be demonstrated that not only were the first translation technological endeavours, such as the 1954 Georgetown experiment, affected by ideological power but rather their very inception was instigated by it. This discussion will lead to a less obvious hypothesis about this earlier period of MT: it will be suggested that the Georgetown experiment had more to do with projecting US power than developing a working MT system. Secondly, the GWoT era will be focused on, and it will be illustrated that like the early MT endeavours, conflict and the pursuit of ideological goals produced translation technologies. However, it will be argued that beyond these similarities, the post-9/11 translation technologies relate to not only combating external threats but were part of an ideological shift in the US that infringed the personal liberties of its citizens.

2 Translation Technology's Absence in Translation Studies

Considering this chapter will grapple with the ideological underpinnings of translation technology, a good point to start is to highlight the underrepresentation of translation technology in Translation Studies. This is because many of the observations, theories and normative approaches that have been formulated have ignored the technological turns in the practice of translation, and thus, they are based on a model of translation that has not changed since James Holmes (2000) seminal paper first published in 1972, *The name and nature of translation studies*. For example, the many discussions and debates (e.g. Kenny, 2009) concerning equivalence have not seen a reappraisal since the event of the professional use of translation memories, which function on the premise that there is absolute equivalence in meaning between source text (ST) and target text (TT) segments. Also, representative of the scarcity of translation technology in the field is the limited specific scholarly publications on translation technology the most recent being O'Hagan's (2020) edited book, *The Routledge Handbook of Translation and Technology*. Also, the main translation technology textbooks such as Austermühl (2014 (first published in 2001)), Bowker (2002) and Quah (2006) that are more accessible to students of translation technology are in many ways outdated. For instance, an issue discussed in Austermühl (2014) are the problems associated with 56k modems. In addition, within the context of general Translation Studies textbooks, translation technology only has a cursory mention. For example, Munday et al. (2022) in their textbook, *Introducing Translation Studies: Theories and Applications*, only offer a basic description of CAT tools and MT without a theoretical engagement of how they have radically changed the very practice of translation. This level of interaction in Translation Studies is not reflective of the impact CAT tools have had on the practice of translation. For example, Tabor (2019) reports that 88% of just over 3000 respondents to a Proz survey use at least one CAT tool to undertake some of their translation jobs. Similarly, in 2020, a large-scale survey of translators and interpreters, which was conducted by Pielmeier and O'Mara (2020), revealed that 66% of the 7,363 participants who completed the survey considered translation memory or computer-aided translation to be the main translation technology they use for client projects. This level of reliance on technology in the professional realm is best summed up by Sin-wai (2015) who asserts that:

> Translators have to work with the help of translation technology. The use of computer-aided translation tools has actually been extended to almost every type of translation work. Computer-aided translation tools are aimed at supporting translators and not at replacing them… Translation competence or knowledge and skills in languages are not enough today. It is more realistic to talk about professional competence, which includes linguistic competence, cultural competence, translation competence, translator competence, and technological competence. (p. 45)

Translation technology is now a part of the very fabric of professional translation, and thus, discussions that aim to explore the forces that mould translation should reflect technology's impact.

3 Making Sense of Translation Technology

In extremely broad terms translation technology is any technological advancement that aids the translation process. The pen, the dictionary and the printing press can be all considered as technologies that have affected translation at various points in history. From this perspective translation aids are in a continual state of flux; consequently, what is presently considered to be a new technology will eventually become outdated and replaced by another development. For example, the introduction of printed dictionaries at one point was a technological advancement which affected the translation process. Bobrick (2003) Query argues 'the general climate of the Reformation and the new technology of the printing press meant that Bible translations dominated book production' (as cited in Munday et al. 2022, p. 32). However, in terms of defining translation technology, there is disagreement, and the terms are problematic. For example, Somers (2003) explains that 'the most widespread term, "Machine Translation", is felt by many to be misleading (who calls a computer a "machine" these days?) and unhelpful. But no really good alternative has presented itself' (p. 1). Austermühl (2014) refers to translation technological developments as electronic tools; for example, he asserts that 'when reading this book, please bear in mind that the term "electronic translation tools" does not refer exclusively to machine translation (MT)' (p. 1), and he continues to explain that the term encompasses all electronic based aids that assist translation. Quah (2006) uses the term 'Translation Technology' in relation to a multitude of computer-based translation aids including, Machine Translation (MT), Machine-Aided Human Translation (MAHT), Human-Aided Machine Translation (HAMT), Computer-Aided Translation (CAT), Machine-Assisted Translation (MAT) and Fully Automated High-Quality (Machine) Translation (FAHQMT). Bowker (2002) uses the term CAT technology as the title of her book; however, its application also encompasses supplementary technological aids such as Optical Character Recognition (OCR) software, corpus tools, terminology management systems and Translation Memory (TM) systems, but excludes MT.

Taking these various aspects into consideration, translation technology can be defined by separating it into two categories: (1) General translation technologies: this category encompasses technologies which have been adapted and employed for translation but were not specifically designed to aid it. These include word-processing tools, digital corpora, digital dictionaries, internet search engines and OCR systems. (2) Specific translation technologies: this category relates to technologies developed for translation such as MT and CAT tools. At this juncture, it is important to explain that the main conceptual difference between them is that with MT the computer is the primary translator and the human aids the computer through post-editing, while with CAT tools the human is the primary translator and is aided by the computer. However, this historical demarcation is almost redundant because modern CAT tools now use MT to generate target text segments when TM matches are not available.

4 The Main Architects of the First Western MT Developments

A relevant starting point in the discussion on the development of MT, which focuses on the Western perspective, and its interaction with ideology and power is to describe the history of its two main architects, Warren Weaver and Léon Dostert whose lives were affected by the same ideologically led global events, World War One and World

War Two. Warren Weaver was born in 1894 in Wisconsin to a German family. He initially set out to study civil engineering in 1912 but switched to differential calculus and probability (Hutchins, 2000). After the US declared war on Germany in 1917, Weaver was eager to join the war effort and eventually did in 1918 and served as a second lieutenant for the Army's Air Service (Weaver, 1970). He returned to academia in 1920 and assumed various roles at the University of Wisconsin including assistant professor, associate professor, professor and Chairman of the Department of Mathematics. In 1931, he gained the directorship of the Natural Science Division of the Rockefeller Foundation, a position he would hold for 27 years (Hutchins, 2000). During the Second World War, he became a member of the Office of Scientific Research and Development, which was headed by Vannevar Bush, and he worked on fire control that '… refers to all the devices and procedures used to assure that any "projectile" (a shell fired from an anti-aircraft gun, a bomb dropped from an airplane, or a torpedo launched against a ship) will in fact hit the desired target' (Weaver, 1970, pp. 77–78). During his World War Two service, he spent time in the UK, met many English scientists and experienced firsthand the bombing of London. It was also during this period of his life that he was exposed to the power of computers, Weaver (1970) notes:

> … during the war it became evident that we were going to have electronic computers of unprecedented speed and logical flexibility, and with 'memory' organs wherein vast amounts of information could be stored, any item of which could be made available to the computer in a fraction of a second (p. 104).

Léon Dostert was born in 1904 in Longwy, a French village, which was seized by German soldiers during World War One. This event led him to learn German and then English after his village was liberated by American soldiers who also sponsored him to study in the US. After his primary and secondary education, he gained a Bachelor of Science from Georgetown University and then a master's degree. Eventually, he was appointed as a Professor of French at Georgetown University. Following the start of the Second World War and the German occupation of France, Dostert still as a French citizen served as an attaché at the French Embassy. He eventually became a US citizen and after Pearl Harbor became a Major in the US Army where he served several roles including being an interpreter for General Dwight Eisenhower (Gordin 2015). After the war, his language skills led him to be appointed to organize simultaneous interpretation for the Nuremberg war crime trials. Gordin (2015) relates a story that it was Dostert who introduced the practice of using booths and headsets to assist interpreters, which he also introduced to the UN. He returned to Georgetown University in 1949 where Gordin (2015) argues that he '… published little (essentially nothing in linguistics) but organized a great deal; most of his efforts were directed to either technological or institutional modernization of language instruction' (p. 231). Demonstrative of his ingenuity, Dostert produced a device, a 'binaural apparatus for teaching languages', to help in the learning of a second language. MacDonald (1967) explains that 'with the aid of this machine, a student can have available for listening two synchronized texts, one in the language he is studying, at one ear, and the other in a language he knows, at the other ear' (p. 11).

5 The Assumptions Underlying the Drive Towards Fully Automated High-Quality Translation (FAHQT)

The Georgetown experiment, which was the first demonstration of a working MT, relied on rudimentary assumptions surrounding language and translation. The basis of these early assumptions revolved around the idea that language can be treated similar to mathematical problems. Also, during the 1940s, computers were being used to solve complex mathematical equations beyond human capability and it was postulated that machines should be therefore able to solve 'simpler' language-based problems. For example, Rafael (2016) suggests that breakthroughs in cryptanalysis:

> … guided the early development of machine translation. Cryptanalysis regards foreign languages as if they were secret codes whose surfaces can be broken to bring forth hidden messages in the form of statistically arranged patterns. Such mathematical patterns are believed to be evidence of 'linguistic universals' supposedly buried in all languages (p. 126).

A pioneer of the idea to use computers for translation, which was based on his exposure to computers during the Second World War, was Warren Weaver who in 1949 produced a memorandum calling to his idea. Weaver (1949) explained in the memorandum how codes embedded in a language can be deciphered without the cryptographer knowing the language and he supposed that:

> … in the manifold instances in which man has invented and developed languages, there are certain invariant properties which are, again not precisely but to some statistically useful degree, common to all languages (p. 2).

Based on this understanding of language he hypothesized that computers could be used for translation. Weaver found support for his assumptions from Dr Andrew Booth (1948), a specialist in computer design, who asserts, 'we have considered this problem in some detail and it transpires that a machine of the type envisaged could perform this function without any modification in its design' (as cited in Weaver, 1949, p. 6). Eventually, the spark in interest Weaver started led to the first MT conference in 1952 held at the Massachusetts Institute of Technology (MIT). It was funded by the Rockefeller Foundation and organized by Yehoshua Bar-Hillel who worked on MT research in MIT's Research Laboratory for Electronics. Moreover, the conference was pivotal in advancing MT research and development because it brought together several specialists, including Léon Dostert from Georgetown University, to discuss the feasibility of using computers to translate (Hutchins, 1997).

6 The Ideological Significance of Language Choice

The choice of language pairs and the direction of translation, Russian to English, used in the Georgetown experiment, the very first demonstration of a working MT system was not an arbitrary decision. Rather from the initial stages the MT system had been specifically developed using the IBM 701 and many of the program rules were unique to produce translations from Russian to English (Garvin, 1967). Moreover, an immediate benefit of the language pairs can be seen in the attention the Georgetown experiment gained in the media and the subsequent funding MT projects received. This is because the experiment took place in January 1954 in the backdrop of the Cold War and almost coincided with the launch of the world's first nuclear-powered submarine, the USS Nautilus (SSN-571). At such a critical moment both these technological based advancements had the potential in varying degrees to disrupt the balance of power and heighten tensions between the US and the USSR. Thus, there was significant sociopolitical currency in selecting Russian as the ST language. Hutchins (2006) argues that:

> For obvious political reasons Dostert decided that the demonstration should translate from Russian into English. Since the end of the War, the enemy was no longer German but Russian, and the lack of knowledge about activities in the Soviet Union was already a matter of major concern (p. 3).

In addition, another relevant factor to note is that even if there was no direct governmental influence over language choice, academics and scientists would have still been influenced by the ideological ambitions of the state by the allure of research grants. For example, Montgomery (2000) explains that while working on another translation project in the same period with Paul Garvin, who was a Russian linguist on the Georgetown experiment, they had discovered the funding for their research was to end unless they could provide the US Air Force with a strong justification. To accommodate this, Montgomery (2000) suggested to the research team to use examples from '… *Pravda* [a Russian political newspaper] article describing the first press interview of a couple of DoD code clerks who had defected to the Soviet Union …' (p. 106). Consequently, the continuation of their research funding was granted. This example, at least in the development of the first MT systems, demonstrates that academics, researchers and scientists aware of the sociopolitical climate can exploit it to be better positioned to gain government funding.

7 'We Transmit Thoughts by Means of Speech': The Georgetown Experiment

The 1954 Georgetown University MT experiment led by the interest generated by the 1952 conference was a manifestation of Weaver's memorandum as it tested his idea that computers could be used for translation the same way they were employed for code breaking. Dostert headed the experiment while Paul Garvin, who was also from Georgetown University, and Peter Sheridan from IBM programmed IBM's newly developed 701 computer to undertake translation tasks (Hutchins, 1997). The demonstration itself involved the apparent translation of 60 sentences from Russian to English covering a variety of subjects including science, politics and law. The operator fed a punch card with the Russian text and the machine ejected a card with an English translation requiring no post editing. The first translated sentence was 'we transmit thoughts by means of speech'. This process and its presentation in the media gave the impression that the 701 analysed the sentence, derived meaning, and then reformulated the same meaning in English, similar to how humans translate. For example, it was reported in the *New York Herald Tribune* on the 8 January 1954 that:

> A huge electric 'brain' with a 250-word vocabulary translated mouth-filling Russian sentences yesterday into simple English in less than ten seconds. As lights flashed and motors whirred inside the 'brain' the instrument's automatic type-writer swiftly translated statements on politics, law, science and military affairs. Once the Russian words were fed to the machine no human mind intervened (as cited in Hutchins 1997, p. 240).

However, the reports did not mention any independent assessments of the quality of the translations by Russian linguists; rather they assumed that what they were being told was accurate. Furthermore, a detailed explanation was not given of exactly how the 701 was able to undertake this extremely complex task, which included producing grammatically correct Russian sentences across a variety of different subjects. Even according to modern standards, the translations produced by MT which require little to no post-editing systems, have been developed for a specific field with a controlled vocabulary. Overall, the details of how the 701 achieved this were either not mentioned or ambiguous descriptions were given. For example, in the *New York Times* on it was stated that:

> In translating, for instance, a word 'A' which precedes a word 'B' in Russian, may be reversed in some cases in English. Each of the 250 words is coded for this inversion. Sometimes words must be inserted in the English text, sometimes they must be omitted, following code instructions. When there are several possible English meanings for a Russian word, the instructions tell the machine to pick out the meaning that best fits the context (as cited in Hutchins 2006, p.8).

A crucial element of this description is that it suggests the computer had the ability to 'pick out the meaning that best fits the context'. How was it able to determine meaning? How was it able to understand the context of the text and apply this to determining meaning? None of these points were clarified, but nevertheless, the reputed results installed high expectations for the future of MT. Hutchins (2006) argues that:

> A persistent and unfortunate effect of the demonstration was the impression given to many observers outside the field of MT that fully automatic translation of good quality was much closer than in fact the case. It was an impression which was to last—in the minds of the general public and indeed with computer scientists outside the MT filed [sic]—for many years (p. 28).

8 Benefits of the Georgetown Experiment

The Georgetown experiment presented a tangible working prototype of MT which had immediate sociopolitical benefits; in terms of American society, the newspaper reports of the experiment gave the public the image that their government could not only intercept Russian communiqués but also almost instantly understand them with the use of this technology. Similarly, it can be postulated that the claims of this experiment would have had an indirect effect on the Soviet Union in that they were led to believe that the US possessed the power to instantly translate whatever they wrote and could be accessed by the US. Beyond the sociopolitical benefits, the project led to additional government funding, especially in the short period after the experiment. For example, The Defense Advanced Research Projects Agency (DARPA) was created in 1957 by the US government in response to the USSR's technological advancements. DARPA served to monitor Soviet technological developments and produce its own that could give the US an advantage in both hot and cold conflicts. In its mission statement, it declares:

> The genesis of that mission and of DARPA itself dates to the launch of Sputnik in 1957, and a commitment by the United States that, from that time forward, it would be the initiator and not the victim of strategic technological surprises. Working with innovators inside and outside of government, DARPA has repeatedly delivered on that mission, transforming revolutionary concepts and even seeming impossibilities into practical capabilities. (DARPA, n.d., para. 2)

Also, Vasconcellos (2000) explains 'at the time, post-sputnik fever was at its height. The U.S. government had been caught short, and one of its priorities was to step up its monitoring of scientific and technical literature in Russian' (p. 94). Also, Kotz (1966) suggests that even though the race between the USSR and the USA to produce MT was not as important as the space race '… the first country to satisfactorily solve the problem of automated translation even for a specific pair of languages will enjoy a great boost in national achievement …' (p. 592).

9 Assessing the Viability of the Georgetown Experiment's Claims

The ability to extract meaning from one language and reproduce it in another is a complex and multi-layered cognitive process that extends beyond systematic and predictable linguistic formulas (Gile 2009). In essence, this process is intertwined with the thinking process and requires the same inference skills to write a story and comprehend a story. Thus, on this basis the notion that a 'machine' was able to mimic this process in 1954 is questionable. Furthermore, current MT systems of various types produce translations through means of analysis, comparison which leads to the exclusion of variables, i.e. current technologies do not attempt to translate through firstly deriving meaning like human translators. Rather, MT systems work by disaggregating the ST into manageable segments and then attempt to compile an identical phrase in the TT by referencing extensive bilingual dictionaries, grammar rules of both language pairs, including syntax and morphological rules and bilingual parallel corpora. In short, the process attempts to replace signs with signs where there are corresponding matches and where there is an inevitable difference the system references grammar and syntax rules and parallel bilingual corpora to exclude and limit the possibilities. Thus, MT can be described as a process of representing meaning from one language in another through the process of eliminating variables through the predictable elements of language, and the reference to extensive corpora to compensate for the aspects of language that are unpredictable or in instances where there is a lack of exact corresponding terms. Taking the necessary modern requirements of MT into account and the limited computer memory storage devices and computing power in 1954, the Georgetown experiment appears to be more of a showcase of the potential of MT rather than a functional MT system, namely because the technology relied upon for text retrieval did not exist during that period. For example, Hutchins (1998) explains that the initial ideas for translation systems that used some form of bilingual parallel databases [an essential component of MT systems] were only realized in the late 1980s after the technology was developed. These considerations suggest that the ST examples used in the Georgetown experiment were formulated to meet the limited computing ability and memory storage of the IBM 701. This means that any variation to the sentences would have left the system unable to produce a translation without additional programming. This proposition is supported by Garvin (1967) who worked on programming the 701; he notes in his summary of the characteristics of the experiment that'the scope of the translation program was clearly specified. Any sentence meeting its narrow specifications could be translated, provided the required entries were present in the glossary' (p. 48). Furthermore, Hutchins (2006) discussion indicates that the program used to produce the translations was only specific for the words and structures used in the experiment and thus would not have been able to generate a translation from different Russian sentences and in essence 'the system demonstrated in 1954 was undoubtedly preliminary, and the output was undoubtedly, in part (the non-chemistry sentences), 'designed' for the particular occasion' (Hutchins, 2006, p. 29). Hutchins also asserts that 'considering the state of the art of electronic computation at the time, it is remarkable that anything resembling automatic translation could have been achieved at all. Despite all its limitations, the demonstration in January 1954 marked the beginning of MT as a research field seen to be worthy of financial support' (p. 30).

10 Repercussions of the Georgetown Experiment's Claims

Despite the manifold immediate sociopolitical benefits of the Georgetown experiment, it did not directly advance the understanding of MT. For example, Bar-Hillel (1962), who was integral in organizing the MT conference that led to the experiment, argues that the 1954 experiment did not offer meaningful information to further MT research. Interestingly, Garvin (1967) echoes this sentiment by stating that 'the actual execution of the program on the 701 computer turned out to be an interesting exercise in nonmathematical programming, but showed nothing about translation beyond what was already contained in the verbal rules' (p. 46). However, the major repercussions of the experiment's claims relate to the negative effect on future MT research. Hutchins (2006) argues that '… the Georgetown-IBM demonstration was damaging both to MT at Georgetown and to MT in general' (p. 29). This was namely due to the inability of new research to produce results that surpassed or even matched those presented at the Georgetown experiment. This had a blowback effect which was embodied in the Automatic Language Processing Advisory Committee (ALPAC) report in 1966. The committee had been established in 1964 following a request by The Department of Defense, the National Science Foundation, and the Central Intelligence Agency to determine if continued research in the development of MT could be justified. Mainly, due to the expectations created by the Georgetown experiment the ALPAC report was extremely critical of the progress of MT and its inability to fulfil its primary role in translating large amounts of Russian text into readable English. For example, the committee found that 'unedited machine output from scientific text is decipherable for the most part, but it is sometimes misleading and sometimes wrong (as is postedited output to a lesser extent), and it makes slow and painful reading' (p. 19). Also, due to the high development costs of MT and the requirement of post-editing the ALPAC report suggested more economically viable options. For example, 'the Committee believes that in some cases it might be simpler and more economical for heavy users of Russian translations to learn to read the documents in the original language' (p. 5).

11 Was the First MT Endeavours Really a Failure?

Based on the ALPAC's findings the initial endeavours of MT had been framed as a failure (Quah, 2006). This is because it was assumed the primary goal of the Georgetown experiment and subsequent research that followed it was to achieve high-quality MT. However, if different primary goals are ascribed to these first endeavours, then the assessment of whether they were a failure or success will change accordingly. To determine the actual project goals, it is necessary to consider three significant factors about the Georgetown experiment: (1) the experiment presented a working MT able to produce high-quality translation unaided by humans; (2) based on the previous discussion on the viability of the Georgetown experiment's claims, it is unlikely that the available computing power would have been able to produce the result the Georgetown experiment purported; (3) the Georgetown experiment occurred during a Cold War period of heightened tensions between the US and the USSR. For example, in 1952, the US was the first country to test a hydrogen bomb, and in March 1954, the US detonated the most powerful nuclear bomb at the time (UN, n.d.). Taking all these factors into account it can be hypothesized that the primary objective of the Georgetown experiment and the immediate subsequent research was not to develop a working TM system per se but to present an illusion that the US had the technology to develop a working MT system that could translate Russian texts instantly. This illusion would create the same reaction as if the US did have the technology because, at the early stages of MT development, there was no way for Russian researchers to assess the viability of the claims and they took the reporting of the Georgetown experiment at face value. For example, Kulagina (2000) explains that 'after having learned about this achievement in the beginning of 1954, D. Ju. Panov organized at the Institute of Precision Mechanics and Computer Technologies … a group which started working on English to Russian MT' (p. 197). Consequently, if creating an illusion of a working MT is taken as the primary objective of the early MT endeavours, then they can be considered a success in that they fulfilled their objective and had the desired pragmatic effect, which boosted the US' perceived power socially and internationally.

In addition, a more recognized benefit of the early MT developments is that it highlighted fundamental gaps in the understanding of language. Behind Weaver's call for the use of computers to translate was an understanding of language that posited it is a consistent code system and thus computers could process language problems the same way they are used to solve mathematical ones. However, in the period following the Georgetown experiment, Bir-Hillel (1960) highlighted the complexities involved in extracting meaning from a text, which directly challenged Weaver's initial view of language. In Appendix III titled *A Demonstration of the Nonfeasibility of Fully Automatic High Quality Translation* in his 1960 article Bar-Hillel suggests that determining meaning is a prerequisite which must occur before translation. On this basis, he rejected the feasibility of computers producing high-quality translations unaided by humans because he claimed that the ability to determine meaning is something machines are unable to undertake and is intrinsically linked to human intelligence. Bar-Hillel (1960) demonstrated this fundamental premise with the following sentence:

> Little John was looking for his toy box. Finally he found it. The box was in the pen. John was very happy. (p. 159)

A prerequisite to understand this sentence is to determine the meaning of 'pen' which is only possible with the knowledge of the dimensions of writing pens and playpens in relation to the size of toy boxes. Even though simple, Bar-Hillel's example highlights the necessity of inference and additional knowledge which extends beyond the text itself and linguistic considerations. Crucially, Bar-Hillel (1962) argued that regardless of future developments, computers would not be able to perform better than humans due to the ambiguity of language, which is alleviated only through human induction and deduction. For example, Bar-Hillel (1962) asserts that 'expert human translators use their *background knowledge*, mostly subconsciously, in order to resolve syntactical and semantical ambiguities which machines will have either to leave unresolved or resolve by some "mechanical" rule which will ever so often result in a wrong translation' (p. 34). The results of the early MT approaches to translation supported Bir-Hillel's reservations. The computer programs attempted to replace a word in the ST with an equivalent word in the TL, i.e. replacing symbols with symbols. Kotz (1966) notes 'the input words in the incoming language would be looked up and substituted for their equivalents in the other language' (p. 592). However, at this juncture, it became apparent that languages do not have absolute corresponding words. Consequently, researchers attempted to overcome the non-equivalence problem by using grammatical and syntactical structures; however, this attempt highlighted more gaps in the understanding of language. For example, Kotz

(1966) explains that '… it became obvious that before starting seriously on machine translation of languages a careful and thorough study of the basic problems of grammar and syntax was required' (p. 593). The awareness of these inherent language problems led researchers to doubt, like Bir-Hillel, the feasibility of high-quality MT. What is crucial to note is that Kotz (1966) did not ascribe this to the limitations of the period's technology but rather to the inherent ambiguities in language, which can lead to multiple meanings even when identical words are sequenced in the same order. Like the doubts Bir-Hillel (1962) raised, there was a realization among researchers that without an interpretive framework, which uses extralinguistic information, a text can have several potential meanings. In this vein, Kotz (1966) suggests that:

> In fact, in order to resolve the ambiguity by means of the linguistic context in the 'neighbourhood' of the ambiguous word or expression we must in theory make this neighbourhood infinitely long, since no common sense or general knowledge of the universe can be expected from a machine (p. 595).

Interestingly, and supportive of Kotz's assertion, Google's state-of-the-art MT system (tested in 2023, September 30) is unable to determine that the pen referred to in Bar-Hillel's sentences mentioned above is a playpen. Consequently, when tasked with translating the sentences into Arabic and Turkish it translates pen, respectively, as قلم and *kalem*, which both refer to writing pens rather than playpens. The results of the Google translation are as follows [emphasis added to both the examples]:

> كان جون الصغير يبحث عن صندوق ألعابه. وأخيرا وجد ذلك. كان الصندوق في <u>القلم</u>. وكان جون سعيدا جدا.

> Küçük John oyuncak kutusunu arıyordu. Sonunda buldu. Kutu <u>kalemin</u> içindeydi. John çok mutluydu.

12 Translation Technology Post9/11

The aim of this section is to illustrate that there is a continued symbiotic relationship between translation technology and the pursuit of ideological power by highlighting the development of translation technologies to aid strategic military operations and advance aspects of the global war on terrorism (GWoT). Similar to the manner the Cold War drove the development of MT in the 1950s, the 9/11 attacks presented a catalyst that instigated further developments in translation technology. These include advancements in MT systems, the creation of a number of field devices and the development of specific software and apparatus to facilitate the US' widespread information mining operation. A case in point, in response to the 9/11 attacks, the US government, in January 2002, established a new sub-office under the directive of DARPA called the Information Awareness Office (IAO), which was to be headed by John Poindexter and would serve to develop new methods and systems that could provide warnings of future terrorist attacks. Dr. Tony Tether (2002), the then Director of the DARPA, in his statement to the Subcommittee on Emerging Threats and Capabilities, outlines the function of IAO:

> One of the great challenges in the war on terrorism is to know our enemy—who he is, where he is, and what he's doing. In order to focus our efforts, I established another new DARPA office, the Information Awareness Office (IAO). IAO is developing the information systems needed to find, identify, track, and understand terrorist networks and vastly improve what we know about our adversaries (p. 10).

The IAO introduced a number of projects that are translation technology-oriented such as Translingual Information Detection, Extraction, and Summarization (TIDES) and Babylon. But, before discussing the nature of these projects it is interesting to note the manner translation and language are approached in the realm of ideological conflict; for example, Charles Wayne (2002), who led the TIDES program speaking at the DARPATech symposium states that:

> Exploiting human language is currently a very labor intensive process. And much of it requires foreign language skills that are in very short supply in the defense, intelligence, and law enforcement communities. It is clear that the U.S. cannot succeed simply by adding more people. To obtain timely, actionable, mission-critical information, we absolutely must have effective language exploitation technology to magnify greatly the capabilities of a necessarily limited set of analysts (p. 1).

Wayne treats language and translation as assets that can be exploited, which is similar to the way other apparatuses of the state are used to advance their ideological objectives. To this end and during the GWoT period, one of the most ambitious and far-reaching projects of the IAO was TIDES, which is an abbreviation for 'Translingual Information Detection, Extraction, and Summarization'. The aim of the project was to create a system that can convert speech and text either stationary or streaming into a digital text format which then can be automatically translated through MT into English (Wayne 2002). Also, crucial to this system is that it enables the mining of translated information, which normally would have been impossible. In short, this system would facilitate the digitization and translation of phone calls, internet streams, media reports (live broadcasts as well as online videos) and intercepted communiqués. In addition, it would facilitate the digitization and translation of all textual information including printed text and handwritten text; it also would have the ability to instantly process information obtained in the field. For example, if military or law enforcement agents seize handwritten documents in a raid, they could take a picture and upload it to the system which in turn would immediately produce a translation in real time. In addition to the technological advancements, there is a major ideological difference between these types of translation technologies and previous endeavours. The earliest translation technological projects during the Cold War focused on achieving ideological goals regarding foreign elements outside of the state. For example, the Georgetown experiment was designed to translate Russian, which was the main language of the US' ideological adversary, the USSR. However, the impact and application of TIDES reach well beyond the extraction of information from foreign adversaries as it also can be used in conjunction with the widespread mining of information from US citizens. For example, commenting on the IAO, Cohen (2010) argues that '... it sought to create a giant network of integrated computer technologies for intercepting, storing, searching, monitoring, reading, and analyzing all private, computerized records of 300 million Americans

…' (p. 21) Thus, the use of this type of technology conflicts with key Western liberal social concepts such as 'the exemption from control of the citizen in respect of his person and property' (Bryce, 1933, as cited in Fukuyama 1992, p. 42). Moreover, Wayne (2002) alludes to this apparent social turn and the ramifications of such a system:

> We want to make a night and day difference——to change the world from the way it is today—where huge volumes of data are available electronically but English speaking operators and analysts can exploit only a small fraction of it—to where the same people can exploit a much larger fraction of the English data plus many other languages (p. 2).

Another type of technology that had been developed by the IOA is handheld personal translators. These were meant to primarily address the shortfall in trained linguists on the battlefield and to an extent circumvent the problems stemming from the mistrust of indigenous interpreters used by the US' occupying armies. For example, Pollachek (2011) argues that a substantial problem US forces encountered once they came into contact with civilians both in Iraq and Afghanistan was the shortage of qualified linguists to aid both combat operations and civil projects. He notes that the earliest handheld translation devices such as the Phraselator worked by using simple pre-set sentences such as 'get out the car', 'Do you have a bomb'? Mike Beaulieu, who is mentioned in Pollachek's article and who is the product director of Machine Foreign Language Translation Systems (MFLTS), also acknowledges this shortfall:

> Unfortunately there aren't enough linguists to go around and not all of them can put on a rucksack and go up and down mountains in Afghanistan and follow troops around, so we have to fill that capability gap with these devices (as cited in Pollachek 2011, para. 5).

The device developed by the IAO to address this problem is called Babylon, which builds on previous technological developments namely the Phraselator. While the previous devices allowed soldiers to speak a number of set phrases through offering an audible translation, the aim of Babylon was to develop a device that offered a one-plus-one-way capacity (Wayne 2002). In that, it allows the soldier to speak any sentence rather than a set phrase and have it immediately translated and presented in an audible format. Also, the project endeavoured to develop it into a two-way translation device through which the soldier can ask questions and a captive, for example, can respond through the device (Wayne 2002). It is important to note that the generation of handheld field translators that emerged during the GWoT period such as the Phraselator not only benefited military operations but had value in projecting the image of US state power, like the Georgetown experiment. For example, reports of the Phraselator in the media during the GWoT period functioned to support its narrative and to bolster the presentation of the US government's effort to defeat global terrorism. For example, Atkinson (2004) states, in the Baltimore Sun:

> He spoke into a hand-held black box, called the Phraselator, which translated his English into Arabic and broadcast it clearly through a speaker… The children pointed to a weapons cache, which included a mortar tube that was ready to be used and rocket-propelled grenades, which Collins destroyed… 'Finding the weapons cache with the kids ... never would have

> happened if I didn't pull out the unit,' said Collins, who noted that several military teams had previously passed through the area without detecting the weapons (para. 2–4).

Similarly, the media's reporting of another handheld translation device, the 'Raytheon TransTalk', has served to also support the GWoT narrative. For example, in a story reported by Fox News (2012), entitled *Star Trek universal translator to join war on terror*, the Raytheon TransTalk is compared to a fictional device called the Universal Translator featured in the 1960s Science fiction TV show Star Trek. To understand the importance and relevance of this comparison it is necessary to explain its fictional context. The device originally made by Captain Spock allowed for instant communication with an unknown alien species that had taken a human captive. In the episode entitled *Metamorphosis* (Coon & Senensky 1967) which the Fox report mentions, an alien entity imprisons Zefram Cochrane, the inventor of the Federation's propulsion system, the warp drive. Using the Universal Translator Captain Kirk communicates with the alien and discovers it has a female personality and is in love with Cochrane and this is the reason she held him captive for over 150 years. In due course, Kirk manages to convince the alien that it and Cochrane are too different for true love to ever flourish and that if she truly loves Cochrane, she should release him. The reference to this fictional portrayal of translation technology relates to the themes of otherness, superiority and domination, which have been discussed in detail following the cultural turn in Translation Studies (e.g. Bassnett & Trivedi, 2002, Pérez, 2014, and Álvarez & Vidal, 1996). This is because the comparison of people occupied by American forces to an alien that can only be communicated to through technology simultaneously degrades the humanity of the occupied while elevating the status of the occupier. It is also reminiscent of the way colonial missions were justified through claims of racial or ideological superiority, and in some cases, both. The similarities between the wars undertaken as part of the GWoT and colonialism are best summed up by Rafael (2016):

> Just as Habsburg Spain sought to conquer the Americas and the Pacific through the conversion of native peoples to Catholicism in the wake of the Reformation, so the U.S. Empire has sought to dominate the world by seeking to convert its peoples into neoliberal forms of governance in the wake of the attacks of 9/11. Both conversion and counterinsurgency seek to rid the world of insurgents, religious as well as political, establishing in their wake a new order of civic life ordered around the broad concerns of the empire (p. 122).

13 Conclusion

The chapter began by outlining the importance of translation technology and its underrepresentation in Translation Studies. It was argued that the use of translation technologies in a contemporary context is inseparable from practical translation and therefore there is a necessity to engage more with translation technology within the discipline. The main architects of the early MT endeavours as well as the rudimentary assumptions regarding language were then outlined. Both Weaver and Dostert's lives were impacted by war and their experiences led them to specific understandings of language and translation, which would have influenced their desire to employ computers for translation. The focus then turned to an analysis of the first demonstration of MT, the Georgetown experiment. It was highlighted how the reporting of the event was ideologically conducive to the US' domestic and global interests. Moreover, contrary to the claim that the first endeavours were a failure it was hypothesized that the primary objective of the experiment could have been to create an illusion that the US had a working MT system rather than actually produce one. Thus, from this perspective, the first endeavours would have been a success. The chapter then turned to technologies used for furthering the GWoT. The primary focus was on translation projects developed by the IAO, which is a subdivision of DARPA. It was argued that the TIDES project is significantly different from previous translation technology developments in terms of its ideological goals and reach; in that the technology is part of a wider trend adopted by US governments that infringe on the personal liberties of Americans. Focus was then given to the development of handheld translation field devices, which address in part the demand for interpreters in conflict zones. The political gain produced in the reporting of these devices was highlighted, and it was also explained that a result of the Fox News report was a comparison of occupied indigenous people to an alien creature. It was suggested that the report relates to themes of otherness, superiority and domination, and has relevance to the notion that the wars and occupations committed under the banner of the GWoT are forms of colonialism.

Acknowledgements I thank Prince Sultan University for supporting this research through the research lab [Applied Linguistics Research Lab-RL-CH-2019/9/1].

References

ALPAC (Automatic Language Processing Advisory Committee). 1966. *Language and machines: computers in translation and linguistics* (Publication 1416). A report by the Automatic Language Processing Advisory Committee, Division of Behavioral Sciences, National Academy of Sciences, National Research Council. https://web.archive.org/web/20110409070141/, http://www.mt-archive.info/ALPAC-1966.pdf

Álvarez R., and Vidal M., C. (eds). 1996. *Translation, power, subversion* (pp. 10 – 24). Multilingual Matters LTD.

Atkinson, B. 2004. A hand-held translator is boon to GI's in Iraq. *The Baltimore Sun*. http://articles.baltimoresun.com/2004-05-18/business/0405180061_1_sarich-hand-held-translator-weapons-cache.

Austermühl, F. 2014. *Electronic tools for translators*. Routledge.

Bar-Hillel, Y. 1960. A demonstration of the nonfeasibility of fully automatic high quality translation. *Advances in Computers* 1: 91–163. https://doi.org/10.1016/S0065-2458(08)60607-5.

Bar-Hillel, Y. 1962. The future of machine translation. *Times Literary Supplement*. https://aclanthology.org/www.mt-archive.info/50/TLS-1962-Bar-Hillel.pdf.

Bassnett, S. & Trivedi, H. (eds.) 2002. *Post-colonial Translation: Theory and Practice*. Routledge.

Bowker, L. 2002. *Computer-aided Translation Technology: A Practical Introduction.* University of Ottawa Press.

Buzan, B. 2006. Will the 'global war on terrorism' be the new Cold War? *International Affairs* 82 (6): 1101–1118. https://doi.org/10.1111/j.1468-2346.2006.00590.x.

Cohen, E. D. 2010. *Mass Surveillance and State Control: The Total Information Awareness Project.* Palgrave Macmillan.

Coon, G., L. & Senensky, R. 1967. Metamorphosis (Season 2, Episode 9) [TV series episode]. *Star Trek.* Desilu Productions.

DARPA n.d. *About DARPA.* http://www.darpa.mil/about-us/about-darpa.

Fukuyama, F. 1992. *The end of history and the last man.* The Free Press.

Garvin, P.L. 1967. The Georgetown-IBM Experiment of 1954: An Evaluation in Retrospect. In *Papers in linguistics in honor of Léon Dostert*, ed. W.M. Austin, 46–56. Mouton.

Gile, D. 2009. *Basic Concepts and Models for Interpreter and Translator Training.* John Benjamins Publishing Company.

Gordin, M. 2015. *Scientific Babel: How Science Was Done Before and After Global English.* The University of Chicago Press.

Holmes, J.S. 2000. The Name and Nature of Translation Studies. In *The Translation Studies Reader*, ed. L. Venuti, 172–185. Routledge.

Hutchins, J. 2000. Warren weaver and the launching of MT: Brief biographical note. In *Early Years in Machine Translation Memoirs and Biographies of Pioneers*, ed. W.J. Hutchins, 17–20. John Benjamins Publishing Company.

Hutchins, J. 1997. From First Conception to First Demonstration: the Nascent Years of Machine Translation, 1947–1954. A Chronology. *Machine Translation*, 12(3): 195–252. http://www.jstor.org/stable/40027329.

Hutchins, J. (1998). The origins of the translator's workstation. *Machine Translation, 13*(4): 287–307. https://www.jstor.org/stable/40007072.

Hutchins, J. 2006. *The first public demonstration of machine translation: the Georgetown-IBM system, 7th January 1954.* Unpublished manuscript. https://open.unive.it/hitrade/books/HutchinsFirst.pdf.

Kenny, D. 2009. Equivalence. In: *Routledge encyclopedia of translation studies*, 2nd ed., M. Baker & G. Saldanha, 96–99. Routledge.

Kotz, S. 1966. Machine translation after fifteen years. *Science Progress (1933–)*, 54(216), 591–599. http://www.jstor.org/stable/43419593.

Kulagina, O.S. 2000. Pioneering MT in the Soviet Union. In *Early Years in Machine Translation Memoirs and Biographies of Pioneers*, ed. W.J. Hutchins, 197–204. John Benjamins Publishing Company.

MacDonald, R.R. 1967. Léon Dostert. In *Papers in linguistics in honor of Léon Dostert*, ed. W.M. Austin, 9–14. Mouton.

Macdonald, N. (1954). Language translation by machine — a report of the first successful trial. *Computers and Automation,* 3(2), pp. 6–11. https://ia904603.us.archive.org/24/items/sim_computers-and-people_1954-02_3_2/sim_computers-and-people_1954-02_3_2.pdf.

Montgomery, C.A. 2000. Is FAHQ(M)T Impossible? Memories of Paul Garvin and other MT Colleagues'. In *Early Years in Machine Translation Memoirs and Biographies of Pioneers*, ed. J.W. Hutchins, 97–110. John Benjamins Publishing Company.

Munday, J., Pinto, S., Ramos, & Blakesley, J. 2022. *Introducing Translation Studies: Theories and Applications* (5th ed). Routledge.

Fox News. 2012. *Star Trek's Universal Translator to Join War on Terror.* http://www.foxnews.com/tech/2012/05/17/star-trek-universal-translator-to-join-war-on-terror.html.

Pérez, M., C. (ed.). 2014. *Apropos of Ideology: Translation Studies on Ideology – Ideologies in Translation Studies.* Routledge.

Pielmeier, H., O'Mara, P. 2020. *The State of the Linguist Supply Chain: Translators and Interpreters in 2020.* CSA Research. https://cdn2.hubspot.net/hubfs/4041721/Newsletter/The%20State%20of%20the%20Linguist%20Supply%20Chain%202020.pdf.

Pollachek, B. 2011. Machine Foreign Language Translation Systems bridge gap between Soldiers, locals. *U.S. Army.* https://www.army.mil/article/54543/machine-foreign-language-translation-systems-bridge-gap-between-soldiers-locals.

Quah, C. K. 2006. *Translation and Technology*. Palgrave Macmillan.

Rafael, V. L. 2016. *Motherless Tongues: The Insurgency of Language Amid Wars of Translation.* Duke University Press.

Sin-wai, C. 2015. Computer-aided translation: major concepts. In: C. Sin-wai (ed.) *Routledge Encyclopedia of Translation Technology*, pp. 32–67. Routledge.

Somers, H.L. 2003. Introduction. In *Computers and Translation: A Translator's Guide*, ed. H.L. Somers, 1–12. John Benjamins Publishing.

Tabor, J. 2019. *CAT tool use by translators: who is using?* Proz. https://go.proz.com/blog/cat-tool-use-by-translators-who-is-using.

Tether, T. 2002. *Subcommittee on Emerging Threats and Capabilities, Armed Services Committee, U.S. Senate.* https://www.darpa.mil/attachments/TestimonyArchived(April%2010%202002).pdf.

UN n.d. *Ending Nuclear Testing.* https://www.un.org/en/observances/end-nuclear-tests-day/history.

Vasconcellos, M. 2000. The Georgetown project Leon Dostert: Recollections of a young assistant. In *Early Years in Machine Translation: Memoirs and biographies of pioneers*, ed. J. Hutchins, 87–96. John Benjamins Publishing.

Wayne, C. 2002. Information Awareness Office (IAO) Human Language Technology TIDES, EARS, Babylon (DARPATech 2002 DARPA). https://web.archive.org/web/20130223163902/http://archive.darpa.mil/DARPATech2002/presentations/iao_pdf/speeches/WAYNE.pdf.

Weaver, W. 1949. Memorandum on translation from one language to another, and on the possibility of contributing to this process by the use of modern computing devices... *Letter to The Rockefeller Foundation.* https://aclanthology.org/1952.earlymt-1.1.pdf.

Weaver, W. 1970. *Scene of change: a lifetime in American science.* Charles Scribner's Sons.

Burcin Kagan Mustafa's research has focused on the impact of beliefs on translation. In addition, he has taught Translation Technology courses at various universities. Currently, he is an Assistant Professor at Prince Sultan University where he teaches Research Techniques and is undertaking a study into the influence of personal ethics on translation.

Revolutionising Translation with AI: Unravelling Neural Machine Translation and Generative Pre-trained Large Language Models

Sai Cheong Siu

Abstract This work explores the technical advancements in artificial intelligence (AI) for translation, with a focus on neural machine translation (NMT) and large language models (LLMs) as primary drivers of progress. The analysis encompasses foundational deep learning techniques, the influential Transformer model, and the strengths and weaknesses of NMT and LLMs in the context of translation. Furthermore, practical recommendations are offered for translation educators and developers on how to harness the power of AI effectively while addressing potential challenges. The aim is to enhance our understanding of AI-driven translation technologies and equip language professionals with the knowledge needed to make informed decisions when using these cutting-edge tools.

1 Introduction

Artificial intelligence (AI) has advanced rapidly in recent years and enabled numerous applications to transform various fields (e.g., LeCun et al. 2015; Zhang et al. 2021). Translation technology has also made significant progress, catalysed by innovative developments such as neural machine translation (NMT) (e.g., Bahdanau et al. 2014; Vaswani et al. 2017) and pre-trained large language models (LLMs) (e.g., Devlin et al. 2018; Brown et al. 2020). These AI-driven techniques have spurred a new wave of tools applicable to translation and language services, including conversational chatbots capable of real-time language translation and communication (e.g., ChatGPT (OpenAI 2022)). Delving into the latest AI developments in translation technology, this work focuses on artificial neural networks that underpin NMT and the generative language models employed in the development of advanced chatbot applications. The aim is to enhance our understanding of how AI facilitates translation and, in turn,

S. C. Siu (✉)
School of Translation and Foreign Languages, The Hang Seng University of Hong Kong, Hong Kong, China
e-mail: scsiu@hsu.edu.hk

Y. Peng et al. (eds.), *New Advances in Translation Technology*, New Frontiers in Translation Studies, https://doi.org/10.1007/978-981-97-2958-6_3

assist language professionals in determining effective ways to leverage cutting-edge, AI-powered applications.

The present work is structured in eight sections. Following this introduction, Sect. 2 provides an overview of deep learning, an AI approach featuring the design and use of multilayer artificial neural networks. Section 3 explains the Transformer model, an architecture that has enabled significant advances in natural language processing (NLP). Section 4 explores two types of AI for translation: NMT, which is designed for translation between languages using neural networks, and generative LLMs, which generate human-like text and power chatbots potentially applicable to translation. Section 5 analyses the strengths and weaknesses of these applications, highlighting their potential and limitations. Sections 6 and 7 offer recommendations for translation educators and developers, respectively, to train language professionals with necessary skills and improve AI tools. Section 8 presents concluding remarks. It is hoped that this work provides insights for language professionals to make informed decisions about incorporating these technologies.

2 An Overview of Deep Learning

Deep learning is a branch of machine learning that uses multilayer artificial neural networks to analyse and process data, with applications in various domains like NLP and computer vision (LeCun et al. 2015). These networks are loosely inspired by biological neural networks and consist of simple units called artificial neurons. The objective is to learn how to extract relevant features from large amounts of data, without the need for handcrafting rules, as seen in symbolic AI, or extensive feature engineering, as is common in other machine learning methods. In the context of NLP, deep learning typically involves four key tasks, as explained in Sects. 2.1, 2.2, 2.3 and 2.4 below. For more insight into deep learning and its applications, refer to Goodfellow et al. (2016) and Zhang et al. (2021). For more information on deep learning in the context of translation technology, see Siu (2023b).

2.1 Model Design

Model design refers to the creation of a model that maps input data to output data based on specific parameters. In machine translation, for example, the input and output are sequences of words or tokens. Token sequences are often represented as high-dimensional vectors using techniques like one-hot encoding or word embeddings, such as Word2Vec or GloVe (e.g., Mikolov et al. 2013; Pennington et al. 2014; Jurafsky and Martin 2023). The number of parameters in a model can range from a few hundred million, as seen in Radford et al. (2019), to over a hundred billion for large models such as GPT-3 (Brown et al. 2020).

2.2 Data Collection

Data collection involves gathering a dataset for training the model. In machine translation, this usually means assembling large datasets of input–output pairs to teach the model how to generate correct translations. These datasets often consist of parallel corpora containing aligned sentences in the source and target languages. In addition to bilingual data, monolingual data may also be utilised, which can be back-translated to form bilingual sentence pairs or used directly for training language or translation models (e.g., Sennrich et al. 2016; Edunov et al. 2018).

2.3 Model Training

Model training involves finding the best values for parameters that minimise the overall loss function, typically measured as the sum or average of errors across all data points in a training set. For efficient computation, the dataset is divided into smaller batches during training. For instance, in supervised learning, where a model is trained on a labelled dataset to predict outcomes based on given inputs, each batch contains a fixed number of input–output pairs, which are processed through the model.

There are two essential processes during training: forward propagation and backpropagation. In the forward propagation, the input is passed through the model, generating an output prediction. The loss function then calculates the error between the predicted output and the true output for each input–output pair in the batch. In NLP and translation, the cross-entropy loss can be used as the loss function (see Jurafsky and Martin (2023)). It measures the difference between the predicted probability distribution of tokens in the output sequence and the corresponding true distribution in the target sequence.

Backpropagation is an algorithm used to compute the gradients of the loss function with respect to the model's parameters. It works by applying the chain rule of calculus recursively, propagating from the output layer back through the model's layers to calculate each parameter's contribution to the loss. The gradients indicate how to adjust the parameters to minimise the loss function. During model training, optimisation algorithms use the gradients to update the parameters and reduce the cross-entropy loss. Examples of optimisation algorithms include stochastic gradient descent (SGD) with random initialisation and momentum (Sutskever et al. 2013), as well as the Adam optimisation method introduced by Kingma and Ba (2014).

2.4 *Model Evaluation*

To assess the performance of a trained model, a separate test dataset that was not used during the training process is utilised. This approach helps to estimate the model's ability to generalise to previously unseen data and detect potential overfitting. Examples of evaluation metrics for machine translation include BLEU (Papineni et al. 2002) and CHRF (Popović 2015), which quantify the similarity between the model-generated output sequences and their corresponding reference sequences. There are also embedding-based metrics that calculate the similarity between the output and reference sentence embeddings. Notable examples of these metrics are BERTScore (Zhang et al. 2019), BLEURT (Sellam et al. 2020), and COMET (Rei et al. 2020). For further details on evaluation metrics for machine translation, refer to Siu (2022).

3 The Transformer Model Explained

The transformer model, introduced by Vaswani et al. (2017), has become a widely used architecture in the field of NLP (Tay et al. 2020). Given the model's importance in NMT and generative LLMs, this section explains its key features.

3.1 *Input and Output of the Transformer Model*

The Transformer model processes a sequence of tokens, such as words, subwords, or characters, based on the chosen tokenisation strategy (Kudo and Richardson 2018; Tay et al. 2021). Each token is represented by a high-dimensional embedding vector.

The output of the model depends on the specific task and implementation. Generally, it produces a sequence of continuous vectors, with each vector representing the learned information at a particular position. These output vectors can be used as features for other models or fed into subsequent layers within the Transformer model. For sequence-to-sequence tasks, where both the input and output are sequences of tokens, the model usually generates tokens one at a time in an auto-regressive manner, decoding them into probabilities for all possible tokens, which are then normalised using the softmax function (Bridle 1990). The model continues to predict the next token in the output sequence until it generates an end-of-sequence token or reaches the maximum output sequence length.

3.2 Key Components of the Transformer Model

The Transformer model comprises several essential components: the encoder and decoder, positional encodings, multi-head self-attention, and position-wise feed-forward networks with layer normalisation and residual connections.

Encoder and Decoder: The original Transformer model features an encoder-decoder architecture. The encoder turns input tokens into hidden states (a set of feature vectors that represent the input), and the decoder generates the output sequence based on these hidden states. Both the encoder and decoder consist of layers. An encoder layer has multi-head self-attention followed by a position-wise feed-forward network (see below). A decoder layer includes an additional multi-head attention component that focuses on the encoder's output, making the model suitable for sequence-to-sequence tasks. Decoder-only transformers, as seen in some LLMs, leave out this extra attention component and just focus on the decoder's input.

Positional Encodings: The Transformer model processes input tokens in parallel, so it needs explicit information about each token's position in the sequence. Positional encodings provide this information by adding position-specific information to the token embeddings. A common method uses sine and cosine functions with varying frequencies, analogous to assigning a unique identifier to each word based on where it is in a sentence.

Multi-head Self-attention Mechanism: Central to the Transformer model, this mechanism captures relationships between tokens in a sequence by calculating multiple attention scores for each token pair using distinct learned projections. These scores are then used to generate an "integrated" embedding for each token, with the other tokens in the input taken into consideration. With this mechanism, the model can consider various aspects of the input simultaneously and identify which parts are important for generating the output. This process is analogous to having different people look at the same sentence, with each person focusing on a different part of the sentence, and then working together to understand the full meaning.

Position-Wise Feed-Forward Networks (FFNs): Position-wise FFNs process the output of multi-head self-attention. Each FFN consists of two linear layers with a ReLU (Rectified Linear Unit) activation function (Krizhevsky et al. 2012) in between. The function acts like a switch, deciding whether a neuron should be "on" or "off". This helps the network focus on the most important information.

Layer Normalisation and Residual Connections: There are two additional techniques that help models learn better: (1) layer normalisation, which makes sure that all the numbers in a group have a similar range, akin to standardising a set of test scores to have the same mean and spread; and (2) residual connections, which provide a path for data to reach later parts of the network by skipping some layers, similar to taking a shortcut through a maze and avoiding unnecessary turns. For more details, refer to Xiong et al. (2020).

3.3 Variants of the Transformer Model

Over time, the Transformer model has been adapted for various tasks and domains, resulting in popular variants and applications like BERT (Devlin et al. 2018), GPT (Radford et al. 2018; 2019), T5 (Raffel et al. 2020), and Vision Transformers (Dosovitskiy et al. 2020; Khan et al. 2022). BERT has revolutionised natural language understanding by leveraging bidirectional context in pre-training and fine-tuning for a wide range of tasks. GPT has become known for its strong generative capabilities, particularly in text generation and completion tasks. T5 has unified various natural language processing tasks under a single text-to-text framework for both pre-training and fine-tuning. Vision Transformers have applied the Transformer architecture to computer vision tasks, showcasing the model's versatility beyond natural language processing. These variants have significantly advanced AI across multiple domains and continue to inspire new developments in the field.

4 AI for Translation: NMT and Generative Pre-trained LLMs

This section discusses two prominent examples of AI for translation: (1) NMT; and (2) generative pre-trained LLMs. Both leverage deep learning techniques are discussed in previous sections, with the Transformer being a popular architecture.

4.1 NMT

NMT often uses an encoder-decoder architecture, which can consist of Transformer or alternative networks like recurrent neural networks (RNNs) and convolutional neural networks (CNNs) (Stahlberg 2020; Siu 2023b). The encoder maps the source text to an internal representation, which the decoder then transforms to predict the next token in the target text. Mathematically, we can define the probability distribution of the next target token y_t as follows:

$$P\left(y_t|\boldsymbol{y}_{<t};\boldsymbol{x};\theta\right) = F\left(y_t,\boldsymbol{y}_{<t},\boldsymbol{x};\theta\right).$$

Here, F represents the NMT model (e.g., a Transformer) that maps the input tokens $\boldsymbol{x}$, previous target tokens $\boldsymbol{y}_{<t}$, and the next token y_t to logit values, which are then transformed into probability values using the softmax function. The model parameters are denoted by θ.

4.1.1 The Transformer Model for NMT

As discussed in Sect. 3, the Transformer model is a popular architecture for NLP. It is designed to overcome the limitations of RNNs and CNNs in handling long-range dependencies and parallelisation (Vaswani et al. 2017).

For NMT, the Transformer encoder comprises multiple encoding layers, with each layer consisting of a multi-head self-attention mechanism and position-wise feed-forward networks with layer normalisation and residual connections. The first layer accepts positional encoding, which provides information about the relative positions of tokens in the input sequence. The multi-head self-attention mechanism enables the model to determine the importance of different tokens in the input sequence by capturing dependencies among words. The position-wise feed-forward networks apply a non-linear transformation to each token independently. The output is an internal representation of the source text used by the decoder.

The decoder consists of multiple layers that resemble the encoder layers but with two key differences. First, it employs a self-attention mechanism that masks future target tokens during training, preventing the decoder from attending to them. Second, it has an additional self-attention component that combines the encoder's output representation of the source text. More specifically, the decoder starts with a self-attention mechanism similar to the one used by the encoder. However, it only attends to the target tokens that have been predicted so far, while future tokens are masked. Then, a second self-attention mechanism is used, which focuses on the output from the encoder. The final output is a sequence of logit values for the next token in the target text, which are then converted into probabilities using the softmax function.

4.1.2 Decoding Methods

Decoding methods in NMT models, such as those used in Bahdanau et al. (2014) and Vaswani et al. (2017), predict the next word in a sequence based on the probabilities of subsequent tokens. Various decoding methods help strike a balance between translation quality and diversity, enhancing the performance of these models.

A simple method is *greedy search*, which selects the token with the highest probability at each step and assumes that each token is independent of each other (Kamath et al. 2019). However, it may generate sub-optimal translations due to the garden-path problem, where the best translation output may initially consist of tokens that have lower probabilities (Koehn 2020). An alternative to greedy search is *beam search*, which maintains multiple candidate translations at each step. Beam search keeps n partial candidate sequences, called beams, where n is the beam width. The beams are expanded by selecting the top-n most probable tokens at each step. Beam search continues until the end-of-sequence token is reached or a maximum sequence length is achieved. The beam with the highest final probability is chosen as the output translation. By exploring more candidates, beam search (using narrow beams) produces better translations compared to greedy search (Koehn and Knowles 2017). However, its computational cost also increases with the beam width.

We may also consider *sampling* to introduce randomness and explore more diverse translations. Sampling with *temperature scaling*, for example, selects tokens based on their probability distribution (Hinton et al. 2015). This method involves a temperature parameter that adjusts the output probability distribution. Another decoding approach is *top-k sampling* (Fan et al. 2018), which selects a token from the top-k most probable tokens at each step, where k is an integer representing the number of tokens to consider. Alternatively, *top-p sampling*, also known as nucleus sampling (Holtzman et al. 2019), chooses tokens from the top-p most probable tokens, where p represents a cumulative probability threshold. This method first sorts the tokens by their probabilities and then selects the smallest set of tokens whose cumulative probability surpasses p. Finally, it samples a token from the chosen set.

4.2 Generative Pre-trained LLMs

Generative pre-trained LLMs have shown remarkable versatility across a wide range of NLP tasks beyond translation. LLMs feature the use of a massive number of parameters and can be classified as encoder-based, decoder-based, or encoder-decoder-based. For example, GPT-3, a decoder-based LLM, has 96 layers with 128 attention heads and an input token dimension exceeding 12,288 (Brown et al., 2020), whereas the "big" Transformer model for NMT, which is an encoder-decoder-based model, comprises 6 encoding layers and 6 decoding layers, with 8 attention heads and an input token dimension of 1024 (Vaswani et al. 2017). Formally, for decoder-based language models like ChatGPT, the probability distribution over the next token given the previous tokens can be denoted as follows:

$$P\left(y_t | \boldsymbol{y}_{<t}; \theta\right) = \text{softmax}\left(F\left(y_t, \boldsymbol{y}_{<t}; \theta\right)\right),$$

where F is the decoder-based model, and θ denotes the model parameters. In this equation, $\boldsymbol{y}_{<t}$ represents the sequence of tokens generated so far by the decoder, which takes these previous tokens as input to predict the next token y_t in the target sequence. Decoding methods for LLMs share similarities with those for NMT models.

LLMs leverage transfer learning through pre-training, fine-tuning, zero-shot, and few-shot learning (e.g., Radford et al. 2018, 2019; and Brown et al. 2020). They are first pre-trained on a vast corpus of text in an unsupervised manner to "learn" language in general, capturing syntactic, semantic, and contextual information embedded in the training data. Then, the models can be fine-tuned for specific tasks using smaller, task-specific datasets. Unlike NMT, which is task-specific and often trained end-to-end on parallel corpora, LLMs learn translation indirectly. Sophisticated models can effectively tackle new tasks without having observed any examples during fine-tuning (zero-shot learning) or with only a limited number of examples (few-shot learning).

GPT-3, for instance, as a decoder-based transformer model, is similar to the decoder for machine translation presented in the Transformer paper, with two differences: (1) it lacks the second self-attention mechanism (i.e., the one taking encoder output as input), and (2) it employs sparse attention in Transformer layers (Brown et al. 2020). For ChatGPT, pre-training is followed by instruction fine-tuning and reinforcement learning with human feedback based on GPT-3 model (see OpenAI (2022) and Ouyang et al. (2022)), enabling the model to follow human instructions and generate more accurate and contextually relevant responses.

When using LLMs as translation tools, the input is a prompt that includes an instruction specifying the task and other relevant information, along with the source text to be translated. The model then predicts the next token iteratively, in a manner similar to NMT, computing probabilities and decoding using the aforementioned methods. Effective prompt engineering plays a crucial role in achieving high-quality translations, as LLMs rely on prompts to understand the context and specific task. The prompt should clearly specify the desired output format and include any additional information that might assist the model in generating an accurate translation. For example, to translate English text into Chinese, the prompt can be framed as "Translate the following text from English into Chinese: '<source_text>'". See Gao et al. (2023b), Peng et al. (2023) and Siu (2023a) on prompting for translation.

Although both NMT and LLMs can be employed for translation, they exhibit different features. First, LLMs have been pre-trained on a diverse range of text, making them potentially more adaptable to different domains and styles, while NMT models may require additional fine-tuning on domain-specific parallel corpora for optimal performance in specialised domains (for more discussion on this "domain mismatch" issue, see Koehn and Knowles (2017)). Second, LLMs can perform zero-shot or few-shot learning, making them more data-efficient (when they need to be developed for translation) compared to NMT models, which typically require large parallel corpora for training. Third, LLMs are capable of handling multiple tasks without the need for dedicated models for each task, unlike NMT models, which are specifically designed for translation and require separate models for other language tasks. Lastly, while NMT models are optimised specifically for translation tasks, LLMs, though capable of generating high-quality translations in some cases, may not always match the performance of dedicated NMT models (e.g., Brown et al. 2020).

5 Strengths and Limitations of NMT and LLMs

This section explores the strengths and weaknesses of NMT and generative pre-trained LLMs in the context of translation tasks.

5.1 *Strengths*

5.1.1 Superior Performance Over Conventional Machine Translation Approaches

NMT systems have demonstrated improvements over their predecessors, such as Statistical Machine Translation (SMT), when sufficient training data are available (Stahlberg 2020). One reason for NMT's success lies in its ability to capture complex linguistic relationships. Unlike SMT, which relies heavily on word alignment and phrase-based methods, NMT learns directly from parallel data to understand context and semantics. The use of deep neural networks and attention mechanisms further equips NMT systems with the ability to handle long-range dependencies and ambiguities in language.

5.1.2 Enhanced Context Awareness Through Transformer Models

The adoption of Transformer models facilitates improved context awareness by utilising self-attention mechanisms, as discussed in Sects. 3 and 4. This capability allows NMT systems and LLMs to weigh the importance of words in a sentence based on their relevance to the output text. Each token in the input sequence has a dynamic internal representation that changes according to the context and other tokens present, enabling the model to adapt to different linguistic situations more effectively. Consequently, the model can dynamically adjust to various contexts, resulting in higher quality translations. This is particularly beneficial in cases where context plays a crucial role, such as preserving the meaning of idiomatic expressions and handling pronoun disambiguation.

5.1.3 Performance and Customisability of LLMs

LLMs, such as ChatGPT, demonstrate promising performance in translation tasks and could potentially surpass NMT systems (Jiao et al. 2023). One of the key strengths of LLMs lies in their customisability, as users can provide more information in the form of prompts to supply additional details about a translation job (Siu 2023a). This feature enables tailored translations that accurately capture the intended meaning and adhere to specific preferences in terms of style or tone. Moreover, LLMs can be fine-tuned further on domain-specific data, which may result in better alignment of training data and user actual inputs and enhance adaptability across subject areas.

5.1.4 Versatility of LLMs as Advanced Assistive Tools for Translators

LLMs can handle a wide range of NLP tasks beyond producing translations, making them valuable tools for translators. As discussed by Siu (2023a), such models can function as interactive editors, suggesting possible edits and modifications to translators' drafts, and facilitate human-in-the-loop collaboration. This approach allows translators to leverage the language fluency and grammatical knowledge embedded in LLMs while maintaining full control over the final translation. LLMs can also generate rough draft translations from scratch, provide explanations for expressions in the source and/or target language, and offer multiple alternative translations for consideration. These features contribute to a more efficient and effective translation process, allowing translators to focus on complex, nuanced translations and delegate repetitive tasks to their AI collaborators. This human–computer partnership paves the way for a mutually enriching translation experience and showcases the potential of LLMs as advanced assistive tools in the translation industry.

5.2 Limitations

While NMT and LLMs have achieved remarkable success in translation, they also present some shortcomings that necessitate further research and development. This section identifies five major areas, including the processing of long sentences (Sect. 5.2.1), support for specialised translation domains (Sect. 5.2.2), support for non-English languages (Sect. 5.2.3), contextual and background analysis (Sect. 5.2.4), and hallucination (Sect. 5.2.5).

5.2.1 Translation of Long Input Sentences

NMT systems may struggle to produce complete and accurate translations when presented with very long sentences (Koehn and Knowles 2017). The following example illustrates how two NMT systems fail to fully translate a long sentence in Chinese (Hong Kong and Macao Affairs Office of the State Council 2023), comprised of over 110 characters, concerning the Central Government's support for Hong Kong's post-pandemic recovery.

- **Source text** 中央始終十分關心香港的疫情形勢，多措並舉支持香港統籌做好疫情防控和經濟社會發展工作，中央有關部門高度重視在疫情常態化防控下恢復内地與香港『通關』的問題，一View 直與特區政府保持密切溝通，深入交換意見，推動兩地防控措施的有效銜接。[Reference translation by the author: The Central Government has consistently paid close attention to the epidemic situation in Hong Kong and has implemented a variety of measures to support Hong Kong in effectively coordinating its epidemic prevention and control efforts, as well as its economic and social development. Relevant central government departments place great importance on the "resumption of normal cross-border travel" between Mainland China and Hong Kong under normalised epidemic prevention and control measures. They have been maintaining close communication and in-depth exchanges of views with the SAR government to promote effective coordination of prevention and control measures between the two regions.]

- **Google Translate** The central government has always been very concerned about the epidemic situation in Hong Kong, and has taken multiple measures to support Hong Kong in coordinating the work of epidemic prevention and control and economic and social development. The SAR government maintains close communication, exchanges views in depth, and promotes the effective convergence of prevention and control measures between the two places.
- **ChatGPT** The central government has always been very concerned about the epidemic situation in Hong Kong. It has taken multiple measures to support Hong Kong in coordinating epidemic prevention and control as well as economic and social development work. The relevant departments of the central government attach great importance to the issue of resuming "cross-border" exchanges between the Mainland and Hong Kong under the normalization of epidemic prevention and control. They have been maintaining close communication with the Hong Kong SAR government, exchanging views in depth, and promoting effective coordination of prevention and control measures between the two regions.

Although the translation provided by Google Translate might seem fluent at first glance, a closer examination reveals that it omits the middle part of the source sentence. The missing part, "中央有關部門高度重視在疫情常態化防控下恢復內地與香港『通關』的問題", corresponds to "The relevant departments of the central government attach great importance to the issue of resuming 'cross-border' exchanges between the Mainland and Hong Kong under the normalization of epidemic prevention and control" in ChatGPT's translation. For NMT in general, problems relating to the translation of long sentences could result from several factors. The training data used to train NMT models may have predominantly contained short sentences, causing the models to struggle with properly translating longer sequences; more data with long, complex sentences are needed. In addition, the encoder and decoder of NMT models might have insufficient capacity (e.g., the number of layers or dimensionality of embeddings) to fully capture the information in the long input sentence, so more advanced model architectures with increased capacity can be explored. The models may also have a hard constraint on the maximum length of input/output sequences, leading them to generate partial translations for sentences that exceed the maximum length. Finally, the attention components of the models that align tokens may have difficulty maintaining alignment over long distances, and developing more sophisticated attention mechanisms that can capture long-range dependencies could lead to better translation results (e.g., Zhang and Feng 2021).

5.2.2 Support for Specialised Translation

NMT engines, especially general-purpose ones, may encounter difficulties when translating specialised documents due to inconsistencies in translation style and the accuracy of domain-specific terminology. Consequently, there has been extensive research on domain adaptation—the process of adapting translation systems to specialised domains (see, for instance, Chu and Wang (2018)). Similar challenges have been observed when using LLMs, such as ChatGPT, for translation tasks (Siu 2023a).

The following short example illustrates stylistic and terminological issues in translating a sentence from a listing document in Hong Kong. The source sentence in English is from an "Important Notice to Investors" (Landrich Holding Limited 2020), advising investors to rely only on information in the prospectus when making investment decisions.

- **Source text** You should rely only on the information contained in this prospectus to make your investment decision. [Reference translation by the author: 程閣下應僅依 賴本招股章, 所載資料作出投資決定。]
- **Google Translate** 您應該僅依 賴本招股說明書中包含的信息來做出投資決定。
- **ChatGPT** 您應該只依 賴於本招股說明書所包含的資訊，以做出您的投資決定。

In both Google Translate and ChatGPT, the pronoun "you" is rendered as "您", which is inconsistent with the common use of "閣下" in Hong Kong IPO prospectuses. The word "prospectus" is translated as "招股說明書", more common in Mainland China than "招股章程" used in Hong Kong prospectuses. Similarly, in Google Translate, the word "information" is translated as "信息" rather than "資料" in the reference translation, with the former more typical in Mainland China and the latter in Hong Kong. These issues in translation style and terminology may stem from the use of Mainland Chinese training data and different usage patterns in general and specialised documents. This could be addressed by training models on specialised texts. For example, the author of this article developed IPOTranslate (Siu 2019), an NMT system trained on sentences extracted from IPO prospectuses. Exposure to the writing style and terminology of these documents allows IPOTranslate to translate the above sentence consistently with the reference translation. This suggests that training on in-domain data and tailoring models to domain-specific language usage and conventions can help address these issues in specialised translation.

5.2.3 Limited Support for Non-english Languages

The performance of LLM-driven applications can be influenced by the composition of languages in the training data. These applications, if trained primarily on English data, tend to perform better in English and have limited support for other languages such as Chinese. As Siu (2023a) explained, for example, ChatGPT was largely trained on English data, and it has limitations in generating Traditional Chinese sentences, despite demonstrating some ability to handle multilingual data. The following example from the paper, a short sentence extracted from the *Hong Kong Fact Sheets* that describes the city's features and population statistics in 2019, illustrates ChatGPT's lack of support for Chinese and suboptimal English-Chinese translation (with a translation provided by Google Translate added here for comparison):

- **Source text** Hong Kong, with a population of about 7.51 million in mid-2019, is a small but dynamic city, which has earned an international reputation as a leading commercial and financial centre as well as a highly efficient entrepot. [Reference translation provided in the original example: 在2019年年中，香港人口約751萬。香港雖然面積小，但朝氣蓬勃、一幹勁十足。香港被譽為全球首屈, 指的商業及金融中心，亦是一個效率超卓的轉口港。]
- **Google Translate** 2019 年年中，香港人口約為751萬，是一座雖小但充滿活力的城市，作為領先的商業和金融中心以及高效的轉口港而享有國際聲譽。
- **ChatGPT** 香港是一座人口约在2019年中期达到750万的小而有活力的城市，不仅因为是一个高效的贸易港口而享有国际声誉，同时也是一个领先的商业和金融中心。

The results indicate that ChatGPT fails to follow the instructions to produce a translation in Traditional Chinese, instead generating a translation in simplified Chinese. The Chinese translation "在 2019 年中期达到 750 万的小而有活力的城市" is also largely unclear, inaccurately translating the number "7.51 million" as "750 万" (7.5 million). Google Translate, however, correctly translates the number with proper use of Traditional Chinese, even though there is still room for improving the overall fluency.

In addition to inadequate support for Chinese, the literature suggests that there is potential for ChatGPT to enhance its non-English translations (Khoshafah 2023), and increasing the proportion of non-English data in the training set might offer a solution (e.g., Anil et al. 2023).

5.2.4 In-Depth Analysis of Context and Background

Although NMT and LLMs have enabled translation systems to consider the context of surrounding words in the input, they tend to struggle when translating texts that require an understanding of nuances extending beyond the immediate input. Tasks involving a comprehensive analysis of paratextual context, background knowledge, or historical context push the limits of current AI technologies, especially when the necessary contextual information is absent from the training data.

The following example, which is longer than the previous ones, is designed to assess the model's ability to translate text requiring a solid grasp of context and background information. It clearly illustrates the significant room for improvement in translation tasks demanding an in-depth analysis of context and background. The source text (HKSAR Government 2023) comes from a speech given by Mr. John Lee, Chief Executive of Hong Kong, a few days before Chinese New Year 2023. The speech announces the resumption of cross-border travel between Mainland China and Hong Kong, following nearly 2 years of COVID-19 border closures.

- **Source text** 今日是年廿七，再過幾日就是大年初一，我們將會送虎迎兔。我先在這裏預祝大家新一年事事如意、身體健康。新一年香港的第一件大事必然是與內地逐步、有序、全面通關。由一月八， 日實施首階段通關到昨日，剛好十天，已經有差不多40萬人次經陸路口岸免檢疫往返兩地，由今日到年三十晚，更會是高峰期。見到兩地人民家庭團聚，在春節前達成重聚的心願，笑容滿面，團團圓圓，温馨感人，我非常欣慰。[Reference translation by the author: Today marks the 27th day of the 12th lunar month, with the Chinese New Year just a few days away. We will soon bid farewell to the Year of the Tiger and welcome the Year of the Rabbit. I would like to take this opportunity to extend my warmest wishes to everyone for a prosperous and healthy New Year in advance. The first significant event for Hong Kong in the New Year is the progressive, orderly, and full resumption of normal travel with Mainland China. Since the implementation of the first phase of travel resumption on January 8 up until yesterday, a span of ten days, approximately 400,000 passengers have travelled quarantine-free between Hong Kong and Mainland China through boundary control points. The peak travel period will continue from today until Chinese New Year's Eve. Witnessing the reunions of cross-boundary families as they fulfil their long-held desire to gather before the Spring Festival, I am deeply touched and filled with immense joy, seeing their beaming smiles and heart-warming celebrations.]
- **Google Translate** Today is the twenty-seventh day of the new year, and in a few days it will be the first day of the new year, and we will send off the tiger and welcome the rabbit. Let me first wish you all the best and good health in the new year. The first major event for Hong Kong in the new year must be the gradual, orderly and comprehensive customs clearance with the mainland. From the implementation of the first phase of customs clearance on January 8 to yesterday, exactly 10 days, almost 400,000 people have traveled to and from the two places through the land port without quarantine. From today to the evening of the 30th of the new year, it will be the peak period. I am very gratified to see the family reunion of people from the two places and their wish to be reunited before the Spring Festival.
- **ChatGPT** Today is the 27th day of the year. In a few days, it will be the first day of the Lunar New Year, and we will be sending off the Year of the Tiger and welcoming the Year of the Rabbit. I would like to take this opportunity to wish everyone a happy and healthy new year. The first major event in Hong Kong in the new year will undoubtedly be the gradual, orderly, and comprehensive clearance with mainland China. From the implementation of the first phase of clearance on January 8th to yesterday, which was exactly ten days, almost 400,000 people have crossed the border without quarantine checks by land. From today until New Year's Eve, it will be the peak period. It is heartwarming to see families from both

sides reunite before the Spring Festival, with smiles on their faces and warmth in their hearts, and I am very pleased about this.

The ChatGPT translation presents two primary issues. Firstly, the model inaccurately translates the expression "年廿七" (the 27th day of the last lunar month) as "the 27th day of the year", a mistake mirrored by Google Translate: "the twenty-seventh day of the new year". This error likely stems from inadequate exposure to training data containing traditional Chinese cultural phrases, resulting in a flawed interpretation of expressions related to dates preceding the Chinese New Year.

Secondly, the model translates "通關" as "clearance", which is, again, similar to the output of Google Translate ("customs clearance"), failing to fully convey the intended meaning within the context of the speech. Clues such as "quarantine inspection" and "Spring Festival" suggest that the term refers to the reopening of borders following the COVID-19 pandemic, rather than "clearance" in a general sense. However, the model lacks the contextual understanding necessary to infer the correct translation.

This example illustrates that while neural models have enabled translation systems to consider local context, they still face challenges in handling texts that call for a comprehensive understanding of background knowledge and context. The translation of complex texts demands in-depth analyses of textual and paratextual context and proper incorporation of external knowledge. As such, human involvement remains crucial in the most nuanced, specialised translation tasks.

5.2.5 Hallucination

Hallucination, or the generation of fictional details, is a well-known shortcoming of LLMs, as discussed in the literature, including reports by OpenAI (2023) and Bubeck et al. (2023). This issue can have significant implications for various use cases, as illustrated by the recent incident where a lawyer cited fabricated cases generated by ChatGPT, which falsely claims to have verified their authenticity, as reported by *The New York Times* (Weiser 2023). The problem could be a key disadvantage of LLMs compared to NMT systems. The latter, being specifically developed for translation and trained on bilingual data pairs, tends to follow the source text more closely and consequently exhibit less hallucination.

The problem of hallucination may become more apparent when an LLM processes input beyond its training data. In these cases, the model may generate fictional details in the target text based on outdated knowledge acquired during pre-training, rather than faithfully translating the source text. For instance, consider the following example from Siu (2023a). The source text was published by the HKSAR Government on 15 March 2023, describing a visit by Mr John Lee, the Chief Executive, to Beijing, accompanied by major government officials:

- **Source Text** 行政長官李家超今日(三月十五日)繼續在北京的訪問行程。他先後拜訪國家科學技術部、文化和旅遊部、海關總署和商務部,與各部門領導就共同關注的事宜交換意見。文化體育及旅遊局局長楊潤雄、政制及内地事務局局長曾國衞、保安局局長鄧炳強、商務及經濟發展局局長丘應樺、醫務衞生局局長盧寵茂教授和創新科技及工業局局長孫東教授亦有出席相關會面。[Reference translation provided in the original example: The Chief Executive, Mr. John Lee, today (March 15) continued his visit in Beijing, where he called on the Ministry of Science and Technology, the Ministry of Culture and Tourism, the General Administration of Customs of the People's Republic of China (GACC), and the Ministry of Commerce to exchange views with the respective leaders on issues of common interest. The Secretary for Culture, Sports and Tourism, Mr. Kevin Yeung; the Secretary for Constitutional and Mainland Affairs, Mr. Erick Tsang Kwok-wai; the Secretary for Security, Mr. Tang Ping-keung; the Secretary for Commerce and Economic Development, Mr. Algernon Yau; the Secretary for Health, Professor Lo Chung-mau; and the Secretary for Innovation, Technology and Industry, Professor Sun Dong, also joined relevant meetings.]

The translation from ChatGPT contains fictional details not present in the source text:

- **ChatGPT** On March 15th, the Chief Executive, Mr. Carrie Lam, continued her visit to Beijing. She visited the Ministry of Science and Technology, the Ministry of Culture and Tourism, the General Administration of Customs, and the Ministry of Commerce, and exchanged views with leaders of these departments on matters of common concern. The Director of the Tourism Bureau, Mr. Yang Runxiong, the Director of the Constitutional and Mainland Affairs Bureau, Mr. Patrick Nip, the Director of the Security Bureau, Mr. John Lee Ka-chiu, the Director of the Commerce and Economic Development Bureau, Mr. Edward Yau Tang-wah, the Director of Health, Professor Sophia Chan Siu-chee, and the Director of the Innovation and Technology Bureau, Professor Alfred Sit Wing-hang, also attended the relevant meetings.

The platform mistakenly insists that the Chief Executive mentioned in the text is Mrs. Carrie Lam, who was in office at the time of the 2021 training data cut-off, before the new government took office in July 2022. The current Chief Executive is Mr. John Lee, who assumed duties after Mrs. Carrie Lam. The tool struggles with the conflict between the presence of the male third-person pronoun "他" in the source text and "Carrie Lam", who is female, as learned from the training data. This leads to the interesting translation of "Mr. Carrie Lam" and inconsistent usage of personal pronouns in the article (e.g., using "She" to refer to "Mr. Carrie Lam"). The job titles and names of government officials in the translation are largely incorrect (e.g., translating " 商務及經濟發展局局長丘應樺 " (the Secretary for Commerce and Economic Development, Mr. Algernon Yau) as "the Director of the Commerce and Economic Development Bureau, Mr. Edward Yau Tang-wah"). Instead of translating according to the source text, the system attempts to translate the names of government officials into the known officials of bureaus with a similar nature in 2021. Notably, Mr. John Lee, the current Chief Executive, appears as "the Director of the Security Bureau" (the correct translation of the post should be "Secretary for Security"), a position he held from 2017 to June 2021, with the post currently held by Mr. Chris Tang Ping-keung.

In contrast, the output of Google Translate adheres more closely to the factual details provided in the source text, with some inaccuracies but fewer instances of hallucination:

- **Google Translate** The Chief Executive, Mr Lee Kar-chao, continued his visit to Beijing today (March 15). He successively visited the Ministry of Science and Technology, the Ministry of Culture and Tourism, the General Administration of Customs and the Ministry of Commerce, and exchanged views with leaders of various departments on issues of common concern. Yang Runxiong, Secretary for Culture, Sports and Tourism, Tsang Kwok-wai, Secretary for Constitutional and Mainland Affairs, Tang Ping-keung, Secretary for Security, Yau Ying-wah, Secretary for Commerce and Economic Development, Professor Lo Chung-mao, Secretary for Medical and Health Bureau, and Professor Sun Dong, Secretary for Innovation, Technology and Industry Attend relevant meetings.

The output is generally based on the source text, without attempting to compare the current officials' names with those prior to 2022. However, there are still discrepancies that would need to be revised during the post-editing stage. These include the correct names of the officials (such as "Mr Lee Kar-chao" and "Yang Runxiong", the latter being a pinyin transliteration for Mr. Kevin Yeung), along with the mistranslation of the post "Secretary for Health", which came into effect in July 2022 but appears as "Secretary for Medical and Health Bureau" in the target text.

6 Recommendations for Translation Educators

As AI-driven translation tools continue to advance rapidly, it is crucial for translation practitioners to adapt their practices to maximise the benefits of these technologies while mitigating their limitations. When leveraged properly with a deep understanding of their capabilities and shortcomings, AI can significantly enhance translator-computer interaction and cooperation in translation. This section provides recommendations for translation educators to help prepare language professionals to work effectively with cutting-edge technologies. For further discussion, please refer to Siu (2023a).

6.1 Focus on Reviewing and Editing Translations

Given the improved fluency of AI-driven translation tools, identifying and correcting issues in their output may become more challenging. It is important to emphasise the critical assessment of AI-based translation output and train students to identify common issues such as omissions, problematic structures in NMT, or hallucinations in LLMs as discussed in Sect. 5. In addition, developing post-editing techniques targeting typical AI errors, and strategies for verifying and improving AI translations using official sources and parallel texts can further enhance students' capabilities.

6.2 Focus on Specialised Translation Domains and Creative Forms of Translation

With AI systems becoming increasingly adept at handling simple translation tasks, human expertise may prove more valuable in specialised domains. These include legal, medical, and technical translation, as well as creative forms of cross-lingual activities such as literary translation, audiovisual translation, game localisation, and marketing content adaptation, with a focus on how translation technology can help solve issues specific to these areas. In the past, conventional translation technology offered limited assistance in creative translation. However, with enhanced capabilities like LLMs, AI tools are now better positioned to provide creative suggestions and edits, as discussed in Siu (2023a). It is, therefore, beneficial for educators to develop curricula and design teaching and learning activities that focus on the use of AI technology in the translation process within these specialised areas. This approach will help students develop expertise and harness the new tools in the context of both specialised and creative translation.

6.3 Provide In-Depth Exploration of AI-Based Translation Technologies

Students can greatly benefit from gaining a deeper understanding of the fundamental principles that underpin the AI technologies used in translation. This goes beyond simply exploring conventional applications such as translation memories and termbases and delves into the intricacies of neural networks, attention mechanisms, and transfer learning. By doing so, students can gain valuable insights into the inner workings of AI translation tools. It is beneficial to teach students how to leverage NMT models using effective prompting and temperature tuning methods. For instance, providing additional information about translation tasks in the prompt and adjusting sampling settings, such as the *k* value in top-k sampling, might be more effective than using default settings provided by developers. Encouraging students to experiment with the optimisation of AI-based translation tools, such as customising pre-trained models using their own data, can further enhance their skills in this area.

6.4 *Enhance Programming and Computational Skills*

Equipping students with basic programming and computational skills can empower them to customise, enhance, and even develop their own AI solutions. For example, translation teachers could introduce students to programming languages such as Python, along with popular machine learning libraries and frameworks. This knowledge would enable students to design and train their own neural networks, explore new decoding methods based on pre-trained weights, or fine-tune models using their own data sets. Familiarising students with data preprocessing and automatic evaluation is also beneficial, as these skills helps them appreciate the crucial role of quality data and evaluation in the development of AI-driven translation applications. The enhancement of programming education can enable students to better understand the limitations of existing tools and build new solutions tailored to their needs.

6.5 *Design More Sophisticated Assessment Tasks*

With the increasing prevalence of AI, simple translation tasks might not adequately assess student abilities, especially given the availability of automatic translation tools that produce moderately accurate drafts. It is, therefore, necessary to incorporate more diverse or challenging assessment tasks into the teaching and learning of practical translation. These tasks should require complex contextual analyses, and students need to demonstrate their ability to verify and correct AI output, along with explaining the rationale behind their corrections. This approach can better assess students' actual performance and encourage them to develop these essential skills for AI-assisted translation. Assessment tasks that simulate real-world challenges, where students work alongside AI tools to manage complex projects utilising various resources and technologies, can also provide a more accurate evaluation of their performance.

7 Recommendations for Developers

To empower language professionals to work effectively with cutting-edge technologies and identify potential areas for new application development, this section presents recommendations for developers. These suggestions, based on Siu (2023a), aim to address the diverse needs of language professionals, enhance the capabilities of AI translation tools, ensure the effective integration of these tools in various cross-lingual communication tasks, and support the continued development of AI applications.

7.1 *Enhance Domain-Specific and Multilingual Support for Models*

To better serve the needs of language professionals in specialised areas and enhance support for multilingual communication, it is crucial to improve domain-specific translation capabilities and multilingual support, especially in LLMs. Developers could build models that are tailored to specific domains, such as legal and technical translation, by incorporating domain-specific data during training and applying domain adaptation methods for better handling of technical expressions. Regarding multilingual support, developers can optimise the use of non-English data and explore possibilities such as zero-shot translation (translating between language pairs without direct parallel data) and cross-lingual transfer learning (learning from one language and apply the knowledge to another). Such strategies can boost the performance of low-resource language pairs (e.g., Gao et al. 2023a).

7.2 *Improve Integration of NMT, LLMs, and Other Tools*

Integrating existing translation technologies with AI-driven tools can more effectively capitalise on the power of AI in the context of translation. For example, incorporating information from translation memory and termbases into prompts may help LLMs reuse translated sentences and terms, ensuring stylistic and terminological consistency. The use of quality estimation models and error detection methods can help address issues such as hallucination, identifying plausible but incorrect translations. Leveraging outputs from multiple sources in this way could enhance translation accuracy, and the development of hybrid systems can take advantage of the strengths of various technologies.

7.3 *Develop AI for Cross-Modal Translation*

With the exponential growth of digital multimedia content, cross-modal translation is becoming increasingly important. It would be advantageous to develop AI solutions that support multimodal, multilingual translation, extending beyond text and speech to encompass images, videos, and other media forms. For example, cross-modal embeddings, such as CLIP (Contrastive Language-Image Pre-training) proposed by OpenAI (Radford et al. 2021), may assist translation systems in learning relationships between modalities, and multimodal language models (e.g., Gong et al. 2023) could facilitate the processing of different media types. The integration of such embeddings and language models into translation applications could improve the quality of multimedia translation. For instance, NMT/LLMs enhanced with multimodal capabilities can capture both text and visual elements in the input, offering a significant advancement over conventional text-based models. Compared with text-only machine translation, these advanced applications could better support tasks like subtitling translation. Furthermore, tools such as speech-to-text (see Xu et al. 2023 for a comprehensive survey) and text-to-image translation (e.g., Li et al. 2023) could streamline communication across modalities.

7.4 Improve Interpretability and User Interaction

Techniques that enhance the interpretability of AI translation tools and improve interaction can help language professionals build trust in AI, ultimately fostering a positive impact on human-AI collaboration. Possible directions include increasing interpretability, for instance, by visualising the next-token prediction process. This could make it easier for users to understand how translations are generated and pinpoint areas for improvement. Moreover, user-friendly interfaces equipped with robust feedback collection mechanisms would allow users to provide instant suggestions regarding the output. This feedback could contribute to further training of LLMs, as seen in the emergence of reinforcement learning with human feedback, exemplified by ChatGPT (OpenAI 2022). Advancements like these would be beneficial for the long-term development of AI applications for translators.

8 Concluding Remarks

This work presents a comprehensive analysis of NMT and LLMs, two major innovations in translation technology. The discussion begins by outlining the four key tasks of deep learning: model design, data collection, model training, and model evaluation. The widely adopted Transformer model is highlighted, including its encoder and decoder, positional encodings, multi-head self-attention, position-wise feed forward networks, layer normalisation, and residual connections.

Building on this foundation, the article explores NMT and generative pre-trained LLMs in the context of translation, with a particular focus on predicting the next target token and decoding methods such as greedy search and sampling. The strengths and limitations of NMT and LLMs are examined in relation to their underlying mechanisms as previously explained. While NMT surpasses conventional approaches and demonstrates enhanced context awareness with the Transformer model, LLMs exhibit promising performance and versatility. However, certain limitations are identified, such as challenges associated with translating long input sentences, providing support for specialised translation and non-English languages, conducting in-depth context and background analysis, and avoiding the generation of fictional details. Illustrative examples are provided to highlight the limitations.

In light of these issues, the article offers recommendations for translation educators. These include emphasising the development of students' skills in reviewing and editing translations, improving their knowledge and skills in specialised translation domains and creative forms of translation, promoting AI literacy (such as understanding how neural networks and decoding methods work), and acquiring programming and computational skills. It is also important to design sophisticated assessment tasks that require demonstration of advanced thinking and translation skills, as it is now easier for students to access moderately accurate drafts prepared by automatic translation tools. Additionally, the article provides recommendations for developers, offering insights into enhancing NMT and LLMs from a development perspective. Suggestions include improving domain-specific and multilingual support, integrating NMT, LLMs, and other applications, exploring cross-modal translation, and focusing on interpretability and user interaction.

The multifaceted analysis of AI for translation presented in this article, from both translation and engineering perspectives, aims to enable language professionals to make informed decisions when using NMT and LLMs. It also encourages translation educators and developers to reconsider how they teach and develop translation technology in light of the new possibilities brought about by these AI advancements, with the goal of facilitating cross-lingual communication through the integration of human intelligence and AI.

Acknowledgements The author acknowledges the insightful comments and valuable suggestions provided by the anonymous reviewer(s).

References

Anil, R., A. M. Dai, O. Firat, M. Johnson, D. Lepikhin, A. Passos, S. Shakeri, et al. 2023. Palm 2 technical report. *arXiv preprint* arXiv:2305.10403.

Bahdanau, D., K. Cho, and Y. Bengio. 2014. Neural machine translation by jointly learning to align and translate. *arXiv preprint* arXiv:1409.0473.

Bridle, J. S. 1990. Probabilistic interpretation of feedforward classification network outputs, with relationships to statistical pattern recognition. In *Neurocomputing*, eds. F. Fogelman-Soulié and J. Hérault, 227–236. Berlin, Heidelberg: Springer.

Bubeck, S., V. Chandrasekaran, R. Eldan, J. Gehrke, E. Horvitz, E. Kamar, P. Lee, et al. 2023. Sparks of artificial general intelligence: Early experiments with GPT-4. *arXiv preprint* arXiv: 2303.12712.

Chu, C., and R. Wang. 2018. A survey of domain adaptation for neural machine translation. *arXiv preprint* arXiv:1806.00258.

Devlin, J., M. W. Chang, K. Lee, and K. Toutanova. 2018. Bert: Pre-training of deep bidirectional transformers for language understanding. *arXiv preprint* arXiv:1810.04805.

Dosovitskiy, A., L. Beyer, A. Kolesnikov, D. Weissenborn, X. Zhai, T. Unterthiner, M. Dehghani, et al. 2020. An image is worth 16x16 words: Transformers for image recognition at scale. *arXiv preprint* arXiv:2010.11929.

Edunov, S., M. Ott, M. Auli, and D. Grangier. 2018. Understanding back-translation at scale. In *Proceedings of the 2018 Conference on Empirical Methods in Natural Language Processing*, 489–500. Association for Computational Linguistics.

Fan, A., M. Lewis, and Y. Dauphin. 2018. Hierarchical neural story generation. In *Proceedings of the 56th Annual Meeting of the Association for Computational Linguistics (Volume 1: Long Papers)*, 889–898. Association for Computational Linguistics.

Gao, P., L. Zhang, Z. He, H. Wu, and H. Wang. 2023a. Improving zero-shot multilingual neural machine translation by leveraging cross-lingual consistency regularization. *arXiv preprint* arXiv: 2305.07310.

Gao, Y., R. Wang, and F. Hou. 2023b. How to design translation prompts for ChatGPT: An empirical study. *arXiv preprint* arXiv:2304.02182.

Gong, T., C. Lyu, S. Zhang, Y. Wang, M. Zheng, Q. Zhao, K. Liu, et al. 2023. Multimodal-GPT: A vision and language model for dialogue with humans. *arXiv preprint* arXiv:2305.04790.

Goodfellow, I., Y. Bengio, A. Courville, and Y. Bengio. 2016. *Deep learning*. Cambridge: MIT Press.

Hinton, G., O. Vinyals, and J. Dean. 2015. Distilling the knowledge in a neural network. *arXiv preprint* arXiv:1503.02531.

HKSAR Government. 2023a. 行政長官出席2022年特區政府施政十件大事評選頒獎典禮致辭. https://www.info.gov.hk/gia/general/202301/18/P2023011800598.htm. Accessed 3 July 2023.

Holtzman, A., J. Buys, L. Du, M. Forbes, and Y. Choi. 2019. The curious case of neural text degeneration. *arXiv preprint* arXiv:1904.09751.

Hong Kong and Macao Affairs Office of the State Council. 2023. 國務院港澳辦發言人:內地與香港 『通關』工作正有序推進. https://big5.hmo.gov.cn/gate/big5/www.hmo.gov.cn/xwzx/xwfb/xwfb_child/202111/t20211104_22957.html.

Jiao, W., W. Wang, J. Huang, X. Wang, and Z. Tu. 2023b. Is ChatGPT a good translator? Yes with GPT-4 as the engine. *arXiv preprint* arXiv:2301.08745.

Jurafsky, D., and J. H. Martin. 2023. *Speech and language processing* (3rd ed. draft). https://web.stanford.edu/~jurafsky/slp3/ed3book_jan72023.pdf. Accessed 2 July 2023.

Kamath, U., J. Liu, and J. Whitaker. 2019. *Deep learning for NLP and speech recognition*, 2019. Cham, Switzerland: Springer.

Khan, S., M. Naseer, M. Hayat, S.W. Zamir, F.S. Khan, and M. Shah. 2022. Transformers in vision: A survey. *ACM Computing Surveys* 54 (10): 1–41.

Khoshafah, F. 2023. ChatGPT for Arabic-English translation: Evaluating the accuracy. https://doi.org/10.21203/rs.3.rs-2814154/v2. Accessed 3 July 2023.

Kingma, D. P., and J. Ba. 2014. Adam: A method for stochastic optimization. *arXiv preprint* arXiv: 1412.6980.

Koehn, P. 2020. *Neural machine translation*. Cambridge: Cambridge University Press.

Koehn, P. and R. Knowles. 2017. Six challenges for neural machine translation. In *First Workshop on Neural Machine Translation*: 28–39. Association for Computational Linguistics.

Krizhevsky, A., I. Sutskever, and G. E. Hinton. 2012. ImageNet classification with deep convolutional neural networks. In *Advances in Neural Information Processing Systems 25*: 1097–1105. Neural Information Processing Systems Foundation.

Kudo, T., and J. Richardson, J. 2018. SentencePiece: A simple and language independent subword tokenizer and detokenizer for neural text processing. In *Proceedings of the 2018 Conference on Empirical Methods in Natural Language Processing: System Demonstrations*, 66–71. Association for Computational Linguistics.

Landrich Holding Limited. 2020. Share Offer. https://www1.hkexnews.hk/listedco/listconews/sehk/2020/0930/2020093000019.pdf. Accessed 3 July 2023.

LeCun, Y., Y. Bengio, and G. Hinton. 2015. Deep learning. *Nature* 521: 436–444.

Li, Y., C. Y. Chang, S. Rawls, I. Vulić, and A. Korhonen. 2023. Translation-enhanced multilingual text-to-image generation. *arXiv preprint* arXiv:2305.19216.

Mikolov, T., K. Chen, G. Corrado, and J. Dean. 2013. Efficient estimation of word representations in vector space. *arXiv preprint* arXiv:1301.3781.

OpenAI. 2022. Introducing ChatGPT. https://openai.com/blog/chatgpt. Accessed 3 July 2023.

OpenAI. 2023. GPT-4 technical report. *arXiv preprint* arXiv:2303.08774.

Ouyang, L., J. Wu, X. Jiang, D. Almeida, C. Wainwright, P. Mishkin, C. Zhang, et al. 2022. Training language models to follow instructions with human feedback. In *Advances in Neural Information Processing Systems 35*: 27730–27744. Neural Information Processing Systems Foundation.

Papineni, K., S. Roukos, T. Ward, T., and W. J. Zhu. 2002. Bleu: A method for automatic evaluation of machine translation. In *Proceedings of the 40th annual meeting of the Association for Computational Linguistics*, 311–318. Association for Computational Linguistics.

Peng, K., D. Liang, Q. Zhong, L. Shen, X. Liu, M. Zhang, Y. Ouyang, et al. 2023. Towards making the most of ChatGPT for machine translation. *arXiv preprint* arXiv:2303.13780.

Pennington, J., R. Socher, and C. D. Manning. 2014. GloVe: Global vectors for word representation. *Proceedings of the 2014 Conference on Empirical Methods in Natural Language Processing*, 1532–1543. Association for Computational Linguistics.

Popović, M. 2015. CHRF: Character n-gram F-score for automatic MT evaluation. In *Proceedings of the Tenth Workshop on Statistical Machine Translation*, 392–395. Association for Computational Linguistics.

Radford, A., K. Narasimhan, T. Salimans, and I. Sutskever. 2018. Improving language understanding by generative pre-training. https://cdn.openai.com/research-covers/language-unsupervised/language_understanding_paper.pdf. Accessed 3 July 2023.

Radford, A., J. Wu, R. Child, D. Luan, D. Amodei, and I. Sutskever. 2019. Language models are unsupervised multitask learners. https://cdn.openai.com/better-language-models/language_models_are_unsupervised_multitask_learners.pdf. Accessed 3 July 2023.

Radford, A., J. W. Kim, C. Hallacy, A. Ramesh, G. Goh, S. Agarwal, G. Sastry, et al. 2021. Learning transferable visual models from natural language supervision. In *International conference on machine learning*, 8748–8763. PMLR.

Raffel, C., N. Shazeer, A. Roberts, K. Lee, S. Narang, M. Matena, Y. Zhou, et al. 2020. Exploring the limits of transfer learning with a unified text-to-text transformer. *The Journal of Machine Learning Research* 21 (1): 5485–5551.

Rei, R., C. Stewart, A. C. Farinha, and A. Lavie. 2020. COMET: A neural framework for MT evaluation. In *Proceedings of the 2020 Conference on Empirical Methods in Natural Language Processing*, 2685–2702. Association for Computational Linguistics.

Sellam, T., D. Das, and A. Parikh. 2020. BLEURT: Learning robust metrics for text generation. In *Proceedings of the 58th Annual Meeting of the Association for Computational Linguistics*, 7881–7892. Association for Computational Linguistics.

Sennrich, R., B. Haddow, and A. Birch. 2016. Improving neural machine translation models with monolingual data. In *Proceedings of the 54th Annual Meeting of the Association for Computational Linguistics (Volume 1: Long Papers)*, 86–96. Association for Computational Linguistics.

Siu, S.C. 2022. COVID-19 MT Evaluator: A platform for the evaluation of machine translation of public health information related to COVID-19. In *Translation and Interpreting in the Age of COVID-19*, ed. K. Liu and A.K.F. Cheung, 85–109. Singapore: Springer.

Siu, S.C. 2023a. ChatGPT and GPT-4 for professional translators: Exploring the potential of large language models in translation. *Available at SSRN:* https://doi.org/10.2139/ssrn.4448091.

Siu, S.C. 2023b. Deep learning and translation technology. In *Routledge Encyclopedia of Translation Technology*, 2nd ed., ed. S.W. Chan, 797–817. London: Routledge.

Siu, S.C. 2019. IPOTranslate: An Online System for English-Chinese Translation of IPO Prospectuses. https://ipotranslate.com/static/IPOTranslate.pdf. Accessed 3 July 2023.

Stahlberg, F. 2020. Neural machine translation: A review. *Journal of Artificial Intelligence Research* 69: 343–418.

Sutskever, I., J. Martens, G. Dahl, and G. Hinton. 2013. On the importance of initialization and momentum in deep learning. In *International Conference on Machine Learning*: 1139–1147. PMLR.

Tay, Y., M. Dehghani, D. Bahri, and D. Metzler. 2020. Efficient Transformers: A survey. *arXiv preprint* arXiv:2009.06732.

Tay, Y., V.Q. Tran, S. Ruder, J. Gupta, H.W. Chung, D. Bahri, Z. Qin, et al. 2021. Charformer: Fast character transformers via gradient-based subword tokenization. *arXiv preprint* arXiv:2106.12672.
Vaswani, A., N. Shazeer, N. Parmar, J. Uszkoreit, L. Jones, A. N. Gomez, Ł. Kaiser, and I. Polosukhin. 2017. Attention is all you need. In *Proceedings of the 31st International Conference on Neural Information Processing Systems*, 6000–6010. NIPS Foundation.
Weiser, B. 2023, May 27. Here's what happens when your lawyer uses ChatGPT. *The New York Times*.
Xiong, R., Y. Yang, D. He, K. Zheng, S. Zheng, C. Xing, H. Zhang, et al. 2020. On layer normalization in the transformer architecture. In *International Conference on Machine Learning*, 10524–10533. PMLR.
Xu, C., R. Ye, Q. Dong, C. Zhao, T. Ko, M. Wang, T. Xiao, et al. 2023. Recent advances in direct speech-to-text translation. *arXiv preprint* arXiv:2306.11646.
Zhang, S., and Y. Feng. 2021. Modeling concentrated cross-attention for neural machine translation with Gaussian Mixture Model. In *Findings of the Association for Computational Linguistics: EMNLP 2021*: 1401–1411. Association for Computational Linguistics.
Zhang, T., V. Kishore, F. Wu, K. Q. Weinberger, and Y. Artzi. 2019. BERTScore: Evaluating text generation with BERT. *arXiv preprint* arXiv:1904.09675.
Zhang, A., Z. C. Lipton, M. Li, and A. J. Smola. 2021. Dive into deep learning. *arXiv preprint* arXiv:2106.11342.

Dr. Sai Cheong Siu is an Associate Professor in the School of Translation and Foreign Languages at The Hang Seng University of Hong Kong. He is the Programme Director of the Bachelor of Translation with Business and the Master of Arts in Translation (Computer-aided Translation). His research focuses on translation technology and artificial intelligence for the creative industries. His publicly-funded projects include "Machine Translation of IPO Documents" and "A Hybrid Approach to the Translation of Government Press Releases", supported by the Innovation and Technology Fund and the Research Grants Council, respectively.

Cloud Technologies in Media Localisation (Subtitling and Revoicing)

Alejandro Bolaños García-Escribano

Abstract The media localisation industry has experienced an increasing presence of cloud-based technologies, leading many stakeholders to embrace and incorporate them into their localisation workflows. Cloud solutions use the internet and off-site storage to operate, thereby enhancing the mobility and flexibility of the workforce. Large media producers also use cloud-based ecosystems to distribute localisation work among translation service providers, who often outsource work to linguists using proprietary cloud-based tools. Cloud technologies are more agile than legacy desktop programs, and software developers are keen to establish close collaborations with end users and academic institutions in their quest for feedback on user experience. This makes cloud-based solutions the perfect allies for fine-tuning technologies and customising the newest tools to the needs of audiovisual translators. The main aim of this chapter is to take stock of the far-reaching implications of cloud technologies in the industry and to investigate their potential in translation studies, particularly translator training environments. A discussion will be provided on how these tools operate and how workflows are (re-)shaped by these new tools. This chapter suggests ways to exploit them, from a pedagogical perspective, in the teaching and learning of media localisation (aka audiovisual translation), specifically subtitling and revoicing.

The original version of the chapter has been revised: The author name has been updated. A correction to this chapter can be found at
https://doi.org/10.1007/978-981-97-2958-6_14

A. Bolaños García-Escribano (✉)
University College London, London, United Kingdom
e-mail: a.bolanos@ucl.ac.uk

Universitat Jaume I, Castelló, Spain

Y. Peng et al. (eds.), *New Advances in Translation Technology*, New Frontiers in Translation Studies, https://doi.org/10.1007/978-981-97-2958-6_4

1 Introduction

Cloud-based platforms have been catalysts for change in the translation industry since the turn of the century. Scholars have previously established that the wider use of cloud technologies has led to a so-called "cloud turn" (Bolaños García-Escribano & Díaz-Cintas, 2020, p. 520). The translation of popular TV series, films, and all sorts of audiovisual programmes is currently being undertaken with cloud software that translation agencies and service providers tend to share exclusively with their pool of translators (usually for free). Several caveats notwithstanding, these cloud tools are supposed to reduce costs, improve security against piracy, increase productivity and enhance connectivity among professionals by providing clients, vendors and end users with an online solution—usually accessed through a browser—that utilises cloud computing to store the files and process the data that are necessary to undertake revoicing or subtitling projects.

Progressively incorporated into translators' workbenches, cloud ecosystems are now widely present across the translation industry (Díaz-Cintas & Massidda, 2019). In the ever-changing landscape of the language industries (Baños & Díaz-Cintas, 2015; Georgakopoulou, 2018), audiovisual programmes—films, series, or commercial videos, among others—are currently being localised with cloud software. Regarding translation project management, these cloud tools often provide end-to-end ecosystems where clients, vendors and end users can easily communicate and share working files via a browser-based platform that utilises cloud computing to process data. Media localisation workflows are directly affected by this migration of work onto cloud environments and are increasingly online. Yet, cloud-based translation ecosystems are far from newcomers and have long been used by language vendors to enhance internet-based access to translation tools for freelance linguists, often developing proprietary platforms to improve the overall productivity and quality of the translation outcome achieved (Bolaños García-Escribano & Díaz-Cintas, 2020).

Alongside the rapid and profound evolution of media localisation workflows came a substantial number of new scenarios and research trends that echoed new viewing habits (Chaume, 2016, 2018), including the so-called "Netflix effect" (Matrix, 2014, p. 219). Younger generations have less of a commitment to live TV, with media scholars such as McDonald and Smith-Rowsey (2016, p. 2) positing that "[Netflix] has become synonymous with the growing, pervasive impact of technology". Nowadays, leading media services offer almost instant access to audiovisual programmes via video-on-demand platforms, video-sharing services, and social media platforms. New consumption habits have led to a significant expansion of practices, such as growing media accessibility services and more mainstream use of English-language dubbing. Fresher consumption trends, irrespective of origin, continue transforming how audiovisual content is distributed globally nowadays, but also the nature of in-demand media localisation services. In light of the sheer volumes of media content being produced nowaday, it would not be too far-fetched to argue that such changes owe to the expansion of new technologies such as cloud computing.

Against this backdrop, and amid the so-called fourth industrial revolution (Schwab, 2017), this chapter seeks a better understanding of how cloud systems have been embedded in the media localisation industry in recent decades. It also establishes that recent advancements in cloud computing have undoubtedly fuelled new ways in which we consume and interact with media—including the instant availability of on-demand videos on the internet that many take for granted nowadays. The emphasis lies on cloud revoicing and subtitling and their impact on the media localisation industry while taking stock of the new applications and scenarios.

2 Cloud Technologies in the Translation Industry

In the culture of the digital age, technology-led changes have deeply transformed the variable nature of translation. Traditional understandings of translation as a form of interlingual rendering of written text are becoming obsolete in the wake of technological advancements (Cronin 2013), and cloud technologies are known to be driving more efficient workflows in a booming industry.

Language services have a considerable size in the international market. Fifteen years ago, the European Commission's Directorate-General for Translation (2009, p. III) predicted "an approximate value of the [European] language industry of 16.5 billion € in 2015", doubling the €8.4 billion generated by European member states in the year of publication of their report. Years later, the 2022 *European Language Industry Survey* (ELIS) collated 1,342 responses from language service providers, independent language professionals, students or representatives of training institutions, language departments and language service buyers. The authors suggest that not only has confidence been restored following the COVID-19 pandemic, but "more than 50% of the language company respondents expected 2021 market growth to be in line with pre-Covid years, and were even more optimistic about their performance (net 71% expecting growth)" (ELIS Research, 2022, p. 6). The translation industry has been one of sustained growth with most predictions exceeding expectations in the midst of a troubled global economic climate (Massey et al. 2023).

Some of the latest Nimdzi's reports (2019, 2020, 2021, 2022) have been equally optimistic about the steady growth of the translation industry, and 2021 even marked the rise of TransPerfect to a position of long-time industry leadership after surpassing a threshold that no other company had met in the language industry—a $1 billion in revenue in a tax year. When it comes to media localisation, production and distribution changes have been profoundly spearheaded by policies such as the European Commission's revised Audiovisual Media Services Directive (2016, 2018) and other legal instruments like the seminal *Convention on the Rights of Persons with Disabilities* produced by the United Nations (2006). Whereas the former requires large media producers to invest in European audiovisual content by imposing a minimum quota (Nikoltchev 2022), the latter establishes the right to access media content for people with sensory disabilities. Both initiatives thereby boost the need for localising media content in a myriad of languages. Consequently, audiovisual materials feature on-demand products and services, with the market experiencing its biggest financial growth in recent years—"24% in 2021 compared to 2020" (Nimdzi 2022, p. 57). In this context, cloud technologies have made inroads into the language industry, facilitating the implementation of swifter turnaround times and thereby increasing efficiency among stakeholders by enhancing international collaboration via the internet.

2.1 Cloud Systems

Cloud computing commenced as a niche market in the late 1990s. Years later, in the age of big data and artificial intelligence, cloud systems have altered the ways in which businesses use applications and store information (Antonopoulos and Gillian, 2017). According to the BSI (2015, p. 2), it has even changed "how organisations should assess and mitigate information security risks because of the significant changes in how computing resources are technically designed, operated and governed."

Clouds allow end-users to manage tasks while storing files in off-site servers, sharing documents via the internet and working simultaneously and remotely on the same platform. Most users now take these everyday computer tasks for granted, but from an epistemological point of view, the essence of cloud computing is a complex matter (Vaquero et al., 2009). There is also a patent lack of terminological consensus arising from the diverging positioning scholars can adopt, i.e., as developers, traders, or end users (Birman et al., 2009). However, the US National Institute of Standards and Technology's definition of cloud computing remains extremely useful for a lay readership. In the words of Mell and Grance (2011, p. 2), cloud computing is "a model for enabling ubiquitous, convenient, on-demand network access to a shared pool of configurable computing resources (e.g., networks, servers, storage, applications, and services) that can be rapidly provisioned and released with minimal management effort or service provider interaction". In terms of how cloud systems work, it is important to note that cloud computing refers to "both the applications delivered as services over the internet and the hardware and systems software in the data centers that provide those services" (Armbrust et al. 2010, p. 50).

More business-oriented understandings of cloud computing have instead capitalised on its efficiency, notably the fact that "it is much cheaper to leverage these resources as services, paying as you go and as you need them, than it is to buy more hardware and software for the data center" (Linthicum 2010, p. 7). According to Armbrust et al. (2010), cloud platforms imply that up-front capital expense is no longer required for end-users, who can purchase the exact amount of time they need to use the tools and services by subscribing to pay-as-you-go systems (aka pay-per-use platforms). This means end-users no longer have to purchase lifetime licenses for desktop-based tools that may become obsolete. The main advantage of cloud computing is, perhaps, the delocalisation of file-based data storage. End-users can reduce hardware expenses and increase data access efficiency by replacing hard drives with hosting services via cloud computing. Furthermore, cloud systems developers offer stable environments that can be more easily fine-tuned on demand, thus enhancing software agility and customisation.

Cloud systems require several components to work, such as data storage and central processing units that can be on- or off-premises. Cloud providers supply developers with the infrastructure necessary to operate a specific application, whereas developers leverage the technology and resources needed and acquire the cloud services they need on a pay-as-you-go basis. Bolaños García-Escribano & Díaz-Cintas's (2020) taxonomy of cloud systems, which draws on Sriram & Khajeh-Hosseini (2010), Linthicum (2010) and Shroff (2010), helps understand where cloud-based translation systems lie, especially in terms of abstraction—that is, whether a given cloud operates as a software, a service, or a platform.

Cloud ecosystems have led to far-reaching changes in the translation profession as much as in educational settings. In the industry, job projects are currently being dealt with within cloud environments. While in the past, translators would set up their workstations by purchasing single-version licenses of specialist software, which represented high up-front costs, today's vendors can provide their workforce with access to complimentary cloud-based private and proprietary software. Long gone are the days when translators would acquire single-version tools in the form of shrink-wrap, desktop-based software with little or no possibility of receiving updates for newer versions of the same software. More innovative systems will inevitably supersede the swift current cloud environments, allowing users to share information and handle projects more efficiently. It is just a matter of time before the ways in which users operate nowadays in cloud-computing environments experience yet a new metamorphosis. This may respond to the challenges posed by security, which remains a concern shared by developers and end-users (Vaquero et al. 2011) because of the multitenancy nature of cloud environments. Two decades into the twenty-first century, in the midst of third-generation internet and artificial intelligence developments, there are many ways for translators to use translation technology, and the likes of OpenAI's ChatGPT (https://openai.com/blog/chatgpt) and similar language models—also deployed using cloud service models—are bound to cause further changes in the uses and applications of language technologies as we know them today. However, these fall beyond the scope of the present chapter.

2.2 *Professional Translation Workbenches*

Whereas basic computerised tools, such as text editors, led to deep transformations in translation workflows and productivity before the turn of the century, the translation industry is now experiencing exponential growth that affects the nature of the translation work required. Among the most in-demand solutions are translation tools designed to enhance efficiency (O'Hagan 2016; Bowker and Corpas-Pastor 2015). Language technologies—including computer-aided tools (Bowker 2002; Chan 2004) and revoicing and subtitling systems in the case of media localisation—allow translators to process greater volumes of work more swiftly (Chan 2017). Traditionally known as "translation workstations" (Quah 2006, p. 93), these technologies have been spearheaded by the internetisation and globalisation of language-related work, accommodating new practices, expectations, and experiences in interlingual communication and, consequently, the translation industry. Linguists thereby have access to a combination of free and paid software (Chan 2014), although vendors and companies can offer them on a complimentary basis.

Despite the vast array of tools available on the market today, further emphasis is placed on two types of computer-aided translation (CAT) tools only—translation memory (TM) and machine translation (MT) (Bowker 2002; Chan 2015; Corpas-Pastor and Durán-Muñoz 2018). Designed to improve productivity and cost-effectiveness, these tools have had a major impact on translation workflows (Gough 2018).

On the one hand, TM operates by suggesting translation options to (human) translators on a segment-by-segment basis, using previous translations already stored in the tool based on the users' previously aligned segments and databases (see, for instance, Bowker 2002). TM cloud platforms are becoming increasingly popular among freelancers and agencies due to their pay-per-use services and lack of installation packages. Additionally, many cloud TM tools now include MT engines or allow for the use of external MT systems via an API (Application Programming Interface), which uses unique identifier codes known as tokens to share content and data between software applications. The most commonly used cloud TM tools available in the market are MateCat (www.matecat.com), memoQ Cloud (www.memoq.com/cloud), Memsource Cloud (https://cloud.memsource.com), SDL Online Editor (http://www.sdltrados.com/products/language-cloud/online-editor), Transifex (www.transifex.com), Wordfast Anywhere (www.freetm.com) and XTM Cloud (www.xtm-cloud.com).

On the other hand, MT systems automate the translation process even further by instantly transferring copious amounts of text from one language to another. MT systems facilitate the "automatic production of a target-language text on the basis of a source-language text" (Kenny 2022, p. 32). Unlike TM systems, MT systems are designed to replace the human translator when generating raw translated output, changing the translator's role to that of a post-editor (Torrejón & Rico 2012; Robert et al. 2022). The development of MT engineering dates back to the mid-twentieth century and has evolved much from early, rudimentary approaches such as first-generation, word-for-word translation systems with no built-in linguistic component (Wilks 2009; Koehn 2010). The most recent and sophisticated approach, neural MT, was introduced in 2016 and is based on deep learning in neural networks and is widely used nowadays (Kenny 2022). Many translation scholars and computational linguists have studied the use of MT systems in translation, focusing on topics such as translation quality (Federico et al. 2014), evaluation metrics (Babych 2014), post-editing effort (O'Brien et al. 2014), potential productivity gains (Federico et al. 2012) and the training of translators-to-be (Gaspari et al. 2015).

The industry landscape depicted by Nimdzi's latest report (2023) and Language Technology Atlas (2022) is one where CAT tools—including TM and MT but also project and quality management systems—are steadily migrating to cloud environments in search of more dynamic and online solutions. Desktop-based software programs continue to be supported by developers and are reliable, but licenses are usually bound to a single version and user or machine, and the latest updates may need to be purchased. Besides, in the height of remote work, particularly fuelled by the COVID-19-led lockdowns imposed by most nation states in 2020 (OECD 2020), translators may no longer have a fixed working space, nor may they be eager to invest in shrink-wrap software, lifetime licenses or ultimately periodical updates of the translation software they use. According to Nimdzi (2022, online), "the majority of the tools are now on the cloud", with most TM tools now offering online or hybrid solutions. As for MT engines, some of the most popular ones are currently available online, too, such as Iconic Translation Machines (https://iconictranslation.com), KantanMT (www.kantanmt.com), Language Studio (https://omniscien.com/language-studio/language-studio-2), Microsoft Translator (https://translator.microsoft.com), Pairaphrase (www.pairaphrase.com), SmartMATE (www.smartmate.co) and SYSTRAN (www.systransoft.com). Lastly, cloud-based project management tools, such as XTRF (www.xtrf.eu), allow vendors to centralise project and quality management systems in more customisable interfaces.

It is worth recalling that translators' workbenches can include other applications to further automate the text creation or revision process (e.g., language spellcheckers, speech, and optical character recognition) or facilitate the decoding or rewriting process (e.g., dictionaries and thesauri). Advancements in the fields of natural language processing, machine learning and artificial intelligence will continue to feature more prominently in future technological developments in the industry.

2.3 *Professional Media Localisation Workstations*

Media localisation practices are usually subsumed under two main umbrella categories: revoicing and subtitling (Bolaños García-Escribano & Díaz-Cintas, 2019, p. 207). In broad terms, whereas the former encompasses practices in which new soundtracks are created and often superimposed (e.g., lip-sync dubbing, voiceover, audio description), the latter preserves the original soundtracks by adding snippets of text onto the screen (e.g., interlingual subtitling, closed captioning, respeaking). Revoicing and subtitling solutions can be categorised depending on two main factors: firstly, the availability and distribution of the program (i.e., commercial, proprietary, or free) and, secondly, the tenancy of the application (i.e., desktop- or cloud-based). Additionally, media localisation software can include language automation functionalities such as TM and MT engines, spellcheckers, and similar built-in or API-integrated tools.

Subtitling, including interlingual and intralingual subtitling (notably *closed captioning*, also known as *subtitling for the deaf and the hard of hearing* in the

UK), has usually been the preferred mode for the testing and implementation of new technological solutions. Specialist subtitling systems (also known as *text-timing editors*) are essential for linguists working on any given subtitling project, and they have been an integral part of the industry since the late 1980s (Kuo 2015). The first subtitling programs were developed with commercial intent and were desktop-based. Software developers then offered software as shrink-wrap products with lifetime licenses, though electronic purchases and pay-per-use schemes soon followed. Among the best-recognised desktop-based subtitling software were EZTitles (www.eztitles.com), FAB (www.fab-online.com), Screen Systems' WinCAPS (www.screensystems.tv), Spot (www.spotsoftware.nl) and TitleVision (http://titlevision.dk). Large vendors developed other applications in-house, including the now obsolete Deluxe's EddiePlus (http://bydeluxemedia.com) and SDI Media's Global Titling System (www.sdimedia.com), which distributed them among freelance linguists. Instances of freeware packages with near-professional functionality have also been widely available on the internet for many years now, including Aegisub (www.aegisub.org), DivXLand Media Subtitler (https://divxland-media-subtitler.en.uptodown.com/windows), Subtitle Edit (www.nikse.dk/SubtitleEdit) and Subtitling Workshop (http://subworkshop.sourceforge.net/index.php).

Revoicing practices—such as dubbing and voiceover—remained largely unaffected by the latest technology until a few years ago. Most revoicing professionals did not have access to any instances of specialist software and had to complete tasks using generic text editors and video players, not least because "dedicated technology is therefore used at a later stage, in the dubbing or recording studio, and its use is not required by translators or dialogue writers" (Baños 2018, p. 10). Exceptions were that the commercial program VoiceQ (www.voiceq.com) and freeware program Capella (www.cappella.tv) allowed for the creation of dubbing tracks with relevant notations[1] with the aid of *bande rythmo* (henceforth, rhythmoband[2]). Other software packages have also been used for audio description production and recording, such as the ones developed by Starfish Technologies (www.starfish.tv/audio-description-video-description). The development of most revoicing tools is indeed recent, coinciding with the spread of cloud technologies, as will be discussed in the next section.

While the usefulness of CAT tools in media localisation remains relatively unexplored, Athanasiadi (2015, 2017) established that subtitlers are interested in integrating subtitling tools with language automation tools such as TM and MT systems. Some developers have ventured into this field with the introduction of video preview players in their traditional CAT tools, including the likes of Kilgray (www.memoq.com), Star AG (www.star-uk.co.uk), Transifex (www.transifex.com) and Wordbee (www.wordbee.com). Internationally known TM system Trados Studio (currently owned by RWS) launched an ad-hoc subtitling app, in early 2019, for professionals to translate pre-timed subtitle templates within the main interface of the TM system.

[1] To know more about the scripting and dialogue writing processes in dubbing, see Spiteri Miggiani (2019).

[2] To know more about rhythmoband, a feature common in the French dubbing industry that is now being widely used in the Anglosphere as well as in other industries, see De los Reyes Lozano (2019).

None of these developments, however, managed to offer text-timing features, which remain essential to originate subtitles even if the industry has recently privileged template-translation practices over text-timing in the interest of efficiency (Georgakopoulou 2006, 2012; Nikolić 2015). Numerous researchers have examined the challenges of integrating MT in subtitling (Bywood et al. 2017), with many focusing on the quality of output (Popowich et al. 2000; Armstrong et al. 2006; Burchardt et al. 2016), post-editing and effort (De Sousa et al. 2011; Georgakopoulou and Bywood 2014; Koponen et al. 2020) and subtitlers' productivity when using MT (Volk 2008; Volk et al. 2010). Ortiz-Boix's (2016) work on language automation tools and post-editing in documentary revoicing is one of the few to explore the use of MT systems in revoicing. The MUSA project (Multilingual Subtitling of multimediA content, 2000–2004) was one of the first to explore the applicability of MT engines to subtitling, but it yielded disappointing results due to the inefficiency of the MT system at the time. Further attempts have followed, with commercially funded, industry-led projects that aim to automatise the production of subtitle templates (Mehta et al. 2021) or even the editing and revision that a human reviewer would undertake of auto-generated translations (Gupta et al. 2021).

Given the multimodal nature of media products, it is worth noticing that the field of automatic speech recognition (ASR) technologies is rapidly advancing, too, with new applications being created and having a noticeable impact on the industry. ASR tools, such as Nuance's Dragon NaturallySpeaking (www.nuance.co.uk), are used to convert spoken language into written text and can therefore be used to create captions or subtitle templates. In respeaking, for instance, a subtitler produces live subtitles by dictating the speech to an ASR tool integrated into a subtitling program (Romero-Fresco 2011). Text-to-speech technologies are also employed to synthesise voices for audio description scripts and create talking subtitles for visually impaired audiences (Verboom et al. 2002). ASR developments are accelerating and are expected to have a noticeable impact on the profession in certain language combinations (e.g., automatic text timing).

3 Embedding Cloud Technologies in Media Localisation Practices

Software in the media localisation industry—where typical workstations differ from those used in other translation practices (Matamala 2005)—has also undergone a progressive and steady migration to the cloud. Over a decade ago, Georgakopoulou (2012) pointed out that the media localisation industry faced the challenge of growing demand for translation services while dealing with budget cuts and shorter time-frames for delivery. To remain competitive and financially viable, vendors have had to adapt and embrace cloud technologies offering translators stable environments to securely and efficiently produce subtitles, dubbing scripts and ensure quality assurance.

According to Nimdzi's (2022) Language Technology Atlas—curated by three female researchers (Akhulkova, Hickey and Hynes)—there are currently over 800 providers of language technology solutions, of which over 400 responded to the surveys. Tools range from editing, translation (business) management, machine translation and interpreting tools to marketplaces and platforms as well as integrators, quality management, ASR and—more importantly for this chapter—media localisation.

Figure 1 constitutes the latest update, at the time of writing, of the Language Technology Atlas regarding media localisation systems and tools. These are categorised under five main types: project and asset management, dubbing editors, subtitling editors, remote recording, and AI-enhanced dubbing tools. Interestingly, most of the dubbing and subtitling editors in this section are now offered on the cloud except for—in order of appearance—Adobe Audition, Magix, nTrack, Nuendo, Pro Tools, Aegisub, AV Manager, Clipomatic, EZTitles, ImAc Subtitle Editor, InView for Subtitling, Kapwing App, PacteraEDGE, Screen Systems (WinCAPS), Subtitle Next, Subtitle Workshop, Subtitle Edit, Title, Titlebee, VisualSubsync, and YesCaption.

The last category (i.e., *AI-enhanced dubbing tools*) is a completely new addition to Nimdzi's atlas, which contrasts with previous versions such as the one from 2019

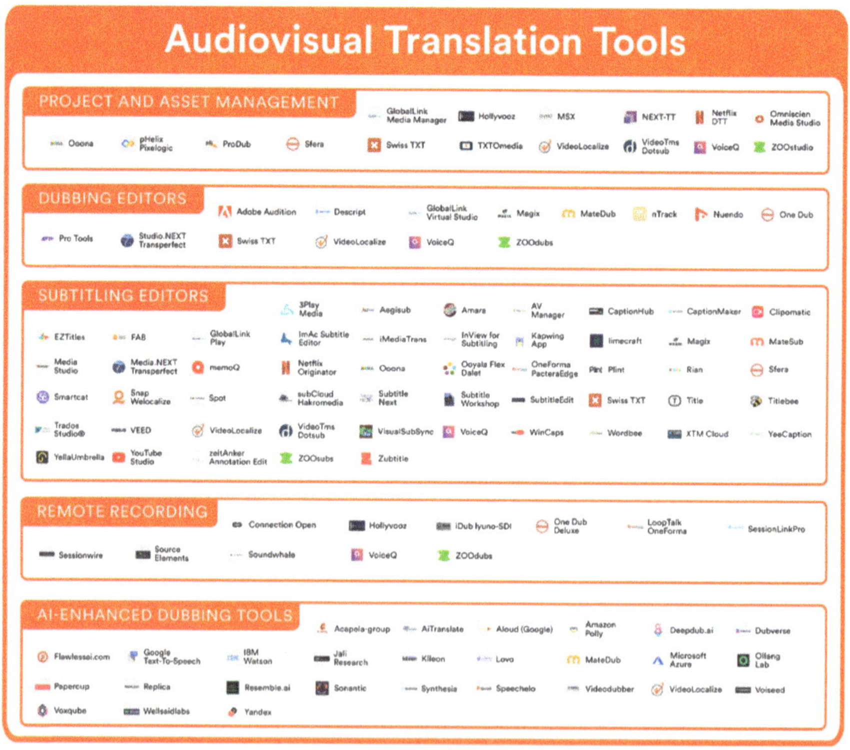

Fig. 1 Language technology Atlas by Nimdzi (2022)

Fig. 2 Language technology Atlas by Nimdzi (2019)

(Fig. 2). In the 3 years that separate both reports, not only have three new categories been added, but the total number of software programs mapped by the researchers has also grown considerably. This is exemplary of the media localisation industry's growth, which needs ad-hoc technology solutions to handle greater volumes of work. It only follows that further attention will continue to be paid cloud ecosystems and artificial intelligence solutions to enhance automation.

As it happens, collaborative projects initiated by specific organisations or volunteer teams were among the first to experiment with subtitling in cloud-based environments. They used online platforms, built specifically for subtitling, which were easy to use and had been designed for volunteers with limited subtitling skills. Amara (https://amara.org), Dotsub (https://dotsub.com), Khan Academy (www.khanacademy.org) and Viki (www.viki.com) are examples of such environments, with TED Talks (www.ted.com) being perhaps the most well-known platform that regularly subtitles videos in multiple languages.

Years after the desktop-based MUSA project was completed, the EU-funded SUMAT (An Online Service for Subtitling by Machine Translation, https://cordis.europa.eu/project/rcn/191,741_en.html) was a cloud-based initiative that ran from 2011 until 2014. It explored the automation of subtitling, using statistical MT functionalities at its core to translate subtitles in seven bi-directional language pairs (Bywood et al. 2017) and yielded positive results despite copyright issues preventing subsequent commercialisations of the system. Similar projects on the use of NMT for the subtitling of educational videos via the internet were TransLectures (Transcription and Translation of Video Lectures, 2011–2014, https://cordis.europa.eu/project/id/287755) and TraMooc (Translation for Massive Open Online Courses 2015–2018, https://cordis.europa.eu/project/id/644333). More recently, Media Studio (www.omniscien.com/media-studio) and MediaWen (www.mediawen.com) have developed automated approaches to subtitling and revoicing. Whereas the former allows users to increase productivity and reduce costs by creating subtitles from screenplay and media files and translating subtitle content using a custom subtitle MT workflow, the latter has developed customisable platforms that provide automatic dubbing and subtitling online solutions.

Cloud environments offer advantages for media localisation businesses. First, they can manage the entire project online, allowing linguists to work from various geographical locations, which can reduce the need for physical offices. Secondly, they allow for leaner, streamlined workflow management that saves time in the editing, post-production, and delivery stages. Thirdly, employees, whether freelancers or in-house staff, can access the platform from any device connected to the internet, which adds flexibility to workflows and can result in higher levels of workforce satisfaction. Fourthly, project managers can monitor progress at any time in the relevant management ecosystems, allowing linguists to work simultaneously within the same online environment without using separate communication channels such as emails and instant chats. Allowing clients to access the online platform can also improve communication and collaboration. Clients can provide feedback and make requests in real time, and the translation team can respond promptly and adjust their work accordingly. This can help to avoid misunderstandings and ensure that the final product meets the client's expectations. Additionally, cloud-based systems can provide transparency and accountability—besides the enhanced security offered by protected offline storage—that can help build trust between the translation team and the client.

Cloud-based systems can strive to offer quick updates whenever bugs or missteps might occur. Thanks to their agile nature, alterations can be implemented centrally, thus promoting a more stable and seamless work environment, which is why developers are often eager to receive user-generated feedback. Enhancements nurtured by the hand-in-hand collaboration between the software developers, researchers and end users help reshape cloud-based systems and exemplify the fruits such collaborations can yield (Bolaños-García-Escribano et al. 2021). Today, there is also greater interactivity and connectivity among linguists and project managers. More ergonomic interfaces and social networking help with professional scenarios in which a substantial number of individuals work together to localise the same audiovisual content in different language combinations and various geographical spaces (Díaz-Cintas 2015). Using end-to-end management systems, linguists collaborate to translate, revise, proofread and deliver work simultaneously. Cloud computing addresses the subsequent need for efficient and sustainable ecosystems where greater volumes of data are generated and shared.

3.1 Cloud Subtitling

Subtitling is known for its capacity to embrace new technologies swiftly (Díaz-Cintas 2015; Matamala 2017; Athanasiadi 2022), so it is no surprise that cloud-based subtitling solutions were developed decades ago. YouTube was one of the pioneers in offering its users automated subtitling and translation features in 2008. The auto-captioning component, introduced in 2019, uses ASR technology (Google's Voice Search) to generate subtitles automatically based on the audio content of the video, while the auto-translate feature relies on Google Translate to provide real-time translations of the captions into different languages. These features have made it easier for content creators to make their videos accessible to viewers who are deaf or hard of hearing or speak different languages (Harrenstien 2009) and have helped to increase the reach and visibility of content on the platform.

Cloud subtitling platforms provide end-to-end services—via browser-based ecosystems—for video subtitling and post-production tasks. In 2009, the first web-based proprietary subtitling system was launched by ZOO Digital (ZOOsubs, www.zoosubs.com), with a wide range of cloud-based subtitling tools following suit. Similar proprietary tools include the likes of Deluxe One (https://one.bydeluxe.com), MediaWen (http://mediawen.com), iMediaTrans' MSX Cloud (www.imjediatrans.com), Plint (https://plint.com), and YellaUmbrella's Stellar (www.yellaumbrella.tv). Large media services provider Netflix also developed its Subtitle Originator (http://originator.backlot.netflix.com) and QC 2.0 (http://meechum.netflix.com) tools to allocate work to their preferred partners. Netflix's Subtitle Originator, for instance, can only be used by professionals who collaborate directly with the streaming giant, whereas Plint's (formerly Nordisk Undertext) subtitling tool, originally conceived as a proprietary tool for employees, can now be purchased by other language service providers. Other platforms, such as eCaption (www.ecaption.eu) and OOONA Tools (https://ooona.ooonatools.tv), are made available on demand to the public.

Even though most cloud subtitling tools permit the production of subtitles from scratch (see Fig. 3), the widespread use of subtitle templates in the industry (Nikolić 2015; Georgakopoulou 2019) had a knock-on effect on the development of subtitle template-translation applications. As seen in Fig. 4, users can open pre-timed files containing ready-made subtitles in the source (or sometimes pivot) language for the subtitler to focus on the translation.

There are also cloud-based subtitling platforms that, though originally developed for in-house labour or to be distributed among freelance linguists, have eventually

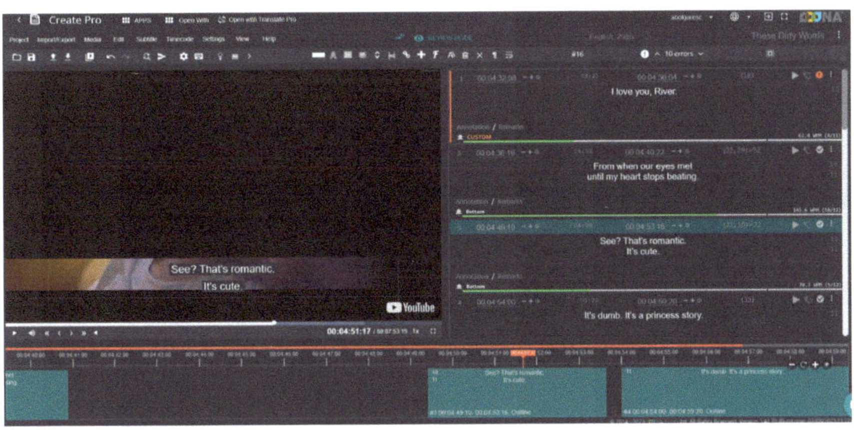

Fig. 3 Text-timing application on OOONA Tools

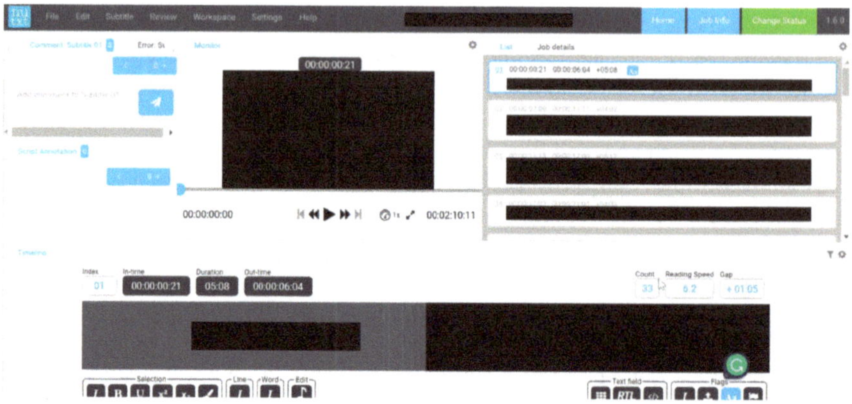

Fig. 4 Interface of Plint's text-timing and template-translation editor (courtesy of Plint)

been made available to would-be subtitlers and trainers through academia-industry collaborations. Examples are Zoo Academy's ZooSubs (www.zoodigital.com/technology/zoosubs) whose text-timing interface can be seen in Fig. 5, and OOONA Edu (https://edu.ooonatools.tv).

Some subtitling systems such as OOONA Tools (see Fig. 6) offer modular solutions with built-in applications to perform tasks such as text-timing, template translation, transcription, revision, conversion and viewing, among other functionalities. These tools, therefore, expand linguists' agency in the subtitle production process and allow users to offer more comprehensive subtitling services to end clients.

Cloud-based subtitling platforms, however, draw heavily on legacy desktop-based programs that pioneered subtitling technology in the previous decades. As a rule of thumb, cloud subtitling tools have the following functionalities:

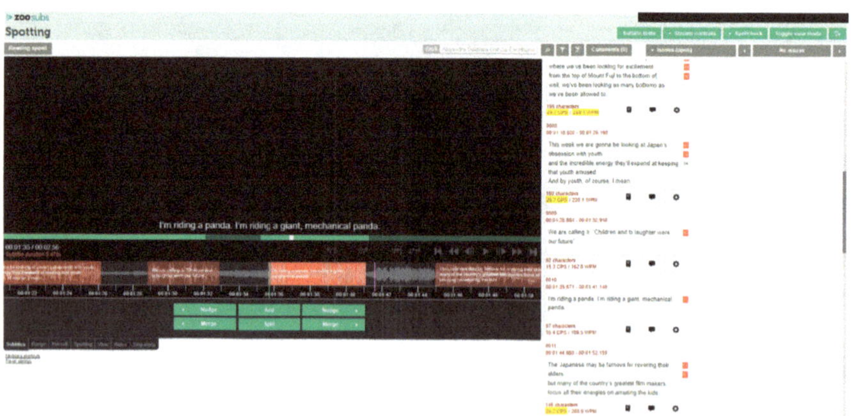

Fig. 5 Text-timing application on ZooSubs

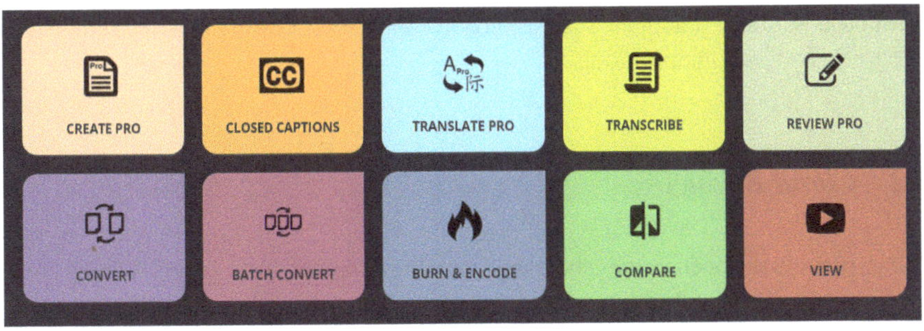

Fig. 6 Dashboard of OOONA Tools

- Annotations and comments: suggestions and terminological references can be discussed and shared as built-in appendices.
- Error checkers: technical and linguistic errors can be automatically checked (and sometimes fixed) using quality check functionalities. These often use the pre-set properties (e.g., characters per line, maximum reading speed, working languages, among others) to amend any errors introduced in the templates.
- Media uploader: users can upload local video files drive or use clips from other cloud-storage services (e.g., Google Drive and Dropbox) and video-streaming platforms (e.g., YouTube).
- Project settings and subtitle configuration: subtitle files can be configured to follow specific parameters (e.g., subtitle duration values and specific subtitle display rates), which can be set up on the system when creating or uploading the files.
- Shortcut customisation: users can set up their hotkeys to minimise the interference with keyboard traps caused by language-specific configurations, browsers, and operating systems.
- Subtitle text editor: interfaces often include basic features, including at least a video player, a text editor (containing timing information) and a waveform display (see Figs. 3, 4 and 5). Additional features that subtitlers would find helpful include shot change detectors, error checkers, space and line counts, display rate meters, font and position toolbars, project configuration menus and change trackers.[3]

Media localisation software developers first focused on creating cloud-based subtitling solutions to echo the greater need for this translation practice in cyberspaces. Many tools have now evolved and often offer appropriate solutions for

[3] Subtitlers ought to observe certain parameters when timing text. Subtitling conventions are often imposed by vendors or clients (e.g., Netflix, 2016/2022), though those conventions are often inspired by academic works on the technical and linguistic considerations of subtitling (e.g., Díaz-Cintas & Remael, 2021). Some important rules include the observation of in and out timecodes in terms of minimum and maximum display values as well as the fact that shot and scene changes trigger certain changes (e.g., snapping to shot change). Also important are the number of characters on each subtitle line and the display rate (i.e., how long the viewer is expected to spend reading each subtitle depending on how long its screen exposure is).

media accessibility practices, such as closed captioning, as well as more widespread integrations of automation tools.

3.2 *Cloud Revoicing*

It has previously been established that viewing changes have recently been instigated by the likes of Netflix, whose "research has shown that dubbed versions of hit shows are more popular than their subtitled equivalents" (Roxborough 2019, online). Following simultaneous advances in ASR technologies, further efforts are now directed at dubbing and voiceover (Green 2018). Although "the dubbing context demonstrates a substantially delayed adoption of technology for the translation" (Bywood 2020, p. 511), the increasing use of artificial intelligence and cloud platforms seems to point in a completely new direction.

Launched in 2003, VoiceQ (www.voiceq.com) pioneered the development of revoicing platforms with their dubbing software. Their platform now integrates cloud solutions for revoicing practices such as dubbing, voiceover and audio description. In 2017, ZOO Digital also launched the cloud dubbing platform ZOOdubs (https://www.zoodigital.com/technology/zoodubs), which was soon followed by Deluxe's One Dub (www.bydeluxe.com/localization) in 2020. More recent is TransPerfect's StudioNext (www.transperfect.com/medianext/services/technology), released in 2020 amid the COVID-19 lockdowns. A closer look at Nimdzi's (2022) Technology Atlas reveals that software developers Videolocalize (https://videolocalize.com) and Matedub (https://matedub.com) offered dubbing editors and are currently tampering with synthetic speech to produce human-sounding, digital dubs employing artificial intelligence. Language automation technologies—such as ASR, MT, and text-to-speech—are being employed in automatic dubbing "to automatically replace the audio track of an original audiovisual text with synthetic speech in a different language, taking into consideration relevant synchronies" (Baños 2023, in press).

According to Chaume and De los Reyes Lozano (2021), cloud dubbing systems reunite all dubbing phases, from scripting to the recording of the dubbed audio track by the voice actors, thereby contributing to the delocalisation of dubbing tasks, which used to involve highly technical processes at dubbing studios (Chaume 2012). In the main interface of Zoo Digital's ZOOdubs platform (see Fig. 7), users can find a basic scripting tool to produce *events* (i.e., text segments that coincide with a given utterance from the video in time). This tool, previously analysed by Chaume and De los Reyes Lozano (2021), offers plenty of features, including glossaries and annotations, which can be extremely useful when it comes to the translation of proper nouns as well as cultural references and quotations, which are usually subsumed under working documents such as Netflix's KNPs (aka key names and phrases[4]). Besides, collaboration among translators and other stakeholders is an integral part

[4] See: < https://partnerhelp.netflixstudios.com/hc/en-us/articles/5110291703443-Terminology-Tool-Overview-Key-Names-and-Phrases-KNP-_ > .

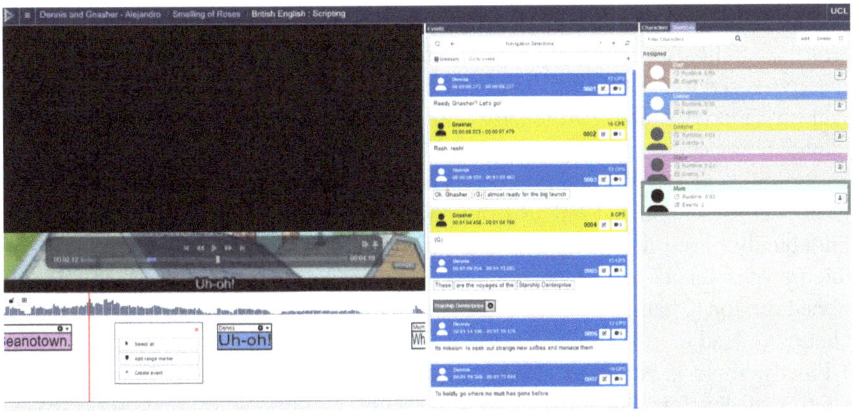

Fig. 7 Scripting tool on ZooDubs

of this cloud dubbing platform, which allows users to allocate, distribute, share, and review work via a project management tool.

For linguists to work on the above interface, a project manager has to create and assign each dubbing task. A dubbing template is often created in the scripting tool using the video's original language (i.e., master template). Events can then be created and tagged to characters or narrators, depending on the origin of each utterance. The resulting events appear on the rhythmoband below the video player. The template needs to be populated with events that respect the isochrony (i.e., in and out timecodes) and the paralinguistic elements that may appear (i.e., dubbing notations). Once finished, the template can be shared with linguists by creating different dubbing streams for translation purposes.

Like their subtitling predecessors, cloud-based dubbing platforms share similar features, and they draw on legacy desktop-based rhythmoband programs but also replicate subtitling interfaces. Among the greatest differences, and apart from a lesser emphasis on timing accuracy, there are extra functionalities such as:

- Annotations and comments: suggestions and terminological references can be shared in the events.
- Character identification: each utterance can be tagged to link it to a particular character from a pre-made list.
- Dubbing audio-tracks: the equivalent of subtitling master templates, freelance translators and adapters can work on the translation and adaptation of the dialogue into the target language, which is subsequently shared with the voice actors for the actual recording, all connected in real-time to the online dubbing tool.
- Notations and pauses: users can add frequently used dubbing notations and pauses to facilitate the enunciation of the script by voice talents.
- Rhythmoband: script events are shown on the video player and the waveform display, in which the text rolls on using proportional lettering to reflect the duration of the utterance.

Whereas most dubbing activities used to be conducted face-to-face in soundproof recording studios, an increasing number of dubbing professionals—notably dubbing directors, script translators, dialogue writers and voice talents—can work from home thanks to cloud dubbing. Particularly fuelled by the COVID-19 lockdowns in 2020, cloud dubbing ecosystems can also be conceived as end-to-end environments where the scripting, auditioning of future voice talents, casting, recording, editing, and mixing can be conducted online from end to end. Cloud dubbing platforms have undoubtedly paved the way for collaborative dubbing (Baños 2020), a context in which professionals work from separate locations to produce and record a single dubbed version (Chaume 2019, p. 112). Alongside automatic dubbing, cloud dubbing is bound to lead to further changes in the industry soon.

Finally, there is common ground between cloud dubbing and cloud subtitling in terms of development. Firstly, there are hybrid solutions, such as SubtitleNext (https://pbteu.com) and Yella Umbrella's Nebula, that rely on desktop-based software programs and communicate with the web-based computerised versions of the tools. Secondly, software developers also seem interested in internal and external integration; indeed, versatile systems offer integration with other cloud- and desktop-based systems to store, review and deliver work. Most tools now offer the possibility of working with templates and converting and reviewing translation files. These are common steps undertaken in the professional world and are therefore offered to end-users, either within the platform or via API integration. Thirdly, automation tools for transcription and interlingual rendering processes are increasingly frequent. Platforms such as CaptionHub (https://captionhub.com) and Matesub (https://matesub.com) can generate closed captions and templates using ASR and MT systems, whereas the likes of Aloud (aloud.area120.google.com) can produce automatic dubs by integrating ASR, MT and text-to-speech technologies. Commercial systems such as OOONA Tools already offer integrated MT engines to translate pre-made subtitle templates but are also tampering with the potential of ASR technologies. These can automatically align text with audio to expedite the spotting task whilst still allowing for subtitle editing, with options on positioning and use of colours in the case of captioning, as well as various other technical attributes that the client or the vendor can set. Though glossaries are becoming further integrated into cloud dubbing and subtitling solutions, TM functionalities remain virtually non-existent, with mainly TM software developers (e.g., Kilgray and looking into integrating video players rather than the other way around.

4 Conclusions

Media localisation practices, such as revoicing and subtitling, involve the use of specialist software, which is gradually being integrated into cloud ecosystems both in the industry (Bolaños García-Escribano 2018; Bolaños García-Escribano & Díaz-Cintas 2020) and at training institutions (Bolaños García-Escribano et al. 2021). In an increasingly globalised world, ground-breaking changes affecting the distribution and consumption of audiovisual material and translation workflows have brought about additional challenges.

Media distributors are expected to release content at a global scale, thus adding to swifter work turnarounds. Work environments are being progressively delocalised, and international communications are increasingly virtual, with global collaborations affecting how media content is localised. Cloud solutions have been embraced to effectively enhance workflows, social networking, and teamwork (Díaz-Cintas and Massidda 2019). The media localisation industry has a long-standing relationship with technology, and the cloud has presented new possibilities for maximising resources. Language technologies such as terminology databases, CAT tools, and ASR technologies have also contributed to more efficient workflows, whereas social interconnectedness facilitates teamwork in a profession previously characterised by individual, solitary work, particularly among freelancers.

This chapter has elaborated on the newly developed cloud-based revoicing and subtitling tools that have entered the market and are reshaping media localisation workstations. In addition, teaching-focused platforms specially designed to train would-be linguists in educational environments are currently being orchestrated by industry stakeholders such as Zoo Academy (www.zoodigital.com/about/zoo-academy) and OOONA Edu (https://ooona.net/ooona-edu). These utilise cloud ecosystems and are expected to pioneer far-reaching changes in how media localisation practices are taught in the future. Additionally, the much-discussed "talent crunch" (Estopace 2017, online) experienced by media localisation stakeholders is also being addressed by companies with in-house training and global certification initiatives such as AVTpro (https://the-poool.com/certification) that endeavour to close the gap between academic training and industry demand. The ways in which cloud technologies impact the training of would-be audiovisual translators are manifold, and further collaboration between those who create new technologies and those who use them would help to preserve and enhance the industry's wealth.

The increasing production and dissemination of audiovisual content and the rising demand for translation will continue to spur software developers to explore new expansion areas. With language automation developments, such as neural MT and ASR—as well as state-of-the-art large language models capable of producing translations (e.g., ChatGPT)—a sizable greater volume of research involving artificial intelligence is expected to be undertaken by media localisation scholars in the upcoming years. Against the backdrop of pervasive artificial intelligence, research efforts have been devoted to establishing how and why human agency is paramount in the language industries (see, for instance, Massey et al. 2022), and future research will probably examine how large language models can be integrated into existing workflows. Yet, training institutions are currently affording greater importance to how new generations of translators are being taught, specifically on the ethical implications arising from the use of automation technologies and on how translation-related skills are honed, how translation can be assessed, and how the curricula can reflect industry changes.

Acknowledgements This research was funded by a "Margarita Salas" postdoctoral research fellowship from Universitat Jaume I (ref. no. MGS/2022/03), financed by the European Union—Next Generation EU).

References

Antonopoulos, N., and L. Gillian. 2017. *Cloud computing: principles, systems and applications*. Berlin: Springer.

Armbrust, M., A. Fox, R. Griffith, A.D. Joseph, R. Katz, A. Konwinski, G. Lee, D. Patterson, A. Rabkin, I. Stoica, and M. Zaharia. 2010. A view of cloud computing. *Communications of the ACM* 53 (4): 50–58. https://doi.org/10.1145/1721654.1721672.

Armstrong, S., Way, A., Caffrey, C., Flanagan, M., Kenny, D., & O'Hagan, M. 2006. Improving the quality of automated DVD subtitles via example-based machine translation. In *Proceedings of Translating and the Computer* 28, 1–13. www.mt-archive.info/Aslib-2006-Armstrong.pdf. Accessed 20 March 2023.

Athanasiadi, R. 2017. The potential of machine translation and other language assistive tools in subtitling: a new era? In *Audiovisual Translation—Research and Use*, ed. Ł Bogucki, 29–49. Oxford: Peter Lang.

Athanasiadi, R. 2022. Technology as a Driving Force in Subtitling. In *New perspectives in audiovisual translation towards future research trends*, ed. L. Mejías-Climent and J.F. Carrero-Martín, 135–164. Valencia: Publicacions de la Universitat de València.

European Commission. 2016/2018. *Audiovisual Media Services Directive*. Directive 2010/13/EU. Brussels: European Commission.

Babych, B. 2014. Automated MT evaluation metrics and their limitations. *Tradumàtica* 12: 464–470. https://doi.org/10.5565/rev/tradumatica.70.

Baños, R. 2018. Technology and Audiovisual Translation. In *An encyclopedia of practical translation and interpreting*, ed. S.-W. Chan, 3–30. Hong Kong: Chinese University Press.

Baños, R. 2020. Insights into the dubbing process: a genetic analysis of the spanish dubbed version of *Ocean's* eleven. *Perspectives* 28 (6): 879–895. https://doi.org/10.1080/0907676X.2020.1726418.

Baños, R., and J. Díaz-Cintas. 2015. Audiovisual translation in a global context: mapping an ever-changing landscape. In *Audiovisual translation in a global context: mapping and ever-changing landscape*, ed. R. Baños and J. Díaz-Cintas, 1–10. Basingstoke: Palgrave Macmillan.

Baños, R. (2023, in press). Main challenges of using automatic dubbing to translate educational YouTube videos. *Linguistica Antverpiensia, New Series: Themes in Translation Studies*, 22.

Birman, K., G. Chockler, and R. van Renesse. 2009. Toward a cloud computing research agenda LADIS 2008 topic cloud computing defined. *ACM SIGACT News* 40 (2): 68–80. https://doi.org/10.1145/1556154.1556172.

Bolaños García-Escribano, A. 2018. The pedagogical potential of cloud-based platforms: a study on the didactics of subtitling in online translator training environments. In *Focusing on Audiovisual Translation Research*, ed. J.D. Sanderson and C. Botella-Tejera, 63–94. Valencia: Publicacions de la Universitat de València.

Bolaños García-Escribano, A., and J. Díaz-Cintas. 2019. Audiovisual translation. In *The Routledge Handbook of Translation and Education*, ed. S. Laviosa and M. González-Davies, 207–225. London: Routledge.

Bolaños García-Escribano, A., and J. Díaz-Cintas. 2020. The cloud turn in audiovisual translation. In *The Palgrave Handbook of Audiovisual Translation and Media Accessibility*, ed. Ł Bogucki and M. Deckert, 519–544. London: Palgrave.

Bolaños García-Escribano, A., J. Díaz-Cintas, and S. Massidda. 2021. Subtitlers on the cloud: the use of professional web-based systems in subtitling practice and training. *Tradumàtica* 19: 1–21. https://doi.org/10.5565/rev/tradumatica.276.

Bolaños García-Escribano, A. (2022). Audiovisual translation migrates to the cloud: industry, technology and education. In: Mejías-Climent & J. Fernando Carrero-Martín (Eds.) *New Perspectives in Audiovisual Translation Towards Future Research Trends*, 19–42. Valencia: Publicacions de la Universitat de València.

Bowker, L. 2002. *Computer-aided translation technology: a practical introduction.* Ottawa: University of Ottawa Press.

Bowker, L, & Corpas-Pastor, G. (2015). Translation technology. In *The Oxford Handbook of Computational Linguistics.* 2nd Ed, Ruslan Mitkov. Oxford: Oxford University Press.

BSI. 2015. *Information Technology—Security Techniques—Code of Practice for Information Security Controls Based on ISO/ IEC 27002 for Cloud Services.* London: British Standards Institution.

Burchardt, A., A. Lommel, L. Bywood, K. Harris, and M. Popović. 2016. Machine translation quality in an audiovisual context. *Target* 28 (2): 206–221. https://doi.org/10.1075/target.28.2.03bur.

Bywood, L. 2020. Technology and audiovisual translation. In *The Palgrave Handbook of Audiovisual Translation and Media Accessibility*, ed. Ł Bogucki and M. Deckert, 503–517. London: Palgrave.

Bywood, L., P. Georgakopoulou, and T. Etchegoyhen. 2017. Embracing the threat: machine translation as a solution for subtitling. *Perspectives* 25 (3): 492–508. https://doi.org/10.1080/0907676X.2017.1291695.

Chan, S.-W., ed. 2015. *The Routledge encyclopedia of translation technology.* London: Routledge.

Chan, S.-W. 2017. *The future of translation technology: towards a world without Babel.* London: Routledge.

Chan, S.-W. 2014. Computer-aided Translation. Major Concepts. In S.-W. Chan (Ed.). *An Encyclopedia of Practical Translation and Interpreting*, 32–67. London: Routledge.

Chaume, F. 2018. Is audiovisual translation putting the concept of translation up against the ropes? *The Journal of Specialised Translation* 30: 84–104.

Chaume, F. 2019. Audiovisual translation in the age of digital transformation: industrial and social implications. In *Reassessing dubbing: historical approaches and current trends*, ed. I. Ranzato and S. Zanotti, 104–124. Amsterdam: John Benjamins.

Chaume, F., & De los Reyes Lozano, J. (2021). El doblaje en la nube: la última revolución en la localización de contenidos audiovisuales. In: B. Reverter Oliver, J. J. Martínez Sierra, D. González Pastor, & J. F. Carrero Martín (Eds), *Modalidades de traducción audiovisual. Completando el espectro* (pp. 1–16). Granada: Comares.

Chaume, F. (2012). *Audiovisual Translation: Dubbing.* Manchester: St. Jerome.

Chaume, F. (2016). Audiovisual translation trends: growing diversity, choice, & enhanced localization. In *Media Across Borders: Localising TV, Film, and Video Games*, M. Á. Bernal-Merino & I. Robert Smith (Eds), 68–84. London: Routledge.

Corpas-Pastor, G, & Durán-Muñoz, I. (Eds). (2018). *Trends in E-Tools and Resources for Translators and Interpreters.* Leiden: Brill/Rodopi.

Cronin, M. 2013. *Translation in the Digital Age. New Perspectives in Translation Studies.* Abingdon: Routledge.

De los Reyes Lozano, J. (2019). Panorama et perspectives de la traduction audiovisuelle en France: zoom sur le doublage. In M.M. Ogea Pozo, & F. Rodríguez Rodríguez (Eds), *Insights into Audiovisual and Comic Translation. Changing Perspectives on Films, Comics and Videogames*, 163–176. Córdoba: UCOPress.

De Sousa, S. C. M., Aziz, W., & Specia, L. 2011. Assessing the post-editing effort for automatic and semi-automatic translations of DVD subtitles. In: *Proceedings of Recent Advances in Natural Language Processing*, 97–103. Hissar: RANLP. www.aclweb.org/anthology/R11-1014. Accessed 20 March 2023.

Díaz-Cintas, J. 2008. Teaching and learning to subtitle in an academic environment. In *The didactics of audiovisual translation*, ed. J. Díaz-Cintas, 89–104. Amsterdam: John Benjamins.
Díaz-Cintas, J. 2015. Technological strides in subtitling. In *The Routledge encyclopedia of translation technology*, ed. S.-W. Chan, 632–643. London: Routledge.
Díaz-Cintas, J., and S. Massidda. 2019. Technological advances in audiovisual translation. In *The Routledge handbook of translation and technology*, ed. M. O'Hagan, 255–270. London: Routledge.
Díaz-Cintas, J., and A. Remael. 2021. *Subtitling: concepts and practices*. London: Routledge.
Directorate-General for Translation. 2009. *The size of the language industry in Europe*. Brussels: European Commission.
ELIS Research. 2022. *European Language Industry Survey 2022. Trends, Expectations and Concerns of the European Language Industry*. https://elis-survey.org/repository. Accessed 20 March 2023.
Estopace, E. 2017. Talent Crunch Hits Media localisation as Amazon, Netflix Accelerate Market Growth, *Slator*. https://slator.com/talent-crunch-hits-media-localization-as-amazon-netflix-accelerate-market-growth. Accessed 20 March 2023.
Federico, M., Cattelan, A., & Trombetti, M. 2012. Measuring user productivity in machine translation enhanced computer assisted translation. *Matecat Publica*tions. www.matecat.com/publications/measuring-user-productivity-in-machine-translation-enhanced-computer-assisted-translation. Accessed 20 March 2023.
Federico, M., Negri, M., Bentivogli, L., Turchi, M. 2014. Assessing the impact of translation errors on machine translation quality with mixed-effects models. In: *Proceedings of the 2014 Conference on Empirical Methods in Natural Language Processing (EMNLP)* 1, 1643–1653. www.aclweb.org/anthology/D14-1172. Accessed 20 March 2023.
García, I. 2014. Computer-aided translation. In *The Routledge Encyclopedia of translation technology*, ed. S.-W. Chan, 68–87. London: Routledge.
Gaspari, F., H. Almaghout, and S. Doherty. 2015. A survey of machine translation competences: insights for translation technology educators and practitioners. *Perspectives* 23 (3): 333–358.
Georgakopoulou, P. 2006. Subtitling and globalisation. *The Journal of Specialised Translation* 6: 115–120.
Georgakopoulou, P. 2012. Challenges for the audiovisual industry in the digital age: the ever-changing needs of subtitle production. *The Journal of Specialised Translation* 17: 78–103. https://doi.org/10.1080/0907676X.2014.979842.
Georgakopoulou, P. 2018. Technologization of audiovisual translation. In *The Routledge handbook of audiovisual translation*, ed. L. Pérez-González, 516–539. London: Routledge.
Georgakopoulou, P. 2019. Template files: the holy grail of subtitling. *Journal of Audiovisual Translation* 2 (2): 137–160. https://doi.org/10.47476/jat.v2i2.84.
Georgakopoulou, P., Bywood, L. 2014. Machine translation in subtitling and the rising profile of the post-editor. *MultiLingual*, January/February: 24–28.
Gough, J. 2018. Investigating the use of resources in the translation process. In *Trends in E-Tools and Resources for Translators and Interpreters*, ed. Gloria Corpas-Pastor and Isabel Durán-Muñoz, 9–36. Leiden: Brill/Rodopi.
Green, S. 2018. How Digital Demand Is Disrupting Dubbing. *M&E Journal*. www.mesalliance.org/2018/03/15/journal-digital-demand-disrupting-dubbing. Accessed 20 March 2023.
Gupta, P., Juneja, R., Nelakanti, A., Chatterjee, T. 2021. Detecting over/under-translation errors for determining adequacy in human translations. ArXiv:2104.00267. Available at: http://arxiv.org/abs/2104.00267
Harrenstien, K. (2009). Automatic Captions in YouTube. *Google Official Blog*. https://googleblog.blogspot.com/2009/11/automatic-captions-in-youtube.html. Accessed 20 March 2023.
Kenny, D. 2022. Human and machine translation. In *Machine translation for everyone: empowering users in the age of artificial intelligence*, ed. D. Kenny and D. Kenny, 23–50. Berlin: Language Science Press.
Koehn, P. 2010. *Statistical machine translation*. Cambridge: Cambridge University Press.

Koponen, M, Sulubacak, U., Vitikainen, K., & Tiedemann, J. 2020. MT for Subtitling: Investigating professional translators' user experience and feedback. In *Proceedings of the 14th Conference of the Association for Machine Translation in the Americas*, 79–92. Online. Association for Machine Translation in the Americas. https://aclanthology.org/2020.amta-research. Accessed 20 March 2023.

Kuo, A.S.-Y. 2015. Professional Realities of the Subtitling Industry. In *Audiovisual Translation in a global context: mapping and ever-changing landscape*, ed. R. Baños and J. Díaz-Cintas, 163–191. Basingstoke: Palgrave Macmillan.

Linthicum, D.S. 2010. *Cloud computing and SOA convergence in your enterprise: a step-by-step guide*. Upper Saddle River: Addison-Wesley.

Massey, G., M. Piotrowska, and M. Marczak. 2023. Meeting evolution with innovation: an introduction to (re-)profiling T&I education. *The Interpreter and Translator Trainer* 17 (2): 1–7. https://doi.org/10.1080/1750399X.2023.2237321.

Massey, G., Huertas-Barros, E., Katan, D. 2022. *The Human Translator in the 2020s* London: Routledge.

Matamala, A. 2017. Mapping audiovisual translation investigations: research approaches and the role of technology. In *Audiovisual translation—research and use*, ed. Ł Bogucki, 11–28. Oxford: Peter Lang.

Matamala, A. 2005. La estación de trabajo del traductor audiovisual: herramientas y recursos. *Cadernos de Tradução* 2(16): 251–68. https://doi.org/10.5007/%25x

Matrix, S. (2014). The Netflix effect: teens, binge watching, & on-demand digital media trends. *Jeunesse: Young People, Texts, Cultures* 6(1): 119–138. https://doi.org/10.3138/jeunesse.6.1.119

McDonald, D., and K. Smith-Rowsey, eds. 2016. *The netflix effect: technology and entertainment in the 21st century*, 1st ed. New York: Bloomsbury Academic.

Mehta, S., Azarnoush, B., Chen, B., Saluja, A., Misra, V., Bihani, B., Kumar, R. 2020. Simplify-then-translate: automatic preprocessing for black-box machine translation. *ArXiv:2005:11197v2*. Available at: http://arxiv.org/abs/2005.11197. Accessed 20 March 2023.

Mell, P., Grance, T. 2011. *SP 800-145. The NIST Definition of Cloud Computing*. Gaithersburg: National Institute of Standards and Technology.

Netflix. 2016/2022. Timed text style guide: general requirements. Available at: https://partnerhelp.netflixstudios.com/hc/en-us/articles/215758617-Timed-Text-Style-Guide-General-Requirements. Accessed 20 March 2023.

Nikolić, K. 2015. The pros and cons of using templates in subtitling. In R. Baños & J. Díaz-Cintas (Eds), *Audiovisual Translation in a Global Context. Mapping and Ever-Changing Landscape*, 192–202. Basingstoke: Palgrave Macmillan.

Nikoltchev, S. (2022). *Investing in European Works: The Obligations on VOD Providers*. Strasbourg: European Audiovisual Observatory.

Nimdzi. 2023. *Language Technology Atlas*. [Report] Nimdzi Insights.

Nimdzi. 2019, 2020, 2021, 2022. *Top 100 Largest Language Service Providers*. [Reports] Nimdzi Insights. www.nimdzi.com/nimdzi-100-top-lsp/. Accessed 20 March 2023.

O'Brien, S., L. Winther Balling, M. Carl, M. Simard, and L. Specia, eds. 2014. *Post-editing of machine translation: processes and applications*. Newcastle upon Tyne: Cambridge Scholars Publishing.

O'Hagan, M. 2016. Massively open translation: unpacking the relationship between technology and translation in the 21st century. *International Journal of Communication* 10: 929–946.

Organisation for Economic Co-operation and Development (OECD). 2020. The territorial impact of COVID-19: managing the crisis across levels of government. [Report] www.oecd.org/coronavirus/policy-responses/the-territorial-impact-of-covid-19-managing-the-crisis-across-levels-of-government-d3e314e1/#section-d1e175. Accessed 20 March 2023.

Ortiz-Boix, C. 2016. *Implementing Machine Translation and Post-Editing to the Translation of Wildlife Documentaries through Voice-over and Off-screen Dubbing. PhD Dissertation*. Barcelona: Universitat Autònoma de Barcelona.

Popowich, F., P. McFetridge, D. Turcato, and J. Toole. 2000. Machine translation of closed captions. *Machine Translation* 15 (4): 311–341. https://doi.org/10.1023/A:1012244918183.
Quah, C.K. 2006. *Translation and technology*. Basingstoke: Palgrave Macmillan.
Robert, I., J.J.J. Ureel, and I. Schrijver. 2022. Translation, translation revision and post-editing competence models: where are we now? In *The human translator in the 2020s*, ed. G. Massey, E. Huertas-Barros, and D. Katan, 44–59. London: Routledge.
Romero-Fresco, P. 2011. *Subtitling through Speech Recognition: Respeaking*. Manchester: St Jerome.
Roxborough, S. 2019. Netflix's Global Reach Sparks Dubbing Revolution: 'The Public Demands It.' *The Hollywood Reporter*. www.hollywoodreporter.com/news/netflix-s-global-reach-sparks-dubbing-revolution-public-demands-it-1229761. Accessed 20 March 2023.
Shroff, G. 2010. *Enterprise cloud computing*. Cambridge: Cambridge: Cambridge University Press.
Spiteri Miggiani, G. 2019. *Dialogue writing for dubbing: an insider's perspective*. Basingstoke: Palgrave Macmillan.
Sriram, I., Khajeh-Hosseini, A. 2010. Research agenda in Cloud Technologies. In *ACM Symposium on Cloud Computing*. http://arxiv.org/abs/1001.3259. Accessed 20 March 2023.
Torrejón, E., and C. Rico. 2012. Skills and profile of the new role of the translator as MT post-editor. *Tradumàtica* 10: 166–178. https://doi.org/10.5565/rev/tradumatica.18.
United Nations. 2006. *Convention on the rights of persons with disabilities and optional protocol*. New York: United Nations.
Vaquero, L.M., L. Rodero-Merino, and J. Cáceres. 2009. A break in the clouds: towards a cloud definition. *ACM SIGCOMM Computer Communication Review* 39 (1): 50–55. https://doi.org/10.1145/1496091.1496100.
Vaquero, Luis M., Luis Rodero-Merino, and Daniel Morán. 2011. Locking the sky: a survey on iaas cloud security. *Computing* 91: 93–118. https://doi.org/10.1007/s00607-010-0140-x.
Verboom, M, Crombie, D., Dijk, E., & Theunisz, M. 2002. Spoken subtitles: making subtitled TV programmes accessible. In *Computers Helping People with Special Needs. ICCHP 2002*, K. Miesenberger, J. Klaus, & W. Zagler (Eds), 295–302. Berlin: Springer.
Volk, M., Sennrich, R., Hardmeier, C., Tidström, F. 2010. Machine translation of TV subtitles for large scale production. In *JEC 2010: Bringing MT to the User*. Denver, Colorado: Association for Machine Translation in the Americas. http://uu.diva-portal.org/smash/get/diva2:420760/FULLTEXT01.pdf
Volk, M. 2008. The automatic translation of film subtitles. a machine translation success story? In *Resourceful Language Technology: Festschrift in Honor of Anna Sågvall Hein*, A. Sågvall Hein, J. Nivre, M. Dahllöf, & B. Megyesi (Eds), 202–214. Uppsala: Acta Universitatis Upsaliensis.
Wilks, Y. 2009. *Machine translation: its scope and limits*. New York: Springer.

Integrating ASR and MT Tools into Cloud Subtitling Workflows: The *¡Sub!* and *¡Sub!2* Projects

Annalisa Sandrelli

Abstract In recent years, cloud-based environments have radically altered traditional subtitling workflows that can now be conducted online by virtual teams of professionals working together from all corners of the Earth. Moreover, automatic speech recognition (ASR) and machine translation (MT) tools are being integrated into audiovisual translation workflows. As a result, new professional profiles are emerging, but the new opportunities offered by technological progress are accompanied by significant challenges. The present chapter illustrates the main results of *¡Sub!: Localisation Workflows that Work* (2020–2021) and its follow-up *¡Sub!2* (2021–2022), two international pilot projects carried out at UNINT university (Italy). A series of experiments was conducted on the *OOONA* cloud subtitling platform to compare three workflows which differed in their degree of automation. 24 subjects were recruited from amongst postgraduate students and recent translation graduates from UNINT and Roehampton universities. There were three subtitling teams working from English into Italian and three teams working from Spanish into Italian, and each team comprised a Project Manager, a Spotter, a Translator, and a Reviser. The teams were required to subtitle three 10-min clips from a science documentary according to the instructions provided for each workflow. As well as submitting the target language subtitles for each clip, the teams were required to document all the steps of the process via a team logbook, screen recordings of work sessions, Quality Assessment forms, and workflow reports. In addition, pre- and post-experiment questionnaires were administered to participants. All the data thus collected has been analysed from a quantitative and qualitative point of view to determine the most efficient workflow, i.e., the one that ensures the best quality output in the tightest turnaround time. The results of the two pilot studies will be used to inform translator training practices, to ensure they are in line with constantly evolving market demands.

A. Sandrelli (✉)
Università degli Studi Internazionali di Roma—UNINT, Rome, Italy
e-mail: Annalisa.Sandrelli@unint.eu

Y. Peng et al. (eds.), *New Advances in Translation Technology*, New Frontiers in Translation Studies, https://doi.org/10.1007/978-981-97-2958-6_5

1 Introduction

Historically, audiovisual translation (AVT) has played a key role in the distribution of films and TV products worldwide, and especially in Europe where there is so much linguistic diversity. Over the last few years, the audiovisual market has been growing steadily with the advent of streaming services, catch-up TV, and multimedia contents on social networks, and in 2020 it expanded exponentially with the coronavirus pandemic, when the number of subscribers to streaming platforms rose to 518 million worldwide (Wyndham 2021). This unprecedented growth created a huge demand for AVT services: however, the process has been so fast that it has not been easy for language service providers (LSPs) to manage it. Thus, the AVT sector has turned to technology for help.

The two projects presented and discussed in this paper (*¡Sub!* and its follow-up *¡Sub!2*) aimed to investigate the integration of automatic speech recognition (ASR) and machine translation (MT) tools into cloud subtitling workflows. An experimental study was carried out on the subtitling of science documentaries from English into Italian and Spanish into Italian according to three workflows which differed in their degree of automation. The aim was to identify the most effective workflow, i.e., the one that produced the best quality output in the shortest turnaround time. Section 2 presents a brief overview of recent research on the role played by ASR and MT technologies in subtitling. Section 3 presents the experimental design of the *¡Sub!* and*¡Sub!2* projects, and Sect. 4 presents key results for both language combinations, i.e., English into Italian and Spanish into Italian.[1] Finally, Sect. 5 discusses our results and presents some conclusions.

2 Automation in Subtitling: A Brief Overview

Recent years have seen major changes in the AVT sector, with demand for translation services increasing exponentially. Video on demand (VOD) streaming services have played a key role in this process, as viewers can freely select the version they want to watch, i.e., dubbed, subtitled, audio described, and so on (Estopace 2017). However, while the massive expansion of the AVT market is undoubtedly positive for the sector, during the Covid 19 pandemic it put mounting pressure on translators to deliver as fast as possible, with less time for quality control and revision. Thus, in recent years the need to accelerate workflows has led language service providers (LSPs) to consider the opportunities warranted by translation technologies that are already widely used in other domains. This has had important repercussions on the organisation of labour and on the skills required of AVT translators. The advent of cloud-based AVT tools has made it possible for teams of professionals to work together remotely, thus helping to source translators with the language combinations and expertise required for each

[1] Results for the English into Italian translation direction have already been reported in Massidda and Sandrelli (2023).

project. In addition, there have been attempts to integrate translation technologies of various kinds into workflows, to streamline and accelerate processes. Therefore, in the current market it is less frequent for individual translators to work off-line for direct clients:

> AVT work has been more frequently performed by an international team working on cloud-platforms often signed under subcontracts and applying a combination of (semi-) automatised assistive processes. In these workflows, the translators are no longer directly in touch with the client, but communication is handled by project managers in different language service providers. (Tardel 2023: 141)

It must be highlighted that, while in other sectors cloud tools and translation technologies have been taken up gradually over a much longer period, in AVT the process has happened piecemeal and rather suddenly. Partial automation of translation processes has driven rates down, and many professionals have been forced to leave this sector (Bond 2018; AVTE 2021a, b). Thus, budget cuts have created a talent crunch (Estopace 2017; Bryant 2021; Berman 2022):

> While these technologies promote faster turnaround times and a boost in productivity, this often does not go hand in hand with sustainable working conditions. This includes among others manageable deadlines and workload, effective communication between colleagues, as well as fair prices to make a living. Undesirable working conditions lead to a lack of qualified audiovisual translators staying in the industry. (Tardel 2023: 141)

The current situation is triggering a vicious circle, as LSPs and individual translators are relying more and more on translation technologies, to increase productivity and stay afloat. From a training perspective, if today's translation trainees are to carve themselves a space in the increasingly machine-driven AVT market, they need not only to develop advanced translation competences, but also to be exposed to different workflows and to become familiar with key technologies, so that they can select and use the most suitable tools for each project and collaborate with colleagues who may be located elsewhere (even in a different country). As AVT workflows do include some tasks which may lend themselves to (partial or full) automation, individual translators and LSPs need to make the most of current technology to free up time and energy for the truly creative aspects of translation. In other words, translation trainees need to become the ideal "augmented translator that puts the human front and centre and uses technology to enhance their capabilities" (AVTE 2021a), as was recently advocated by the European Federation of Audiovisual Translators in their *Machine Translation Manifesto*.

Clearly, academia has been looking at these recent developments with great interest. Research has been focused largely on the two types of technology with the most obvious potential application to AVT, namely ASR and MT, the former to transcribe spoken content and the latter to translate it. However, given the wide variety of audiovisual genres and the technical constraints of the various AVT modes, the uptake of these technologies is not as straightforward as it may seem. In particular, a few recent studies have shown that there are still significant limitations that need to be overcome before such tools can be fully integrated into subtitling workflows. This section presents a brief overview of such studies.

In relation to ASR, the first aspect that needs to be stressed is that, for the time being, efficient tools are only available for major languages, thanks to the research and capital investment put into them. Moreover, such tools only work relatively well under specific conditions, namely with clean audio, no voice overlapping and standard accents. This means that for some audiovisual genres their output may not be very accurate. Some subtitling systems already incorporate ASR for autocaptioning, namely, to transcribe dialogue and automatically generate time codes:

> [A]automatic speech recognition (ASR) technology has known a vertiginous progress in transforming original speech into written text, which can then be used to create intralingual subtitles or templates for translation into multiple languages [...]. (Díaz Cintas and Massidda 2019: 260)

Of course, automatically generated captions must be revised by humans, not only to detect and correct transcription errors, but also to check the time codes, i.e., the quality of the spotting. As Tardel (2020: 81) points out, "[I]it remains unclear whether a corrupt ASR transcript might still facilitate subtitling processes, and under which circumstances, or the role which the visual part of the video plays during computer-assisted transcription and translation". Indeed, this was one the key research questions of the *CompASS* project, funded by the EU and carried out at the University of Mainz in collaboration with ZDF Digital (Tardel 2020). More specifically, the team investigated the use of ASR to produce automatic intralingual captions for films (i.e., subtitles in the same language of the soundtrack), which were then automatically translated into English to produce a template file that could be used to translate the subtitles into other languages (again, via machine translation). An experiment compared the performance of 12 professional subtitlers and 13 translation students involved in transcription and translation tasks carried out in different conditions, i.e., working directly from the soundtrack, with the help of an ASR transcript and with the help of a script produced by a human. Eyetracking and keylogging technologies were used to collect data on temporal, technical and cognitive efforts (respectively, task duration, the use of the mouse or keyboard, and processes such as monitoring, reading and attention distribution). The main results were that the availability of an ASR script reduced the technical effort involved in the transcription task (in other words, less time was spent typing), but did not speed up task completion, nor did it have a positive impact on duration in the translation task. It must be highlighted that in this experiment recognition accuracy was an issue, with word error rate scores (WER) relatively high in both English and German, the two languages involved in the experiment. Therefore, it can be concluded that "[…] written assistance in AVT could be a contributor to decreased effort, if the quality of transcripts meets certain levels" (Tardel 2020: 100).

In a recent study by Karakanta et al. (2022), 22 professional subtitlers working from and into several Western European languages took part in an experiment in which they post-edited automatically generated subtitles (the software used was *MateSub*). The participants had an average of over two years' experience as subtitlers and a slightly longer experience in post-editing MT output. The clips used in the experiment were short (about 3 min each), but they contained "[…] elements which are particularly challenging both for human subtitlers and automatic systems, such as background noise, slang, overlapping speech and multi-speaker events" (Karakanta et al. 2022: 263). After post-editing the subtitles, the subjects filled in a questionnaire. While their overall user experience can be evaluated as ranging from neutral to positive, most respondents stated that they had identified major speech recognition and spotting errors, as well as several translation errors (especially in the translation of slang and colloquial expressions). Technical issues with the subtitles were also mentioned by many respondents, who pointed out that the subtitles did not seem to respect shot changes, they were often not properly synchronised and segmentation did not seem to follow widely accepted subtitling conventions. However, they did point out a positive aspect, i.e., the potential time-saving warranted by the automatic insertion of time codes. In summary, if automatic spotting and segmentation could be improved, most of the participants would welcome such a development, as it would partially automate the most tedious part of the job.

Finally, a recent study carried out by Tuominen et al. (2023) investigated the use of automatically generated subtitles to translate news programmes from Finnish into English. Experimental data and data from a focus group and a questionnaire suggest that automatic subtitles did help comprehension for viewers with little or no knowledge of Finnish, but their quality was perceived as inadequate by many participants, owing to mistranslations, excessive speed, and timecoding and segmentation issues which resulted in excessive cognitive load. Overall, the participants felt that automatic subtitles would be useful in the absence of subtitles produced by a human translator but also expressed concerns about information accuracy. One of the key problems that emerged from this study is that automatic subtitles may not be especially suitable for unscripted broadcasts and news programmes, as speed and features of spoken language such as hesitations, interruptions, ellipsis and other disfluencies mean that such genres do not lend themselves well to speech recognition, and even less so to machine translation. Moreover, even if recognition accuracy were to improve dramatically, it must be taken into account that ASR tools produce verbatim transcripts, which in the case of programmes that include very fast speech result in subtitles that are too fast for viewers. As some condensation is required to facilitate reading, human post-editing is thus deemed essential in all cases.

This brief overview of a handful of recent studies was not meant to provide a comprehensive picture of this fascinating and fast-developing field of research, but merely to highlight some of the aspects that were also investigated in our own projects, described in the following section.

3 The *¡Sub!* and *¡Sub!2* Projects: Experimental Design

The *¡Sub!: Localisation Workflows that Work* project and its follow-up *¡Sub!2* (2020–2022) were carried out by a research team based at UNINT university in Rome, with the participation of an international partner.[2] The two pilot projects were funded by the UNINT Research Fund and received the support of four industry partners, namely *OOONA*, *Captionhub*, *Matesub* powered by *Translated*, and *Sub-Ti Ltd*.[3]

As was mentioned in §1, the main objective was to try and determine whether current ASR and MT technologies can help subtitlers work faster without compromising quality. This was investigated by means of an experimental study on the subtitling of science documentaries from English into Italian and Spanish into Italian. The original plan was to recruit participants, train them up for a few weeks in a traditional face-to-face setting, and then run a series of online experiments using the *OONA* subtitling platform and a range of other tools. However, when the desk research phase was completed in early 2020, the coronavirus pandemic struck and made it necessary to re-design the whole project, draw up a new plan, move all activities online and prolong the duration with a follow-up (*¡Sub!2*).

This section provides an overview of our experimental design and illustrates our materials, methods, tools, and subjects. Let us begin by explaining the choice of science documentaries as source materials for the subtitling experiments. Science documentaries generally feature voiceover narrations and structured interview segments, whereas it is less frequent to find adlibbing, overlapping voices, background noises or loud music in the soundtrack. Moreover, the language used in documentaries tends to be relatively standard, without too many colloquialisms or dialects (even though there are often technical terms and acronyms). Because of all these characteristics, ASR tools are likely to perform better (i.e., to achieve better recognition) when used to transcribe science documentaries than TV series or films, which tend to feature a wider variety of characters (with different voices and accents), communicative situations and language registers. Clearly, an accurate transcript is a good starting point for machine translation, while the presence of many speech recognition errors can produce a snowballing effect in the MT process. Therefore, it was hypothesised that science documentaries would lend themselves relatively well to automated processes.

One of our industry partners, *Sub-Ti Ltd*, provided us with working copies of two documentary films that had been screened at the 2019 Turin *Cinemambiente* film festival. The English-language film was titled *Do you trust this computer* (dir. Paine 2018) and was focused on the pervasiveness of AI technology in our society. The Spanish-language one was titled *Empatía* (dir. Antoja 2017) and was about veganism and the ethical treatment of animals. The subtitling company also provided us with the Italian subtitles produced by their translators and used in the festival screenings of

---

[2] The UNINT team included Annalisa Sandrelli (Chief Investigator), Lorenzo Blini, Fiorenza Mileto and Claudio Russello; the international partner was Serenella Massidda (Roehampton University).

[3] *OOONA*: https://ooona.net/; *CaptionHub*: https://www.captionhub.com/; *Matesub*: https://matesub.com/; *Sub-ti*: https://www.subti.com/.

the two films. These "official" subtitles were used as a benchmark in the qualitative stage of our study (see §4). The first 30 min of both films were edited into three 10-min video clips for use in the experiments.

In April–May 2021 24 MA translation students and recent graduates from UNINT and Roehampton universities were recruited for the two language combinations involved in the experiment (12 for English into Italian and12 for Spanish into Italian). The participants were volunteer translators and translation students who agreed to commit a few hours of their time every week for a period of six weeks (a total of approximately 25 h), in exchange for free training in all the tools and techniques they would be required to use. Participants were informed that they would take part in an online experiment in which they would work together in teams on a cloud subtitling project. Before the beginning of the experimental phase, they filled in a pre-experiment questionnaire aimed at collecting information on their language competences and background in translation and, more specifically, in AVT. For reasons of space, it is not possible to summarise here all the data gathered on the subjects. However, it must be mentioned that the participants recruited for the English into Italian direction were, on average, older than their counterparts who were going to subtitle the Spanish film (27 vs. 24 years of age, respectively). Moreover, although all the subjects had received some training in translation, the English subjects were recent graduates who were already working professionally, while the Spanish subjects were students in their second and final year of MA in Translation and Interpreting. Finally, while 58% of the English subjects had professional or semi-professional experience in AVT, the percentage went down to 50% for the Spanish subjects. Based on the information they provided about their experiences and training, participants were allocated to a subtitling team and assigned a role: each team was made up of four members, namely a Project Manager, a Spotter, a Translator, and a Reviser.

In the first week of the "course" a live class was held on *Zoom* to explain the logistics of the project, to brush up on key subtitling principles (including technical parameters and subtitling conventions) and to introduce post-editing techniques for MT output. All the reference materials, slides, subtitling guidelines, technical instructions and so on were made available via a dedicated *Google Classroom* course. In the second week, subjects were trained in the use of the *OOONA* cloud subtitling platform (a 3-h session) and were then allowed to use it for autonomous practice for as long as they wanted in the third week, when they subtitled a range of practice videos. Then, in weeks 4, 5, and 6 the actual subtitling experiments took place.

All the teams experienced three workflows which differed in their degree of automation. The 'traditional' workflow (WF1) entailed using only cloud subtitling tools, the 'semi-automated' one (WF2) also integrated an ASR tool for automatic captioning, and the 'fully automated' one (WF3) included both ASR and MT. More specifically, the *OOONA* cloud subtitling tools used for the experiment were *Create Pro* and *Translate Pro*: the former was used to produce the source language subtitles (in English and Spanish, respectively), while the latter was used to produce the Italian target language subtitles. However, as no ASR or MT tool was fully integrated into the platform when the experiments took place (April–May 2021), two external tools were used: the English and Spanish automatic captioning tools in *CaptionHub* were

Table 1 Workflow order by group

Group	Week 4	Week 5	Week 6
A	WF1	WF2	WF3
B	WF2	WF3	WF1
C	WF3	WF1	WF2

used to transcribe the original language soundtrack and produce the SL subtitles with automatic spotting, while the machine translation tools provided by *MateSub* were used to translate the SL subtitles into the TL (Italian, in this case) in the fully automated workflow.

As can be seen in Table 1, each team was exposed to a different workflow in the same week. Thus, in week 4 group A began with the traditional workflow (WF1), while group B adopted the semi-automated one (WF2) and group C worked according to the fully automated workflow (WF3); this all changed in week 5 and then again in week 6. Thus, each subtitling team was exposed to the three workflows, but in a different order.

The instructions for each workflow included a detailed explanation of tasks for each team member, expected deliverables, reporting procedures, and so on. Each participant was to fill in a logbook with information about their work sessions, including duration, technical problems, translation difficulties, coping strategies, and so on, to ensure that each step would be documented in this "diary". In addition, the subjects, who all worked remotely and in isolation, were instructed to record their work sessions via screencasting software (*Ocam*),[4] so that the subtitling process could be monitored. This method was chosen because "[T]the creation of screen recording video does not require translators to do anything they would otherwise not be doing during the natural course of translation task completion" (Angelone 2020: 34). Participants were also instructed to keep a record of any communications (e-mail messages, text messages, voice messages, and so on) taking place within the team and all this information was summarised in a workflow report at the end of each week. The workflow reports and the logbooks provided us with a glimpse into team dynamics.

In all the workflows the Project Manager assigned tasks and distributed files to the other team members. The subtitling process was broken down into steps to be carried out in a specific order, namely the creation of a SL dialogue list, spotting and creation of a SL subtitle list, translation into the TL, and revision of the TL subtitles. However, the process was not linear; in fact, it could be described as an iterative process overseen by the Project Manager. Each member carried out their individual task(s) and submitted their output to the Project Manager, who checked the material(s) and then forwarded it to the team member who would carry out the next step in the workflow.

While the basic process was the same in the three workflows, the materials and the tools made available to the teams varied slightly, and so did the tasks that had to be

[4] *Ocam*: https://ohsoft.net/eng/.

carried out. In the traditional workflow (WF1) the team was given just a video clip and a post-production script in a pdf format (as often happens in real-life scenarios), which had to be converted to a more flexible file format and then checked against the video to detect any inaccuracies (errors and/or omissions). The Spotter used this material to produce a subtitle list in the source language (English or Spanish), by inserting all the relevant time codes manually and adapting the SL transcript to comply with guidelines and parameters (i.e., number of characters per line, reading speed, gaps between subtitles, and so on). This SL subtitle file was checked (and, if necessary, corrected) by the Project Manager and was then forwarded to the Translator. The latter produced the target language subtitles, using all the necessary resources and reference materials (to be documented in the logbook); of course, specific translation issues could be discussed with the other team members. The PM checked the translation and then sent it to the Reviser, who corrected any linguistic or technical errors they noticed and filled in a Quality Assurance (QA) form to quantify and describe such corrections. A final quality check was carried out by the PM who then uploaded all the materials (SL subtitles, TL subtitles, QA form, screen recordings, team logbook, and workflow report) to the dedicated online project repository.

In the partially automated workflow (workflow 2) teams were provided with a video clip and a SL subtitle file generated automatically by *CaptionHub*. Therefore, the Spotter's task was not to carry out the spotting manually, but to check the accuracy of the transcript (to detect any recognition errors) and of the spotting and segmentation (to make sure the subtitles complied with the technical parameters set for the project). The rest of the workflow was the same as in WF1.

Finally, in the fully automated workflow (WF3) the teams were given a video clip, a file of automatically generated SL subtitles (as in WF2) and a file of machine translated TL subtitles produced by *MateSub* (via *ModernMT*). In this workflow it was necessary to check the performance of the ASR tool (transcription and automatic captioning), and then to post-edit the output of the MT tool. Clearly, if transcription errors were detected in the SL subtitles, they had to be flagged up by the team member who had identified them, because they were bound to have reverberated on the MT process. After the experiment, all the participants filled in a post-experiment questionnaire that was designed to elicit their opinions.[5]

As can be seen from this brief overview, each member had clear tasks in each workflow and communication and teamwork were very important in each step. The following section illustrates the main results of the experiment for both language directions.

[5] More specifically, there were questions about the subjects' motivations and expectations before the course, their evaluation of the overall experiment and about the usefulness (or otherwise) of their prior training and professional experience.

4 Results

As was mentioned in §3, several types of data were collected over the three weeks of experiments: the SL and the TL subtitles produced by each team for each workflow, the team logbooks, the workflow reports, the QA forms, and the screen recordings of all the work sessions. As the key aim of the study was to identify the workflow that produced the best results in the shortest time, it was decided to analyse each workflow from a quantitative and a qualitative point of view.

The first step was to calculate the duration of each workflow for each team in every week. The data on duration entered by participants in the logbooks were checked against the screen recordings provided and any discrepancies or inaccuracies were cleared with the PM of the group in question. The time spent by each team member on their tasks was added up to calculate overall workflow duration. Figures 1 and 2 below show the data presented by group and by language direction (English into Italian and Spanish into Italian, respectively). It is immediately noticeable that the subtitling teams working from English into Italian were generally faster than their colleagues working from Spanish into Italian, which could be expected to an extent, as the English subjects were graduates with more professional experience than their Spanish counterparts (see §3). There were marked differences in the teams working in the same language direction, which demonstrates the importance of the human factor, i.e., team composition and teamwork. Group B for English and group C for Spanish were, on average, faster than the other groups working in the same language direction. Moreover, it is also interesting to see that the workflow tackled in the final week of the experiment was always the fastest: this is significant, because the teams experienced the three workflows in a different order (see §3). In other words, the subtitling teams tended to work faster over time regardless of the workflow, as teamwork improved and familiarity with tools and procedures increased.

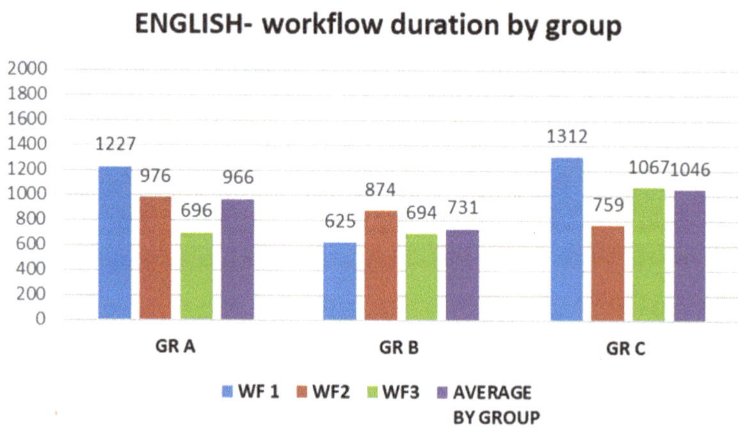

Fig. 1 Duration by group (English into Italian)

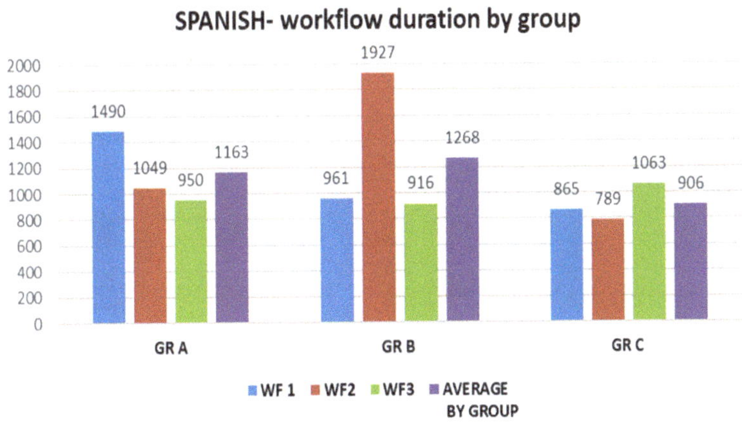

Fig. 2 Duration by group (Spanish into Italian)

When the same data are re-arranged by workflow (see Figs. 3 and 4), other aspects emerge. The fastest workflow on average for both English and Spanish was WF3, i.e., the fully automated one, with 819 and 976 min, respectively. However, in absolute terms the fastest workflow for English was the traditional one (WF1) as carried out by group B (625 min), while for Spanish it was the partially automated one (WF2) carried out by group C (789 min). Noticeably, in both cases this was the third and last workflow tackled by the two teams in question. In addition, although the fully automated workflow was on average the most time-efficient, when it was tackled in the first week it was actually the slowest (1,067 and 1,063 min for group C in English and Spanish, respectively). These results seem to suggest that, although there are potential time gains with the fully automated workflow (WF3), there is a learning curve and the integration of ASR and MT tools does not immediately produce good results.

Moreover, these data only tell us how long it took to produce the TL subtitles, but not how good (or bad) their quality was. Therefore, a qualitative analysis was carried out in which the subtitles produced by each team in each workflow were evaluated on the basis of linguistic and technical parameters. All the parameters are presented in Table 2 below, which shows an example of the QA Form that Revisers had to fill in for every workflow. Linguistic errors were translation errors (i.e., when the meaning of the original was distorted), omissions, or additions of irrelevant content ('semantics' error). The 'punctuation' category included both the absence of punctuation and punctuation marks used incorrectly. Calques and wrong collocations were classified as 'use of the TL' errors, while issues concerning the level of formality of the target language were classified as 'register' errors. As the subjects worked on science documentaries, there was a relatively high number of technical terms and when these were rendered incorrectly in the TL, they were categorised as 'terminology' issues. Finally, issues with spelling, morpho-syntactic aspects, or subtitle segmentation were also detected in the output. Technical errors included spotting issues, issues affecting

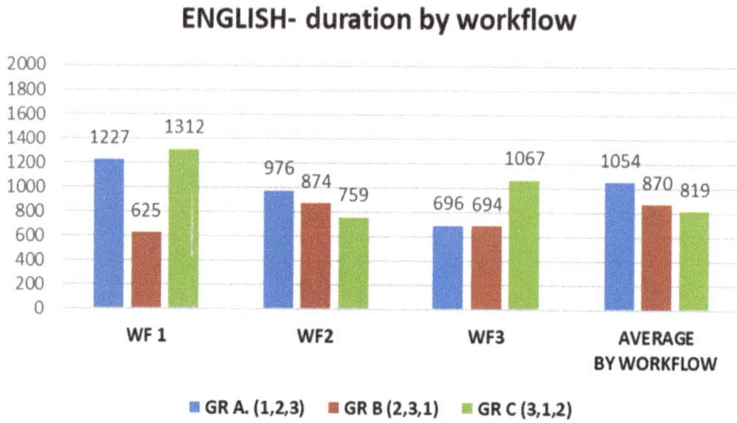

Fig. 3 Duration by workflow (English into Italian)

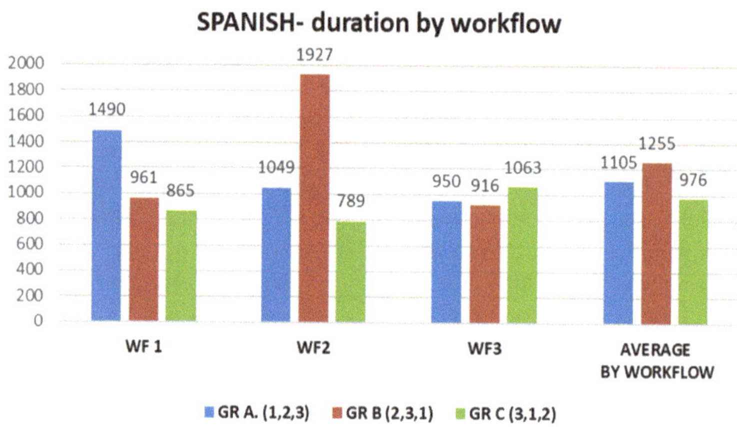

Fig. 4 Duration by workflow (Spanish into Italian)

reading speed, non-compliance with guidelines, and the absence of subtitles when there is visual or audio information in the film.

As was explained in §3, the Reviser for each team filled in a QA form at the end of every workflow with information on the errors that had been detected and corrected in the output. During the qualitative analysis stage, all the TL subtitle files and related QA forms were checked and any additional errors identified by the research team were added to the forms. Moreover, the TL subtitles produced by all the teams were compared with the benchmark, i.e., the "official" subtitles produced by Sub-Ti Ltd and screened at the film festival (see §3). These comparisons made it possible to identify several patterns in the errors made by the teams.

The most common technical errors that were encountered in our data were issues of reading speed (in many cases over the recommended limit of 180 words per minute),

Table 2 Quality assessment (QA) form

Linguistic issues	Errors	Technical issues	Errors
Semantics	2	Spotting (lack of sound synch)	0
Punctuation	0	Spotting (lack of synch in shot change)	0
Use of the TL	12	Minimum gap between subtitles	0
Register	0	Subtitling conventions	15
Terminology	1	Reading speed	10
Spelling	1	Subtitle length	5
Line breaks	0	No subtitle for audio	0
Morphosyntactic issues	0	No subtitle for video	0
TOTAL	**16**	**TOTAL**	**30**
COMMENTS		**COMMENTS**	
Very good translation overall. All the changes were made for the sake of clarity		Several time codes were changed to improve reading speed, as OOONA flagged several errors in red. Several commas at the end of subtitles were also identified and deleted, in accordance with the guidelines	

spotting problems (mostly to do with the 'in' time code, i.e., the time the subtitle first appears on the screen), and errors in the application of subtitling conventions (for example, bad subtitle segmentation or bad positioning). As regards the linguistic aspects of the subtitles, the most frequent problems were cases in which the meaning of the original had been distorted through a translation error, an omission or an addition, calques and wrong collocations, punctuation issues and some terminology problems related to the specific domains discussed in the two films.

The breakdown of results can be seen in Table 3, which presents the data by group and by language. It is immediately apparent that the subtitling teams working from Spanish into Italian produced a much higher number of errors than their English counterparts, irrespective of the group and workflow. Once again, this could be attributed to the more limited AVT experience of the Spanish subtitling teams. The other aspect that is immediately apparent is a noticeable learning effect in both language combinations, i.e., all the subtitling teams initially made a high number of errors and then got gradually better, with the last workflow they tackled producing the best results for each team. Interestingly, both the semi-automated (WF2) and fully-automated (WF3) workflows resulted in a high number of errors when they were tackled in the first week of the experiment (groups B and C for both language directions). Finally, the semi-automated workflow (WF2) produced the best result in absolute terms for both languages, with only 12 and 23 errors in English and Spanish, respectively.

If the same data are presented by workflow (see Table 4), the most accurate one on average was also the slowest: the traditional one for English (WF1, 24.3 errors and a duration of over 17 h and a half) and the semi-automated one for Spanish (WF2), 51.3 errors for a duration of almost 21 h. The semi-automated workflow, which entailed the use of an ASR tool to produce automatic transcription and captioning of the SL

Table 3 Errors by group and language

English		Linguistic errors	Technical errors	Total errors	Average errors	Average duration
A	WF1	21	7	28	21	16 h 6 min
	WF2	7	12	19		
	WF3	8	8	16		
B	WF2	47	22	69	41.6	12 h 11 min
	WF3	16	14	30		
	WF1	15	11	26		
C	WF3	42	10	52	27.6	17 h 26 min
	WF1	3	16	19		
	WF2	9	3	12		
Spanish		Linguistic errors	Technical errors	Total errors	Average errors	Average duration
A	WF1	17	66	83	66	19 h 23 min
	WF2	5	50	55		
	WF3	18	42	60		
B	WF2	26	50	76	62	21 h 8 min
	WF3	19	43	62		
	WF1	14	33	47		
C	WF3	14	43	57	53	15 h 6 min
	WF1	8	71	79		
	WF2	8	15	23		

soundtrack, produced reasonably good results for both languages, but not when it was the first workflow tackled by the teams (groups B in English and Spanish, with 69 and 76 errors, respectively). The fully automated workflow (WF3) was the fastest for both languages and produced good results for English (not in the first week, i.e., group C), but proved challenging for the Spanish subtitling teams, regardless of the week when they were exposed to it.

These results seem to indicate that, while the integration of an ASR tool into the workflow may simply require some time to adapt, the use of an MT tool is a much more complex issue, as subtitlers need to have good post-editing skills to make the most of the output produced by the machine. Indeed, many of the errors identified in the subtitles produced in the fully automated workflow (WF3) were caused by poor post-editing. There were many cases of *under-editing*, i.e., when the text produced by the MT tool was considered acceptable and errors were not rectified by the Translator, Reviser or Project Manager. The opposite, i.e., *over-editing*, was also frequent, when an acceptable translation suggested by the software was rejected and an error was introduced by the Translator, Reviser or Project Manager. Other errors that were encountered in the TL subtitles produced in WF3 were issues of

Table 4 Errors by workflow and language

English		Linguistic errors	Technical errors	Total errors	Average errors	Average duration
WF1	A	21	7	28	24.3	17 h 34 min
	B	15	11	26		
	C	3	16	19		
WF2	A	2	12	19	33.3	14 h 30 min
	B	47	22	69		
	C	9	3	12		
WF3	A	8	8	16	32.6	13 h 39 min
	B	16	14	30		
	C	42	10	52		
Spanish		**Linguistic errors**	**Technical errors**	**Total errors**	**Average errors**	**Average duration**
WF1	A	17	66	83	69.7	18 h 25 min
	B	14	33	47		
	C	8	71	79		
WF2	A	5	50	55	51.3	20 h 55 min
	B	26	50	76		
	C	8	15	23		
WF3	A	18	42	60	57.7	16 h 16 min
	B	19	43	62		
	C	14	43	57		

language register, i.e., when the translation suggested by the machine (and accepted by the subtitler) was not semantically wrong but was inappropriate in relation to the level of formality of the text. Finally, the MT tool also produced several errors in the use of Italian prepositions, which were not detected (and therefore were left uncorrected) by the participants. It must be stressed that, unlike the older types of machine translation tools, the output of neural machine translation tends to look very plausible, which means that subtitlers need to be trained to detect issues of the kind mentioned above in order to perform good quality post-editing. Being aware of the limitations of MT in relation to a specific language combination and, more specifically, being familiar with how a specific MT tool works, facilitates revision and makes post-editing more accurate.

5 Discussion and Conclusions

This study compared three workflows adopted in a cloud subtitling experiment, which differed in terms of the degree of automation and involved teams of subtitlers collaborating remotely. The key principle adopted in all the workflows was the division of labour, with the subtitling process broken up into discrete steps and with each team member in charge of a specific aspect working in isolation and remotely. Clearly, this was somewhat artificial, in the sense that in real-life there can be many more variations in the way subtitling workflows are organised (see Tardel 2023 for a full discussion of possible workflow models); however, it was also necessary to carry out a manageable experiment. In all three workflows teamwork and communication played a key role. Although the basic process and roles were the same, the workflows differed in terms of the technologies made available to participants. The traditional workflow (WF1) was meant to simulate the most common way of managing a cloud subtitling project when the client provides the video and a post-production dialogue list (often in an unsuitable format that needs to be converted before the translators can start working). The semi-automated workflow (W2) simulated those situations in which the SL dialogue list is not provided by the client and therefore needs to be generated directly from the soundtrack: rather than transcribing everything manually, an ASR tool which could also create the relevant time codes was used. Finally, the fully automated workflow (WF3) simulated a scenario in which both an ASR tool and an MT tool are available and therefore team members need to check the output of both and make any necessary corrections and adjustments, both linguistic and technical. Typically, this scenario would apply when there is a very tight deadline and LSPs must try to speed up the subtitling work as much as possible. Two different language directions were taken into account in the study, namely English into Italian and Spanish into Italian, to reflect expertise in the research team and to detect possible language-related differences in the performance of the tools.

A quantitative and qualitative analysis was carried out on the data collected during the experiment, to determine the most time-efficient workflow, the most accurate workflow and the workflow with the best time-quality ratio. Some interesting trends have emerged, but before they are summarised and discussed, it must be stressed that this study has a number of limitations. Firstly, the amount of data that was generated in the project is possibly excessive and not all the data are easy to manage. More specifically, the screen recordings that were obtained from participants were certainly useful in determining the exact duration of the work sessions, but the sheer volume of recordings (over 45 h for English and over 55 for Spanish) meant that it was not possible within the timeframe of the projects to exploit them to the full. Therefore, they were only used for reference in the qualitative part of the analysis to check what had happened in specific situations. Secondly (and more importantly), the study was never intended to establish the general efficiency and effectiveness of ASR and MT tools in AVT. The study was conducted on a small sample of translators (24 overall), working on a specific genre (science documentaries) in two specific language directions and using specific tools selected by the research team.

Therefore, any result or conclusion can only be considered valid in this scenario and is not directly applicable to other situations, although some principles may be generalisable.

Interestingly enough, the first result to have emerged from our study is the importance of the human factor. Even though the whole project was meant to evaluate the usefulness of technology in subtitling, what is striking is the very marked differences in both quantitative and qualitative terms in the results achieved by the subtitling teams. The English subjects, who were older and more experienced in AVT, adapted to all workflows better than their Spanish counterparts. Moreover, some subtitling teams performed better than others working in the same translation direction, which points to the importance of team composition and teamwork. The other interesting result is that there is a clear learning effect, as all the teams worked gradually faster and better, obtaining the best results in the last week of the experiment, regardless of the level of automation in the workflow they carried out. While this may seem like a foregone conclusion, it is nevertheless reassuring to see such improvements over a short period of time (only three weeks in the experimental conditions).

In relation to the key research questions explored in the *¡Sub!* and*¡Sub!2* project, it can be concluded that the semi-automated workflow produced relatively good results, when not tackled in the first week of the experiment. In other words, there was certainly a learning curve, but once the subjects became familiar with auto captioning, it was relatively easy to integrate the ASR tool into the process. By contrast, the adoption of a fully automated workflow (WF3) did seem to reduce turnaround times, but initially produced low accuracy because of the challenges of post editing MT output. Moreover, the poor results achieved by all the Spanish subtitling teams in this workflow show that good translation skills (obviously a pre-requisite to work in the sector) are not sufficient when subtitlers are required to integrate MT tools into their working processes. In other words, a very wide set of advanced competences is required if subtitlers are to use ASR and MT tools to their advantage, i.e., to facilitate (not hamper) the process. Indeed, this was actually mentioned by several participants in their answers to the post-experiment questionnaire.[6] They pointed out pointed out that dedicated training in post-editing MT output applied to AVT is required to find a balance between *over-editing* and *under-editing* and make the most of the suggestions provided by the tool. They also stressed that one of the key benefits of the experiment was the development of teamwork and communication skills, which points to the need to replicate similar activities in the translation training classroom where group work is perhaps not always given sufficient space. It is hoped that this study has provided some empirical data to contribute to the discussion on the role of ASR and MT tools in AVT workflows. Of course, it would be interesting to replicate the experiment with variations. For example, experiments could be set up to work on a different AVT genre. Professional subtitlers with more experience could be recruited, and different language combinations could be taken into account. A different cloud subtitling platform could be used, or different automation tools

[6] For reasons of space, this paper does not report in detail on this part of the study (it will be the object of a future publication).

could be used. Computer Assisted Translation (CAT) tools could be used instead of (or together with) MT tools. In short, this is only the beginning and, although in recent years research in this field has taken off, the role of automation in AVT is still more or less uncharted territory. What is clear is that recent technological developments do have the potential to facilitate the subtitlers' work and even improve quality, provided that translators, software developers and AVT researchers engage in constructive dialogue to ensure that the human element is always at the core of the process.

References

Angelone, Erik. 2020. The impact of screen recording as a diagnostic process protocol on inter-rater consistency in translation assessment. *The Journal of Specialised Translation-JosTrans* 34: 32–50. https://jostrans.org/issue34/art_angelone.pdf Accessed on 20 September 2023

Antoja, Ed, director. 2017. Empatía. FAADA and La Diferencia.

AVTE. 2021b. Not enough translators? AVTE knows why. Audiovisual Translation Europe. https://avteurope.eu/2021/11/30/not-enough-translators-avte-knows-why/. Accessed on 20 September 2023.

AVTE. 2021a. *Machine Translation Manifesto.* Audiovisual Translators Europe. https://avteurope.eu/wp-content/uploads/2021/09/Machine-Translation-Manifesto ENG.pdf. Accessed on 20 September 2023.

Berman, Jeff. 2022.CWMF: Talent Crunch is Creating a Localization Challenge. *M+E Daily* April 06, 2022. https://www.mesaonline.org/2022/04/06/cwmf-talent-crunch-is-creating-a-localisation-challenge/. Accessed on 20 September 2023.

Bond, Esther. 2018. Why People Leave the Language Industry. *Slator,* 27 Jul 2018. https://slator.com/why-people-leave-the-language-industry/. Accessed on 20 September 2023.

Bryant, Miranda. 2021. Where have all the translators gone?. *The Guardian*, 14 November 2021. https://www.theguardian.com/tv-and-radio/2021/nov/14/where-have-all-the-translators-gone. Accessed on 20 September 2023.

Díaz-Cintas, Jorge and Serenella Massidda. 2019. Technological advances in audiovisual translation. In *The Routledge Handbook of Translation and Technology*, ed. M. O'Hagan, 255–270. London: Routledge (Routledge Handbooks in Translation).

Estopace, Eden. 2017. Audiovisual Translation Hits a Sweet Spot as Subscription Video On-Demand Skyrockets. Slator, 23 Nov 2017. https://slator.com/audiovisual-translation-hits-sweet-spot-subscription-video-on-demand-skyrockets/. Accessed on 20 September 2023.

Karakanta, Alina, Luisa Bentivogli, Mauro Cettolo, Matteo Negri and Marco Turchi. 2022. Post-editing in Automatic Subtitling: a Subtitlers' Perspective. In *Proceedings of the 23rd Annual Conference of the European Association for Machine Translation*, 261–270. Ghent: European Association for Machine Translation.

Massidda, Serenella and Annalisa Sandrelli. 2023. ¡Sub! localisation workflows (th)at work. *Translation and Translanguaging in Multilingual Contexts* 9(3): 298–315. Amsterdam/Philadelphia: John Benjamins Publishing Company.

Paine, Chris, director. 2018. Do you trust this computer, Papercut Films.

Tardel, Anke. 2020. Effort in semi-automatized subtitling processes: speech recognition and experience during transcription. *Journal of Audiovisual Translation* 3 (1): 79–102.

Tardel, Anke. 2023. A proposed workflow model for researching production processes in subtitling. *Trans-kom* 16 (1): 140–173. Url: https://www.trans-kom.eu/bd16nr01/trans-kom_16_01_09_Tardel_Subtitling.20230706.pdf. Accessed on 20 September 2023.

Tuominen, Tiina, Maarit Koponen, Kaisa Vitikainen, and YleUmut Sulubacak, and Jörg Tiedemann. 2023. Exploring the gaps in linguistic accessibility of media: The potential of automated subtitling as a solution. *The Journal of Specialised Translation-JosTrans* 39: 77–98. https://jostrans.org/issue39/art_tuominen.pdf Accessed on 20 September 2023.

Wyndham, Anna. 2021. Streaming Boom Changes Buyer Perception of Subtitling, Dubbing. Slator, 31 May 2021. https://slator.com/streaming-boom-changes-buyer-perception-of-subtitling-and-dubbing/. Accessed on 20 September 2023.

Annalisa Sandrelli joined UNINT as a Lecturer in English in 2008, after teaching in Trieste, Bologna at Forlì, and Hull. A trained conference interpreter and film translator, she has taught Interpreting, Audiovisual Translation, and Respeaking. Research interests: Interpreting Studies, Audiovisual Translation, EU English, and Computer Assisted Interpreter Training (CAIT).

Industry Insights About Translation Technologies: Current Needs and Future Trends

Roser Sánchez-Castany

Abstract Globalisation and technological innovation have sparked significant structural changes in the language industry in the last decade. Faced with this reality, we find ourselves at a critical moment to reflect on the technological needs and trends of this dynamic sector. In order to provide as accurate a picture as possible, we have reviewed leading industry stakeholders' publications on the state of the language industry, with a twofold aim: to identify (1) the existing professional profiles that require technology-related skills and know-how and (2) the current technological trends. All the publications reviewed confirm that the language industry is highly technologised and that traditional profiles now require high levels of technology-related skills. However, there is yet to be a clear answer as to where the profession is heading, given the relentless process of technological change taking place in the sector. Language service providers and independent professionals are well aware that new technologies may be developed that will have a disruptive effect on the way translation services are performed and delivered.

1 Introduction

As a natural response to the globalisation and technologisation in which we live today, the language industry has undergone profound structural changes in recent decades (O'Hagan 2020, 1–2). Among other factors, this is due to the evolution, use and consolidation of technology in this industry and the immediacy demands of today's society. All these factors place professional translation on a wheel that is spinning increasingly fast. As a result, the vast amount of content generated daily and requiring translation is overwhelming, as well as the range of languages and locales. It would be unthinkable for the language industry to take on such volumes without using technology.

R. Sánchez-Castany (✉)
Translation Technologies, Universitat Jaume I, Castelló de la Plana, Spain
e-mail: castan@uji.es

Y. Peng et al. (eds.), *New Advances in Translation Technology*, New Frontiers in Translation Studies, https://doi.org/10.1007/978-981-97-2958-6_6

Some years ago, only some industry stakeholders —which can include language service providers (LSPs), vendors, project managers (PMs), terminologists, translators, localisers, post-editors, interpreters, revisers, quality assurance specialists and consultants (Angelone et al. 2020, 1)— would have considered using technologies such as machine translation (MT) in a translation workflow. In contrast, it is now possible that more than 99% of the world's translations are in the hands of machines (van der Meer 2020, 300).

According to Graphical Research (2021, online), the global language services industry is growing at an annual rate of 2.07% and is expected to reach 40.8 billion euros by 2028. The consolidation of some LSPs in the top positions of the main rankings (Hickey, 2022; CSA Research, 2022; Slator, 2022) is a fact, and this industry is becoming more significant year after year. This trend is often reproduced even in the lowest positions on the lists. What is more, for the first time in history, the language industry has a billion-dollar company (Hickey 2022, online), and Europe is currently the highest revenue-generating region in the world, ahead of North America and Asia, most likely due to its rich cultural and linguistic diversity. Yet it remains unclear to what extent technology has penetrated the provision of translation services.

This study is part of a larger research project whose main goal is to assess technological training in Translation & Interpreting undergraduate degrees in Spain through the combination of different empirical studies. When it comes to the Spanish academic context, conclusive evidence is needed concerning the adequacy of translation technology (TT) training for market demands in undergraduate translation programmes.[1] In this study, the concept of TT is based on O'Brien and Rodríguez Vázquez's (2019, 264) proposal: "In its broadest sense translation technology is understood to include a large array of computer tools that help translators do their jobs, including word processors; spell, style and grammar checkers; the World Wide Web; corpus compilation and analysis tools; terminology management tools; translation memory tools (TM); translation management systems (TMS); and machine translation (MT)." In a research project conducted by Sánchez-Castany (2022, 2023a,b), whose main goal was to investigate the current TT teaching–learning environments in Spanish universities, empirical data suggested that Spanish undergraduate translation degrees offer TT modules in all cases. However, most of them include rather traditional technologies, such as word processors, terminology management systems, computer-assisted translation (CAT) tools and, to a lesser extent, general MT architectures. Additionally, data indicated that TT is usually presented in independent modules, and it is not common to integrate them into practical translation classes.

Understanding market trends could allow higher education programmes to respond to specific industry needs and can subsequently prepare students to provide value-added services in an area of specialisation (Olohan 2007; Mellinger 2017). While analysing whether translation curricula in Spain are in line with the industry demands falls outside the scope of the present paper, we do hope that it will serve to lay the groundwork for future research in that direction. The study presented in

[1] This study focuses on "translation technologies" only, and interpreting technologies are not under the remit of this research.

this paper falls within the framework of Sánchez-Castany's aforementioned work, as its goal is twofold: (i) to broadly reflect on the profiles in greatest demand in the language industry that require technology-related skills and know-how through the analysed publications; and (ii) to identify which technology trends are driving this dynamic and fast-changing industry on a global scale.

The following section sets out the research approach adopted in this study. Then, Sect. 3 presents the findings of the literature review and their discussion, while the study's main conclusions are covered in Sect. 4.

2 Research Approach

2.1 Grey Literature: Market Research and Industry-Related Publications

To achieve the goals mentioned earlier, we decided to delve into industry-related studies and reports through a comprehensive grey literature review (Fink 2005, 3). Grey literature is understood as text-based output that is not formally published by commercial or academic publishers (i.e., not a book or academic journal; Carpenter, 2005). This paper focuses on language industry stakeholders' publications that may offer valuable information on TT in the language industry worldwide. Some authors argue that traditional or narrative literature reviews, unlike systematic ones, need more transparent and replicable explicit methodology or guidelines (Ferrari 2015). For this reason, following the recommendations of Jesson et al. (2011), we have tried to systematise the sample selection and rationale, the analysis, and the synthesis of the information. There have been very few attempts in our field to take stock of the studies and reports published by industry stakeholders, a gap this study aims to bridge.

Market research is intended to provide context to inform companies' decision-making processes (Hague et al. 2004, 2), and it usually tries to characterise and describe an industry, with a focus on its performance, trends, expectations and/or challenges. If there is one thing that characterises market research in our field, compared to studies conducted within academia, it is precisely its scarcity (Hu 2018). In the language industry, some stakeholders, such as LSPs and associations, publish studies or reports on the state of the market. In this grey literature, figures are difficult to compare, given the industry's diversity, global spread, shifting exchange rates, varying understandings of what should be measured and the fact that leading LSPs are privately managed and not obliged to share performance data (Drugan 2013, 9). However, reviewing this grey literature is yet another way in which the market can be studied. It can provide relevant new insights not usually covered in academic publications, since they include reliable and updated data about industry aspects to which academia may have limited or no access at all, such as companies' needs, business turnover or investment prospects.

2.2 *Sample Selection and Description*

We defined three criteria for selecting the publications we were going to review. First, given the lack of financial resources available for this research, we selected those publicly available and free of charge. The second and third criteria were the language and date of publication. We reduced the sample to those published in English between 2020 and 2022,[2] regardless of the geographic scope on which they were focused. Publications written in a language other than English, those without a publication date and blog posts were discarded.

No databases collect these publications, so compiling the corpus through systematically consulting databases, as suggested in most systematic review procedures (*cf.* Jesson et al. 2011; Page et al. 2021), was not possible. However, we systematised the bibliography search as much as possible, selecting the most relevant industry sources. First, we narrowed the list down to (i) specialised companies and organisations that conduct market research on the language industry and publish rankings of LSPs. To do this, we consulted popular industry magazines and blogs, such as Futures of Work,[3] Multilingual[4] and Gartner.[5] Not all market research is available in open access, as is the case for Slator,[6] CSA Research[7] and Graphical Research,[8] from which we were only able to obtain a few publications. We also consulted academic works in recent years that refer to those reports, such as Lambert and Walker (2022), Firat (2021), Angelone et al. (2020), O'Hagan (2020) and Moorkens (2020), among others. Then, we consulted (ii) public institutions and (iii) professional associations that periodically publish studies and reports of this type, such as the European Master's in Translation (EMT) Network,[9] the Globalization and Localization Association (GALA),[10] the European Union of Associations of Translation Companies (EUATC)[11] and the Translation Automation User Society (TAUS).[12] Finally, we checked the websites of the (iv) LSPs included in the three main industry rankings (*cf.* Hickey 2022; CSA Research 2022; Slator 2022). As the reader will note, the sources are very diverse, which may lead to widely varying perspectives or points of view on the industry.

[2] The broader research project in which this study is included has been carried out from 2020 to 2022, although the analysis and interpretation of data have extended to 2023. Academic references extend beyond this period of time to reflect the reality of the industry from the point of view of academia.

[3] https://futuresofwork.co.uk/. Accessed 20 September 2022.

[4] https://multilingual.com/magazine/. Accessed 20 September 2022.

[5] https://www.gartner.es/es/smarterwithgartner.htm. Accessed 20 September 2022.

[6] https://slator.com/. Accessed 20 September 2022.

[7] https://csa-research.com/. Accessed 20 September 2022.

[8] https://www.graphicalresearch.com/. Accessed 20 September 2022.

[9] https://commission.europa.eu/resources-partners/european-masters-translation-emt_en. Accessed 20 September 2022.

[10] https://www.gala-global.org/. Accessed 20 September 2022.

[11] https://euatc.org/. Accessed 20 September 2022.

[12] https://www.taus.net/. Accessed 20 September 2022.

The final publication sample covered the following aspects: understanding industry market trends, developments, expectations, concerns, obstacles and challenges; characterising the demographics, behaviours and attitudes of industry stakeholders; and identifying changes in business practices. The author' final aim in collecting this information is to understand the industry and set several roadmaps from a global and changing industry landscape perspective. In terms of the topics covered, while some of the selected publications focus on the most cutting-edge technologies in the sector, such as neural machine translation (NMT) and AI, others include a wide range of general questions about the state of the industry. What was crucial for us was that all of them related at some point to the technological aspects of the profession and/or the industry.

Table 1 presents a list of the 18 publications selected in descending order by year of publication. For clarity's sake, when presenting and discussing the findings, they were coded as P01-18 to identify the publication (P) from the sample (n = 18) being cited. This code has been added to the bibliographic citations when they appear in the text (for example, "P01: EUATC 2022"). More information about the publications can be found in the appendix, with a comprehensive table that includes data on the publication's commissioner, the country or region the publication focusses on, its main goals, the type of publication or method to gather and analyse data, and the sample used.

The nature of the publications in our sample is quite diverse, as it includes online survey reports, market research studies, company reports and accounts, white papers—on technological matters, in this case—or post-conference papers, from which we could obtain reliable and updated data. This diversity results in a significant disparity between the methodological approaches adopted and the samples used to conduct the studies included in our sample, which may constitute a methodological challenge for our study. For instance, certain publications deal with a relatively large sample, such as EUATC's annual ELIS reports, which include the results of online surveys targeting language service companies, independent language professionals, representatives of training institutions and students, and language departments and language service buyers, with 809 responses in 2020, 907 in 2021 and 1342 in 2022; two other online surveys offered by CSA Research, with 7363 responses from translators and interpreters in 2020, and 393 responses in 2022; and a Nimdzi market research published in 2022 about the 100 largest LSPs, for which 167 valid responses were collected from LSPs of all sizes, and interviews were conducted with more than 30 of the most significant players in the language industry. Other publications, primarily from LSPs, do not include explicit information on either the methodological approach or the data sample used. However, they seem to be the result of LSPs' expertise and know-how.

Table 1 List of publications selected with bibliographic data

ID	Publication title	Author(s)	Organisation	Year
P01	European Language Industry Survey (ELIS)	EUATC	ELIA, EMT, EUATC, FIT EUROPE, GALA, LIND, Women in Localization	2022
P02	The Viability of the Freelance Linguist Profession	Hélène Pielmeier	CSA Research	2022
P03	The 2022 Nimdzi 100: The Ranking of Top 100 Largest Language Service Providers	Sarah Hickey	Nimdzi Insights, LLC	2022
P04	Market Guide for AI-Enabled Translation Services	Bern Elliot, Gabriele Rigon, Adrian Lee and JC Martel	Gartner	2022
P05	Imminent Research Report 2022	Translated	Imminent (Translated's Research Center)	2022
P06	European Language Industry Survey (ELIS)	EUATC	ELIA, EMT, EUATC, FIT EUROPE, GALA, LIND, Women in Localization	2021
P07	Language Services Industry Survey and Report 2021	ATC UK and Nimdzi	ATC UK and Nimdzi Insights, LLC	2021
P08	Nimdzi Language Technology Atlas: the Definitive Guide to the Language Technology Landscape	Yulia Akhulkova, Sarah Hickey and Rosemary Hynes	Nimdzi Insights, LLC	2021
P09	Machine Translation	TransPerfect	TransPerfect	2021
P10	Annual Report	RWS	RWS Holdings plc	2021
P11	Annual Report and Accounts 2021	Keyword Studios	Keyword Studios plc	2021
P12	Annual Report	Appen	Appen Limited	2021
P13	ZOO Digital Goup PLC. Final Results FY21	ZOO	ZOO Digital Group plc	2021
P14	Reinventing the Translation Industry	Andrew Joscelyne and Şölen Aslan	TAUS	2020
P15	The State of the Linguist Supply Chain	Hélène Pielmeier and Paul O'Mara	CSA Research	2020
P16	Global Multilingual Commerce: Components of a Winning Cross-Border Strategy	TransPerfect	TransPerfect	2020
P17	The Nimdzi 100	Nimdzi	Nimdzi Insights, LLC	2020
P18	European Language Industry Survey (ELIS)	EUATC	ELIA, EMT, EUATC, FIT EUROPE, GALA, LIND, Women in Localization	2020

2.3 Data Analysis and Presentation

The data analysis procedure was based on a qualitative content analysis approach, as explained by Saldanha and O'Brien (2014, 190), using Atlas.ti 8. We first identified the main themes we were looking for in the publications: technology integration in the workflow, workflow automation, technological trends and investment intentions, technology development, training in TT, profiles in demand and the impact of AI. We then carefully read all the publications included in the sample, looking for patterns. After the analysis stage, we summarised the concepts and findings from different publications according to their similarities and differences to synthesise the review's findings. Finally, we grouped the information by type of technology or tool.

In order to enrich the discussion, whenever pertinent, the findings were compared against the results of previous academic studies that have addressed some of the topics highlighted in this review. It should be borne in mind that, in academia, as suggested by Plaza-Lara (2014, 93–94), Rodríguez De Céspedes (2020, 124) and Márquez Garrido (2022, 20), among others, many publications are the product of the professional experience of researchers who wish to record their own knowledge of the working reality of the translator. Other researchers, given their lack of knowledge of the profession in situ, make their contributions based on previous research works in translatology and translation teaching. There appears to be a gap in the literature in terms of conducting broader empirical studies from an industry perspective, with most of those published having certain geographical, temporal, methodological, sampling or sectoral limitations. However, our research does not aim to fill this gap but rather to provide an up-to-date overview of the technological trends and profiles that require technology-related skills in this industry, according to the selected literature.

3 Findings and Discussion

This section presents the results from the analysis of the 18 publications included in the sample and a discussion of our findings, taking into account prior academic works. Section 3.1 includes an overview of the most common job profiles that are in need of technological skills and know-how, and Sect. 3.2 presents the main technological trends observed in the publications of the sample.

3.1 Main Profiles that Require Technology-Related Skills and Know-How

One of the main ideas observed across our publication sample is that LSPs will still need to hire human translators and localisers to translate texts. However, given the unstoppable force of the technological changes we see in the industry, it seems that technologies will reshape the future of translation and the profiles of professionals (Briva-Iglesias and O'Brien, 2022). As a result, there will be a need for specialists with experience and pointed expertise to perform technology-related tasks, such as preparing data, corpora annotation, curating MT training, evaluating MT engines, and fine-tuning MT processes.

We identified three professional profiles that require technology-related skills and know-how: (1) translation and localisation professionals; (2) MT post-editors; and (3) project managers (PM). Despite these profiles being traditionally found in our industry (see, for example, Gouadec 2007; Orlando 2016; or Robinson 2020), TT is nowadays entirely in play in these professional profiles. In addition, according to the information gathered, other profiles will gain momentum in the following years, such as data management and processing professionals, which will be covered in the trends section (see Sect. 3.2).

3.1.1 Translation and Localisation Professionals

The translator and localiser,[13] as defined by Gouadec (2007, 111), is "someone who carries out all of the tasks that make up the provision of a translation to a client (work provider)". Despite the date of the reference, it is fully valid for today's times. Not surprisingly, as highlighted in the 2021 ELIS (P06: EUATC 2021) and according to the 2022 Nimdzi ranking of LSPs (P03: Hickey 2022, online), the service most commonly provided by LSPs is translation and localisation (98.1%).

LSPs are increasingly adopting technologies that help optimise translation speed and outputs. According to the 2022 ELIS (P01: EUATC 2022, 23), only 3% of LSPs reported not using CAT tools, and only 12% of independent language professionals reported never using any TM or CAT tool. This is an idea that has been widely acknowledged in academia in empirical studies on the industry, as shown by Plaza-Lara (2014, 25–46), Bowker (2015, 88–90), Sánchez-Gijón (2016, 154) or Mellinger (2017, 2018), among others.

As we can observe in some of the analysed publications from leading LSPs, such as Translated (P05: 2022), RWS (P10: 2021), TransPerfect (P09: 2021) and Keyword (P11: 2021), companies have always embraced new TT to adapt to new trends in workflows and business management. As a result, CAT tools or MT (mainly NMT) systems are now part of their working environments, as noted by Ginovart Cid (2020, 171) and Cadwell et al. (2018, 318), among others. Some companies have even developed or acquired proprietary software tools, such as XLoc[14] (Keyword) and Trados Studio[15] (RWS), to name but a few. It seems surprising to see, nonetheless, that these tools do not appear to be integrated into undergraduate translation teaching–learning environments to prepare students with the necessary technological skills and

[13] See Bond (2018) for other titles to refer to these professionals.

[14] https://www.xloc.com/. Accessed 20 September 2022.

[15] https://www.trados.com/es/. Accessed 20 September 2022.

competencies, at least in Spain (Plaza-Lara 2014; Sánchez-Gijón 2016; Sánchez-Castany 2022).

3.1.2 Machine Translation Post-Editors

The profile of the MT post-editor, understood as a linguist who "works on material translated by some sort of machine translation engine" (Gouadec 2007, 111), was also mentioned a number of times in our sample of publications.

Both academia (see Way 2020 and Cid et al. 2019), among others) and industry stakeholders agree that MT has been integrated into the regular translation and localisation workflows in many domains (e.g., e-commerce, life sciences, social media sectors and IT). Our analysis shows that the number of companies providing MT and PE increases yearly, and it is the second service offered by LSPs (79.0%) (P03: Hickey 2022, online). This is also highlighted in the Association of Translation Companies (ATC) and Nimdzi survey and report on the UK language services industry, according to which the most requested services in the UK are technology-related: MT and PE (78%), publishing (75%), subtitling (71%), desktop publishing (71%) and remote interpreting (71%) (P07: 2021, 14).

However, we found some reluctance among certain LSPs and independent linguists regarding MT and PE. For example, 30% of LSPs participating in the 2021 ELIS stated that they had no intention to implement MT (P06: EUATC 2021, 71). Moreover, 40% of ATC and Nimdzi survey respondents stated that MT no longer contributes significantly to their revenue, even though more than half of the surveyed LSPs use MT tools (P07: 2021, 22, 30). As for independent language professionals, the 2022 ELIS reported that they identified PE tasks as the most significant change –taking into account its increase– in the language industry (P01: EUATC 2022, 16).

Yet this is still an issue of considerable controversy and conflicting positions. On the one hand, this survey and other analysed publications confirm that MT is today the most widely used technology among independent language professionals, as another tool in their translation process, after TM and terminology management systems (P01: EUATC 2022, 23). This fact is supported in a CSA Research report ("One in five translators (22%) use MT even when clients don't ask for it") (P15: Pielmeier and O'Mara 2020, 42) or in the latest Nimdzi ranking ("Of course, the majority of translators use MT, but rather as just another tool in their translation process") (P03: Hickey 2022, online). In fact, according to a study conducted by Cadwell et al. (2018, 318), translators sometimes find MT useful and can have positive experiences with it. On the other hand, linguists do not always get excited about correcting MT output. As stated by the aforementioned CSA Research report, translators sometimes rate MT as a delaying tool compared to other translation tools, "most likely tied to the fact that MT's output isn't consistently good enough to speed up translations" (P15: Pielmeier and O'Mara 2020, 44).

Despite the fact that MT post-editors appear to represent a core profile for the language industry, scientific academic evidence suggests that the undergraduate education that students receive in this field, at least in Spain, does not usually provide the required skills. A more extensive discussion about this topic can be found in the work by Piqué and Colominas (2013), Cid-Leal et al. (2019) and Sánchez-Castany (2022), among others.

3.1.3 Project Managers

According to Gouadec (2007, 118), PMs supervise the running of a project and carry out tasks such as deciding on the workflow; managing human resources, software, hardware, documentation, etc.; preparing the source materials for translation; supplying the translators with a complete translation or localisation kit; checking and controlling translation quality and approving interim and final versions; and looking after the administrative and financial side of the project. In short, in Walker's (2023, 1) words, "project management is about risk management: proper planning and organisation will in most places remove (or at least mitigate) the chance of things going wrong".

According to our data sample, the need for human PMs has increased sharply over the past years and is still growing. Despite the general trend to automate processes in the language industry's business models (see Sect. 3.2.2), counting on PMs seems to be crucial due to both the increase in LSPs subcontracting professionals and the large size and technicality of projects, expressed in terms of number of words, number of languages, and number and complexity of tools used and procedures (Risku et al. 2019). The role of technologies for PM tasks is crucial, as stated by the ATC and Nimdzi survey, where 91% of the respondent LSPs said they used a TMS and 70% used a business management system (BMS) (P07: 2021, 30). Moreover, according to the 2022 ELIS, 59% of LSPs' full-time staff are directly involved in production tasks (in a PM role, as a linguist, multimedia expert or language engineer), and recruitment intentions for PM functions remain high (P01: EUATC, 2022, 30).

In Spanish undergraduate degrees, as in the case of the MT post-editors profile, undergraduate translation degrees offer very little training in project management skills, as stated by Plaza-Lara (2018) and Quijano Peña (2022), among others, and even less in the technological skills that PMs should master (Sánchez-Castany 2022).

3.2 *Main Technological Trends*

The technology industry represents one of the leading language services markets and is also recognised as the fastest-growing segment, a statement supported by many academic sources, such as O'Hagan (2020), Angelone et al. (2020) and O'Brien and Rossetti (2021). Driven mainly by a shift among companies towards digital, the technology sector has been boosted throughout the COVID-19 health crisis. In fact, for many LSPs, the pandemic and the 2021 recovery exposed weak points, but it also pushed innovation, brought technological and process changes —such as automation services, AI or cloud-based technology— and created new jobs and research opportunities (P07: ATC and Nimdzi 2021, 15).

In reviewing our publication sample, we identified four leading technology trends at the heart of the main LSP investments: MT, process automation, AI and cloud-based technologies.

3.2.1 MT at the Centre of the Business

MT is no longer disruptive. The hype around its revolution has died down, as stated by Nimdzi: "Large and medium-sized LSPs alike are reporting that while the use of MT has increased, the perceived benefits from MT have plateaued" (P17: 2020, 32). The publications analysed agree that MT is clearly destined to be an integral part of the professional translation landscape, and industry stakeholders are discussing how to properly keep on integrating this technology into the industry's business model (P01: EUATC 2022, 26). LSPs are looking for high-quality results and high-efficiency levels, so they —especially those in the first ranking positions— invest time in training these technologies, namely preparing and cleaning datasets, or technically developing customisation initiatives (P03: Hickey 2022, online). For example, this is reflected in some LSPs developing their own TMX editors to help prepare and refine data to be used with MT systems, developing their in-house solutions for MT, improving NMT technology, or increasing the size of MT and data teams. Meanwhile, undergraduate education seems to be lagging behind when it comes to training students in these new skills, although there are already voices advocating for highly-technological linguistic profiles, such as the case of the "language engineer" proposed by Briva-Iglesias and O'Brien (2022). We must bear in mind that there are many professionals who do not limit their training in translation and/or TT to an undergraduate level, but take a specialised master's degree.[16]

Not only is it worth highlighting the increase in the use of MT, but also higher levels of final client acceptance. MT systems have reached such a high level that big tech players (e.g. Google, Microsoft and Amazon) appear to have lost interest in optimising their MT engines even further, as reflected by Nimdzi (P17: 2020, 33). According to the 2022 ELIS, 65% of surveyed LSPs see the NMT quality improvement and development as an opportunity rather than as a threat, while the independent professionals have mixed feelings about that: only 35% of them see it as an opportunity, and 41% as a threat (P01: EUATC 2022, 11).

In addition, how to get paid for PE tasks has become a hotly-debated topic, as there needs to be more alignment between what the market needs and what linguists want and can provide. Many professionals participating in the 2021 ELIS argue that

[16] It is worth noting some MA programmes in Europe that focus in technical and technological training in the field of translation, such as the MA in Tradumatics: Translation Technologies offered by Universitat Autònoma de Barcelona (https://www.uab.cat/web/estudiar/official-master-s-degrees/general-information-1096480962610.html?param1=1345695508762) and the MA in Multilingual Communication Technology offered by Université de Genève (https://www.unige.ch/fti/en/enseignements/ma-tim/).

the concerns regarding the economic climate and the rise of MT are their main cause of stress, as paying post-editors based on how many corrections they make to MT-translated texts does not help to improve this situation, but rather worsens it (P06: EUATC 2021, 56). There is an assumption in the industry that people can buy PE services relatively cheaply. However, this differs from what professional translators want, as they do not always look favourably on correcting MT output and are not always willing to work either at any rate or under any conditions (Collantes et al. 2018; Cadwell et al. 2018). From an academic perspective, many researchers have focused their work on these and other ethical issues in the profession regarding the use of TT, such as Moorkens (2022) and Kenny et al. (2020).

Regarding local public agencies, it seems that they have a less-developed technology approach, except where technology is already wholly mature —i.e. a stage of development where it is highly advanced, well-established, and stable, as is the case with CAT tools and TMS— or where it is an integral or necessary part of the organisational structure —e.g. centralised procurement platforms (P01: EUATC 2022, 24). International public agencies, on the contrary, appear to be forerunners in virtually all technologies (P01: EUATC 2022, 24). An excellent example of this penetration is the technological initiatives —most of them related to MT and post-editing projects— that have been carried out in organisations such as the Directorate-General for Translation of the European Commission (Lesznyák 2019; Rossi and Chevrot 2019; Vardaro et al. 2019; Rodríguez Vázquez 2020; Stefaniak 2020; Svoboda and Sosoni 2022) and some United Nations organisations (Elizalde et al. 2012; Servant 2014; Pouliquen 2015; Cadwell et al. 2016).

3.2.2 A Clear Commitment to Process Automation

Most of the publications analysed agree that automation came into the professional outsourcing scene some years ago to boost further linguistic content delivery, particularly in project management processes and tasks related to quality assurance. This is something that has also been echoed by academia, as in Pym and Torres-Simón's (2021) research about the significant impact of automation-driven changes in the translation profession. According to the aforementioned LSP rankings, the industry is becoming larger every year, and its operations need to be increasingly structured. To cope with this paradigm, coupled with ever-larger volumes and ever-tighter budgets and time restrictions (do Carmo 2020), LSPs are increasing automation wherever possible to reduce costs and boost efficiency. Indeed, one of the leading innovation trends in the industry revolves around how to translate more content faster, at higher quality levels, and at lower costs (P03: Hickey 2022, online; P08: Akhulkova et al. 2021, online).

LSPs seek to centralise their translation projects from start to finish and control every step in the process. Currently, the remote working conditions imposed by the COVID-19 health emergency have considerably accelerated the implementation of automated processes throughout the workflow. As a result, more and more companies (both large and medium-sized) are launching or reactivating self-service platforms that offer a translation service with less or no human intervention, which adds a new dimension to existing marketplaces (e.g., Proz[17] or Translatorscafe).[18] In fact, according to the 2022 ELIS, 45% of LSPs claimed that more than 25% of their projects are carried out using automated workflows (P01: EUATC 2022, 27). Indeed, TMS and BMS are increasingly important in the relationship between LSPs, freelance professionals and their end-customers. For example, the ATC and Nimdzi survey showed that 91% of companies use a TMS, and 70% use a BMS (P07: 2021, 30) and, according to the 2020 ELIS, this trend is increasing amazingly on an annual basis (P18: EUATC 2020). We believe that this upcoming trend should be reflected in TT undergraduate training, as specific technological skills that are not currently covered, at least in Spanish universities, will have to be included in the curricula (Quijano Peña 2022).

3.2.3 Data and AI Consolidation

The use of AI in a myriad of applications is becoming more ubiquitous. In everyday life, AI applications are used in mobile phones, intelligent speakers, recommender systems, and many other applications (P09: TransPerfect 2021, 1). According to Nimdzi, there are considerable opportunities for AI in the manufacturing space in Europe (P17: 2020, 28), and they estimate that the segment often referred to as "data for AI services" —i.e. services ranging from multilingual data collection, annotation, and training of AI models— reached nearly USD 2 billion in 2021 (P03: Hickey 2022, online). All these increasingly varied applications have earned a place at the vanguard of advances in human development and have caused the translation market to be more dynamic than ever. In fact, some of the biggest LSPs, such as Appen (P12: 2021), TransPerfect (P16: 2020; P09: 2021) and Translated (P05: 2022), admit to combining their AI technology, processes and systems with their expertise and crowdsourcing to support global projects. Massey and Kiraly (2019) mention some outstanding new developments in the AI field that will contribute to reshaping our industry and society. This is the case of ChatGPT (Wenzlaff and Spaeth 2022; Swennen 2023), which has recently caused concern among professionals and academics. Overall, the publications analysed agree that developments in the AI market, the regulatory environment, and rapidly-changing client needs and end-user expectations could impact LSPs' business models, required product offerings and strategic decisions across markets.

Regarding translation, AI means professionals can train machines to translate the way they want their translations done. Translation is often a time-consuming and costly process. Hence, advances in AI enable a broad range of new translation use cases and enhance existing ones —for instance, machine learning (ML), NMT, AI-based CAT and QA tools— improving quality, increasing savings, and enabling outcomes that were previously not possible due to cost or delays. Unfortunately,

[17] https://www.proz.com/. Accessed 20 September 2022.

[18] https://www.translatorscafe.com/cafe/. Accessed 20 September 2022.

according to some analysed reports (e.g. P04: Elliot et al. 2022, online), small and medium-sized LSPs have limited access to emerging AI-enabled translation use cases that offer better outcomes and efficiencies. The same applies to independent professionals, as they do not usually have the technical or financial means to integrate all these technological advances into their daily work.

In general terms, most of the advances in the translation industry are being used to improve existing workflows and create new business and consumer markets (P04: Elliot et al. 2022, online). Therefore, as stated in the latest Nimdzi ranking, if LSPs are looking for high-quality results, they need to invest time in nurturing AI tools from the start: creating and preparing datasets, training NMT systems, technically rolling out a customisation initiative at a given enterprise, data annotation, labelling and scoring, working with natural language processing (NLP) systems and language models, powering TMS and BMS (P03: Hickey 2022, online). As stated by TAUS: "[...] of all the variables that compose the pattern of business, global range, and technology, data wins the highest accolade for sheer importance" (P14: Joscelyne and Şölen 2020, 16). While, in general, independent linguists still see this emerging field primarily as a threat, according to the 2022 ELIS this may change as these services become mainstream (P01: EUATC 2022, 11).

The technological savviness of the professionals performing data cleaning and training tasks will underpin their ability to perform the work. This may require a professional not necessarily native to the language services ecosystem, such as computer scientists or NLP specialists (Briva-Iglesias and O'Brien 2022). However, artificial intelligence (AI) experts unanimously agree that true mastery of language will remain beyond the reach of machines, at least for the foreseeable future (Joscelyne and Şölen 2020; Hohenstein et al. 2023).

3.2.4 Towards Cloud-Based Technologies

Globalisation leads independent linguists, LSPs and clients to be even more connected, and so must the services they offer and demand. According to the analysed publications, cloud-based systems have become popular in recent years. Therefore, it is not surprising to see that it was one of the key trends observed in the grey literature studied, given the growing tendency towards turning traditional desktop tools into cloud-based ones. As stated in the 2022 ELIS, "the boundaries between CAT, MT and TMS are blurring as tools become more and more embedded and multifunctional" (P01: EUATC 2022, 28). For example, according to the ATC and Nimdzi survey, 70% of LSPs in the UK reported using specific cloud-based tools to manage term bases and glossaries (P07: 2021, 30). In many cases, these processes or tools are embedded in the workflows of the LSPs themselves, which, as previously mentioned (see Sect. 3.2.2), tend to automate processes and manage them through online management systems.

A similar observation could be made regarding quality management and assessment steps. The review process measures the quality of the translated or localised content (Drugan 2013). Traditionally, it has been considered a highly-customised task aimed at finding mistakes (P03: Hickey 2022, online). This stage of translation projects, however, became less of a concern to LSPs, possibly due to the broader embedding of quality management software into TMS. In fact, according to a Gartner report, it is common for LSPs to automate project management tasks to the point of establishing "policies that enable new and existing content to be divided into 'tiers' of 'acceptable translation quality' —with specific metrics outlining 'acceptable quality' for each tier" (P04: Elliot et al. 2022, online). Besides, according to the 2022 ELIS, automated language QA tools seem to be one of the technologies with the most significant growth potential amongst LSPs (P01: EUATC 2022).

Other cloud-based technologies that are gaining importance among LSPs and end-clients are STT and chatbots. According to another Nimdzi report, there are many companies in the language industry working with video content that are already taking advantage of out-of-the-box solutions, which are used to caption pre-existing content, increase productivity and speed up the translation and localisation process (P08: Akhulkova et al. 2021, online). Meanwhile, chatbot use and demand are increasingly widespread. The chatbot market has matured quickly in recent years, becoming a natural part of LSPs' technological offer (P08: Akhulkova et al. 2021, online).

As to how this technology may affect the industry and, consequently, professionals and LSPs, it seems that it will not be as disruptive as other technologies (i.e. NMT or AI) — at least for the time being. Moving to the cloud implies using tools that, in many cases, are already part of the linguists' toolkit. As a result, the adaptation process to these technologies might be much smoother.

4 Final Considerations

In general, all the publications surveyed appear to agree that human translation is still the service most in demand, followed by PE and ahead of other services such as localisation, transcreation or interpreting. Yet questions continue to arise, the most important of which is *where* the profession is heading. The answer is far from clear, not least because technology will continue to evolve. The potential outcomes of the technological future are not predetermined, but rather a consequence of the actions taken by industry stakeholders, who shape them through their visionary ideas and innovative creations. Market stakeholders are aware that new technology could be developed that may reduce the need for traditional human translation services or disrupt how they are performed and delivered.

Our grey literature review shows that technology is leading the way concerning investment and innovation plans. Nowadays, projects can only be understood using technologies in all their phases, from start to finish. Big LSPs, such as RWS, Appen, Keyword, Lionbridge, Translated and ZOO, to name but a few, plan to increase their investment in product, engineering and ML to enable their product-led strategy. Therefore, one could imagine LSPs' recruiters moving towards the search for linguist profiles that can adapt to multiple scenarios and help with ML tasks, improve MT services and work towards the seamless integration of technology in the workflows.

Given the rapid technological evolution, LSPs and professionals must be equipped with technological skills that allow them to adapt smoothly to this change. It is the responsibility of all stakeholders in the language industry to contribute to ensuring that technologies do not become a source of further instability in the profession, employment and rates, something particularly frightening for independent linguists.

Studying industry business models, needs, and trends can make it easier for professionals to adapt their profiles, roles and training to market demands. Furthermore, having a deep knowledge of the industry could help professionals and trainers know what to expect from the profession. This study has allowed us to continue to shed light on the importance of TT for the language services industry and its presence in university training programmes. Our findings, in line with prior work (*cf.* Austermühl 2013, 327; Piqué and Colominas 2013, 310), make us believe that the growing technologisation observed in the language industry does not seem to be reflected in the Spanish undergraduate translation curricula. Al-Batineh and Bilali's (2017) work on the current situation in the Middle East and the North African regions appears to point in the same direction. As can be inferred from our analysis, adequate training is vital for professionals to understand and cope with all the technological skills and know-how they will require as future professionals. Moreover, being aware of this data is crucial for informing higher training institutions as well, as it could help determine the path of evolution in the training of future professionals.

We are aware that, despite contributing to the field by providing an insightful overview of TT's role in the industry, our study has a number of limitations. Firstly, it should be noted that the analysis and interpretation of the data have been carried out by the researcher and there was no second coding process. Secondly, as mentioned earlier in this paper, the publications analysed were published between 2020 and 2022. However, the rapid evolution of the market and technology may cause some publications in the sample to become obsolete more quickly than others. In addition, the publications reviewed here were diverse in nature (case studies, white papers, annual accounts, market studies) and approach (qualitative, quantitative, mixed methods). This diversity has made it quite challenging to systematically analyse the publications in the sample and select the most relevant information. Similarly, although the information obtained from many of the texts included in the analysis provided us with a complete picture of the industry's view of itself, it must be noted that some publications come from multi-million dollar companies with an overly futuristic view of the industry. Their status may have influenced the content they produced and the conclusions they came to.

Finally, we believe that the conclusions of these studies —and this review, by extension— may have been different if the data were sourced from independent professionals and small companies from the language industry. For this reason, future avenues for research could include expanding the data sample with reports from smaller sources, as well as studying real job offers to identify which TT skills are truly requested from translators. In this regard, it would be very enriching for this research to carry out our own market research —perhaps national in an initial phase and international at a later stage— following the trends and profiles identified in this first study.

References

Akhulkova, Yulia, Sara Hickey, and Rosemary Hynes. 2021. *Nimdzi Language Technology Atlas: the Definitive Guide to the Language Technology Landscape*. Nimdzi. https://www.nimdzi.com/language-technology-atlas/. Accessed 20 September 2022.

Al-Batineh, Mohammed, and Loubna Bilali. 2017. Translator training in the Arab world: Are curricula aligned with the language industry? *The Interpreter and Translator Trainer* 11 (2–3): 187–203. https://doi.org/10.1080/1750399X.2017.1350900.

Angelone, Erik, Maureen Ehrensberger-Dow, and Gary Massey. 2020. *The Bloomsbury Companion to Language Industry Studies*. London: Bloomsbury Academic.

Appen. 2021. *2021 Annual Report*. Appen Limited. https://appen2021.qreports.com.au/. Accessed 20 September 2022.

ATC and Nimdzi. 2021. *ATC UK Language Services Industry Survey and Report 2021*. ATC and Nimdzi. https://www.nimdzi.com/uk-language-services-industry-report/. Accessed 20 September 2022.

Austermühl, Frank. 2013. Future (and not-so-future) trends in the teaching of translation Technology. *Revista Tradumàtica. Tecnologies De La Traducció* 11: 326–337. https://doi.org/10.5565/rev/tradumatica.46.

Bond, Esther. 2018. The stunning variety of job titles in the language industry. *Slator*. https://slator.com/features/the-stunning-variety-of-job-titles-in-the-language-industry/. Accessed 20 September 2022.

Bowker, Lynne. 2015. Computer-aided Translation—Translator Training. In *The Routledge Encyclopedia of Translation Technology*, ed. Chan Sin-wai, 88–104. New York: Routledge.

Briva-Iglesias, Vicent, and Sharon O'Brien. 2022. The Language Engineer: A Transversal, Emerging Role for the Automation Age. *Quaderns de Filologia: Estudis Lingüístics* XXVII: 17-48. https://doi.org/10.7203/QF.27.24622.

Cadwell, Patrick, Sheila Castilho, Sharon O'Brien, and Linda Mitchell. 2016. Human factors in machine translation and post-editing among institutional translators. *Translation Spaces* 5 (2): 222–243. https://doi.org/10.1075/ts.5.2.04cad.

Cadwell, Patrick, Sharon O'Brien, and Carlos Teixeira. 2018. Resistance and accommodation: Factors for the (non-) adoption of machine translation among professional translators. *Perspectives* 26 (3): 301–321. https://doi.org/10.1080/0907676X.2017.1337210.

Carpenter, Brian B. 2005. GrayLit network: A science portal of technical papers. *Reference Reviews* 19 (5): 40–41. https://doi.org/10.1108/09504120510604292.

Cid, Ginovart, and Clara. 2020. The Professional Profile of a Post-editor according to LSCs and Linguists: A Survey-Based Research. *Hermes, Journal of Language and Communication in Business* 60: 171–190. https://doi.org/10.7146/hjlcb.v60i0.121318.

Cid, Ginovart, Carme Colominas Clara, and Antoni Oliver. 2020. Language industry views on the profile of the post-editor. *Translation Spaces* 9 (2): 283–313. https://doi.org/10.1075/ts.19010.cid.

Cid-Leal, Pilar, María Carmen. Espín-García, and Marisa Presas. 2019. Traducción automática y posedición: Perfiles y competencias en los programas de formación de traductores. *MonTI. Monografías De Traducción e Interpretación* 11 (11): 187–214. https://doi.org/10.6035/MonTI.2019.11.7.

Collantes, Carlos; Javier Mallo, Carla Parra Escartín, Héctor Quiñones Tapia, and Rocío Serrano. 2018. Pásate al lado oscuro: ventajas de la traducción automática para el traductor profesional. *La linterna del traductor* 17: 33–39. http://www.lalinternadeltraductor.org/n17/ventajas-traduccion-automatica.html.

CSA Research. 2022. *The Largest Language Service Providers: 2022*. CSA Research. https://csa-research.com/Featured-Content/For-LSPs/Global-Market-Study-2022/Top-100-LSPs. Accessed 20 September 2022.

de Céspedes, Rodríguez, and Begoña. 2020. Beyond the margins of academic education: Identifying translation industry training practices through action research. *The International Journal of*

Translation and Interpreting Research 12 (1): 115–126. https://doi.org/10.12807/ti.112201.2020.a07.
do Carmo, Felix. 2020. 'Time is money' and the value of translation. *Translation Spaces* 9 (1): 35–57. https://doi.org/10.1075/ts.00020.car.
Drugan, Joanna. 2013. *Quality in professional translation*. New York: Bloomsbury.
Elizalde, Cecilia; Bruno Pouliquen, Christophe Mazenc, and José García-Verdugo. 2012. TAPTA4UN: collaboration on machine translation between the World Intellectual Property Organization and the United Nations. In *Proceedings of Translating and the Computer 34.*
Elliot, Bern; Gabriele Rigon, Adrian Lee, JC. Martel. 2022. *Market Guide for AI-Enabled Translation Services*. Gartner. https://www.gartner.com/doc/reprints?id=1-2AAOC19B&ct=220613&st=sb&submissionGuid=c92857e8-50cb-4618-87f9-224d0cab3ac5&utm_medium=email&_hsmi=217172203&_hsenc=p2ANqtz-_idCHDYp00OafC7HIaGVTFxkI-C24r7rbZ51D7bFFcQW-oiXT3SOECADk4cTlhO3hC0aE1r8bOt0jgEp4d4EfSEnTtqQ&utm_content=217172203&utm_source=hs_automation. Accessed 20 September 2022.
EUATC. 2020. *European Language Industry Survey (ELIS) 2020 Before & After COVID-19*. European Commission. https://ec.europa.eu/info/sites/default/files/2020_language_industry_survey_report.pdf. Accessed 20 September 2022.
EUATC. (2021). *European Language Industry Survey (ELIS)*. European Commission. https://ec.europa.eu/info/sites/default/files/about_the_european_commission/service_standards_and_principles/documents/elis_2021_european_language_industry_survey.pdf. Accessed 20 September 2022.
EUATC. 2022. *European Language Industry Survey (ELIS)*. European Commission. https://elis-survey.org/wp-content/uploads/2022/03/ELIS-2022-report.pdf?utm_source=elis-repository&utm_medium=website&utm_campaign=elis-report22&utm_id=elis-report-22. Accessed 20 September 2022.
Ferrari, Rosella. 2015. Writing narrative style literature reviews. *Medical Writing* 24 (4): 230–235. https://doi.org/10.1179/2047480615Z.000000000329.
Fink, Arlene. 2005. *Conducting research literature reviews: From the Internet to paper*, 2nd ed. London: Sage Publications Ltd.
Firat, Gökhan. 2021. Uberization of translation. Impacts on working conditions. *The Journal of Internationalization and Localization* 8(1): 48–75. doi:https://doi.org/10.1075/jial.20006.fir.
Márquez Garrido, Rocío. 2022. *Análisis de las competencias traductológicas de los egresados de estudios de Posgrado especializados. Panorama actual en España y expectativas del mercado laboral*. Dissertation. Universidad de Córdoba.
Gouadec, Daniel. 2007. *Translation as a profession*. Amsterdam/Philadelphia: John Benjamins.
Graphical Research. 2021. *Europe Machine Translation Market Report, 2028*. Graphical Research.
Hague, Paul N., Nicholas Hague, and Carol-Ann Morgan. 2004. *Market Research in Practice: A Guide to the Basics*. Kogan Page Limited.
Hickey, Sara. 2022. *The 2022 Nimdzi 100: The Ranking of Top 100 Largest Language Service Providers*. Nimdzi Insights, LLC. https://www.nimdzi.com/nimdzi-100-top-lsp/. Accessed 20 September 2022.
Hohenstein, Jess, Rene F. Kizilcec, Dominic DiFranzo, Zhila Aghajari, Hannah Mieczkowski, Karen Levy, Mor Naaman, Jeffrey Hancockm and Malte F. Jung. 2023. Artificial intelligence in communication impacts language and social relationships. *Scientific Reports* 13: 5487. doi: https://doi.org/10.1038/s41598-023-30938-9.
Hu, Wan. 2018. *Education, Translation and Global Market Pressures. Curriculum Design in China and the UK*. Singapore: Palgrave Macmillan.
Jesson, Jill, Lydia Matheson, and Fiona M. Lacey. 2011. *Doing Your Literature Review: Traditional and Systematic Techniques*. London: Sage Publications Ltd.
Joscelyne, Andrew, and Şölen Aslan. 2020. *Reinventing the Translation Industry*. De Rijp: TAUS.
Kenny, Dorothy, Joss Moorkens, and Felix do Carmo. 2020. Fair MT. Towards ethical, sustainable machine translation. *Translation Spaces* 9(1): 1–11. doi:https://doi.org/10.1075/ts.00018.int.

Lambert, Joseph, and Callum Walker. 2022. Because we're worth it: disentangling freelance translation, status, and rate-setting in the United Kingdom. *Translation Spaces* 11 (2): 277–302. https://doi.org/10.1075/ts.21030.lam.

Lesznyák, Ágnes. 2019. Hungarian translators' perceptions of neural machine translation in the European Commission. In *Proceedings of MT Summit XVIII: Translator, Project and User Tracks*, eds. Mikel Forcada, Andy Way, John Tinsley, Dimitar Shterionov, Celia Rico, and Federico Gaspari, 16–22). https://aclanthology.org/volumes/W19-67/.

Massey, Gary; Donald Kiraly. 2019. The future of translator education: a dialogue. *Cultus: the journal of intercultural mediation and communication* 12: 15–34. https://www.cultusjournal.com/files/Archives/Cultus_2019_12_002_Kiraly_Massey.pdf.

Mellinger, Christopher D. 2017. Translators and machine translation: Knowledge and skills gaps in translator pedagogy. *The Interpreter and Translator Trainer* 11 (4): 280–293. https://doi.org/10.1080/1750399X.2017.1359760.

Mellinger, Christopher D. 2018. Problem-based learning in computer-assisted translation pedagogy. *HERMES Journal of Language and Communication in Business* 57: 195–208. https://doi.org/10.7146/hjlcb.v0i57.106205.

Moorkens, Joss. 2020. A tiny cog in a large machine. Digital Taylorism in the translation industry. *Translation Spaces* 9(1): 12–34. doi:https://doi.org/10.1075/ts.00019.moo.

Moorkens, Joss. 2022. Ethics and machine translation. In *Machine translation for everyone: Empowering users in the age of artificial intelligence*, ed. Dorothy Kenny, 121–140. Berlin: Language Science Press. doi:https://doi.org/10.5281/zenodo.6759984.

Nimdzi. 2020. *The Nimdzi 100. The size and state of the language industry in 2020, including the ranking of the TOP 100 largest language service providers.* Nimdzi Insights, LLC. https://www.nimdzi.com/2020-nimdzi-100/. Accessed 20 September 2022.

O'Brien, Sharon, and Alessandra Rossetti. 2021. Neural machine translation and evolution of the localisation sector: Implications for training. *Journal of Internationalization and Localization* 7 (1/2): 95–121. https://doi.org/10.1075/jial.20005.obr.

O'Brien, Sharon, and Silvia Rodríguez Vázquez. 2019. Translation and technology. In *The Routledge Handbook of Translation and Education*, ed. Sara Laviosa and Maria González-Davies, 264–277. Oxon: Routledge.

O'Hagan, Minako. 2020. *The Routledge handbook of translation and technology*. Abingdon/New York: Routledge.

Olohan, Maeve. 2007. Economic Trends and Developments in the Translation Industry. *The Interpreter and Translator Trainer* 1 (1): 37–63. https://doi.org/10.1080/1750399X.2007.10798749.

Orlando, Marc. 2016. *Training 21st century translators and interpreters: At the crossroads of practice, research and pedagogy*. Berlin: Frank & Timme.

Page, Matthew J., Joanne E. McKenzie, Patrick M. Bossuyt, Isabelle Boutron, Tammy C. Hoffmann, Cyntia D. Mulrow, Larissa Shamseer, Jennifer M. Tetzlaff, Elie A. Akl, Sue E. Brennan, Roger Chou, Julie Glanville, Jeremy M. Grimshaw, Asbjørn Hróbjartsson, Manoj M. Lalu, Tianjing Li, Elizabeth W. Loder, Evan Mayo-Wilson, Steve McDonald, Luke A. McGuinness, Lesley A. Stewart, James Thomas, Andrea C. Tricco, Vivian A. Welch, Penny Whiting, and David Moher. 2021. The PRISMA 2020 statement: An updated guideline for reporting systematic reviews. *Systematic Reviews* 10: 89. https://doi.org/10.1186/s13643-021-01626-4.

Peña, Quijano, and Paula. 2022. La gestión de proyectos de traducción: Una tarea pendiente en los planes de estudio del Grado en Traducción e Interpretación en España. *Hikma* 21: 287–319. https://doi.org/10.21071/hikma.v21i2.14327.

Pielmeier, Hélène, and Paul O'Mara. 2020. *The State of the Linguist Supply Chain.* CSA Research. https://cdn2.hubspot.net/hubfs/4041721/Newsletter/The%20State%20of%20the%20Linguist%20Supply%20Chain%202020.pdf. Accessed 20 September 2022.

Pielmeier, Hélène. 2022. *The Viability of the Freelance Linguist Profession.* CSA Research. https://insights.csa-research.com/reportaction/305013395/Toc?SearchTerms=viability. Accessed 20 September 2022.

Piqué, Ramón, and Carme Colominas. 2013. Les tecnologies de la traducció en la formació de grau de traductors i intèrprets. *Revista Tradumàtica. Tecnologies De La Traducció* 11: 297–312. https://doi.org/10.5565/rev/tradumatica.43.
Plaza-Lara, Cristina. 2018. Project Management: Defining Competences for Translator Trainin. In *Understanding Translator Education*, ed. Łukasz Bogucki, Paulina Pietrzak, and Michal Kornacki, 193–210. Berlin: Peter Lang.
Plaza-Lara, Cristina. 2014. *La enseñanza de la traducción asistida por ordenador: análisis didáctico-curricular y propuesta de integración de la subcompetencia instrumental profesional en el aula.* Dissertation. Universidad de Málaga.
Pouliquen, Bruno. 2015. SMT in various United Nations agencies. In *Machine Translation Summit.*
Pym, Anthony, and Ester Torres-Simón. 2021. Is automation changing the translation profession? *International Journal of the Sociology of Language* 2021 (270): 39–57. https://doi.org/10.1515/ijsl-2020-0015.
Risku, Hanna; Jelena Milosevic, and regina Rogl. 2019. Changes in the field of translation project management: Findings of a longitudinal ethnographic study. Unpublished working paper. https://uscholar.univie.ac.at/detail/o:1177557.pdf.
Robinson, Douglas. 2020. *Becoming a Translator. An Introduction to the Theory and Practice of Translation.* Abingdon/New York: Routledge.
Rossi, Caroline, and Jean-Pierre Chevrot. 2019. Uses and perceptions of machine translation at the European Commission. *The Journal of Specialised Translation* 31: 177–200. https://jostrans.org/issue31/art_rossi.pdf.
RWS. 2021. *Annual Report 2021.* RWS Holdings plc. https://www.paperturn-view.com/?pid=MjE215072. Accessed 20 September 2022.
Saldanha, Gabriela, and Sharon O'Brien. 2014. *Research Methodologies in Translation Studies.* London: Routledge.
Sánchez-Castany, Roser. 2023b. Integrating Technologies in Translation Teaching: A Study on Trainers' Perceptions. *The Interpreter and Translator Trainer* 17 (3): 479–502. https://doi.org/10.1080/1750399X.2023.2237330.
Sánchez-Castany, Roser. 2022. Teaching translation technologies: an analysis of a corpus of syllabi for Translation and Interpreting undergraduate degrees in Spain. In *The Human Translator in the 2020s*, eds. Gary Massey, Elsa Huertas Barros and David Katan, 27–43. London: Routledge. https://doi.org/10.4324/9781003223344.
Sánchez-Castany, Roser. 2023a. Thematic analysis applied to translation research: analysis of technological contents in Translation and Interpreting degrees in Spain. *Bellaterra Journal of Teaching & Learning Language & Literature* 16(3). https://doi.org/10.5565/rev/jtl3.1139
Sánchez-Gijón, P. 2016. La posedición: Hacia una definición competencial del perfil y una descripción multidimensional del fenómeno. *Sendebar* 27: 151–162. https://doi.org/10.30827/sendebar.v27i0.4016.
Servant, F. 2014. Bridging the Online Language Barriers with Machine Translation at the United Nations. In *W3C workshop: New Horizons for the Multilingual Web.*
Slator. 2022. *The Slator 2021 Language Service Provider Index*. Slator. https://slator.com/the-slator-2021-language-service-provider-index/. Accessed 20 September 2022.
Stefaniak, Karolina. 2020. Evaluating the usefulness of neural machine translation for the Polish translators in the European Commission. In *Proceedings of the 22nd Annual Conference of the European Association for Machine Translation*, ed. European Association for Machine Translation, 263–269. https://aclanthology.org/2020.eamt-1.28.
Keywords Studios. 2021. *2021 Annual Report and Accounts.* Keywords Studios plc. https://www.keywordsstudios.com/content/uploads/2022/04/38183-KW-AR21-WEB.pdf. Accessed 20 September 2022.
Svoboda, Tomáš, and Vilelmini Sosoni. 2022. Institutional translator training in language and translation technologies. In *Institutional Translator Training*, ed. Tomáš Svoboda, Łucja Biel, and Vilelmini Sosoni, 73–91. New York: Routledge.

Swennen, Anja. 2023. Research on relevant and diverse issues in teacher education. *European Journal of Teacher Education* 46 (1): 1–5. https://doi.org/10.1080/02619768.2023.2173118.
Translated. 2022. *oXXIgen. Imminent Research Report 2022.* Sandpoint: Translated.
TransPerfect. 2020. *Global Multilingual Commerce: Components of a Winning Cross-Border Strategy.* Akeneno and Translations.com.
TransPerfect. 2021. *White Paper. Machine Translation.* Translations.com. https://globallink.translations.com/sites/default/files/2021-02/machine_translation_whitepaper.pdf. Accessed 20 September 2022.
van der Meer, Jaap. 2020. Translation Technology - Past, Present and Future. In *The Bloomsbury Companion to Language Industry Studies*, ed. Erik Angelone, Maureen Ehrensberger-Dow, and Gary Massey, 285–309. London: Bloomsbury Academic.
Vardaro, Jennifer, Moritz Schaeffer, and Silvia Hansen-Schirra. 2019. Translation Quality and Error Recognition in Professional Neural Machine Translation Post-Editing. *Informatics* 6 (3): 41. https://doi.org/10.3390/informatics6030041.
Rodríguez Vázquez, Silvia. 2020. Traducción automática y posedición en la DGT: de la teoría a la práctica. *Puntoycoma* 167: pp. 13–27. https://ec.europa.eu/translation/spanish/magazine/documents/pyc_167_es.pdf.
Walker, Callum. 2023. *Translation Project Management.* London: Routledge.
Way, Andy. 2020. Machine translation: Where are we at today? In *The Bloomsbury Companion to Language Industry Studies*, ed. Eric Angelone, Maureen Ehrensberger-Dow, and Gary Massey, 311–332. London: Bloomsbury Academic.
Wenzlaff, Karsten, and Sebastian Spaeth. 2022. Smarter than Humans? Validating how OpenAI's ChatGPT Model Explains Crowdfunding, Alternative Finance and Community Finance. *SSRN*. doi:https://doi.org/10.2139/ssrn.4302443.
ZOO. 2022. *Annual Report 2022.* ZOO Digital Group plc. https://www.paperturn-view.com/uk/zoo-digital/zoo-digital-annual-report-2022-online?pid=MjY264364&p=3. Accessed 20 September 2022.

What Kind of Translation Literacy Will Be Automation-Resistant?

Nune Ayvazyan, Ester Torres-Simón, and Anthony Pym

Abstract Automated language processing is advancing rapidly, notably through neural machine translation and automatic text production using various large-language-model (LLM) generative pre-trained transformer (GPT) technologies. These are destined to have an impact on any language-intensive profession, especially translation. The nature of that impact will in turn limit and orient the knowledge and skills that translators can market effectively, both in work with the technologies and in language tasks where the technologies flounder in one way or another. The empirically based O*Net database can help identify the knowledges and skills of translators that are likely to be exposed to automation, and thereby point to those that might be expected to remain automation-resistant. That analysis in turn enables some recommendations to be advanced for the future of translator training, notably with respect to the use of spoken communication skills, the gaining and maintenance of trust, and the ability to draw on automation at key points in translation workflows in which professionals will still have a place.

Study carried out as part of the project *Literacies and the future of occupations* (PID2021-122575NB-I00) financed by the Spanish Ministry of Education and Innovation (MCIN/AEI/10.13039/501100011033). Parts of this report have been published in Spanish in Pym and Torres-Simón (2021a).

N. Ayvazyan (✉) · E. Torres-Simón · A. Pym
Universitat Rovira i Virgili, Tarragona, Spain
e-mail: nune.ayvazyan@urv.cat

E. Torres-Simón
e-mail: ester.torres@uab.cat

A. Pym
e-mail: anthony.pym@urv.cat

E. Torres-Simón
Universitat Autònoma de Barcelona, Barcelona, Spain

Y. Peng et al. (eds.), *New Advances in Translation Technology*, New Frontiers in Translation Studies, https://doi.org/10.1007/978-981-97-2958-6_7

1 Introduction

Translators and interpreters work on language. This means that when language work is affected by automation, translation and interpreting are near the front line of any real or imagined battle: there is now no more vital or compelling question facing the profession than how to adjust to automation. That question is especially pressing given the pace of change. Just when we thought that the neural machine translation systems dating from 2016 were the main instance of automation we had to grapple with, the application of large language models (LLMs) to automated text generation (technically "generative pre-trained transformer" technology or GPT) from late 2022 has brought automated language processes to a new level, not just in translating but also in revising and adapting texts to user-specified receptor profiles. The challenge now is to predict the consequences for long-term translator employment and thereby to adapt our training to a new professional environment.

The rollercoaster history of machine translation is well known. Times have definitely changed, however, when we calculate that professional translators are producing much less than 1% of all the words translated by automated systems (Pym and Torres-Simón 2021b, p. 41). What does that mean? First, it suggests that any study that only looks at the work of paid professionals—and that has so far been the focus of much of translation studies—is doing very little to grasp the actual uses of translation as the general social activity it has become. Second, it challenges any assumption that the human translator will forever be needed simply because the quality of the output is different: the work of algorithms appears to be free and on-demand, whereas professionals need pay and take time, making their translations luxury products. Many translators, along with their instructors, are asking whether this could spell the end of their profession.

Here we place these anxieties against the background of wider historical processes of automation. After all, technology has been automating human skills since the beginning of humanity. From that perspective, we then attempt to identify the literacy components (knowledges and skills) that automation might be transforming. Once we have identified them, we will formulate some suggestions for training translators.

2 What Do We Know About Automation and Translation Literacy?

To assess the effects of automation on translation processes, we have to know how translators can do what they do. Our term for this is *translation literacy*, understood analytically as a combination of basic metalanguage, knowledge, and skills concerning how to translate (Takeda and Yamada 2019) and pedagogically as a process that starts by challenging students' preconceptions of translation as a "linguistic matching game" (Baer 2023, p. 8). As such, it builds on models of "translation competence" that have evolved over time. The early PACTE model (PACTE 2000) included an "instrumental sub-competence" for tools like email and the Internet, as well as resources such as dictionaries and corpora, none of which was specific to translation. The European Masters of Translation model (EMT Expert Group 2009) then incorporated machine translation, translation memories and terminology management. Their 2017 model (EMT 2017) recognized that machine translation and translation memories were changing the role of the human translator. At the same time, it emphasized "personal and interpersonal" and "service provision" skills that might be automation-resistant in that they concern activities machines could not really do. As well as working with technology, human translators were seen as excelling in human communication skills. In a further revision (EMT 2022), the limits of technology become part of a narrative where human skills are more necessary than ever, specifically linguistic, sociolinguistic, cultural and transcultural skills.

These developments have led to two approaches among trainers. On the one hand, technologically aware pedagogies dating from Somers (1997) and O'Brien (2002) have emphasized the need to work *with* machine translation, particularly by training students in post-editing. On the other, some pedagogies have insisted more on the *limits* of automation (Kenny 2018; Rodríguez de Céspedes 2019) and, like the 2017 EMT model, call for more training in person-to-person communication and complex cognitive processing (Deming and Kahn 2018). This apparent conflict is easily resolved: translators can be trained to work with automation *and* to excel where technologies fail.

For both those strategies, translators need to work with machine translation and know its shortcomings. The current term for this is *machine-translation literacy*, popularized by Bowker and Buitrago Ciro (2019) as a set of skills developed among a wide group of people, in the same way as we talk about "numerical literacy", "computer literacy", "health literacy" or, at the origin, "literacy" as the ability to read and write. The 2022 EMT model does indeed emphasize machine translation and data literacy in this way, but the term can also embrace work with automatic text generators. At the same time, Krüger and Hackenbuchner (2022, p. 384) have introduced the concept of *professional MT literacy* as "the full range of MT-related competences professional translators (and other language professionals) may require in order to participate successfully in the various phases of the MT-assisted professional translation process". This is the part of general translation literacy that we are interested in here, extending it into generative AI.

3 What Do We Know About the Use of Generative AI?

The application of large language models in ChatGPT dates from November 2022. Since translation is one of the things that this technology can do, concerns were quickly raised about confidentiality. Lyu et al. (2023) warn against the risk of accidentally disclosing private information; they suggest that translators should anonymize start texts[1] and then de-anonymize target texts—although it is hard to see how this would make the information significantly less confidential. Although translation studies has long addressed issues of confidentiality (Bennett 2021), specific concerns over technology were virtually absent from the codes of ethics until the TAC code in 2019 (Ren 2019).

The advent of GPT has spawned a series of performance assessments. Hendy et al. (2023) offer an analysis of various GPT models in comparison with neural machine translation when translating in 18 directions, including high- and low-resource languages. They find that GPT models can produce very competitive translation quality for high-resource languages but are only partially effective for low-resource languages. Ghosh and Caliskan (2023) report on the performance of ChatGPT when translating between English and six low-resource languages. They note that the technology reproduces gender stereotypes with respect to professions. Jiao et al. (2023) use BLEU scores for translations of isolated sentences and find that GPT-3 and GPT-4 do not perform better than the main neural machine translation systems. Peng et al. (2023) go further by considering parameters including "temperature" (the degree of randomness in a generated text, ranging from highly predictable to highly creative), task information, domain information, and prompts that are task-specific or domain-specific. They find that ChatGPT performs best at a lower temperature and when the task information is emphasized; it produces hallucinations for non-English-centric MT tasks; and the application of powerful chain-of-thought prompts results in a negative effect by translating word-by-word.

More directly concerned with changes in professional literacies, Eloundou et al. (2023) explore the extent to which many occupations are likely to be affected by AI text generation. They find that 76.5% of the tasks of translators and interpreters are "exposed" to automation, where "exposure" is "a measure of whether access to a GPT or GPT-powered system would reduce the time required for a human to perform a specific DWA [Detailed Worker Activity] or complete a task by at least 50%" (2023, p. 7). That is, the main criterion is time saving, which may clearly then lead to task-displacement of various kinds. The analysis should be a wake-up call: translation and interpreting are top of the list as the occupations where the greatest percentage of tasks can be automated.[2]

There are very few empirical studies on the effect of translation technologies on human employment. Yilmaz et al. (2023) report on a sample of 28,158 translation transactions on an online market platform between January 2016 and May 2017, before and after the release of the neural version of Google Translate. They found an overall drop of 13% to 20% in translations involving analytical tasks, while the demand for "interactive tasks that entail adaptation of meaning to cultural

---

[1] The term "start text" is used here instead of "source text" because translators these days work from client instructions, machine translation, translation memories, and term bases, all of which are also "sources".

[2] Note that for exposure to "GPT-power software", about 15 other professions, including mathematicians, accountants and clinical data managers, are considered 100% exposed (Eloundou et al. 2023, p. 15).

and emotional elements and influencing people" (2023, p. 4), broadly characterized as "transcreations", remained stable. Yilmaz et al. conclude that AI *can* replace human tasks, but that the impact varies depending on the cultural and emotional skills required for a specific task. A more positive view is expressed in Borgonovi et al. (2023), reporting on online job vacancies for language professionals between 2014 and 2019. The general finding is that "the introduction of higher quality machine translation systems did not lead to decreases in the demand for language professionals" (2023, p. 44). In fact, machine translation was found to complement the employment of professional translators and enhance the market demand for digital skills, post-editing skills, and "transversal skills and knowledge skills—skills that allow language professionals to deliver high quality translations of text that machine translation tools cannot deliver with accuracy" (2023, p. 45), especially in high-stakes settings.

4 Methodology: Seeking Answers in an Industry-Derived Database

Here we adopt the broad approach used by Eloundou et al. (2023), drawing on the same database but focusing exclusively on translators and interpreters. Eloundou et al. (2023) work from the United States Department of Labor's Occupational Information Network (O*Net) (2023). O*Net covers many occupations (923 were updated in 2022). For each occupation group, it names and evaluates the importance of 33 "knowledges", 52 "abilities" and 35 "skills". Eloundou et al. (2023) went through that list and estimated whether GPT would reduce the worker's time by at least 50%— there are no estimations of effects on quality. Since there were numerous items to evaluate, they had GPT do the categorizing for them. That is, they asked GPT to say what GPT can and cannot do. The resulting estimates are very rough, to the extent that one might legitimately doubt—on methodological grounds alone—the claim that translators and interpreters are the most "exposed" to GPT automation.

O*Net nevertheless has several things going for it. Its data are publicly available (National Center for O*NET Development 2023); it is based on a survey of what "job incumbents" say about their activities; it enables comparisons across a very wide range of occupations; and it rates the importance and level of each knowledge, ability and skill. None of the translation competence models offers all these features.

That said, O*Net also has some disadvantages. First, the database refers to the United States labour market only, which differs in important ways from the labour markets in societies where translation is needed for public governance (as in Europe and Canada) or for virtually all international trade (as in China). The American market has a greater proportion of interpreters working in the legal and healthcare systems. Second, since the main analytical categories have been developed for *all* occupations and over several decades, there is no specific weighting of the role of technologies (Handel 2016). And third, the number of survey respondents is very uneven across occupations. There were responses from at least 15 people working in each occupation, with an estimated average of "39 respondents per item within each of the 809 occupations in the first complete database" (Handel 2016, p.160). That would seem to be rather few informants for an occupation like translation and interpreting, which is heterogeneous in terms of tasks and salaries, especially since it has relatively low percentages of full-time or in-house employment (Pym et al. 2012). That said, O*Net is worth pursuing on an exploratory basis, especially because it allows comparisons across occupations.

Since the database has a huge amount of data that has been collected over decades, a focused reduction is necessary to address our specific concerns with exposure to automation. Here we therefore focus on the occupation Interpreters and Translators as it appears in the 2017 (updated in 2018) and 2023 O*Net data (Occupational Information Network, 2018, 2023). From there we extract data on the relative importance of knowledges, language skills, information-processing skills, social communication skills and "core" tasks. We include only the items that have an importance score of above 50, along with their descriptors.

We use this focused database for two related kinds of analysis:

- Since our first use of the 2017 O*Net database was an analysis of the effects of neural machine translation (Pym and Torres-Simón 2021a), we are now able to compare the *changes* to the knowledges, abilities and skills that have been made in the period from 2017 to 2023. This roughly coincides with the impact of neural machine translation, such that a drop in importance might signal increased exposure to machine translation and a rise in importance could then be interpreted as filling gaps left by machine translation.
- Like Eloundou et al. (2023), we then ask whether automation of the skills and abilities can reach a time saving of at least 50%, calling the shots based on what we know as practitioners of translation—we have not asked ChatGPT to assess its own capabilities. The problems involved nevertheless preclude any simple numerical calculations, none the least because time savings are always in a trade-off with potential loss of product quality. For that reason we present this analysis as no more than a general discussion.

Our aim is to use these two approaches as sets of indicators of what an automation-resistant literacy might look like and how translator training could adjust accordingly.

5 Results: Relative Exposure to Automation

In the following sections, we group our results in accordance with the major pertinent categories presented in the O*Net database: knowledges, language skills, information-processing skills, social communication skills and core tasks. In each section, we first present and compare the "importance" scores from the 2017 and 2023 databases, then we discuss the relative exposures to automation and other factors that might bear upon the various changes in importance.

5.1 Knowledges

The knowledges listed as being needed by translators and interpreters are at once obvious (with respect to languages and service provision) and rather peculiar (with respect to the rest). Table 1 lists the items, the descriptors, and the importance scores from 2017 and 2023, with the major changes marked in bold.

Obviously, basic language knowledge is still what is considered most important. Nevertheless, it can be automated to increasing degrees: it is not particularly automation resistant. But not so the rest. The remaining kinds of knowledge seem to suggest the fields the unknown respondents were working in: law, communications, education and electronics serve to remind us that there are many potential fields involved and that translators have to know something about the field they are working in. Electronic tools certainly help locate specialized knowledge fast, but the message is nevertheless clear enough: human translators know more than languages.

When one compares the importance scores for 2017 and 2023, there are *major* reductions in Foreign Languages, Communications and Media and Computers and Electronics, with the last two slipping below our cut-off point. On the other hand, Public Safety and Security now rises above the cut-off point. It is not hard to see the reduced importance of foreign languages as an acceptance that machine translation can do this part fairly well. The weaker drop in English Language, generally the target language, could then indicate that the results of automation require checking and revision. And the rise in Public Safety and Security would also be a consequence of automation: the more electronic information is stored, the more data leaks can happen, and the more employees are required to manage that risk.[3]

5.2 Language Skills

The basic language skills in the repertoire are the classical four (Table 2), all considered to be of great importance. Again, this should be news to no one. Perhaps surprisingly, there are no major changes here from 2017 to 2023. Very surprisingly, what is really missing here is the ability to translate (the same strange absence occurred in EMT Expert Group 2009).

On the face of it, machine translation and LLM technologies should be able to automate the basics of what is included here—if and when we somewhat naively overlook "*full* attention" as a part of listening, "*effectively*" as a criterion for speaking, and "*understanding*" as a synonym of "processing". Machine translation cannot really adjust to those qualifiers, although GPT can do a good job of meeting "the needs of the audience" when used with clear prompts. More important, the risks of errors and the corresponding value of trustworthiness seem not to be considered

[3] The reduced importance of Communications and Media and Computers and Electronics remain more difficult to interpret. It might be assumed that there are more non-translation experts who handle those things, but we would need more information before hazarding a guess.

Table 1 Knowledges pertinent to written translation (O*Net importance weight and descriptors)

Importance 2017	Importance 2023	Knowledge	Descsription
98	92	English language	Knowledge of the structure and content of the English language including the meaning and spelling of words, rules of composition, and grammar
98	**78**	Foreign language	Knowledge of the structure and content of a foreign (non-English) language including the meaning and spelling of words, rules of composition and grammar, and pronunciation
77	72	Customer and personal service	Knowledge of principles and processes for providing customer and personal services. This includes customer needs assessment, meeting quality standards for services, and evaluation of customer satisfaction
62	**51**	Law and government	Knowledge of laws, legal codes, court procedures, precedents, government regulations, executive orders, agency rules, and the democratic political process
62	**39**	Communications and media	Knowledge of media production, communication, and dissemination techniques and methods. This includes alternative ways to inform and entertain via written, oral, and visual media
60	60	Education and training	Knowledge of principles and methods for curriculum and training design, teaching and instruction for individuals and groups, and the measurement of training effects
56	**48**	Computers and electronics	Knowledge of circuit boards, processors, chips, electronic equipment, and computer hardware and software, including applications and programming

(continued)

Table 1 (continued)

Importance 2017	Importance 2023	Knowledge	Descsription
51	56	Clerical*	Knowledge of administrative and clerical procedures and systems such as word processing, managing files and records, stenography and transcription, designing forms, and other office procedures and terminology
40 +	**52**	Public safety and security	Knowledge of relevant equipment, policies, procedures, and strategies to promote effective local, state, or national security operations for the protection of people, data, property, and institutions

*In 2023, this item is listed as "administrative" with the same descriptor
+Calculations for items not considered initially in the 2017 research are based on raw data (National Center for O*NET Development 2023) and percentages might show slight variations (±2 points error margin)

Table 2 Language skills and abilities pertinent to written translation (O*Net importance weight and descriptors)

Importance 2017	Importance 2023	Skill/ability	Description
78	75	Active listening	Giving full attention to what other people are saying
78	78	Speaking	Talking to others to convey information effectively
75	72	Reading comprehension	Understanding written sentences and paragraphs in work related documents
69	69	Writing	Communicating effectively in writing as appropriate for the needs of the audience

here. One question in the 2023 O'Net database reads, "How serious would the result usually be if the worker made a mistake that was not easily correctable?". The answers are "extremely serious" for 51% of the respondents and "fairly serious" for 36%. So automation might cut the time-on-task by half, but those qualifiers "full", "effectively" and "understanding" are by no means trivial considerations—when the criteria are not met, the consequences can be serious.

5.3 Information-Processing Skills

The skills and abilities listed under Information Processing (Table 3) cover a wide range of items and could easily be expanded (the list of items below our cut-off point includes Inductive Reasoning, Originality, Speed of Closure, and so on). There has been little historical change in this category. Note that many of the items concern spoken more than written translation, raising challenging questions about the extent to which the two can or should be separated.

This list is intriguing because, in principle, the only thing machine translation and LLM technologies do is process information. Yet one struggles to imagine that machine translation can apply Critical Thinking (as described here), and one would hope that this is the kind of thing that might be expected of translators when post-editing or text tailoring. At the same time, GPT is remarkably good at information ordering and generating for-and-against argumentative texts, so these would indeed be skills and abilities that are exposed to automation. In fact, this whole group is the category that could be most affected by the general use of LLM technologies, although aspects like problem sensitivity, monitoring performance and verifying results require specific prompts, which in turn creates a new skill set for the writing, ordering and interpretation of prompts. The spectre of full automation of these items suggests a mode of exposure that opens new kinds of employment.

5.4 Social Communication Skills

The social communication skills considered pertinent to translation (Table 4) are rather restricted in nature and have remained virtually unchanged across the years of comparison. None of them has been automated to any significant degree. The same would also hold for a bunch of skills and abilities that sit on 50: Complex Problem Solving, Coordination, Instructing, Learning Strategies and Time Management, Auditory Attention, Category Flexibility, Fluency of Ideas, Inductive Reasoning, Originality, Speed of Closure, and Time Sharing.

Although these all appear to be automation-resistant skills, their low scores indicate that they are considered of relatively little importance for translation and interpreting. Further, below the 50-point cut-off level, the O*Net repertoire includes a long list of social communication skills that are considered of even less importance: Negotiation, Persuasion, Resolving Conflicts, Communicating with Persons Outside the Organization, and so on. Machines do not do these things—so these are names for a substantial set of automation-resistant skills. Note that these are also the management skills of big companies, the ones that are most growing in an age of automation (Pym and Torres-Simón 2021b, pp. 47–48).

5.5 *Core Tasks*

O'Net not only gives a list of skills, but also collects what tasks professionals consider "core" to the profession. As it is hard to decide whether Information Processing Skills have been automated or not, we decided to investigate these core tasks and the importance placed on them (see Table 5).

The core tasks seem not to have changed much since 2017. "Compiling information on content and context of information to be translated and on intended audience" was the only task not relevant enough in 2017 as to be considered "core" (it was listed as "supplemental"). Current technologies can conceivably perform all the tasks in this list except for one: "Follow ethical codes that protect the confidentiality of information", which happens to be the most important core task. Ethics and confidentiality have clearly maintained their priority position in an age where electronic information is liable to leak. The other core tasks might then be automatized if and when there is an available human who is skilled in the writing of prompts: "Identify and resolve conflicts related to the meanings of words, concepts, practices, or behaviors", "Compile terminology and information to be used in translations, including technical terms such as those for legal or medical material" and "Compile information on content and context of information to be translated and on intended audience".

6 Conclusions: Proposals for Translator Training

In their analysis of the 2017 O*Net data, Ubalde and Alarcón (2020) concluded that "hard verbal-reasoning skills" were being automated and that "interactive and multilingual skills" were more automation-resistant. Paradoxically, they also found that these automation-resistant skills were less rewarded on the American labour market. One cannot assume that a kind of literacy that is automation-resistant will therefore have a high market value.[4] Our analysis here is nevertheless a little different. We find that many of the hard reasoning skills (mostly in Table 3) are quite germane to the work of translators and interpreters and are *not* necessarily being automated. On the other hand, a good number of the interactive skills (Table 4), the ones that Ubalde and Alarcón (2020) find are automation-resistant but not well rewarded, are indeed automation-resistant but are not considered particularly important in this field. This may be why they are not well rewarded on the market.

How does this help find a future for translators and interpreters? It is not enough to privilege skills that machines cannot acquire—automation-resistance is not sufficient. We must also pay close attention to the importance scores and think through how they might relate to professional activities.

What we extract from the O*Net data is that language skills are still crucial. However, as noted, language work itself is not inherently resistant to automation.

[4] In the US context, this might be interpreted as systemic under-payment of the interpreters working in the courts and in healthcare, many of them working with Spanish.

Table 3 Information-processing skills and abilities pertinent to written translation (O*Net importance weight and descriptors)

Importance 2017	Importance 2023	Skill/ability	Description
69	69	Information ordering	The ability to arrange things or actions in a certain order or pattern according to a specific rule or set of rules (e.g., patterns of numbers, letters, words, pictures, mathematical operations)
66	66	Critical thinking	Using logic and reasoning to identify the strengths and weaknesses of alternative solutions, conclusions or approaches to problems
66	66	Problem sensitivity	The ability to tell when something is wrong or is likely to go wrong. It does not involve solving the problem, only recognizing there is a problem
63	66	Monitoring	Monitoring/assessing performance of yourself, other individuals, or organizations to make improvements or take corrective action
60	**53**	Selective attention	The ability to concentrate on a task over a period of time without being distracted
56	53	Active learning	Understanding the implications of new information for both current and future problem-solving and decision-making
53	53	Deductive reasoning	The ability to apply general rules to specific problems to produce answers that make sense

Table 4 Social-communication skills and abilities pertinent to written translation (O*Net importance weight and descriptors)

Importance 2017	Importance 2023	Skill/ability	Description
53	53	Social perceptiveness	Being aware of others' reactions and understanding why they react as they do
53	50	Coordination	Adjusting actions in relation to others' actions
53	53	Service orientation	Actively looking for ways to help people
53	53	Judgment and decision making	Considering the relative costs and benefits of potential actions to choose the most appropriate one

What may resist automation is a set of skills covering "critical thinking", "interaction" or "transcreation": the ability to tailor translations to specific domains. Although this process resembles traditional post-editing, the increasing persuasiveness of AI-generated texts makes it more challenging to identify and rectify such issues. On the other hand, the application of task-specific prompts becomes a crucial skill. Further,

Table 5 Core tasks of "Interpreters and Translators" (O'Net descriptors)

Importance 2017	Importance 2023	Task
97*	97	Follow ethical codes that protect the confidentiality of information
95*	93	Translate messages simultaneously or consecutively into specified languages, orally or by using hand signs, maintaining message content, context, and style as much as possible
88*	87	Listen to speakers' statements to determine meanings and to prepare translations, using electronic listening systems as necessary
84*	86	Compile terminology and information to be used in translations, including technical terms such as those for legal or medical material
80*	85	Refer to reference materials, such as dictionaries, lexicons, encyclopedias, and computerized terminology banks, as needed to ensure translation accuracy
81*	84	Check translations of technical terms and terminology to ensure that they are accurate and remain consistent throughout translation revisions
81*	83	Identify and resolve conflicts related to the meanings of words, concepts, practices, or behaviors
68* (NOT CORE)	**81**	Compile information on content and context of information to be translated and on intended audience

Calculations for items not considered initially in the 2017 list are based on raw data (National Center for O NET Development 2023) and percentages might show slight variations (±2 points error margin)

domain-specific knowledge is still pivotal and automation-resistant in that it enables humans to post-edit AI-generated translations that align with specific requirements and standards, ensuring high levels of accuracy and coherence. In this scenario of rapid change and great uncertainty, customer service provision becomes key for fine-tuning AI-generated translations and generally improving customer experience. In the era of automation, where confidentiality counts and ethical considerations are increasingly prominent, the importance of a translator well-versed in handling technology safely has become paramount.

On that basis, we present a shortlist of proposals for translator training, all of which require adaptation and experimentation.

6.1 Teach Languages and Translation Skills as a Basis for Trust

In general, the language knowledges and skills that are considered to be of most importance in the translation profession are precisely the ones that seem the *least* automation-resistant, with a remarkable drop appearing in the importance of knowing foreign languages. So should we just give up on teaching languages altogether?

That is indeed what could be happening in parts of the translator-training community. The European Masters in Translation network has accepted member programs where under 20% of the contact hours are on language-specific translation, especially in the United Kingdom (Torres-Simón and Pym 2019). The first revised competence model elaborated by the same European Masters in Translation (EMT 2017) not only recognized the usefulness of machine translation in the translation process but also placed increased emphasis on precisely the "personal-interpersonal" and "service provision" skills that appear to be not just the most automation-resistant but also the least language-specific.

One argument that is used here in defence of language teaching broadly runs as follows: For as long as our technologies make mistakes and have to be corrected, we need human revisers. And to correct a translation error, you have to know the languages concerned. In other words, since there are still mistakes, we do not have to change anything fundamental in our syllabi and curricula.

That argument is not only reactionary, suggesting that nothing substantial need change, but also flounders empirically. Temizöz (2013), for example, found that engineers with no special training in translation are remarkably good at picking up technical errors in machine translations that concern their specialized area of knowledge. So our argument here cannot really assume that language teaching is necessary simply because automation leads to errors. Further, what counts is clearly not just knowing languages, but also knowing how to apply non-literalist translation solutions in specific language pairs. This is an area where there appears to be something of a gap in the O*Net descriptors.

To explain our position here, let us consider a few parallel occupations. When we visit a family doctor, their basic activity is linguistic: they listen, talk, and perhaps write something on a piece of paper. It is the same for a lawyer: they basically talk, write, and charge fees. But when those professionals access information, put it in a new order and adapt it to a new user, their information-processing and social-communication skills are highly rewarded not just because those activities are well executed, but also because they are based on access to a highly specialized and complex knowledge base: medicine and law. The *access* to the knowledge may be highly automatized these days (in searches of case law, for example, and in accessing data on medicines), but the *mastery* of the knowledge itself is still highly valued, especially in high-stakes situations. So too with translation, we propose: the algorithms can locate good candidate translations automatically, but mastery of translation enables choice between those linguistic variants, enhanced adaptation to pragmatic situations, and incorporation into linguistic exchanges at various levels of human-assessed risk. In other words, mastery of language-pair-specific translation allows one to "identify and resolve conflicts related to the meanings of words, concepts, practices, or behaviors", as one of the core-task descriptors puts it (with an importance score of 83)—which is perhaps as close as we come to a specific translation skill. If you throw away knowledge of languages and mastery of translation solutions in a specific language pair, it is like training a doctor who knows no medicine or a lawyer who does not know the law—television actors could perform the remaining tasks just as well. Even when they are not highly rewarded in direct terms for knowing languages or being able to translate from scratch, translators still need those things. That is why translators and interpreters can be seen as being trustworthy, as indeed can lawyers and doctors. And that trustworthiness, once won, is why all their other skills are potentially of value. Once trust is lost, none of the other skills of value.

Justa Holz-Mänttäri (1984) theorized this long ago: translators work with clients who have expertise in the various fields concerned, while the expertise of the translator, their knowledge base and field of mastery, is language-pair-specific interlingual communication. If we do not know the languages, and know them extremely well, and know the many ways in which translation solutions operate between them, we have no basis for everything else we can offer.

6.2 *Teach Translation Technologies*

Another kind of reactionary argument insists that all the skills and abilities should be developed without any translation technologies because, if not, the human translation ability will be lost. This might be a little like teaching young children how to write by hand and learn multiplication tables so they will have something to fall back on if ever their keyboards and calculators are taken away. No matter how great the exposure to automation, such things still have to be taught, it seems.

There is nothing wrong with that argument, as long as the technologies are *also* taught. Our position is not that maximum exposure to automation is always required. Instead, we hasten to point out the ways in which new technologies create doubts and false expectations among clients and users of translations. Translators are called upon not only to correct such misapprehensions, but also to give advice as to how automation should enter the workflow. This means knowing the technologies, not just to use the right keys but also on the deeper, critical level of making strategic use of the workflows available and then exercising prudence when new risks arise. Remember that their highest-value core task is listed as "follow ethical codes that protect the confidentiality of information". To protect confidentiality, you have to know about the technologies that will attack it.

This also concerns skills in *communicating* the consequences of automation to employer groups, who tend to see technology as a cost-reducing factor. To do this, translators need the social-communication skills (Table 4) that are not directly rewarded in themselves. The skills can partly be seen as *means* to substantial rewards—we need to be good at them so that our other virtues can be appreciated. This logic is captured in a recommendation by the Fédération Internationale des Traducteurs (FIT): "these professionals should act as language services advisors or language consultants, advising their customers on the best approach to a particular assignment and explaining the benefits or drawbacks of certain translation methods" (FIT 2017, p. 2). To do that, you must know the technologies.

6.3 Sell Trustworthiness Rather Than Words

Automation means translators should not be paid by the numbers of words they produce, since that part is highly exposed to automation. They should be paid for their time. This is another of the recommendations by the Fédération Internationale des Traducteurs: translators "should seek to charge for their services on an hourly or project basis and not per word, line or page translated" (FIT 2017, p. 2).

In the space of training, this means translators must know not just how to post-edit, but also how to act as authorities, *authorizing* the results of post-editing. This "notary" function sells trustworthiness more than either words or hours, and it may be limited to the high-stakes areas where high levels of trust are required: at key points in the legal, medical, pharmaceutical fields, for example, or wherever corporate image counts.

Communication skills are needed to build trust, and trust can then be converted into higher rewards for non-automatized skills.

6.4 Engage in Automation-Related Activities

If communication skills help build trust, then there is no need to place post-editing beneath the dignity of professional translators (Kenny 2018). It should have its place among the services on offer.

Language automation is used in sectors where professional translators were not previously employed: much language learning, tourism, gist translation for everyday purposes, multilingual conversations, right through to the security surveillance that can check on them all. That list does not help anyone seeking to make a living out of translation: it maps out the places one should *not* want to go. It can nevertheless be opposed to the areas where automation helps to create new kinds of professional activities, notably in post-editing, the writing of prompts, project management, terminology, database management, marketing and cross-cultural consulting.

The list of non-exposed activities is growing shorter, as LLM technologies produce usable results for pre-editing, controlled writing, revision, summarizing and text adaptation. Those are areas where students should explore the technologies rather than struggle against them.

6.5 Emphasize Spoken Communication Skills

We have listed *spoken* communication skills as being automation-resistant, almost by definition. These are broadly the skills that Ubalde and Alarcón (2020) find automation-resistant but under-rewarded in the US data. They certainly appear in the O*Net descriptors of the translator's work, where 80% of the informants say they have face-to-face discussions every day, 29% say they must deal with "unpleasant, angry, or discourteous individuals" every day, and 50% say it is important or extremely important to "work with external customers or the public" (O*Net 2023). These skills may be important but under-rewarded in American courts and hospitals, but advanced spoken communication literacy is also the key to customer relations and teamwork in large language-service providers. Indeed, the larger the company, the more important these social skills become (Deming 2017).

Those spoken skills can be developed through group projects and extended role-play activities (Pym 2019). They are nevertheless sometimes compromised by the scission that has historically separated interpreting from written translation in our training programs, encouraging the supposition that translators do nothing but write. That has to be revised. If translators are to use their languages effectively, gaining trust and explaining technologies, they have to be good at talking with people.

6.6 Do More Than Translate

At the same time, automation can and should push us towards professional activities with higher value added, many of which are on the borders of translation or blend translation with other skill sets. Alongside automation, we thus find a proliferation of new names for new things that translators can do. Bond (2018) scoured LinkedIn for the job titles of people who work for language service providers, coming up with over 600 different titles—while the O*Net database still considers Interpreters and Translators as the only title on offer. Some of the newer names for occupations play on concepts wider than translation, such as localization (localization manager, localization strategy consultant) or transcreation (in marketing), and then there is a wide range of titles that emphasize the importance of addressing clients' specific needs, and indeed intensive communication with clients (something the larger companies do indeed tend to recognize). For instance, here are some of the job titles derived from the simple idea of solving clients' problems (still from Bond 2018): *solutions architect, director of client solutions, solutions consulting and director of technology solutions, cloud solutions architect*, or *solutions manager for machine intelligence*. The people doing those jobs may have a background in translation and probably work with technologies and give advice on automation, but they are certainly not spending their whole day post-editing machine translation or correcting GPT output.

Throughout history, translators have regularly had more than one occupation: "translators can do more than translate" (Pym 1998, p. 161). The fact that they continue to do so is shown in studies where only about a third of our graduates work as translators for any length of time (Hao and Pym 2022). Their skills are also used in education and a wide range of communication activities, only some of which are seriously exposed to automation.

No one should suggest that the new names for occupations and the diversity of employment are a direct consequence of automation. There are numerous factors behind each of the developments. The basic message should nevertheless remain clear: as automation handles many everyday translation tasks and can be expected to handle them better each day, there is no need to lament the loss of any profession. Translators should seek well-paid work on high-stakes communicative situations, using combinations with the many neighbouring literacies.

And we should train them to get there.

References

Baer, B.J. 2023. Is there a translation in this class? A crash course in translation literacy. In *Teaching translation: pedagogical contexts and reading practices*, ed. B. Baer and M. Woods, 3–12. Routledge.

Bennett, P. M. 2021. Ethics in translation practice: A comparison of professional codes of conduct" *Verba Hispanica*, 29(1), 31–52.

Bond, E. 2018. The stunning variety of job titles in the language industry. Slator. https://slator.com/features/the-stunning-variety-of-job-titles-in-the-language-industry.

Borgonovi, F., J. Hervé, and H. Seitz. 2023. Not lost in translation: The implications of machine translation technologies for language professionals and for broader society. *OECD Social, Employment and Migration Working Papers No. 291*. https://doi.org/10.1787/e1d1d170-en

Bowker, L., and J. Buitrago Ciro. 2019. *Machine Translation and Global Research: Towards Improved Machine Translation Literacy in the Scholarly Community*. Emerald Publishing.

Deming, D.J. 2017. The growing importance of social skills in the labor market. *The Quarterly Journal of Economics* 132 (4): 1593–1640.

Deming, D.J., and L.B. Kahn. 2018. Skill requirements across firms and labor markets: evidence from job postings for professionals. *Journal of Labor Economics* 36 (S1): S337–S369.

Eloundou, T., S. Manning, P. Mishkin, and D. Rock. 2023. GPTs are GPTs: An early look at the labor market impact potential of large language models. https://arxiv.org/abs/2303.10130.

EMT Expert Group. 2009. *Competences for Professional Translators, Experts in Multilingual and Multimedia Communication*. https://ec.europa.eu/info/sites/info/files/emt_competences_translators_en.pdf.

EMT. 2017. *Competence Framework 2017*. https://ec.europa.eu/info/sites/info/files/emt_competence_fwk_2017_en_web.pdf.

EMT. 2022. *Competence Framework 2022*. https://commission.europa.eu/system/files/2022-11/emt_competence_fwk_2022_en.pdf.

FIT. 2017. FIT position paper on the future for professional translators. Fédération Internationale des Traducteurs. https://www.fit-ift.org/publications/papers.

Ghosh, S., and A. Caliskan. 2023. ChatGPT Perpetuates Gender Bias in Machine Translation and Ignores Non-Gendered Pronouns: Findings across Bengali and Five other Low-Resource Languages. https://arxiv.org/abs/2305.10510.

Handel, M.J. 2016. The O*NET content model: strengths and limitations. *Journal of Labour Market Research* 49: 157–176.

Hao, Y., and A. Pym. 2022. Where do translation students go? A study of the employment and mobility of Master graduates. *The Interpreter and Translator Trainer* 17 (2): 211–229. https://doi.org/10.1080/1750399X.2022.2084595.

Hendy, A., M. Abdelrehim, A. Sharaf, V. Raunak, M. Gabr, H. Matsushita, Y. Jin Kim, M. Afify, and H. Hassan Awadalla. 2023. How good are GPT models at machine translation? A comprehensive evaluation. https://arxiv.org/abs/2302.09210.

Holz-Mänttäri, J. 1984. *Translatorisches Handeln: Theorie und Methode.* Suomalainen Tiedeakatemia.

Jiao, W., W. Wang, J. Huang, X. Wang, and Z. Tu. (2023, March 19) Is ChatGPT A Good Translator? Yes With GPT-4 As The Engine. https://arxiv.org/abs/2301.08745.

Kenny, D. 2018. Sustaining disruption? the transition from statistical to neural machine translation. *Tradumàtica* 16: 59–70.

Krüger, R. and J. Hackenbuchner. 2022. Outline of a didactic framework for combined data literacy and machine translation literacy teaching. *Current Trends in Translation Teaching and Learning*. E.375–432.https://doi.org/10.51287/cttl202211.

Lyu, C., J. Xu, and L. Wang. 2023. New Trends in Machine Translation using Large Language Models: Case Examples with ChatGPT. https://arxiv.org/pdf/2305.01181.pdf.

National Center for O*NET Development (2023). O*NET® Database Releases Archive. O*NET Resource Center, www.onetcenter.org/db_releases.html.

Occupational Information Network (2018). Details Report for 27-3091.00—Interpreters and Translators (updated 2018). O*NET 22.0 https://www.onetonline.org/link/details/27-3091.00.

Occupational Information Network (2023). Details Report for 27-3091.00—Interpreters and Translators (updated 2023). O*NET 27.2 27–3091.00—Interpreters and Translators (onetonline.org).

PACTE. 2000. Acquiring translation competence: hypotheses and methodological problems in a research project. In *Investigating Translation*, ed. A. Beeby, D. Ensinger, and M. Presas, 99–106. John Benjamins.

Peng, K., L. Ding, Q. Zhong, L. Shen, X. Liu, M. Zhang, Y. Ouyang, and D. Tao (2023). Towards making the most of ChatGPT for machine translation. https://arxiv.org/abs/2303.13780

Pym, A. 1998. *Method in Translation History*. Routledge.

Pym, A., and E. Torres-Simón. 2021b. Is automation changing the translation profession? *International Journal of the Sociology of Language* 270: 39–57. https://doi.org/10.1515/ijsl-2020-0015.

Pym, A. 2019. Teaching translation in a multilingual practice class. In *Translator education: The evolving curriculum*, ed. D. Sawyer, et al., 75–79. Benjamins.

Pym, A., and E. Torres-Simón. 2021a. Efectos de la automatización en las competencias básicas del traductor: la traducción automática neuronal. In A. Vidal Suñé and A. Alarcón Alarcón (Eds.) *Ocupaciones y lenguaje. Indicadores y análisis de competencias lingüísticas en el ámbito laboral*, pp. 479–509. Publicacions de la Universitat Rovira i Virgili.

Pym, A., F. Grin, C. Sfreddo, and A. L. J. Chan (2012). *The status of the translation profession in the European Union.* European Commission.

Ren, W. 2019. Ethical Challenges Posed by and Ethical Principles Proposed for Machine Translation. *Shanghai Journal of Translators, 5*, 46–52. (任文.机器翻译伦理的挑战与导向.《上海翻译》)

Rodríguez de Céspedes, B. 2019. Translator education at a crossroads: the impact of automation. *Lebende Sprachen* 64 (1): 103–121.

Temizöz, Ö. (2013). *Postediting machine-translation output and its revision. Subject-matter experts versus professional translators.* PhD thesis, Universitat Rovira i Virgili.

Torres-Simón, E., and A. Pym. 2019. European Masters in Translation. A Comparative Study. In D. Sawyer, F. Austermühl and V. Enríquez Raído *Translator Education: The Evolving Curriculum*, pp. 75–97. Benjamins.

Ubalde, J., and A. Alarcón. 2020. Are all automation-resistant skills rewarded? an analysis of linguistic skills in the US labour market. *The Economic and Labour Relations Review*. https://doi.org/10.1177/1035304620903152.

Yilmaz, E. D., I. Naumovska, and V. A. Aggarwal. 2023. AI-driven labor substitution: evidence from google translate and ChatGPT. INSEAD Working Paper No. 2023/24/EFE. https://doi.org/10.2139/ssrn.4400516.

Nune Ayvazyan is a Lecturer in Translation at Universitat Rovira i Virgili in Tarragona, Spain. She holds a Ph.D. in Translation and Intercultural Studies from the Universitat Rovira i Virgili. Her current research interests are in the use of new technologies in teaching translation and languages, and in multilingual policies.

Ester Torres-Simón is a lecturer in Korean and Translation at Universitat Autònoma de Barcelona, Spain. Her focus of research is on literary circulation and the use of technology for research dissemination and translation teaching.

Anthony Pym is Distinguished Professor of Translation and Intercultural Studies at the Rovira i Virgili in Tarragona, Spain, and Extra-ordinary Professor at Stellenbosch University, South Africa. His research interests are in sociological approaches to intercultural communication.

Computational Terminology

Els Lefever and Ayla Rigouts Terryn

Abstract This chapter introduces the reader to the concept of computational terminology, i.e., to automatic ways of managing domain-specific vocabulary. The chapter begins by elucidating the concept of terminology and its pivotal role for translators and interpreters. Subsequently, it delves into automatic terminology extraction, initially addressing monolingual methods before progressing to multilingual approaches. This section aims to furnish readers with detailed insights into these processes and how they have evolved, highlighting their current capabilities and limitations. Following this, the discussion shifts to the integration of terminology in neural machine translation, exploring how contemporary neural systems grapple with terminological challenges and the strategies employed to mitigate them. The possibilities and challenges of domain adaptation are discussed, followed by a brief overview of strategies for terminology injection, such as lexically constrained decoding. Expanding the scope, the chapter then explores areas beyond term extraction and translation, encompassing related research fields such as term variation detection, ontology building, acronym detection, automatic definition generation, and named entity recognition. The final section of the chapter adopts a pragmatic perspective, cataloguing essential tools for computational terminology, ranging from commercial offerings to research-based, open-source solutions. Ultimately, the chapter aims to acquaint readers with this dynamic research area, selectively focusing on information most pertinent to its potential users.

E. Lefever (✉) · A. R. Terryn
Ghent University, Ghent, Belgium
e-mail: els.lefever@ugent.be

A. R. Terryn
e-mail: ayla.rigoutsterryn@kuleuven.be

Y. Peng et al. (eds.), *New Advances in Translation Technology*, New Frontiers in Translation Studies, https://doi.org/10.1007/978-981-97-2958-6_8

1 Introduction

Terminology is the specialised vocabulary that defines domain-specific concepts (International Organization for Standardization 2019) and consists of both single- and multi-word **terms**. Terminology can refer to either the collection of all terms in a domain, or the study of terms. Terms exist in any domain in which people can specialise, and these domains can be defined very broadly (e.g., *medicine*, *sports*, *law*), or more narrowly (e.g., *heart failure*, *soccer*, *corruption*). Likewise, terms in these domains can be defined more broadly or narrowly, depending on how specialised and domain-specific a concept needs to be to be considered terminological. Examples in the domain of linguistics can include terms that many non-linguists know (e.g., *noun phrase*, *grammar*), as well as more specialised terms (e.g., *semiotics, SVO,* and *dependency grammar*).

The decision on how to delimit a domain and how to define which instances should be considered terms will depend on the intended use for the terminology. **Translators** are among the professionals who spend most time researching and managing terminology. According to Bowker, "[m]anaging terminology effectively can help to improve linguistic quality, reduce costs, and shorten turn-around times for translation" (2015, p. 305). She adds that terminology can also play an important role in corporate branding and that managing terminology well can help translators to avoid legal liabilities. In 2005, it was estimated that translators spend 20–50% of their time researching terminology (Fähndrich 2005). Even though domain expertise is important, it is not always feasible to find a translator with domain expertise and translation skills for the relevant language pair. Even when translators do get to translate in a domain for which they have specialised, it can be hard to keep up with quickly evolving terminology. Moreover, **machine translation** has been shown to struggle with terminology as well, even the latest neural models (Haque et al. 2020). Therefore, translators often have to rely on their research skills to find correct cross-lingual equivalents for terms.

Generally, translators prefer "authoritative" and "comprehensive" resources (Kageura and Abekawa 2013, p. 288). In the case of terminology, this could mean well-managed and up-to-date (multilingual) **term banks**, also called **termbases**. An example is the IATE termbase, which stands for *Interactive Terminology for Europe*.[1] At the date of writing (June 2023), this termbase contains almost 7.5 million terms in 20 languages and is actively maintained by EU translators and terminologists. A typical term record will contain one or more terms in multiple languages, with a potential indication of the preferred term. A good term record will also contain a definition and reference, as well as one or more examples of the term used in context. However, regardless of how helpful such an impressive termbase can be to translators, it cannot always fulfil the *comprehensive* and *authoritative* criteria that translators want. It is almost impossible to keep a termbase up-to-date and complete in a world where new terms are created all the time to keep up with all new developments in specialised communication. And although new entries in IATE tend to

[1] https://iate.europa.eu/home.

be created by well-trained professionals, there are a lot of contributors and not all entries can be regularly submitted to quality control, so translators may not always trust a term record, even in such a high-quality termbase. Moreover, with so many possible domains and language pairs, a relevant high-quality bilingual termbase will simply not always be available.

Consequently, translators often rely on unstructured resources: collections of specialised texts (specialised corpora) and web searches (León-Araúz et al. 2020) to manage terminology themselves. In a 2017–2018 survey of translators in Belgium and the Netherlands, 56% of those engaging in terminology management replied that "they compile their own termbases or terminology lists based on source texts and their translations for future use" (Verplaetse and Lambrechts 2019, p. 16). However, identifying terms (and cross-lingual equivalents, i.e., term translations) in texts is not an easy task. As discussed, delimiting a domain and defining what terms are, is not straightforward. Specialised **terminology management systems** can greatly help to maintain a termbase, and often such specialised software is integrated into CAT-tools (Computer Assisted Translation). However, many translators "still insist on archiving their terminology data bases in the form of Excel spreadsheet files" (Popiolek 2015, p. 350), despite the existence of dedicated term management tools that can be integrated into the translation environment to automatically suggest the stored translations whenever relevant. Whether the terms are managed with a dedicated tool or not, they must be selected first. **Terminology extraction** is the task of identifying terms in texts (corpora). Since doing so manually takes a lot of time and effort, there has been a lot of research into **automatic terminology extraction** (ATE). As results are never flawless, this is still considered a semi-automatic process that requires human validation for quality assurance. The research domain dedicated to the automatic processing of terminology (including but not limited to automatic terminology extraction) is often referred to as **computational terminology**.

The remainder of this article is structured as follows. The next section (Sect. 2) is dedicated to research on computational terminology, discussing monolingual terminology extraction (Sect. 2.1), multilingual terminology extraction (Sect. 2.2), terminology in neural machine translation (Sect. 2.3), and other computational terminology (Sect. 2.4). In Sect. 3, we briefly discuss existing tools for computational terminology, ranging from separate, dedicated tools, to integrated functionality in other tools (e.g., corpus analysis tools). A summary with a look towards potential future evolutions in the field is given in the conclusion (Sect. 4).

2 Computational Terminology

2.1 Monolingual Terminology Extraction

The task of automatic term extraction is challenging for a couple of reasons. First, there is no clear working definition of what a term exactly is. Whereas a lot of theoretical research has been performed on defining the concept of terminology (Temmerman 2000), it is not easy to operationalise these definitions and implement practical guidelines for distinguishing terms from general vocabulary. An attempt to overcome this issue has been made by Rigouts Terryn et al. (2020), who proposed a labelling scheme distinguishing between Specific Terms, Common Terms, out-of-Domain Terms, and Named Entities. The authors show that providing separate labels for various term categories can improve inter-annotator agreement for indicating terms in text. An additional advantage is that the extracted terms can be tailored for different applications. Translators, for instance, will be mainly interested in Specific Terms, whereas Out-of-domain Terms might be irrelevant for domain-specific automatic ontology creation. Similarly, Hätty and Schulte im Walde (2018) asked laypeople to identify terms, specifying four tasks: "highlight domain-specific phrases", "create an index", "define unknown words for creating a translation lexicon", and "create a glossary". They showed that laypeople share a general understanding of termhood, but that inter-annotator agreement was often high. This was especially the case for more specific tasks, ambiguous terms, and multi-word terms.

A related challenge is the creation of high-quality gold standard datasets, as manually indicating terms is a notoriously difficult, but also time-consuming and thus expensive activity. As a result, manually labelled data sets are scarce, and rarely cover multiple languages or domains. Examples of available datasets that have been manually annotated and are frequently used in research are GENIA (Kim et al. 2003), ACL RD-TEC 2.0 (Qasemizadeh and Schumann 2016) and ACTER (Rigouts Terryn et al. 2020). The former two focus on a single domain (biology and computational linguistics respectively) in English. ACTER contains annotations in four domains (corruption, dressage, heart failure, wind energy) and three languages (English, French, Dutch). All data sets and annotation guidelines are publicly available.[2]

As it is so cumbersome to manually annotate terms in text, the proposed approaches for automatic term extraction have often been evaluated on precision (how accurate the result of the term extraction is), and not on recall (how many of the relevant terms have been extracted by the system), which only gives a limited insight in the actual performance of the term extraction system.

---

[2] GENIA: http://www.geniaproject.org/genia-corpus.
ACL RD-TEC 2.0: http://pars.ie/lr/acl_rd-tec.
ACTER: https://github.com/AylaRT/ACTER.

2.1.1 Rule-Based Methods

The first generation of terminology extraction systems relies on rule-based methodologies. Three types of approaches can be distinguished based on the information that is used to discriminate terms from general vocabulary in text. Systems can either incorporate linguistic information, statistical information, or a combination of both. The latter systems are the so-called hybrid systems, which still obtain competitive performance to more recent machine learning approaches.

Linguistic information usually includes tokenisation (splitting up sentences into tokens, viz. words, numbers, punctuation marks, etc.), lemmatisation (providing the base form of a word as found in a dictionary), part-of-speech tagging (defining the grammatical category of words) and chunking (detecting constituents by combining part-of-speech tags). This linguistic information is then used to manually define syntactically valid term patterns (e.g., terms can have underlying noun-noun patterns as in *wind energy*, adjective-noun as in *global warming*, noun-preposition-noun as in *head of state*, etc.).

A first source of useful **statistical information** for terminology extraction starts from the hypothesis that domain-specific terms appear relatively more frequently in domain-specific corpora than in general background corpora. Statistical measures such as Log-likelihood (Rayson and Garside 2000) or C-Value (Frantzi and Ananiadou 1999) build on this intuition and include relative frequencies in specialised and general corpora in their formulas to measure the so-called *termhood* (Kageura and Umino 1996), viz. how domain-specific terms are. A second statistical measure often included is *unithood*, which calculates the strength of cohesion between the various parts of multiword terms. Often the extracted terms are sorted by termhood measures, and a threshold is defined as a cut-off point for which terms will be considered for the final term list.

Hybrid systems, such as TExSIS (Lefever et al. 2009; Macken et al. 2013) combine both types of information, and generate candidate terms relying on linguistic patterns, after which these candidate terms are filtered with statistical measures (see Fig. 1). Other examples of rule-based systems are TermoStat (Drouin 2003), Termolator (Meyers et al. 2018) and TermSuite (Cram and Daille 2016).

2.1.2 Machine Learning Approaches

A second strand of term extraction research applies machine learning techniques, where large numbers of characteristics of term candidates are calculated (so-called features) and combined to model how terms look like. These systems combine linguistic, statistical, and other features, such as word shape features (e.g., presence of uppercase characters, word length, prefix and suffix, etc.), features based on external resources (e.g., terminologies and ontologies, Wikipedia) or topic modelling features (Šajatović et al. 2019). During the training phase, the model learns the optimal feature combination to identify terms in text. Machine learning approaches can follow a similar setup as the rule-based approaches, and start by listing potential candidate

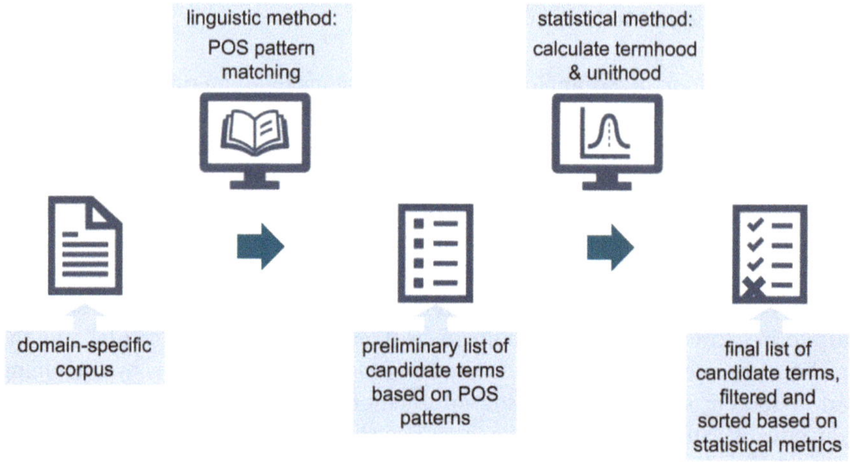

Fig. 1 Hybrid automatic terminology extraction

terms, and then calculate features for each candidate in that list to classify them as terms or non-terms (Ljubešić et al. 2019; Rigouts Terryn et al. 2021). Conversely, there are also sequential approaches (Kucza et al. 2018; Rigouts Terryn et al. 2022b), which don't start by extracting lists of candidate terms, but rather classify candidate terms in the original context. These approaches go over each consecutive word (or character, or sequence of words) in the original text, to tag it as being (part of) a term or not.

More recently, **neural approaches** have been investigated as well. Artificial neural networks are inspired by the working of the human brain and consist of layers of artificial neurons that process input values into a single output value. When they incorporate multiple hidden layers between the input layer and output layer, using such neural networks is referred to as deep learning. The latest generation of deep learning algorithms, such as Transformers like BERT (Devlin et al. 2019), are applied to train large language models and have obtained significant improvements for various NLP tasks. When an input sentence is processed by such a large language model, a contextualised embedding is produced for every token in the input. These word embeddings are numeric vectors that consider the contexts of words in large text corpora, allowing words with similar meanings to have similar representations. Neural approaches to automatic terminology extraction then use these word embeddings as features.

Researchers have relied on pre-trained GloVe (Amjadian et al. 2018; Zhang et al. 2018) or Word2Vec (Mikolov et al. 2013) embeddings, but domain-specific embeddings have been trained as well (Amjadian et al. 2018), and both have even been combined (Drouin et al. 2020; Hätty et al. 2020). Important drawbacks of this neural-based methodology are that it is very data-hungry (requires large domain-specific corpora to train on), computationally expensive, and that current embedding-based approaches cannot handle multi-word terms well. Another important limitation is that deep learning algorithms function as black boxes, meaning that results are neither interpretable nor predictable.

It is difficult to make general statements about the **performance** of state-of-the-art term extraction systems, as scores depend on the type of annotations (e.g., binary labels or fine-grained labels), but also on domain and language. Rigouts Terryn et al. (2021) show that classification results for Dutch clearly outperform French and English, probably because of the different compounding rules in Dutch (i.e., compounds are written as one orthographic string, whereas compound in English and French are written with spaces between the composing parts). This is also reflected in the different F1-scores (harmonic mean of precision and recall) for single-word terms (59%) and for multi-word terms (42%), and even more striking for the recall scores (69% vs. 39% for single-word and multi-word terms, respectively). Concerning domains, it appeared easier to extract terms for heart failure and dressage than for wind energy and corruption. A possible explanation could be that the former two domains contain a lot more specialised terminology, and that the latter two domains also contain more common terms that are part of general vocabulary.

Remaining issues identified in monolingual terminology extraction research are the extraction of rare terms, ambiguous terms (that also have a non-specialised use), and term variation. Most systems provide the result of the term extraction in a flat list of unique terms, and do not consider morphological relationships between terms to combine the various full forms of the same term.

2.2 *Multilingual Terminology Extraction*

Term extraction can also be applied in a multilingual setting. The first component remains as monolingual term extraction on various (monolingual) corpora, but, subsequently, the resulting terms are aligned with their translational equivalents. In multilingual term extraction, a distinction is typically made based on the type of multilingual corpus being used, viz. parallel corpora (Sect. 2.2.1) or comparable corpora (Sect. 2.2.2).

2.2.1 Bilingual Term Extraction from Parallel Corpora

A first strand of bilingual terminology extraction systems extracts bilingual term lists from parallel corpora, viz. collections of direct translations. These systems broadly consist of two modules: a module performing monolingual term extraction and a module aligning the translation equivalents from these monolingual term lists, resulting in a bilingual term list. Foo (2012) makes a distinction between "align-extract" and "extract-align" systems, depending on whether the monolingual candidate terms are extracted first, or alignment happens first. In the latter case, multilingual information can be used during the monolingual extraction process.

An example of a hybrid system performing bilingual ATE is **TExSIS** (Macken et al. 2013). In a first step, statistical word alignment is performed with GIZA++ (Och and Ney 2003). Subsequently, chunk-based alignment is performed, which generates candidate terms from linguistically motivated chunks. By means of a bootstrapping technique, confident term pairs are retrieved allowing the extraction of rules for corresponding term patterns across languages (e.g., PoS-pattern rule for French-Dutch: Noun + Adjective < > Adjective + Noun). Next, the specificity of the candidate terms is determined by combining various *termhood* and *unithood* filters. Other examples of bilingual ATE systems are **LUIZ** (Vintar 2010), which first identifies term candidates monolingually and then uses a bilingual lexicon to align translations, and **Sketch Engine** (Kilgarriff et al. 2014), which first applies monolingual term extraction, and then computes co-occurrence statistics (e.g., logDice) for aligned candidate term pairs.

Besides GIZA++ and Moses phrases tables (Koehn et al. 2007), which remain the most popular alignment methodologies (Ivanović et al. 2022), more recent alignment methods, such as awesome-align, which extracts word alignments from multilingual BERT and fine-tunes mBERT on parallel corpora for better alignment quality (Dou and Neubig 2021) and ASTrED, which performs tokenisation and word alignment before calculating syntactic similarity between sentences (Vanroy et al. 2021), are gaining popularity.

As parallel corpora are hardly available for very specialised domains or novel subjects, and constructing parallel data is very labour-intensive and time-consuming, researchers have started investigating the term extraction from comparable corpora.

2.2.2 Bilingual Term Extraction from Comparable Corpora

Comparable corpora are bilingual or multilingual text collections that are similar but not translations. The degree of similarity can differ. Some comparable corpora can be cross-lingually aligned at document-level (e.g., Wikipedia documents in various languages), whereas others cannot be aligned at all and can contain more variation in the content across languages. State-of-the-art approaches are again neural approaches, where cross-lingual and multilingual embeddings are trained. Cross-lingual word embeddings (Ruder et al. 2019) are obtained by aligning monolingual embeddings for two different languages in a shared embedding space, usually by means of a bilingual seed lexicon. This method, however, is often outperformed by truly multilingual contextualised embeddings, that are produced by multilingual language models such as mBERT (Devlin et al. 2019) trained on multilingual corpora from the start. Bilingual terminology extraction is operationalised here as **bilingual lexicon induction** (BLI), where the task consists of first performing monolingual term extraction and then finding cross-lingual equivalents (or translations) in both monolingual term lists. A popular approach to find equivalents is to retrieve the *nearest neighbours* of a term in the multilingual semantic vector space, obtained by calculating the distance between the embeddings of the terms.

Important **challenges** for bilingual lexicon induction are the representation of rare words, domain-specific words, and most important, the linking of multi-word terms. For multi-word expressions, the meaning is non-compositional, and combining the vectors of the composing words does not achieve good results. Recent approaches have tried to address this issue by creating vectors for multi-word expressions (Liu et al. 2022). Another important challenge for BLI is the lack of manually annotated training and evaluation benchmarks sets. Existing data sets such as MUSE (Conneau et al. 2018), are widely used by the research community, but have been created (semi-) automatically. Creating a high-quality gold standard for BLI is challenging for several reasons. A first issue is that finding cross-lingual equivalents (translations) in a non-aligned comparable corpus is very time-consuming and requires a lot of expertise. In addition, the notion of equivalence has raised a lot of debate in the field of translation studies (Kerremans and Temmerman 2016; Panou 2013), as it is not trivial to decide whether a translation has the exact same meaning as the corresponding source term.

Whereas BLI for specialised terminology extraction is still in its infancy, a recently organised shared task on bilingual term alignment in comparable specialised corpora (Adjali et al. 2022), and an upcoming 2023 edition, show the interest of the community in this task. As the winning system only obtained a precision of 28%, there is still a lot of room for improvement for term extraction from comparable corpora. Despite the modest performance of current BLI methodologies, we are convinced that the resulting bilingual term lists could be a useful asset for translators. Defining translations from scratch is more difficult that starting from a list of translation suggestions (Bollegala et al. 2015). As a result, translators could greatly speed up finding translation equivalents when using bilingual lexicons derived from comparable corpora.

2.3 Terminology in Neural Machine Translation

Since translating terminology is such a challenge, it is important to know how terminology is handled by machine translation (MT). In this section, we will focus on neural machine translation (NMT), since it has largely replaced previous generations of MT systems because of its superior performance in most scenarios. To illustrate: to the best of our knowledge, only neural systems were submitted to the WMT2022 shared task on general MT (Kocmi et al. 2022). It is important to note that NMT systems, like most systems that rely on neural networks, require a lot of (parallel) training data to work well, and that they tend to reach the best accuracy when the training data is very similar (in terms of domain, style, vocabulary) to the texts you want to translate.

To improve term translation accuracy of MT, ideally, a system would be trained on large amounts of domain-specific texts, so that it can learn the specific vocabulary of that domain. However, since this requires large, domain-specific, parallel corpora, this scenario is not always feasible. Large parallel corpora are rarely available for very specific domains, and, even when they are, there is no guarantee the corpus will contain sufficient occurrences of all the latest and most specific terminology for an NMT system to learn this terminology. Consequently, a lot of research efforts have been devoted to **domain adaptation** of MT, where a general system, trained on general data, is fine-tuned on a smaller parallel corpus of domain-specific data. This ensures the system has enough training data to obtain a good general translation accuracy, while still benefitting from the domain-specific knowledge in the smaller corpus. There are many possible strategies which will not be discussed in detail here, but we refer the interested reader to a recent survey on the topic by Chu and Wang (2022).

Domain adaptation can have a positive impact on the accuracy of terminology translations, but there is also research that focuses more specifically on terminology in NMT. In a 2022 study at the European Commission's translation department, it was found that there was "significant variability among participating languages and a general unpredictability of machine translation when it comes to translating terms, confirming that when it comes to MT there is no one-size-fits-all-solution" (Stefaniak 2022, p. 134). That unpredictability is a recurring problem with NMT. Multiple strategies have been developed that attempt to incorporate existing (curated) bilingual term lists into NMT output. There are different approaches for **terminology injection**, which must consider ways to, first, increase the chances that an unpredictable neural system will use the provided terms and not some other options, and second, make sure the injected terms are in the correct form considering the context. A relatively simple technique that can be used is substituting sequences based on exact matches with a bilingual dictionary. While this approach guarantees that each term in the dictionary will result in a translation with its equivalent as present in the dictionary, it will often result in ungrammatical sentences, especially for highly inflected languages (Dougal and Lonsdale 2020). *Lexically constrained decoding* (e.g., Post and Vilar 2018, p. 1314) is another popular approach. In this case, the "beam search" of NMT, which calculates the best potential equivalent from several options, is constrained to a predefined list of options. However, this presupposes that one of the options in the predefined list will be part of the beam search, and "[a]lthough the output is constrained, probabilities in play at this point mean that the final output may or may not contain the constrained sequences" (Dougal and Lonsdale 2020, p. 4820). A final example of an approach for terminology injection is to create artificial training data based on bilingual termbases and train (or fine-tune) an NMT system on this data. Zhang and Zong (2016) propose such an approach with "pseudo sentence pair synthesis".

In conclusion, NMT performance on terminology has not been extensively researched, but the existing research shows that NMT often struggles with terminology translation and that the output is unpredictable (Stefaniak 2022). While it is possible to train systems on domain-specific data to increase performance, sufficiently large domain-specific parallel corpora are rarely available as training data, and often not even for fine-tuning. Therefore, terminology injection is researched as a strategy to make use of existing bilingual termbases to improve the term translations of NMT. Nevertheless, automatic translation of terminology remains a large challenge.

2.4 Computational Terminology

Though we have focused on automatic terminology extraction and automatic terminology translation in this chapter, there is other related research in the field of computational terminology as well. In this section, we will very briefly discuss a few of them.

A first area of research that has not been mentioned yet is the automatic detection of **term variation** and of **relations between terms**. When constructing termbases, it is nice to be able to start from an automatically extracted list of candidate terms, but, ideally, a termbase will also be structured such that multiple variations of terms for the same concept can be combined (e.g., different spellings, abbreviations, synonyms etc.), and that relations between terms can be indicated (e.g., synonyms and antonyms, hypernyms and hyponyms, cfr. Lefever 2016). Again, automatically preparing this information can help to speed up the process. For instance, the TermSuite tool (Cram and Daille 2016) is designed to both extract candidate terms, and to cluster variants (both at a morphological level and at a syntactic level). In this research, a rule-based approach with regular expressions is used to find these variants. Besides such pattern-based approaches, this task has also benefited from the rise of word embeddings and language models, so semantic similarity between terms can also be calculated by comparing the embeddings for those terms (e.g., Lanza et al. 2020). Another related task is automatic **acronym detection** or disambiguation (see, e.g., Link et al. 2022; Spasic 2018). Once relations between terms are known, they can be visualised to make the most of this information. For instance, the NetViz tool was developed to visualise terms in relation to other terms, as shown in Fig. 2, where this method is applied to the domain of karstology (Pollak et al. 2020). The task of finding relations between terms can be taken a step further with **automatic ontology building**. This task is defined as "analysing the collected text for a specific domain; identifying the relevant terms, concepts and their relationships; mapping and representing the ontology by representation language [...]; and finally evaluating the constructed ontology" (Al-Aswadi et al. 2020, p. 3901). Again, strategies range from rule-based, linguistic strategies, to neural machine learning approaches. We refer the interested reader to the work of Al-Aswadi et al. (2020) for more information on this topic. A final example of research that can be considered part of computational terminology is **automatic definition detection** (e.g., Kang et al. 2020), to help enrich termbases with more relevant information.

Before moving on to the next section, it is also worth mentioning **named entity recognition** as a task that is closely related to ATE. The boundary between terms and named entities is not necessarily always clear. To illustrate, we will take the GENIA dataset as an example. In the original paper on the GENIA annotated corpus (Kim et al. 2003), the authors appear to refer to the annotation of biomedical terms and named entities almost interchangeably. Other researchers that use this annotated dataset also refer to either named entity recognition (e.g., Goyal et al. 2018), or automatic term extraction (or automatic term recognition) (e.g., Astrakhantsev et al. 2015; Kucza et al. 2018), though their aim is the same. When annotating the ACTER

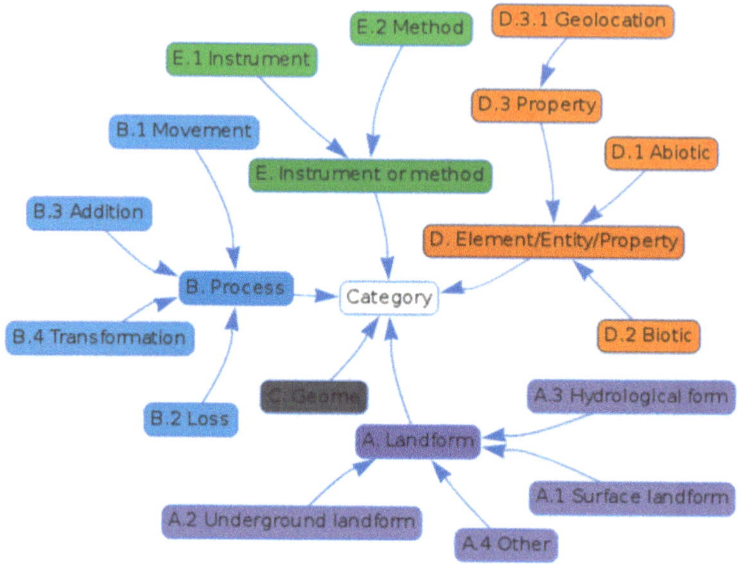

Fig. 2 Taxonomy of categories visualized in NetViz" from Pollak et al. (2020, p. 58)

dataset (Rigouts Terryn et al. 2020), where separate labels were used for terms and named entities, the annotators also reported sometimes hesitating between these categories. This may be worth noting in case researchers fail to find relevant work written from either the perspective of ATE or named entity recognition because they are only using one of the search terms.

In conclusion, while the focus of this chapter is more on ATE and automatic term translation, the research field of computational terminology is much broader than that, and full of remaining research challenges.

3 Terminology Tools

This section gives an overview of some frequently used term extraction tools. It is important to mention, however, that we do not aim to provide an exhaustive list, but rather present some examples of what type of ATE tools are available today.

Most commercial term extraction tools or computer-assisted translation tools that support term extraction, such as MultiTerm Extract or SketchEngine, rely on statistical or rule-based hybrid methodologies.

RWS MultiTerm Extract[3] is part of RWS MultiTerm, a commercial terminology management tool that supports storing, extracting and managing multilingual terminology, and communicates with RWS Trados Studio. It is probably the best-known

[3] https://www.trados.com/products/multiterm-desktop/.

terminology tool in the translation industry. The underlying methodology is purely statistical (frequency-based), meaning that no linguistic information is taken into account to generate candidate terms. As a result, frequent nonsense word sequences can be proposed as candidate terms. Advantages are that users can validate and manage the resulting terms by inspecting monolingual and bilingual concordance, and that the tool supports all languages.

Another well-known tool is **Sketch Engine**[4] (Kilgarriff et al. 2014), created by Lexcial Computing Ltd. Sketch Engine is in fact a corpus analysis tool, which also offers monolingual and bilingual term extraction functionalities. Both single-word and multi-word terms can be extracted, and term lists can be downloaded in CAT-friendly formats, such as TBX or CSV files. OneClick Terms (Baisa et al. 2017) is the more specialised term extraction environment linked to Sketch Engine and offers both monolingual and multilingual term extraction from parallel corpora. For the monolingual extraction, a hybrid methodology is applied: first, syntactically valid candidate terms are extracted, and next, statistical filters are applied to select domain-specific terms from a given corpus. Advantages of OneClick Terms is that the user is provided with a lot of additional information about the term (e.g., frequency information, concordances and collocations containing the term). The main disadvantage is the lack of a dedicated term management tool.

In addition to the commercial tools, various research demos for term extraction are available as well. Again, most research term extractors rely on a rule-based hybrid methodology. Examples are TermoStat[5] or TerMine (Frantzi et al. 2000). An exception is provided by D-Terminer[6] (Rigouts Terryn et al. 2022a), a more recent open access online demo for both monolingual and multilingual automatic term extraction (from parallel corpora) for four languages: Dutch, English, French and German. The monolingual term extraction is based on a recurrent neural network incorporating pretrained embeddings. Terms can be tagged in context in the domain-specific corpus uploaded by the user, but a term list can be downloaded as well. As for the bilingual term extraction, users have to upload a parallel corpus in the form of a translation memory (.tmx format).

Another interesting tool is **TermSuite,**[7] developed by the University of Nantes in the framework of the TTC Terminology Extraction project (Rocheteau and Daille 2011). Termsuite extracts monolingual and bilingual dictionaries applying distributional and compositional methods. The tool is available for English, French, Italian, German, Spanish, Latvian, Chinese and Russian. A final example of a freely available tool is **AntConc,**[8] which has limited keyword extraction capabilities, in combination with other options for corpus analysis, such as a concordancing.

[4] https://www.sketchengine.eu/.

[5] http://termostat.ling.umontreal.ca/.

[6] https://lt3.ugent.be/dterminer/.

[7] http://termsuite.github.io/documentation/introduction/.

[8] https://www.laurenceanthony.net/software/antconc/.

To conclude this brief overview, it is worthwhile mentioning an interesting tool in the related domain of CAI (Computer-assisted Interpreting). InterpretBank[9] (Fantinuoli 2016) offers a user-friendly interface where interpreters can manage documents and term glossaries, with a link to external resources, such as IATE, and a pilot version integrating automatic speech recognition is available for English. Terms can easily be consulted, even in the booth, without the prerequisite of an internet connection. Finally, monolingual and multilingual glossaries can be extracted automatically based on domain-specific documents or web pages.

4 Conclusion

In conclusion, terminology is a crucial part of all specialised communication and can pose challenges for language professionals, who do not always have domain expertise. Translators and interpreters specifically can spend a lot of time and energy finding correct cross-lingual equivalents for terminology. The research field of computational terminology is dedicated to studying ways to process terminology automatically. In this chapter, we focused on the subfields of automatic term extraction and automatic term translation. Monolingual automatic term extraction is used to identify terms in collections of texts, using either rule-based or machine learning approaches. Multilingual term extraction goes one step further and attempts to identify cross-lingual equivalents for terms as well. This can be done starting from parallel (aligned) corpora (which are difficult to obtain, but lead to better results), or comparable (unaligned) corpora (which are easy to obtain, but very challenging for this task). Regarding automatic term translation, neural machine translation, while outperforming previous generations of machine translation systems, still struggles with terminology. Strategies to improve this include domain adaptation (training the systems on domain-specific data) and term injection (including information from existing bilingual termbases).

Although computational terminology is not a very large discipline within the field of natural language processing, it is a productive one, with many tasks beyond term extraction and term translation. In this chapter, we briefly touch upon a few of these, including term variation detection and ontology building. Regardless of the task, there are a couple of recurring challenges in the field of computational terminology. First, the distinction between terms and general vocabulary is not a straightforward one and can be task-dependent. Second, terminology typically does not occur in texts as frequently as general vocabulary. As a result, it can be difficult to find sufficiently large collections of texts, with sufficient occurrences of terms, to obtain enough information for the automatic processing of terms. Another challenge is that terms can consist of multiple words, and many natural language processing techniques do not handle multi-words as well as single words. A final challenge is that some terms

---

[9] https://www.interpretbank.com/site/index.html.

are ambiguous: they only gain a terminological meaning when used in a domain-specific context, but the word(s) also have a general meaning. This complicates any approach based on some form of statistics (which includes neural approaches).

To conclude, the thriving domain of computational terminology still faces important research challenges. Recent work is mainly focussing on the investigation of machine learning approaches for aligning translational equivalents in monolingual term lists extracted from comparable corpora, and correct translation of domain-specific terms in neural machine translation. Despite the progress made in automatic term extraction, translators and interpreters still seem reluctant to use term extraction tools. A possible explanation might be that commercial tools do not always offer a user-friendly interface that integrates the latest state-of-the-art methods for automatic term extraction and validation. Therefore, we believe there are still a lot of opportunities for user-friendly CAT-tools offering high-quality terminology extraction and management support.

References

Adjali, O., E. Morin, and P. Zweigenbaum. 2022. Building comparable corpora for assessing multi-word term alignment. In *Proceedings of the 13th Conference on Language Resources and Evaluation (LREC 2022)*, 3103–3112.

Al-Aswadi, F.N., H.Y. Chan, and K.H. Gan. 2020. Automatic ontology construction from text: A review from shallow to deep learning trend. *Artificial Intelligence Review* 53 (6): 3901–3928. https://doi.org/10.1007/s10462-019-09782-9.

Amjadian, E., D. Z. Inkpen, T. S. Paribakht, and F. Faez. 2018. Distributed specificity for automatic terminology extraction. *Terminology. International Journal of Theoretical and Applied Issues in Specialized Communication* 24(1): 23–40. https://doi.org/10.1075/term.00012.amj.

Astrakhantsev, N., D. Fedorenko, and D. Yu. Turdakov. 2015. Methods for automatic term recognition in domain-specific text collections: A survey. *Programming and Computer Software*, 41(6): 336–349. https://doi.org/10.1134/S036176881506002X

Baisa, V., J. Michelfeit, and O. Matuška. 2017. Simplifying terminology extraction: OneClick terms. In *Proceedings of the 9th International Corpus Linguistics Conference.*

Bollegala, D., G. Kontonatsios, and S. Ananiadou. 2015. A Cross-lingual similarity measure for detecting biomedical term translations. *PLOS ONE* 10(6). https://doi.org/10.1371/journal.pone.0126196.

Bowker, L. 2015. Terminology and translation. In *Handbook of Terminology*, ed. H. J. Kockaert, and F. Steurs, vol. 1, pp. 304–323. John Benjamins.

Chu, C., and R. Wang. 2022. A survey of domain adaptation for neural machine translation. In *Proceedings of the 27th International Conference on Computational Linguistics*, 1304–1319.

Conneau, A., G. Lample, M. Ranzato, L. Denoyer, and H. Jégou. 2018. *Word translation without parallel data.* arXiv:1710.04087.

Cram, D., and B. Daille. 2016. TermSuite: Terminology extraction with term variant detection. In *Proceedings of the 54th Annual Meeting of the Association for Computational Linguistics: System Demonstrations*, 13–18. https://doi.org/10.18653/v1/P16-4003.

Devlin, J., M.-W. Chang, K. Lee, and K. Toutanova. 2019. BERT: Pre-training of deep bidirectional transformers for language understanding. arXiv:1810.04805 [Cs], https://doi.org/10.48550/arXiv.1810.04805.

Dou, Z.-Y., and G. Neubig. 2021. Word alignment by fine-tuning embeddings on parallel corpora. In *Proceedings of the 16th Conference of the European Chapter of the Association for*

Computational Linguistics: Main Volume, 2112–2128. https://doi.org/10.18653/v1/2021.eacl-main.181.

Dougal, D. K., and D. Lonsdale. 2020. Improving NMT quality using terminology injection. In *Proceedings of the 12th Conference on Language Resources and Evaluation (LREC 2020)*, 4820–4827.

Drouin, P. (2003). Term extraction using non-technical corpora as a point of leverage. *Terminology. International Journal of Theoretical and Applied Issues in Specialized Communication* 9(1): 99–115.

Drouin, P., J.-B. Morel, and M.-C. L. Homme. 2020. Automatic term extraction from newspaper corpora: Making the most of specificity and common features. In *Proceedings of the 6th International Workshop on Computational Terminology (COMPUTERM 2020)*, 1–7.

Fähndrich, U. (2005). Terminology project management. *Terminology. International Journal of Theoretical and Applied Issues in Specialized Communication* 11(2): 225–260. https://doi.org/10.1075/term.11.2.02fah.

Fantinuoli, C. 2016. InterpretBank. Redefining computer-assisted interpreting tools. In *Proceedings of the 38th Conference Translating and the Computer*, 42–52.

Foo, J. 2012. *Computational terminology: Exploring bilingual and monolingual term extraction.* Thesis, Linköping Institute of Technology at Linköping University.

Frantzi, K., S. Ananiadou, and H. Mima. 2000. Automatic recognition of multi-word terms: The C-value/NC-value method. *International Journal of Digital Libraries* 3 (2): 117–132.

Frantzi, K.T., and S. Ananiadou. 1999. The C-value/NC-value domain-independent method for multi-word term extraction. *Journal of Natural Language Processing* 6 (3): 145–179.

Goyal, A., V. Gupta, and M. Kumar. 2018. Recent named entity recognition and classification techniques: A systematic review. *Computer Science Review* 29: 21–43. https://doi.org/10.1016/j.cosrev.2018.06.001.

Hätty, A., D. Schlechtweg, and M. Dorna. 2020. Predicting degrees of technicality in automatic terminology extraction. In *Proceedings of the 58th Annual Meeting of the Association for Computational Linguistics*, 72883–72889.

Hätty, A., and S. Schulte im Walde. 2018. A laypeople study on terminology identification across domains and task definitions. In *Proceedings of the 16th Annual Conference of the North American Chapter of the Association for Computational Linguistics: Human Language Technologies*, 321–326.

Ivanović, T., R. Stanković, B. Š. Todorović, and C. Krstev. 2022. Corpus-based bilingual terminology extraction in the power engineering domain. *Terminology. International Journal of Theoretical and Applied Issues in Specialized Communication.* https://doi.org/10.1075/term.20038.iva.

Kageura, K., and T. Abekawa. 2013. The place of comparable corpora in providing terminological reference information to online translators: A strategic framework. In *Building and using comparable corpora*, ed. S. Sharoff, R. Rapp, P. Zweigenbaum, and P. Fung, 285–301. Springer.

Kageura, K., and B. Umino. 1996. Methods of automatic term recognition. Terminology. *International Journal of Theoretical and Applied Issues in Specialized Communication* 3(2): 259–289.

Kang, D., A. Head, R. Sidhu, K. Lo, D. Weld, and M. A. Hearst. 2020. Document-level definition detection in scholarly documents: existing models, error analyses, and future directions. In *Proceedings of the First Workshop on Scholarly Document Processing*, 196–206. https://doi.org/10.18653/v1/2020.sdp-1.22.

Kerremans, K., and R. Temmerman. 2016. How Terminological equivalence differs from translation equivalence: Quantitative and qualitative comparisons of term variants and their translations in a parallel corpus of EU texts. In *Corpus-Based Approaches to Translation and Interpreting: From Theory to Applications*, 43–63. Peter Lang.

Kilgarriff, A., V. Baisa, J. Bušta, M. Jakubíček, V. Kovář, J. Michelfeit, P. Rychlý, and V. Suchomel. 2014. The sketch engine: Ten years on. *Lexicography* 1 (1): 7–36. https://doi.org/10.1007/s40607-014-0009-9.

Kim, J.-D., T. Ohta, Y. Tateisi, and J. Tsujii. 2003. GENIA corpus—a semantically annotated corpus for bio-textmining. *Bioinformatics* 19 (1): 180–182.

Kocmi, T., R. Bawden, O. Bojar, A. Dvorkovich, C. Federmann, M. Fishel, T. Gowda, Y. Graham, R. Grundkiewicz, B. Haddow, R. Knowles, P. Koehn, C. Monz, M. Morishita, M. Nagata, T. Nakazawa, M. Novák, M. Popel, M. Popović, and M. Shmatova. 2022. Findings of the 2022 conference on machine translation (WMT22). In *Proceedings of the Seventh Conference on Machine Translation (WMT)*, 1–45.

Kucza, M., J. Niehues, T. Zenkel, A. Waibel, and S. Stüker. 2018. Term extraction via neural sequence labeling a comparative evaluation of strategies using recurrent neural networks. In *Proceedings of Interspeech 2018, the 19th Annual Conference of the International Speech Communication Association*, 2072–2076. https://doi.org/10.21437/Interspeech.2018-2017.

Lanza, C., A. Hazem, and B. Daille. 2020. Towards automatic thesaurus construction and enrichment. In *Proceedings of the 6th International Workshop on Computational Terminology (COMPUTERM 2020)*, ed. B. Daille, K. Kageura, and Rigouts Terryn, Ayla, 62–71. European Language Resources Association.

Lefever, E. 2016. A hybrid approach to domain-independent taxonomy learning. *Applied Ontology* 11 (3): 255–278. https://doi.org/10.3233/AO-160170.

Lefever, E., L. Macken, and V. Hoste. 2009. Language-independent bilingual terminology extraction from a multilingual parallel corpus. In *Proceedings of the 12th Conference of the European Chapter of the Association for Computational Linguistics on - EACL '09*, 496–504. https://doi.org/10.3115/1609067.1609122.

Link, N.B., S. Huang, T. Cai, J. Sun, K. Dahal, L. Costa, K. Cho, K. Liao, T. Cai, and C. Hong. 2022. Binary acronym disambiguation in clinical notes from electronic health records with an application in computational phenotyping. *International Journal of Medical Informatics* 162: 1–8. https://doi.org/10.1016/j.ijmedinf.2022.104753.

Liu, J., E. Morin, S. Peña Saldarriaga, and J. Lark. 2022. From unified phrase representation to bilingual phrase alignment in an unsupervised manner. *Natural Language Engineering* 29: 1–26. https://doi.org/10.1017/S1351324922000328.

Ljubešić, N., D. Fišer, and T. Erjavec. 2019. KAS-term: Extracting slovene terms from doctoral theses via supervised machine learning. In *Text, Speech, and Dialogue. TSD 2019*, vol. 11697. Springer. http://arxiv.org/abs/1906.02053.

Macken, L., E. Lefever, V. Hoste. 2013. TExSIS: Bilingual terminology extraction from parallel corpora using chunk-based alignment. *Terminology. International Journal of Theoretical and Applied Issues in Specialized Communication* 19(1): 1–30.

Meyers, A.L., Y. He, Z. Glass, J. Ortega, S. Liao, A. Grieve-Smith, R. Grishman, and O. Babko-Malaya. 2018. The termolator: Terminology recognition based on chunking, statistical and search-based scores. *Frontiers in Research Metrics and Analytics* 3: 19. https://doi.org/10.3389/frma.2018.00019.

Mikolov, T., W. Yih, and G. Zweig. 2013. Linguistic regularities in continuous space word representations. In *Proceedings of the 2013 Conference of the North American Chapter of the Association for Computational Linguistics: Human Language Technologies*, 746–751.

Och, F.J., and H. Ney. 2003. A systematic comparison of various statistical alignment models. *Computational Linguistics* 29 (1): 19–51.

Panou, D. 2013. Equivalence in translation theories: A critical evaluation. *Theory and Practice in Language Studies* 3 (1): 1–6. https://doi.org/10.4304/tpls.3.1.1-6.

Pollak, S., V. Podpečan, D. Miljkovic, U. Stepišnik, and Š. Vintar. 2020. The NetViz terminology visualization tool and the use cases in karstology domain modeling. In *Proceedings of the 6th International Workshop on Computational Terminology (COMPUTERM 2020)*, 55–61.

Popiolek, M. 2015. Terminology management within a translation quality assurance process. In *Handbook of Terminology*, ed. H. J. Kockaer, and F. Steurs, vol. 1, 341–359. John Benjamins Publishing Company.

Post, M., and D. Vilar. 2018. Fast lexically constrained decoding with dynamic beam allocation for neural machine translation. In *Proceedings of the 2018 Conference of the North American*

Chapter of the Association for Computational Linguistics: Human Language Technologies, vol. 1. Long papers, 1314–1324. https://doi.org/10.18653/v1/N18-1119.
Qasemizadeh, B., and A.-K. Schumann. 2016. The ACL RD-TEC 2.0: A language resource for evaluating term extraction and entity recognition methods. In *Proceedings of the Tenth International Conference on Language Resources and Evaluation (LREC'16)*, 1862–1868.
Rayson, P., and R. Garside. 2000. Comparing corpora using frequency profiling. In *Proceedings of the Workshop on Comparing Corpora, 38th Annual Meeting of the Association for Computational Linguistics*, 1–6.
Rigouts Terryn, A., V. Hoste, and E. Lefever. 2020. In no uncertain terms: A dataset for monolingual and multilingual automatic term extraction from comparable corpora. *Language Resources and Evaluation* 54 (2): 385–418. https://doi.org/10.1007/s10579-019-09453-9.
Rigouts Terryn, A., V. Hoste, and E. lefever. 2021. hamlet: hybrid adaptable Machine Learning approach to Extract Terminology. *Terminology. International Journal of Theoretical and Applied Issues in Specialized Communication* 27(2): 40. https://doi.org/10.1075/term.20017.rig.
Rigouts Terryn, A., V. Hoste, and E. Lefever. 2022a. D-terminer: Online demo for monolingual and bilingual automatic term extraction. In *Proceedings of the TERM21 Workshop*, 33–40.
Rigouts Terryn, A., V. Hoste, and E. Lefever. 2022b. Tagging terms in text: A supervised sequential labelling approach to automatic term extraction. *Terminology. International Journal of Theoretical and Applied Issues in Specialized Communication* 28(1). https://doi.org/10.1075/term.21010.rig.
Rocheteau, J., and B. Daille. 2011. TTC termsuite—a UIMA application for multilingual terminology extraction from comparable corpora. In *Proceedings of the IJCNLP 2011 System Demonstrations*, 9–12.
Ruder, S., I. Vulić, and A. Søgaard. 2019. A survey of cross-lingual word embedding models. *Journal of Artificial Intelligence Research* 65: 569–631. https://doi.org/10.1613/jair.1.11640.
Šajatović, A., M. Buljan, J. Šnajder, and B. D. Bašić. 2019. Evaluating automatic term extraction methods on individual documents. In *Proceedings of the Joint Workshop on Multiword Expressions and WordNet (MWE-WN 2019)*, 149–154.
Spasic, I. 2018. Acronyms as an Integral part of multi-word term recognition—a token of appreciation. *IEEE Access* 6: 8351–8363. https://doi.org/10.1109/ACCESS.2018.2807122.
Stefaniak, K. 2022. Machine translation and terminology: the experience of the European commission. In *Proceedings of the International Conference New Trends in Translation and Technology NeTTT 2022*, 134–141.
Temmerman, R. 2000. *Towards New Ways of Terminology Description, The Sociocognitive Approach*, vol. 3. John Benjamins Publishing Company.
Vanroy, B., O. De Clercq, A. Tezcan, J. Daems, and L. Macken. 2021. Metrics of syntactic equivalence to assess translation difficulty. In *Explorations in Empirical Translation Process Research*, ed. M. Carl, vol. 3, 259–294. Springer International Publishing. https://doi.org/10.1007/978-3-030-69777-8_10.
Verplaetse, H., and A. Lambrechts. 2019. Surveying the use of CAT tools, terminology management systems and corpora among professional translators: General state of the art and adoption of corpus support by translator profile. *Parallèles* 31(2): 3–31. https://doi.org/10.17462/para.2019.02.01.
Vintar, S. 2010. Bilingual term recognition revisited. Terminology. *International Journal of Theoretical and Applied Issues in Specialized Communication* 16(2): 141–158.
Zhang, J., and C. Zong. 2016. *Bridging neural machine translation and bilingual dictionaries*. arXiv:1610.07272.
Zhang, Z., J. Petrak, and D. Maynard. 2018. Adapted TextRank for term extraction: a generic method of improving automatic term extraction algorithms. *ACM Transactions on Knowledge Discovery from Data* 12 (5): 1–7.

Els Lefever is associate professor NLP at the LT3 Language and Translation technology team at Ghent University. She has a strong expertise in machine learning of natural language and multilingual NLP, with a special interest for computational semantics, multilingual terminology extraction, emotion and irony detection, and language modelling for low-resourced languages.

Ayla Rigouts Terryn is assistant professor NLP who focuses on cross-lingual and domain-specific NLP research specifically. She investigated translation revision competence at Antwerp University and obtained her Ph.D. at Ghent University on machine learning approaches to automatic term extraction. In 2021, she started as assistant professor at KU Leuven and her research has concentrated on cross-lingual lexico-semantic properties in language models.

Pedagogy and Students' Feedback on Translation Technology

Plain Language in the Age of Neural Machine Translation: An Opportunity for Translators

Lynne Bowker

Abstract Plain language writing and neural machine translation are two trends that are taking hold in the world of professional communication. Often considered independently of one another, these two trends have the potential to produce even better results when combined. This chapter explores the potential of combining plain language and NMT by comparing two types of guidelines—plain language guidelines and guidelines for writing for (machine) translation—and concludes that the two are compatible and can be usefully integrated into a single set of guidelines that can support the production of texts that are both reader- and NMT-friendly. The chapter ends by suggesting that translators are well placed to capitalise on the trends of plain language writing and NMT by incorporating plain language communication into their service offering. To better support the next generation of language professionals, opportunities to develop plain language skills must also be integrated into the translation curriculum.

1 Introduction

At least two broad trends can be observed currently in the world of professional communication. Firstly, the use of translation technologies, and particularly neural machine translation (NMT) is increasing. For instance, among the 866 respondents to the 2017 European Language Industry Survey (ELIS Research 2017), approximately 43% of companies and 33% of individual language professionals claimed to be using machine translation (MT) in their workflow. Six years later, among the 1776 respondents to the 2024 European Language Industry Survey (ELIS Research 2024), over 71% of language service companies and 55% of individual translators claim to have implemented MT. Secondly, the use of plain language is growing in a variety of contexts, including in governmental and administrative texts, but also in some types of legal texts (e.g. contracts) and health texts (e.g. patient information) (Maaß 2020; Stoll et al. 2022). For the most part, these two broad trends are unfolding in parallel,

L. Bowker (✉)
Université Laval, Quebec, QC, Canada
e-mail: lynne.bowker.1@ulaval.ca

Y. Peng et al. (eds.), *New Advances in Translation Technology*, New Frontiers in Translation Studies, https://doi.org/10.1007/978-981-97-2958-6_9

with little discussion about ways in which they could intersect or complement one another. The overall goal of this chapter is to consider how plain language and MT can be used together, and to advocate for the inclusion of plain language in the service offering of practicing translators, as well as in translator education.

This chapter opens with an introduction to MT and considers why the approach of using controlled language, which typically improves translation quality when combined with rule-based MT, is less effective when combined with NMT. Next, we introduce the notion of plain language and explore ways in which this overlaps with techniques aimed at writing for translation and NMT. We then propose that translators are well placed to offer plain language expertise, both as a standalone service and as an intermediary step for improving NMT output. Finally, we reflect on possibilities for incorporating plain language training into translator education, with a particular emphasis on combining plain language and translation technology.

2 Machine Translation

MT research was launched following the release of "Weaver's Memorandum" by American mathematician Warren Weaver (1949). Although many of Weaver's specific suggestions, such as treating language as a problem of cryptography, were not ultimately useful for developing working systems, the memorandum was a catalyst for MT research. For nearly fifty years, researchers focused their efforts on developing what are now known as rule-based machine translation (RBMT) tools (Hutchins and Somers 1992). Essentially RBMT systems employ large bilingual dictionaries and detailed sets of painstakingly programmed grammar rules in an attempt to process language in a way that partially resembles how people process language. However, unlike computers, people can also draw on additional types of information, such as pragmatic information, cultural information, subject-field knowledge and real-world knowledge. Much of the additional information that is useful for helping people to disambiguate texts cannot be programmed into a computer easily. As a result, RBMT systems often produced translations of mediocre quality (Poibeau 2017).

By the turn of the new millennium, however, the technological landscape had changed considerably. Computers were cheaper, smaller, faster, and more powerful. Meanwhile, many people were using word processors to create texts in electronic form, and the Internet and World Wide Web made it easy to share and access these texts. This new situation allowed developers to conceive of a completely different way of approaching MT— one that was not based on linguistics but which instead played to the strengths of computers, such as their ability to pattern match and perform rapid calculations. The new approach to MT was data-driven, and developers began by compiling immense corpora of previously translated texts which were aligned (typically at the sentence level) with their corresponding source texts to create parallel corpora. These translations had been done by professional translators and so they contained many examples of high-quality translation solutions. The data-driven MT systems could consult these examples and use this data to inform decisions about how to translate new texts. Early data-driven approaches included example-based machine translation (EBMT) (Carl and Way 2003) and statistical machine translation (SMT) (Koehn 2010). However, since 2016, the dominant paradigm has been neural machine translation (NMT) (Pérez-Ortiz et al. 2022). NMT systems use artificial neural networks combined with artificial-intelligence-based machine learning techniques. The large parallel corpus acts as a training corpus from which the NMT system learns. Data-driven approaches, and NMT systems in particular, have proven to be more successful than RBMT, producing higher quality translations, although there remains room for improvement.

2.1 MT and Controlled Language

When searching for ways to improve the translation quality of RBMT systems, researchers discovered that restricting the domain of application could be helpful. For instance, researchers working on the TAUM-Météo project found that weather forecasts presented a naturally occurring sublanguage in which there was a limited vocabulary and a restricted syntax (Thouin 1981). However, such naturally occurring sublanguages are relative rare. Therefore, researchers also experimented with deliberately engineering and enforcing a style of writing known as controlled language (Kittredge 2022). Simplified Technical English is an example of a controlled language developed to prepare technical documentation, such as maintenance manuals used in the aviation industry (ASD 2021). A controlled language has a list of authorised terms and authorised grammatical structures. Terms or structures not on the authorised list cannot be used. Controlled language drastically reduces the potential for ambiguity through techniques such as:

- eliminating synonymy (e.g. use "ignore" not "disregard");
- restricting a word-form to having only one part-of-speech (e.g. use "check" only as a noun and not as a verb); and
- forbidding modifier stacks with more than three elements (e.g. say "bolts that attach the transmission housing to the engine" instead of "engine transmission housing attachment bolts").

Since the ambiguity of natural language caused by lexical, syntactic and semantic phenomena (e.g. synonymy, polysemy, homonymy, and homography) poses a major stumbling block for RBMT, tightly controlling the language used in the source text proved to be effective for improving the quality of the translation. Indeed, improving MT quality and thereby reducing overall translation time and cost through the use of MT was a key motivation behind the Xerox company's decision to develop the controlled language known as Multinational Customized English (Ruffino 1982). Xerox reported that the combination of controlled language and RBMT shortened the overall time required for translation by up to five times. Two other well-known controlled languages that were developed primarily to aid translation are Perkins Approved Clear English (Pym 1990) and Caterpillar Technical English (Kamprath et al. 1998). However, while technical documentation may be a good fit for controlled language, not all types of text can be so tightly constrained, and so controlled language is not widely applied to non-technical texts.

Additionally, controlled language may no longer be a good solution—even for technical documentation—now that data-driven NMT is the prevailing approach. For instance, Marzouk and Hansen-Schirra (2019) conducted an experiment where they took a set of source texts and revised those texts by applying controlled language rules. They then used an NMT system to translate both versions (i.e., the original texts and the texts with controlled language rules applied). In Marzouk and Hansen-Schirra's (2019) experiment, the original source texts proved to be more similar to the type of language found in the training corpus. However, once the source texts had been reworked by applying controlled language rules, these revised texts less closely resembled the training corpus content. Recall that a data-driven system learns from the examples contained in the corpus, so that in order for an NMT system to learn how to translate controlled language, there must be many examples of controlled language in the training corpus. Since this highly controlled style of writing is not widely used, it does not feature heavily in many training corpora. Therefore, the machine translations of the original texts were of higher quality than the machine translations of the controlled language versions of those same texts. Marzouk and Hansen-Schirra (2019) therefore conclude that the benefits offered by combining controlled language with RBMT are not present when combining controlled language with NMT. However, a new type of simplified writing is emerging that could be more compatible with NMT: plain language.

3 Plain Language

In plain language writing, the writer tries to simplify the text for the benefit of the reader; however, plain language is less restrictive than controlled language. Unlike controlled language, which includes very specific terms and rules that must be applied, plain language has guidelines, rather than strict rules, and it falls somewhere between standard language and controlled language. In the words of Cutts (2009: ix), plain language is

> … the writing and setting out of essential information in a way that gives a cooperative, motivated person a good chance of understanding it at first reading, and in the same sense that the writer meant it to be understood.

There are a number of different motivations for seeking to provide a text in plain language, all of which focus on improving the reader's experience in some way:

> *Meeting a legal or moral obligation.* The use of plain language can be centred around the reader's right to understand the content. This may include readers who have a lower level of literacy, or who may be accessing the text through a non-dominant language. It may also include readers who have some cognitive impairment, although in some cases plain language is not sufficiently accessible for this target readership, who may instead require the text to be simplified even further into Easy Language (Maaß 2020).

Reaching non-expert audiences. Researchers whose work focuses on specialised topics may nonetheless wish to share their findings with a broader audience. This type of outreach is sometimes referred to as science communication or research communication, and it can include preparing a summary of the research results in plain language. A growing number of academic journals, particularly in the health sciences, now encourage authors to provide a plain language summary alongside a more traditional scientific abstract (Stoll et al. 2022).

Optimising search engines. Organisations with online content may be motivated to use plain language as part of a search engine optimisation strategy. By ensuring that the language used on the website corresponds to the language typically used by the target audience to search for a given topic, an organisation can increase the discoverability of their content and help to drive traffic to their website (Enge et al. 2023).

A motivation that is mentioned less often, but which will undoubtedly gain increasing relevance given the growing prevalence of NMT, is the use of plain language to facilitate interlingual (machine) translation.

Facilitating (machine) translation. Translating a well-written source text is much easier than trying to make sense of a convoluted or poorly constructed text. In other words, the principle of "garbage in, garbage out" (GIGO)—an expression that is used by computer scientists to describe the fact that problematic input data results in nonsense output—applies very well to translation too. Because plain language texts strive for clarity in wording, structure and design, these texts will be easier for both people and NMT systems to translate well. In addition, because plain language is closer to standard language than is controlled language, the plain language texts will more closely resemble the contents of the training corpus, which should lead to a better quality of NMT output. Indeed, as the adoption of plain language continues to grow, there will likely be more and more examples of plain language in training corpora, which will further support high-quality translation of plain language texts (Steigerwald et al. 2022).

As more organisations begin to promote the benefits of writing in plain language, guidelines are emerging that can help writers to choose constructions that are easier for readers to understand, or to avoid those formulations which could cause confusion or lead to misunderstandings. Some plain language guidelines may be tailored to a particular text type or context of use (e.g. legal contracts, patient health information), while others may be more generally applicable to many texts. For instance, as summarised in Stoll et al. (2022), some of the most commonly recommended guidelines for writing plainly in English include:

- use short sentences
- use the active voice
- avoid jargon
- explain abbreviated forms.

It is also important to recognise that the notion of plain language is not tied to a particular language but can be applied to any language. While some guidelines (e.g. use short sentences) may be applicable to many languages, other guidelines may be more language-specific in order to address a particular feature of a given language. For example, the recommendation to avoid long stacks of modifiers is very relevant for English, but less so for French since this type of pre-modification is not common in French. For examples of plain language guidelines developed for languages other than English, see Romanik et al. (2022) and Da Cunha (2022) for examples of guidelines for plain Polish and plain Spanish, respectively.

A related approach that is not described as plain language per se, but which seeks to increase the translatability of texts, is the notion of writing for translation. For instance, Piehl et al. (2019) developed a set of guidelines on writing for translation that is targeted at employees of the bodies of the European Union (EU), whose texts are likely to be translated into at least some of the EU's 24 official languages. Meanwhile, the Translation Centre for the Bodies of the European Union (2021), recognising that NMT is increasingly being used as part of the translation workflow, developed guidelines that focus specifically on writing for MT.

Since both plain language guidelines and writing for (machine) translation guidelines essentially aim to improve the experience for the intended reader, comparing these two types of guidelines is an initial step that can be used to investigate whether plain language is compatible with NMT. In the following section, we analyse some plain language guidelines alongside guidelines for writing for (machine) translation to see whether they overlap or differ.

4 Guidelines for Plain Language and Guidelines for Writing for (Machine) Translation

As noted previously, plain language is used in various settings. In this section, we will focus on the research communication setting as an example and compare the plain language guidelines provided by scholarly publishers to the guidelines for writing for (machine) translation from the EU. First we examine separately the guidelines for (a) preparing plain language summaries, (b) writing for translation, and (c) writing for NMT, before going on to compare these various sets of guidelines to identify areas of convergence and divergence.

4.1 Guidelines for Preparing Plain Language Summaries for Scholarly Journals

Organisations such as UNESCO (2021) and Science Europe (2022) advocate for researchers to share their findings with the broader public. In this context, plain language plays an important role in making specialised content accessible to non-experts. A growing number of scholarly publishers are also beginning to encourage the production of plain language summaries, which they publish alongside the research article. In these cases, the publisher's website often contains some tips or suggestions for how to write a plain language summary; however, these guidelines are often quite general and abstract. For instance, Table 1 presents examples of the guidelines provided by two major publishers of scholarly journals (i.e., two members of the so-called "big five" academic journal publishers):

- **Taylor & Francis**: an international company originating in the United Kingdom that publishes more than 2700 journals across science, technology, engineering, mathematics, medicine, humanities, social science, behavioural science, education and law.
- **SAGE Publishing**: a US-based academic publisher that publishes over one thousand journal titles covering business, humanities, social sciences, science, technology and medicine.

We can see that the guidelines address both content and form. With regard to content, both sets suggest that authors should include information about the motivation for the study, the methods used, the findings, and the impact or relevance of the work. Both sets of guidelines also emphasise the importance of making sure that the plain language summary is objective and factual, rather than speculative or opinion-based. While content-related guidance is important for making the summaries useful for readers, the linguistic guidance will more directly impact the translatability of the text and will therefore be our main focus here.

In terms of form, both sets of guidelines note that a plain language summary is distinct from the scientific abstract and requires a different style of writing. The SAGE guidelines stress the importance of thinking carefully about and understanding the needs of the target audience. Both sets of guidelines impose a maximum length of between 250 and 300 words, and SAGE also recommends using a title that is in plain language and different from the title of the academic article. With regard to specific suggestions that writers can use to create a reader-friendly plain language summary, the following points were common to both sets of guidelines:

- Use short sentences
- Use the active voice
- Avoid jargon (and explain technical terms if you must use them)
- Avoid abbreviated forms.

Some additional recommendations suggested by one of the publishers include:

- Use person-centred language (Taylor & Francis)
- Avoid superlatives (SAGE)
- Avoid metaphors (SAGE)
- Avoid non-essential statistics and use whole numbers (SAGE).

Finally, both sets of guidelines suggest testing the quality of the plain language summary by asking a non-expert reader to read the text and confirm that it is understandable.

Table 1 Guidelines for writing plain language summaries that have been prepared by two major scholarly publishers

Taylor & Francis (https://authorservices.taylorandfrancis.com/publishing-your-research/writing-your-paper/how-to-write-a-plain-language-summary/)	SAGE Publishing (https://us.sagepub.com/en-us/nam/plain-language-summaries)
• The PLS should be included in the manuscript under its own heading ("Plain Language Summary") and placed after the Abstract and before the Introduction. The recommended length for text PLS is 250 words or less • In addition, the PLS should: – Be distinct from the abstract and written in easy-to-understand language rather than complex words – Provide answers to the questions: Why was the study done? What did the researchers do and find? What do the results mean? What is the objective influence on the wider field? – Keep statements factual and avoid providing opinions or speculation on the study's findings and significance. It is of primary importance that the PLS not be misleading – Use the active voice rather than the passive voice (for example, "Dr Smith's team report several improvements" rather than "Several improvements were reported by Dr Smith's team") – Use short, clear sentences and phrase sentences in neutral language, remaining as objective as possible – Use person-centered language rather than focusing on the condition/illness or disability Avoid jargon, complex grammatical structures, or abbreviations. If you need to use a technical term or abbreviation, explain it the first time you use it • Once your PLS is complete (or during the writing process), ask someone who doesn't have any knowledge of the subject to read the PLS and provide feedback. They should find it interesting and be able to understand the study, its conclusions, and the potential impact of the research	• PLS sit after the academic abstract. They consist of a plain language title (~50 words) and a clear summary of the article using non-technical language, making it accessible to a wider network of readers (~300 words) • Plan your PLS – Think carefully about your intended audience Consider why your research should matter to them; what details may need to be expanded so that the reader can understand how your research was carried out, and what the findings mean – It should be balanced and accurate, avoiding speculation, exaggeration, or personal opinions • Convey the message of your research in plain language. Writing a PLS requires a different set of skills than producing a scholarly article – Use short concise sentences – Use simplified terms – Avoid jargon and acronyms – Write in an active voice – Avoid superlatives and metaphors if possible • Present your data – Avoid complicated statistics or non-essential numbers – Use whole numbers, displayed as absolute numbers, percentages, or natural frequencies (e.g. 1 out of 10 people) – Do not expect readers to do any calculations • Check the quality of your PLS – Have a member of your target audience read your PLS and explain it back to you. Use their feedback to ensure your reader will have an accurate understanding of your article

4.2 Guidelines for Writing for Translation and Writing for NMT

Translation is a booming business (e.g. DePalma et al. 2019), but if texts are poorly written, it can be time-consuming and labour-intensive for translators to decipher the intended meaning, and it can also be costly to fix translation errors that arise from these poorly constructed texts (European Commission 2012). For organisations that know in advance that their texts will need to be translated, it makes sense to help authors prepare high quality source texts because clarifying a confusing phrase or correcting a typo or punctuation problem in the original text is quicker and cheaper than tracking down and fixing the problem in dozens of translated versions.

To our knowledge, no scholarly publisher has yet prepared guidelines specifically intended to facilitate (machine) translation. However, such guidelines have been prepared by other organisations where translation is commonplace. For instance, the EU and its various institutions, agencies and bodies make up one community where millions of pages are translated into the 24 official EU languages (European Commission 2023). Given the high volume and large number of language combinations, the EU has been motivated to prepare guidelines to help writers prepare texts that are translation-friendly for both human translators and NMT tools that are integrated into the translation workflow. Table 2 presents two sets of guidelines—one for writing for translation (Piehl et al. 2019) and the other for writing for NMT (Translation Centre 2021)—that have been drafted for use in the EU. In both cases, the guidelines are meant to supplement existing guidance for clear writing by drawing attention to particular linguistic features that may cause problems for translators or NMT systems.

Since the guidelines for writing for NMT are meant to build explicitly on the guidelines for writing for translation, it is not surprising to see relatively little overlap between these two sets of guidelines. Indeed, they have only three points in common, and it is likely that these points have been reiterated in the NMT guidelines because they correspond to some of the most significant hurdles for NMT systems, and so they bear repeating:

- Use terminology consistently
- Avoid abbreviations and acronyms
- Avoid long sentences.

The following items appear only in the set of guidelines on writing for translation, but we can assume that these are also meant to be applied in cases of writing for NMT also since this is indicated in the preamble for the latter set of guidelines:

- Plan your text
- Organise content with informative headings and include only one idea per paragraph
- Show your train of thought by using connectors and linking related sentences
- Make sentence structure unambiguous; avoid using several relative clauses
- Avoid empty verbs, cut excess nouns

Table 2 Guidelines for writing for translation and for machine translation prepared for use within the bodies of the European Union

Writing for translation (Piehl et al. 2019) (https://cdt.europa.eu/en/news/writing-translation)	Writing for NMT (Translation Centre 2021) (https://cdt.europa.eu/en/news/writing-machine-translation)
• Plan your text and limit the content to the necessary information • Emphasize what is important, and organize the content in a clear structure with informative headings. Limit each paragraph to one idea • Show your train of thought by using connectors and linking related sentences • Make sentences structure unambiguous. Avoid using several relative clauses in the same sentence • Avoid long sentences. Use vertical lists for clarity when you need to include several items in a single sentence • Avoid empty verbs and cut out excess nouns. Empty verbs are those which must be supported by a noun to make the action of a sentence clear (e.g. instead of saying "carry out an assessment" say "assess") • Use the active voice wherever possible • Beware of noun strings. In long strings of nouns, it can be difficult to correctly identify the relationships between the different elements (e.g. "efficiency monitoring of material exploitation and the recycling industries") • Use technical terms and expressions consistently. Always use the same term to refer to the same concept • Avoid culture-specific expressions • Avoid jargon; use plain words instead • Avoid abbreviations and acronyms	• When writing for machine translation, it is important to follow the principles of clear writing in general, above all keeping in mind the purpose of the text and the reader. Along with these more general guidelines, there are some specific points that relate to writing for NMT • Decide on your terminology and use it consistently throughout the text. Using synonyms can confuse the NMT system and result in different translations of the same concept, which can be wrong or too general • Use pronouns sparingly. For clarity, it may be better to repeat a noun rather than using a pronoun. In languages that have grammatical gender, the NMT system may generate a pronoun with the wrong gender, making it unclear what is being referred to • Avoid abbreviations and acronyms. NMT systems struggle to deal with shortened forms and they may be translated incorrectly • Make sure that sentences are neither too long (more than 60 words) nor to short (fewer than 7 words) – Sentences that are very long are usually complex and it is challenging for NMT systems to understand how different parts of the sentence relate to one another. Convey one idea per sentence to avoid confusion – Sentences that are very short offer little or no context and may not be understood correctly by NMT systems • Avoid unnecessary line breaks (returns). NMT systems will treat the elements on either side of a line break separately, even if they are meant to go together as part of the same phrase or unit of meaning • Punctuate properly. NMT engines rely on punctuation to get clues about meaning, so it is important to punctuate the text accurately • Avoid writing whole sentences in upper case (i.e. capital letters) • Use words instead of special symbols (e.g. use "and" instead of "&")

- Beware of noun strings
- Avoid culture specific expressions.

Finally, the following items feature exclusively on the writing for NMT list. These items do not appear elsewhere because they are unlikely to pose problems for human readers/translators, but they can trip up NMT systems.

- **Use pronouns sparingly**. NMT systems process one sentence at a time and cannot easily identify the antecedent of a pronoun that appears elsewhere in a text.
- **Avoid using very short sentences**. While most guidelines for clear writing advise writers to avoid using long sentences, NMT systems can also encounter problems when the sentence is too short (e.g. under seven words). Very concise sentences may omit optional items such as relative pronouns or other clues that could help to clarify the relationship between different elements in the sentence.
- **Avoid writing in all capital letters**. People may use all capitals to emphasise a particular section of text, but computers do not understand text the way that people do, so emphasis is not relevant to the way that they process the text. However, the use of a capital letter to indicate the start of a sentence or a proper noun could be helpful to a computer (e.g. to distinguish between the proper noun *Polish* and the common noun *polish*), but it would be obscured if a sentence is written in all capitals. While people also use capital letters to signal that a word is at the start of a sentence or is referring to a proper noun, they can also use other knowledge to arrive at these conclusions in cases where all capitals are used.
- **Avoid special symbols**. Some special symbols may not be part of the character set of another language, so when possible, use a word rather than a symbol (e.g. use "and" instead of "&").
- **Punctuate properly**. While proper punctuation is helpful to readers, it is even more critical for NMT systems, who cannot rely on real-world or other knowledge to determine the intended meaning. For example, an NMT system might come up with a different translation for "a small business owner" (a business owner who is small) versus "a small-business owner" (the owner of a small business), whereas a human reader would most likely be able to determine the correct meaning based on the broader context, even if the sentence was not punctuated properly.

Finally, there is just one case where a guideline for writing for translation conflicts with a guideline for writing for NMT. The writing for translation guidelines advise authors to use vertical lists (e.g. bulleted lists) rather than presenting lists horizontally in the running text. However, the writing for NMT guidelines note that authors should avoid unnecessary line breaks because machine translation systems do not recognise material on a new line as being part of a larger unit.

4.3 Comparing the Two Types of Guidelines

Section 4.1 compared two sets of scholarly publisher's guidelines for writing plain language summaries, while Sect. 4.2 compared the EU's guidelines for writing for translation with those for writing for NMT. Let us now consider whether these two types of guidelines are compatible and whether they can be integrated to create single set of guidelines that could result in plain language summaries that are both reader-friendly and NMT-friendly.

First, we must recognise that different publishers will likely produce slightly different sets of guidelines, as we have already seen in Table 1. For instance, one publisher recommends minimising statistics, while the other encourage the use of person-centred language. Such decisions may be linked to the type of subject fields covered, or to wider editorial policies that go beyond the plain language summaries. The important thing to note for the present discussion is that none of the specific recommendations in the plain language summary guidelines that were examined would introduce obstacles for NMT. Therefore, in this section, we will focus on identifying recommendations that could make the existing plain language summary guidelines more NMT-friendly.

Our first recommendation is to expand the preamble about taking the needs of the intended audience into consideration. None of the guidelines from the scholarly publishers explicitly comment on what the reader's needs might be, but given that English is the dominant language in scholarly publication, even though most of the world's citizens speak other languages, it seems likely that many people will interact with the plain language summary either through an additional language or via (machine) translation. Therefore, it could help to specify in the preamble that readers may intend to translate the plain language summary into another language with the help of NMT. An explicit statement could make authors more aware of the benefits of writing in an NMT-friendly way. Table 3 shows the original preamble taken from the SAGE website on the left, along with our suggested modification on the right.

In addition, we recommend increasing the maximum word count for plain language summaries. Both sets of publisher's guidelines set a maximum length for the summary at between 250 and 300 words, which is similar to the length of traditional scientific abstracts. However, both the plain language guidelines and the writing for NMT guidelines recommend that authors explain specialised concepts/terms and disambiguate opaque linguistic constructions such as long noun strings. Such explanations and disambiguation require space. When authors must adhere to a low word count, they may choose constructions that are concise rather than clear. Sacrificing clarity for brevity goes against the principles of writing plain and translatable language, so we recommend extending the length of plain language summaries to 500 words to give authors the space to write in way that is friendly to both readers and NMT systems.

Table 3 The current preamble about the purpose of plain language summaries from SAGE (left) and the proposed expansion (underlined text) to include a reference to translatability

Original preamble about writing plain language summaries from the SAGE Publishing website (https://us.sagepub.com/en-us/nam/plain-language-summaries)	Expanded preamble to include specific mention of the increased translatability of plain language summaries
In recent years, there have been calls to make scholarly articles more accessible to non-specialist audiences. Research has always helped shape the public realm, empowering people across all sectors of society to make informed decisions. Academic or topic-specific jargon can hinder the general understanding and impact of such publications, which is where Plain Language Summaries (PLS) or Plain Language Summaries of Publications (PLS-P) can be very helpful	In recent years, there have been calls to make scholarly articles more accessible to non-specialist audiences. Research has always helped shape the public realm, empowering people across all sectors of society to make informed decisions. Academic or topic-specific jargon can hinder the general understanding and impact of such publications, which is where Plain Language Summaries (PLS) or Plain Language Summaries of Publications (PLS-P) can be very helpful. In addition, plain language can also increase the translatability of your summary, making it easier for speakers of other languages to engage with your work with the help of automatic translation tools

Our third recommendation is to expand this list of tips for writing plain language summaries to include items from the writing for NMT guidelines. A preliminary integrated list of guidelines (for English) could read as follows:

- Avoid jargon. If you must use technical terms, explain them and then use them consistently.
- Avoid acronyms and abbreviated forms.
- Use the active voice.
- Avoid very long sentences (e.g. more than 50 words) and very short sentences (e.g. fewer than 7 words). Sentences that are too long or too short are difficult for readers and NMT systems to process.
- Break up strings of three or more nouns (e.g. instead of "sensitive protein function monitoring system", use "a sensitive system that monitors protein function").
- Use pronouns sparingly. NMT systems process one sentence at a time and may not be able to identify the noun that the pronouns is replacing. This is particularly problematic in languages that have grammatical gender. Where possible, repeat nouns instead of using pronouns.
- Avoid writing in all capital letters. NMT systems use case to help disambiguate text.
- Avoid special symbols and use words instead (e.g. use "and" not "&"). Some special symbols may not be part of the character set of another language and could be mishandled by NMT systems.
- Avoid culture-specific idiomatic expressions.
- Avoid unnecessary line breaks.
- Punctuate the text properly. NMT tools use punctuation to disambiguate the text.

5 Incorporating Plain Language into Translation Service Offerings

The guidelines found on the scholarly publishers' websites aim to support researchers to write plain language summaries of their own work. However, as noted previously, many publishers currently indicate that plain language summaries are optional, rather than required. Unfortunately, as observed in Bowker (2023), the uptake of this option appears to be quite low at present, with relatively few authors choosing to add a plain language summary to their work. There could be several possible reasons for this low uptake. For instance, the guidelines are not currently very detailed or very concrete and may not be easy to follow for people who are not trained to write in this way, especially in an additional language. Moreover, some of the linguistic terminology used in the guidelines may not be immediately familiar to researchers (e.g. modifier stacks, active voice). As Maaß (2020) points out, writing in plain language is a skill that must be developed and honed. In addition, some researchers may feel that preparing a plain language summary is not the best use of their time, but they may be willing to outsource this task to someone better able to execute it. Indeed, some third party services are already beginning to emerge to fill this space, such as Kudos (https://www.growkudos.com/), a platform for science communication. Meanwhile, some scholarly publishers already offer language-related services, such as editing or translation, and it is possible that plain language writing could be a future service offering. As a market poised for growth—not only in the scholarly publishing sector, but also more broadly—plain language writing could be a valuable skill for translators to incorporate into their own service offering.

Translators are no strangers to adapting to changing realities and markets. Following the widespread adoption of desktop computers and the World Wide Web, some translators added software and website localisation skills to their repertoire. Once data-driven MT systems were capable of generating reasonable quality draft translations, some translators began to offer post-editing services. Indeed, Briva-Iglesias and O'Brien (2022) argue that translators have adapted and expanded their service offering to such a degree over the years that the term "translator" does not sufficiently represent the variety of activities involved in the profession today, and they note that traditional translation tasks are not the only possible job opportunities in the language services sector. Indeed Briva-Iglesias and O'Brien (2022: 41) emphasise that the profile of someone with a degree in translation includes transversal competences and skills that can enable a "traditional translator" to also become a "language engineer" and to offer added value in the global value chain of the automation age. This is echoed by Stasimioti (2023), who observes that in the current job market, employers are actively seeking to hire tech-savvy linguists.

While Briva-Iglesias and O'Brien (2022) do not explicitly include plain language writing or editing in their discussion, we have endeavoured in this chapter to highlight the benefits to be gained by combining plain language skills and NMT. The need for plain language is growing, and will likely increase even further as more governments begin to legislate a requirement for plain language communication in texts aimed at regular citizens (e.g. McClure 2022). However, writing in simplified language—whether plain, controlled or easy language—is not simple. Unfortunately, as pointed out by Maaß (2020), the terminology itself does not help, since terms such as *plain* and *easy* give the impression that anyone can do it. In reality, it requires both training and practice to become a proficient writer in these simplified languages, although it will be more straightforward to obtain a level of proficiency in plain language than in either a controlled or easy language, which are more restrictive.

The investment required to learn to write in a controlled language or easy language will pay off if a translator aims to develop a sub-specialisation in this type of writing. However, there is likely to be a higher return on investment for almost any translator who takes the time to polish their plain language skills. In part, this is because, as noted previously, there is already some overlap between plain language guidelines and what might simply be considered good writing skills (which a translator has already developed). As we have already emphasised, the demand for plain language is increasing, so a versatile translator can extend their service offering by incorporating plain language writing. In addition, savvy translators could also market a related service—one where they revise a client's initial source text in order to turn it into a plain language text (a sort of intralingual translation), so that it can be translated more efficiently. While this two-step process might at first glance appear to be more cumbersome, it brings some advantages. First, it ensures that the texts destined for both source- and target-language audiences are reader friendly. Second, in cases where the client intends to have the source text translated into multiple target languages, producing a plain language version first can save both time and money since removing any ambiguities from the source text just once is likely to be much quicker and cheaper than correcting any resulting problems in multiple target texts.

6 Incorporating Plain Language Training into Translator Education

To better prepare translators to be able to add plain language skills to their service offering, plain language training can be incorporated into translation education programs. Currently, translator competence frameworks such as the European Master's in Translation Competence Framework (EMT 2022) do not explicitly identify plain language skills as a necessary skill, although they emphasise the need for students to learn relevant writing and editing skills more broadly, including being able to implement relevant style guides or conventions, and being able to summarise, rephrase, restructure or shorten a message and adapt it to market needs. In addition, the EMT framework emphasises that students should know how to identify and adapt to new societal and language industry demands, new market requirements and emerging job profiles—a point that is echoed by Briva-Iglesias and O'Brien (2022: 41–42), who state

> the solution lies in training for sectors with growing relevance for the future (and, as we have seen, already in the present) that have technology as the backbone and where the human factor is essential… [and] … where we must keep up with the pace and rhythm of the market, to train new language engineers and give them the knowledge and skills that will enable them to stand out in the market, add to the value chain and work in a sustainable way in a sector that will be increasingly marked by automation and technology. Though suggesting new types of training is beyond the scope of this paper, training programs will certainly need to be looked at in the near future.

In this spirit, we believe that plain language training, including the explicit connection between plain language and NMT, could be a valuable addition to the curriculum in translator education programs. There are several options for integrating this content. For instance, many translation programs already include courses on writing, editing or revision, and such courses could be a good place to introduce both plain language guidelines and guidelines for writing for NMT, and to provide students with exercises to practice producing reader- and translation-friendly texts.

As noted previously, the concept of plain language can be applied to any language, so translators will need to familiarise themselves with the style of plain language in all of their working languages. While some plain language guidelines may be widely applicable, others may be language-specific. Since translators may be hired to translate a plain language source text into a plain language target text, students will benefit from the inclusion of plain language texts as one genre to be worked with in practical translation courses. Indeed, some exercises could combine intra- and interlingual translation by asking students to begin with a source text written in standard language and to convert it into a plain language text before translating it into the target language.

Finally, because plain language can be combined with translation technologies, there is also an opportunity to address relevant plain language skills in technology courses. For instance, students can learn about tools such as plain language checkers (e.g. Hemingway, https://hemingwayapp.com/), which offer feedback about ways to simplify texts. In addition, students can experiment with pre-editing and compare the machine-translated versions of standard texts with the machine-translated versions of plain language texts. By comparing the translations of standard and plain language texts, students can learn to identify constructions that pose stumbling blocks for NMT systems, and can avoid these constructions in future writing.

7 Concluding Remarks

The use of both plain language and of NMT is increasing, and this chapter has considered the benefits of combining these two approaches. Using the example of plain language writing guidelines provided by scholarly publishers and comparing these to guidelines prepared by the EU for writing for (machine) translation, we demonstrate that the two approaches appear to be compatible. We posit that combining the two types of guidelines into a single integrated set could help writers to produce texts that are both reader- and NMT-friendly. However, we note that authors who do not have training or experience writing in plain language may not be comfortable, motivated or well placed to produce plain language texts. In contrast, translators are very well positioned to add plain language writing and writing for NMT to their service offering, but to set up the next generation of language professionals for success, these skills should also be integrated into translator education programs. As underscored by Briva-Iglesias and O'Brien (2022), translation technology is here to stay, and language professionals are faced with three options: resistance, collaboration, or reinvention. Resistance will be a losing battle, whereas collaboration and reinvention hold potential for a brighter future. Incorporating plain language writing skills and writing for NMT into a translator's toolbox are promising forms of reinvention and human–computer collaboration.

References

Aerospace, Security and Defence Industries Association of Europe (ASD). 2021. *ASD simplified technical english specification, ASD-STE100*, Issue 8. https://asd-ste100.org/.

Bowker, L. 2023. Combining plain language and machine translation for science communication. In *Proceedings of the 10th Language Technology Conference*, 21–23 Apr 2023, Poznań, Poland.

Briva-Iglesias, V., and S. O'Brien. 2022. The language engineer: A transversal, emerging role for the automation age. *Quaderns de Filologia: Estudis Lingüístics* XXVII: 17–48.

Carl, M., and A. Way, eds. 2003. *Recent advances in example-based machine translation*. Dordrecht: Springer.

Cutts, M. 2009. *Oxford guide to plain english*, 3rd ed. Oxford: Oxford University Press.

Da Cunha, I., ed. 2022. *Lenguaje claro y tecnología en la administración*. Editorial Comares: Granada.

DePalma, D., H. Pielmeier, and P. D. O'Mara. 2019. The language services market: 2019. https://insights.csa-research.com/reportaction/305013045/Marketing.

Enge, E., S. Spencer, and J.C. Stricchiola. 2023. *The art of SEO: Mastering search engine optimization*, 4th ed. Sebastopol, CA: O'Reilly Media Inc.

ELIS Research. 2017. 2017 language industry survey: Expectations and concerns of the European language industry. https://elis-survey.org/.

ELIS Research. 2024. European language industry survey 2024. https://elis-survey.org/.

EMT Board and Competence Task Force. 2022. European Master's in Translation competence framework 2022. https://commission.europa.eu/news/updated-version-emt-competence-framework-now-available-2022-10-21_en.

European Commission. 2012. *Quantifying quality costs and the cost of poor quality in translation*. Luxembourg: Publications Office of the European Union.

European Commission. 2023. 2022 in figures. https://cdt.europa.eu/en/news/2022-figures

Hutchins, W.J., and H.L. Somers. 1992. *An introduction to machine translation*. London: Academic Press Ltd.

Kamprath, C., E. Adolphson, T. Mitamura, and E. Nyberg. 1998. Controlled language for multilingual document production: Experience with Caterpillar technical English. In: *CLAW '98: Proceedings of the Second International Workshop on Controlled Language Applications*, Carnegie Mellon University, Pittsburgh, May 21–22. https://aclanthology.org/www.mt-archive.info/90/CLAW-1998-Kamprath.pdf.

Kittredge, R. 2022. Sublanguages and controlled languages. In *The oxford handbook of computational linguistics*, 2nd ed., ed. R. Mitkov, 454–472. Oxford: Oxford University Press.

Koehn, P. 2010. *Statistical machine translation.* Cambridge: Cambridge University Press.
Marzouk, S., and S. Hansen-Schirra. 2019. Evaluation of the impact of controlled language on neural machine translation compared to other architectures. *Machine Translation* 33: 179–203.
Maaß, C. 2020. *Easy language—plain language—easy language plus.* Berlin: Frank & Timme.
McClure, T. 2022. New Zealand passes plain language bill to jettison jargon. *The Guardian*, Oct 20. https://www.theguardian.com/world/2022/oct/20/new-zealand-passes-plain-language-bill-to-jettison-jargon.
Pérez-Ortiz, J.A., M.L. Forcada, and F. Sánchez-Martínez. 2022. How neural machine translation works. In *Machine translation for everyone*, ed. D. Kenny, 141–164. Berlin: Language Science Press.
Piehl, A., I. Vihonen, and B. Ehrenberg-Sundin. 2019. Writing for translation. Translation Centre of the Bodies of the European Union, Luxembourg. https://cdt.europa.eu/en/news/writing-translation.
Poibeau, T. 2017. *Machine translation.* Cambridge: The MIT Press.
Pym, P. J. 1990. Pre-editing and the use of simplified writing for MT: An engineer's experience of operating an MT system. In *Proceedings of Translating and the Computer 10: The Translation Environment 10 Years on*, ed. P. Mayorcas, Aslib, London, 80–96. https://aclanthology.org/1988.tc-1.11/.
Romanik, W., T. Piekot, and R. Tymiński. 2022. Adaptation of informed consent for anaesthesia to plain language standard. *NOWOTWORY Journal Oncology* 72: 265–273.
Ruffino, J.R. 1982. Coping with machine translation. In *Practical experience of machine translation*, ed. V. Lawson, 57–60. Amsterdam: North-Holland Publishing Company.
Science Europe. 2022. Position statement: Science communication for greater research impact. *Science Europe.* https://doi.org/10.5281/zenodo.6645074.
Stasimioti, M. 2023. Everyone wants to hire tech-savvy linguists. Slator, Mar 23. https://slator.com/everyone-wants-to-hire-tech-savvy-linguists/.
Steigerwald, E., V. Ramírez-Castañeda, D.Y.C. Brandt, A. Báldi, J.T. Shapiro, L. Bowker, and R.D. Tarvin. 2022. Overcoming language barriers in academia: Machine translation tools and a vision for a multilingual future. *BioScience* 72 (10): 988–998. https://doi.org/10.1093/biosci/biac062.
Stoll, M., M. Kerwer, K. Lieb, and A. Chasiotis. 2022. Plain language summaries: A systematic review of theory, guidelines and empirical research. *PLoS ONE.* https://doi.org/10.1371/journal.pone.0268789.
Thouin, B. 1981. The Meteo system. In *Translating and the computer: Practical experience of machine translation*, ed. V. Lawson, 39–44. London: Aslib.
Translation Centre for the Bodies of the European Union. 2021. Writing for machine translation. Translation Centre of the Bodies of the European Union, Luxembourg. https://cdt.europa.eu/en/news/writing-machine-translation.
UNESCO. 2021. Recommendation on open science. UNESCO. https://en.unesco.org/science-sustainable-future/open-science/recommendation.
Weaver, W. 1949. Weaver's memorandum. https://aclanthology.org/1952.earlymt-1.1.pdf.

Lynne Bowker is Full Professor and Canada Research Chair in Translation, Technologies, and Society at the Université Laval. In 2022–2023, she was a NAWA-funded visiting researcher at the Adam Mickiewicz University in Poland working on research at the intersection of plain language and machine translation.

Acquiring Artificial Intelligence (AI) Terminology in the Specialised Translation Class: A Gamified Strategy

Gloria Corpas Pastor and Marta Alcaide-Martínez

Abstract Nowadays, the field of artificial intelligence (AI) is experiencing unprecedented growth in almost all aspects of modern life (e.g., entertainment, e-commerce, marketing, education, fraud prevention, facial recognition, navigation, voice assistants, and chatbots). Even if we are not yet fully aware of its potential or wealth, AI is already present in our daily lives. As a result, we are witnessing the exponential growth and demand for quality translations in the AI domain worldwide. This chapter presents a novel technology-assisted methodology to train university translation students. We advance a corpus-based gamification approach to enhance students' acquisition of domain-specific AI terminology in line with the requirements of the current and future labour market. In order to assess the impact of our technologised approach, a pilot study has been conducted with undergraduates of the Bachelor's Degree in Translation and Interpreting offered by the University of Malaga (Spain). Our main goal is to ascertain the benefits (and possible drawbacks) of introducing a protocolised gamification methodology in the specialised translation classroom. To the best of our knowledge, this is one of the first empirical studies focusing on gamification applied to the acquisition of AI-specific terminology for translators.

1 Introduction

Nowadays, the field of artificial intelligence (AI) is experiencing unprecedented growth in almost all aspects of modern life (e.g., entertainment, e-commerce, marketing, education, fraud prevention, facial recognition, navigation, voice assistants, and chatbots). Even if we are not yet fully aware of its potential or wealth, AI is already present in our daily lives. Core to all AI-enhanced applications are algorithms and neural networks designed to mimic human intelligence. In fact, notions

G. Corpas Pastor (✉) · M. Alcaide-Martínez
IUITLM, University of Malaga, Malaga, Spain
e-mail: gcorpas@uma.es

M. Alcaide-Martínez
e-mail: marta-alcaide@uma.es

Y. Peng et al. (eds.), *New Advances in Translation Technology*, New Frontiers in Translation Studies, https://doi.org/10.1007/978-981-97-2958-6_10

like "intelligence", "consciousness", "knowledge", "representations", and "learning" lie at the heart of AI's recent (and variegated) developments.

These and other common terms (e.g., *agent, blackboard, environment,* and *hallucination*) have acquired novel uses within this specialised domain, i.e., more specific senses that reflect, in a way, a fresh look at such complex phenomena from an interdisciplinary AI-based perspective (cf. Yang et al. 2019; Zhuang et al. 2020). At the same time, new AI concepts arise which require neological term-building formation patterns (e.g., *affective computing*, *chatbot*, *hyperparameter*, and *transformer model*), which is one of the main challenges of specialised translation. Against this backdrop, translation students and professionals need to keep abreast of how AI is constantly changing our world, and how all these processes, concepts, techniques, and applications are conventionally "named".

One of the main goals of AI is to improve the lives of humans by helping them to perform increasingly complex tasks, from innocuous facial recognition for smartphones to drug side-effect prediction or bomb disposal. Thus, the demand for the translation of documents on AI rises every day, which also reflects the rapid expansion and growth of this domain worldwide.

Translating texts on AI[1] is not a simple task. Documents pertaining to this domain not only present the usual problems of specialised translation (see Fiola 2013; Postolea 2016; Ghențulescu 2017; Baker 2018), but also reflect the terminological idiosyncrasies of this burgeoning field. This entails that the language and terminology employed are in a constant state of flux, so translators need to keep up to date and invest time in the documentation phase (Puaschunder 2019). Since terminology is deemed to be a cornerstone in the realm of specialised translation (Faber Benítez 2009; Rogers 2015), a substantial amount of expert knowledge in AI is needed in order to ensure the provision of high-quality translations.

The interdependence between terminology and translation is crucial, given that the quality of a specialised translation hinges on the translator's mastery of the domain-specific terminology.[2] This study explores the potential of gamification for the teaching of specialised translation, with special reference to fast-developing domains such as AI and its applications. Although there is some previous work on gamification and translation (cf. Gutiérrez-Artacho and Olvera-Lobo 2016; Chen 2019; Alcalde Peñalver and Santamaría Urbieta 2020; Alcaide-Martínez and Taillefer 2022; Meyers 2022, among others), very few studies (Soyoof et al. 2022; Octaberlina

[1] For the purposes of this paper, we will conceive AI as the set of algorithms and systems that enable machines and programs to mimic human intelligence, i.e., to be able to learn autonomously from their environment in order to react and act accordingly (Yang et al. 2019; Aggarwal et al. 2022). Pinpointing the exact origin of the term *artificial intelligence* (AI) is not easy, as there were several approaches to the concept before it was officially coined (cf. Grewal 2014; Haenlein and Kaplan 2019). The first definition of AI was provided by John McCarthy, who defined it as "the science and engineering of making intelligent machines, especially intelligent computer programs" (McCarthy 2007, p. 2).

[2] As domain-specific terminology constitutes a core part of the translator's and interpreter's expertise, a myriad of tools has been advanced to enhance its teaching, learning, extraction, acquisition, and storage in long-term memory (Steurs et al. 2015).

2023) have actually targeted the application of gamification for the acquisition of domain-specific terminology.

We argue that gamification is an active methodology that can be effectively applied in the learning-teaching process with a view to engaging students in dynamic, entertaining, and innovative ways to acquire and translate specialised terminology. Thus, we propose a novel technology-assisted methodology that uses a corpus and a set of gamified activities (GAs) to facilitate the learning of domain-specific terminology among undergraduate students of Translation and Interpreting.

The rest of this paper is organised as follows. Section 2 provides a brief overview of gamification and presents our protocol to create the set of GAs. Section 3 describes an experiment conducted in order to test the effectiveness of GAs for specialised translation and, more specifically, for the acquisition and translation of domain-specific AI terminology. Section 4 outlines our conclusions and future research avenues. Following the conclusions, we include a section comprising bibliographic references that underpin our research, as well as a section of Appendices housing the Pre-task and Post-task questionnaire.

To the best of our knowledge, this is one of the first studies to apply corpus-based gamification to the translation of domain-specific texts on AI, with a view to facilitating learning and enhancing the performance of undergraduate students of specialised translation.

2 Creating Gamified Activities for Specialised Translation

In this section, we present gamification as a technological tool for engaging student learning in the specialised translation classroom. We followed a techno-didactic approach based on corpora and aimed at easing the learning of domain-specific terminology in the fledgling and specialised field of AI. First, the basic notions of gamification as a teaching methodology are introduced. Then, a corpus-based protocol to create the four GAs is presented.

2.1 Gamification and Game-Like Elements

Gamification can be defined as the method of introducing game design elements and principles to non-game settings with the intention of boosting user motivation and engagement (Deterding et al. 2011a, b). However, it is relevant to remark that gamification is not limited to the application of gamification platforms such as Kahoot!, and games or game-like elements such as prizes, points, or levels. Analogously, Werbach and Hunter (2012) underline that gamification does not just consist of designing games, but of using game elements to augment users' experiences and reach targeted goals. It also involves the thorough consideration and implementation of behavioural and psychological theories, along with the analysis of user data and opinions, as reported by Deterding et al. (2011a, b). Hence, a fuller comprehension of gamification demands on a multidisciplinary approach that integrates analysis of data, psychology, and game design elements (Hamari et al. 2014).

The game elements that constitute a fundamental part of gamification as an active methodology and of any gamified experience can be broadly classified into three distinct categories: dynamics, mechanics, and components. To provide illustrations of the constituent elements that comprise each of these categories, we direct attention to the pyramid diagram devised by Alcaide-Martínez and Taillefer (2022, p. 286). In this pyramid (see Fig. 1), the elements are organised in descending order from the most general and non-tangible (emotions, narrative, peer relationships, etc.) to the specific props that are part of the gamified system (avatars, badges, levels, etc.). Each of the dynamics, mechanics, and components has a different function and impact on the gamified system and its users. For this reason, it is crucial to incorporate the appropriate elements according to the objectives to be achieved and the profile of the participants. While an element such as the leaderboard could perhaps be very motivating for a group of students, it could have the opposite effect on industry professionals, or vice versa. Thus, knowing the potential users of your gamification design will make it more effective (Kapp 2012).

Gamification has gained significant traction across diverse fields, including education, economics, business, and tourism. The adoption of gamification may lead to certain drawbacks, such as heightened competitiveness, a shift in focus from the task matter, and challenges regarding design, but the benefits of its employment are plentiful and can surpass the drawbacks if applied with care, adding adequate elements and keeping in mind the objectives and characteristics of the intended users. Some of these benefits are increased motivation and participation, higher productivity, improved social interactions, entertaining learning stored in long-term memory, enhanced problem-solving skills, reduced stress when tackling a demanding task,

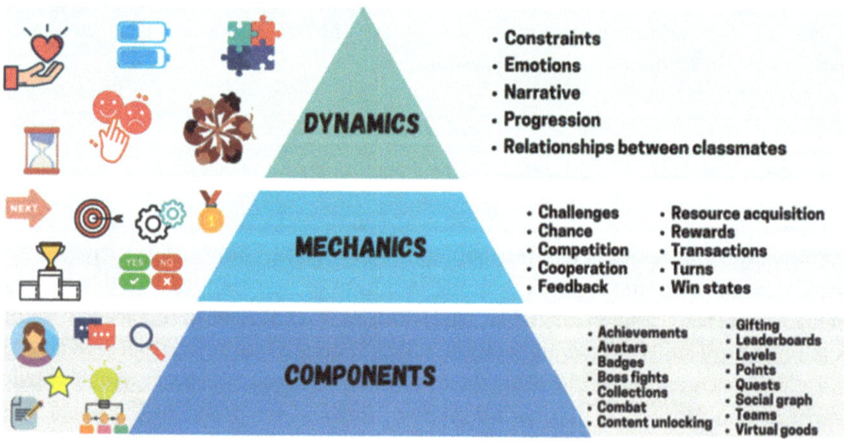

Fig. 1 Pyramid diagram of gamification elements (*Source* Alcaide-Martínez and Taillefer 2022, p. 286)

and so forth (Hamari et al. 2014; Marín et al. 2015). Despite the potential advantages of gamification in the area of translation, there is scarce academic research that examines this topic. Just a few studies have been conducted to investigate the connection between gamification and translation, such as the papers mentioned in the Introduction.

2.2 *A Two-Step Protocol*

We have devised a corpus-based protocol to create GAs for the specialised translation of AI texts. It draws on corpus linguistics as a convenient way to acquire terminology and domain knowledge in the field of AI. Corpora are widely used in translation to fine-tune the expert knowledge necessary when rendering specialised texts from the source to the target language (see Corpas Pastor 2008; Corpas Pastor and Seghiri Domínguez 2016). Our protocol comprises two phases: (i) compilation of a specialised corpus on the subject of AI (AI-Cor corpus) and extraction of contextualised and non-contextualised terminology (AI-seeds) in Sketch Engine, and (ii) design of four GAs for the specialised translation class.

2.2.1 Compilation of a Specialised Corpus and AI-Seeds Extraction on Artificial Intelligence

With the aim of developing our technological gamified didactic proposal based on corpora for translation practice, we have used Sketch Engine to compile an ad hoc monolingual corpus on AI (AI-Cor corpus)[3] composed only of documents written in English. According to Corpas Pastor (2004), an ad hoc corpus is a virtual corpus distinguished by the quality and appropriateness of the texts. The quantity of constituent texts is thus not a determining factor, so its compilation is relatively fast. Such corpora are usually compiled for a specific purpose or assignment in any direction and are very helpful for translators and interpreters. The decision to create a specialised monolingual corpus for the scope of this chapter stems from the fact that it is a strongly recommended option for domain-specific terminology extraction for translators, as it represents a very reliable source of information which can be exploited in a variety of ways, thanks to corpus management tools such as Sketch Engine (Varela Vila 2009). Thus, we have compiled our specialised corpus following the collection criteria outlined by Varela Vila (2009), as specified below.

- Size: Our corpus encompasses 52 documents. Other relevant statistics are tokens (573,360), words (429,909), and sentences (21,502). The corpus is not particularly large, but it is sufficiently representative for the purpose of this chapter.

[3] AI-Cor corpus, available on Sketch Engine <https://app.sketchengine.eu/#dashboard?corpname=user%2FMartaAlcaide%2Fai_cor>.

- Expertise degree: This is a highly specialised corpus formed by research papers retrieved from Google Scholar in PDF format. These articles are published by prestigious publishers such as Elsevier and Springer, and indexed in renowned databases, e.g., Scopus and Dialnet. All these factors, combined with the subject matter of the selected research, ensure a high level of specialisation and accuracy.
- Subject matter: The subject of our specialised corpus is AI, an emerging specialised domain. The selected texts examine AI, its applications, and its impacts on different sectors (medicine, economics, education, tourism, etc.). Domain-specific terminology in this area of expertise can be found in all texts.
- Publication date: The agreed date range for the inclusion of a text in our corpus was 2015–2023. We have collected texts from the last eight years, making it a current and recent corpus. We have decided not to add texts published before 2015 in order to accurately reflect the current state of this specialised language.
- Language: All the constituent documents of our corpus are written in English. In their selection, we have not restricted the author's place of origin to English-speaking countries. In order to better prepare students and professionals in the field of translation, we consider it necessary for them to be acquainted with different varieties of English, so our corpus comprises papers written by authors from Italy, Malaysia, France, Hong Kong, Taiwan, the UK, the USA, India, Germany, Russia, Japan, and New Zealand, to name but a few.
- Genre: The compiled corpus is made up of specialised scientific articles analysing and describing AI, its uses, applications, and consequences in a variety of disciplines.

Through Sketch Engine, it was possible to compile our corpus with the listed criteria very easily and quickly by following three simple steps: (1) description of the corpus (name, monolingual or multilingual, language(s) of the texts, and brief description); (2) uploading of 52 PDF documents obtained from Google Scholar; and (3) automatic corpus creation.

For the exploitation and the extraction of AI-seeds contextualised in sentences and paragraphs, we also used Sketch Engine. Three main functions, accessible from the dashboard, were employed for the retrieval of domain-specific terminology from the AI-Cor corpus, namely the following: "Keywords. Terminology extraction", "Wordlist. Frequency list", and "Concordance. Examples of use in context".

From the generated lists, we manually selected the single-word and multi-word terms (*chatbot*, *algorithm*, *deep learning*, *deep neural networks*, etc.) that we deemed to be the most significant and essential within the domain of AI for translation practice in the classroom. This selection process was primarily based on the review of two glossaries: *Glossary of human-centric artificial intelligence* by Estévez Almenzar et al. (2022) published by the Publications Office of the European Union and the glossary on artificial intelligence of the Council of Europe.[4]

[4] Glossary on artificial intelligence, online <https://www.coe.int/en/web/artificial-intelligence/glossary>.

2.2.2 Design and Development of Gamified Activities

We have created a set of GAs through selected AI-seed words (raw and contextualised in sentences and paragraphs extracted from our AI-Cor corpus) and specific parameters (concrete platforms, and dynamics, mechanics, and components of gamification) which are particularly suitable for our research purposes.

In particular, four AI-seeds-based GAs were developed on three different technological platforms, because each platform provides different functionalities and this contributes to a higher degree of engagement. As a way of illustration, the study conducted by Chaiyo and Nokham (2017) exemplifies how different platforms elicit varying levels of motivation, concentration, enjoyment, and engagement among students. In their case, when comparing Kahoot!, Quizizz, and Google Form, they found that the first two platforms produced a more positive effect. Using a single platform may result in a lack of variety in the exercises, consequently preventing the full benefits of gamification. For each of the activities, the appropriate dynamics, mechanics, and components of gamification offered by each of the platforms have been selected. GA1 and GA2 have been designed on Genially, an online tool that has a multitude of templates for gamification, as well as infographics, presentations, interactive images, and so on. It is possible to start creations from scratch or modify any of the templates available for the free plan. A plethora of elements can also be added, both from the platform itself and from external sources, to make the activities and content more dynamic and engaging.

GA3 has been developed on Quizizz, a free educational website for creating gamified online quizzes. In the free plan, up to five types of questions can be generated (multiple choice, fill-in-the-blank, draw, open-ended questions, and survey), and presentations can also be done. It incorporates highly motivating game elements such as music, points, leaderboards, jokers, and memes. Finally, GA4 has been modelled on Wordwall, a tool that enables the production of activities in a quick, simple, and attractive way. In its free plan, users have up to 18 different activity templates that can be filled in with the desired content. Once the activity has been created, the template can be changed, as the platform adapts the uploaded content to all its available templates. This is very useful, as the same activity can be experienced in different ways and therefore arouse the curiosity of the users. Furthermore, the platform also has elements such as different music per template, lives, and timer.

This set of GAs has two main objectives: (1) in our chapter, the GAs aim to serve learners who have been exposed to the Gamified Seminar[5] as a means to acquire general and terminological knowledge (gamified documentation process) on the specialised subject of AI prior to translating a text on this field, and (2) to provide the scientific and academic community with gamified resources for the practice of translating an upcoming topic, specifically designed for translators-to-be and professionals.

---

[5] In Sect. 3, the two-day seminar (Traditional and Gamified Seminar) and the methodology implemented to test the effectiveness of the four proposed GAs are explained in detail.

GA1: The Millionaire Translator

GA1 has been elaborated from an existing template on Genially. This activity is inspired by the television quiz show known as *Who Wants to Be a Millionaire?*, as it presents the same dynamic. We have also inserted the music of the television show in order to increase student's motivation. GA1 is composed of ten multiple-choice questions. Correct translations have been extracted from online reference dictionaries such as Reverso Context, Linguee, and Collins Dictionary. Incorrect translations consist of terms invented by the authors of this chapter or not equivalent to the original term. GA1 will be projected on the digital whiteboard. There are three different types of questions:

- Type 1: Students have to choose the correct Spanish translation of the given English term specific to the field of AI. To do so, they can use the context to help them. The context is hidden in the document symbol, but accessible to the students. By hovering the mouse over the document symbol, students will be able to read an English sentence containing the term extracted from AI-Cor. In class, the sight translation of the sentence could be done.
- Type 2: Students have to pick out the English translation of the given term in Spanish. For this purpose, they can use the context, in which we have removed the term concerned.
- Type 3: The Spanish translation of a term is given and participants have to choose the corresponding translation in English using the context.

Following the pyramidal figure of Alcaide-Martínez and Taillefer (2022, p. 286; see also Fig. 1), in this GA we have incorporated the following elements:

- Dynamics: Emotions, progression, and peer relationships, as students will have to work as a team to agree on the correct answer in order to progress further. Teams will be made up of 3–4 students. All students will assume identical roles, except for one student who will be designated as the spokesperson.
- Mechanics: Challenge, chance, competition, cooperation, feedback, and rewards, since participants are challenged to cooperate and get the correct translation right with their team while competing with the other teams. After clicking on one of the answers, students receive immediate feedback and the teacher may choose to award a prize to the winning team.
- Components: Achievements, leaderboards, levels, points, and teams, because students are grouped into teams that will have to succeed in finding the equivalent translation of the term to move on to the next level and receive points. Points increase with each level. A tally of points could be made on the board for each team.

A sample of each type of question in GA1 can be seen in Figs. 2, 3, and 4, accessible via the following link: https://view.genial.ly/645e59163ed7fb0011ccd7ae/interactive-content-the-millionaire-translatormarta-alcaide-martinez.

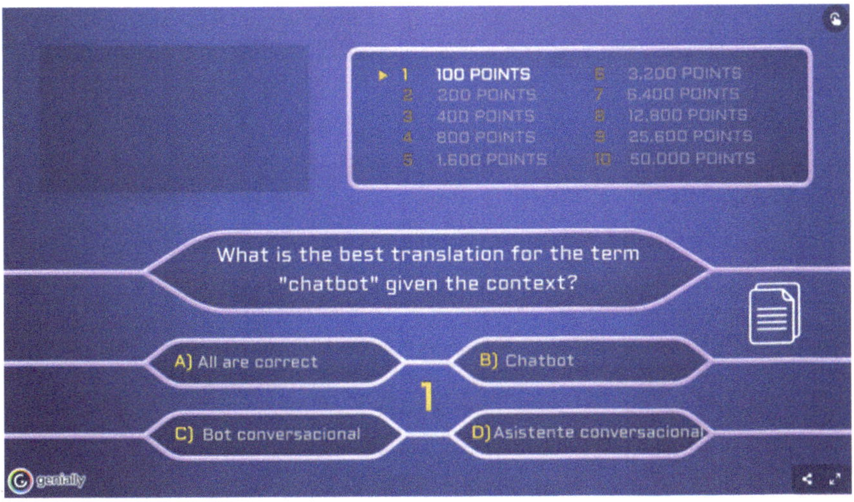

Fig. 2 Type 1 question of GA1: The millionaire translator

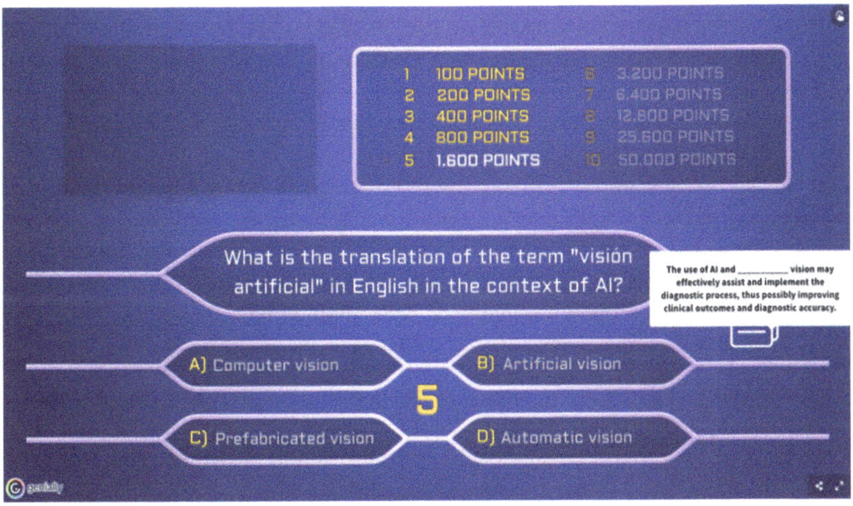

Fig. 3 Type 2 question of GA1: The millionaire translator

GA2: Transmissing Word

GA2 has also been developed on Genially from a free one-slide template. Transmissing word consists of eight questions of the same type. Each slide presents a sentence with two gaps that teams must complete. For each gap, three options are provided. In order to select the correct terms and complete the sentences successfully, participants will have to read and contrast the translation into Spanish of the

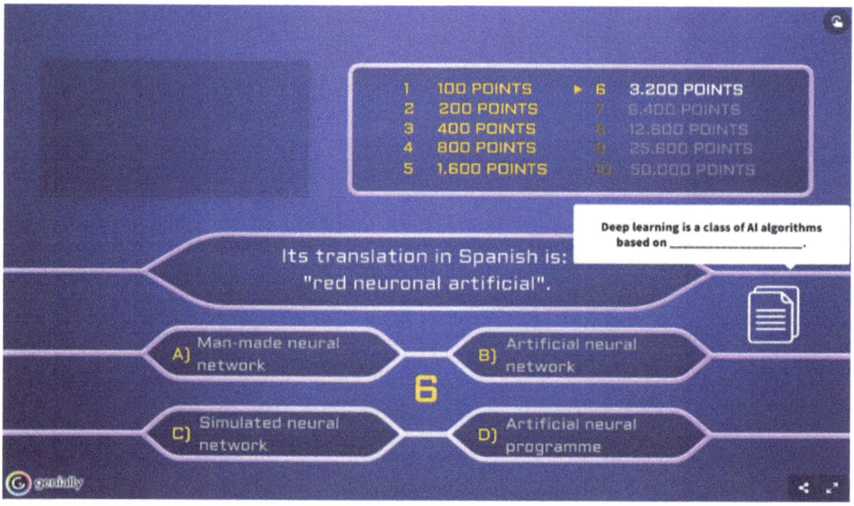

Fig. 4 Type 3 question of GA1: The millionaire translator

sentence (at the bottom written with orange lettering) with the original sentence in English retrieved from our AI-Cor corpus. Contrasting the original English sentence with the Spanish-translated one will be the only way to fill in the gaps correctly, as several options fit grammatically but not semantically in the gaps. When clicking on the correct option, the term is embedded in the sentence, while an error beep sounds if the wrong options are pressed. GA2 will be projected on the digital whiteboard, so learners will not be able to click on all the options until they find the correct choice. AI-Cor is an English monolingual corpus, so the Spanish translations are by the authors of this chapter.

The elements of gamification that have been applied in GA2 are as follows.

- Dynamics: Emotions, progression, and classmate relationships, because learners will be motivated to work in teams to progress through the different questions.
- Mechanics: Challenge, chance, competition, cooperation, and feedback, as teams with 3–4 members will be challenged to be the first to raise their hand to answer and have the chance to get it right after having previously agreed on the answers with their groups. The correct answers will then be checked.
- Components: Achievement, points, and teams, as trainees will have to work quickly and as a coordinated team to be able to contrast the original sentence with the translation and choose the correct terms to score the points and become the winning team.

We have also introduced some visual AI-related elements to make it more eye-catching. Figure 5 illustrates the second slide of GA2, accessible via the following link: https://view.genial.ly/645e985a3ed7fb0011cd73c8/interactive-content-transmissing-word.

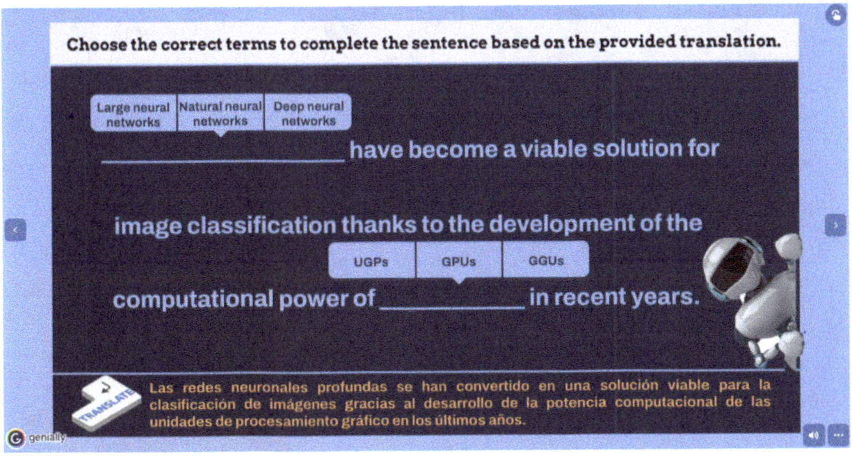

Fig. 5 Second slide of GA2: Transmissing word

GA3: AI-Transelection

GA3 has been made on Quizziz. AI-Transelection is a gamified quiz composed of six multiple-choice questions plus a bonus one. It has three types of questions: (A) questions with two options worth 5 points, (B) questions with three options worth 10 points, and (C) bonus question with three options worth 20 points. Learners have 1.5 minutes to answer Type A questions and 2 minutes to answer Type B and C questions. In every inquiry, a real English sentence containing AI-seeds from our corpus is displayed, with the instructions to select the optimal Spanish translation from the provided choices. Among the options, there is only one correct answer. In the rest of the choices, we have introduced typical translation errors, such as omissions and false meanings. It will be explained to students that there are more ways of translating the given sentences, but they will have to select the one which does not contain any errors or omissions. GA3 will be projected on the digital whiteboard and also each student will have to access it with their own device. As our corpus is in English, the translations added to the quiz are by the authors of this chapter.

In GA3 we have integrated the following game-specific elements.

- Dynamics: Emotions and progression, since students will be curious and engaged, and will have to be attentive in order to answer the questions before the time runs out and they have to move on to the next one.
- Mechanics: Challenge, opportunity, competition, feedback, resource acquisition, and rewards, as learners will have to choose the correct answer individually and as quickly as possible. They will have only one attempt at each question and will be able to see the correct answer instantly after clicking on one of the options. During the quiz, students will receive jokers and boosters. A reward can be given to the winning student.

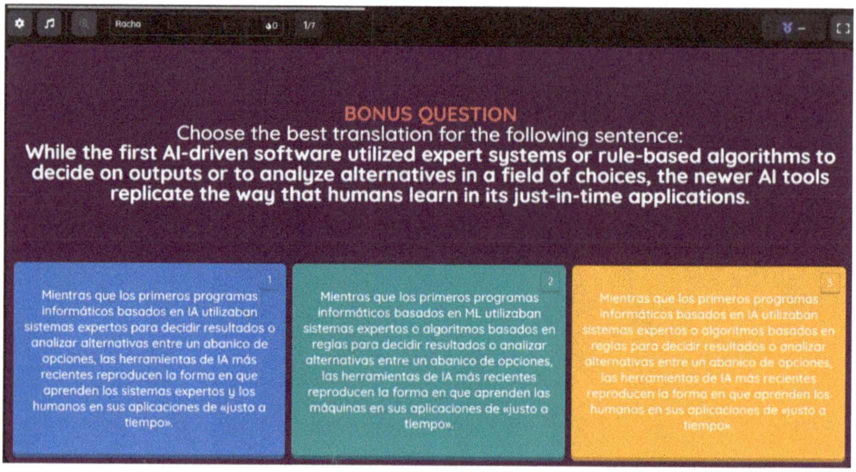

Fig. 6 Bonus question of GA3: AI-transelections

- Components: Achievement, avatars, leaderboards, points, and virtual goods, given that students are assigned a random image when they join the quiz and have to manage to answer in the shortest time possible to get the most points and appear at the top of the leaderboard. They will be able to earn virtual goods as a streak booster.

A sample of GA3 can be seen in Fig. 6, which is available via this link: https://quizizz.com/join/quiz/6461306b2552da001daf5ac2/start?studentShare=true.

GA4: TransAIacronyms

GA4 was developed on Wordwall with the aim of providing translation practice with some of the most commonly used acronyms in the context of AI. GA4 is made up of 13 acronyms in English that students have to associate with their corresponding full term given in Spanish. In this way, they need to translate the term mentally in order to discover the respective acronym. They are given ten minutes and five lives. GA4 will be projected on the digital whiteboard.

The following gamification elements have been used.

- Dynamics: Emotions, progression, and peer relationships, since trainees will have to work well as a team (3–4 students) to discover the answer before the rest of the teams so that they can get the points and move on to the next acronym.
- Mechanics: Challenge, chance, competition, cooperation, feedback, and rewards, as translators-to-be are challenged to match the English acronym to its corresponding full term in Spanish and only have five chances. In addition, they will have to be coordinated as teams to compete and become the winners to gain greater

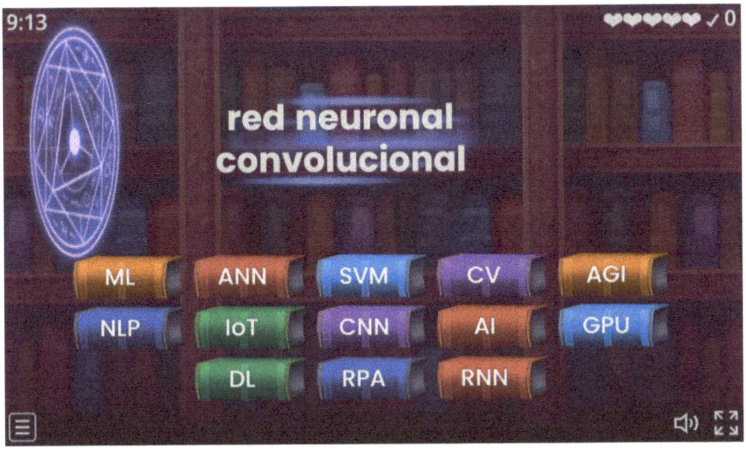

Fig. 7 Example of GA4: TransAIacronyms

translation skills. After clicking on an acronym, learners will automatically see whether they got it right or wrong.

- Components: Achievements, leaderboards, points, and teams, as teams will have to be able to agree on an answer promptly to raise their hand before the other teams and score a point. The tally will be done on the board.

Figure 7 depicts GA4, which is available at https://wordwall.net/es/resource/56495606.

3 Testing Students' Performance and Perceptions

The second part of our paper describes a pilot study we conducted in order to evaluate the effectiveness and usefulness of our corpus-based gamified methodology, as well as students' performance and perceptions (including attitudes and acceptance). To this end, we prepared a seminar divided into two parts, each of them organised around traditional/non-gamified activities and gamified activities, and two online questionnaires (pre- and post-tasks). In each part of the seminar, the participating sample of trainees had to translate a short text on the specialised domain of AI. Subsequently, the domain-related terminology of the texts was extracted and divided into three categories (domain-specific terminology, semi-specialised terminology, and banal terms with new meanings). Last, the translation accuracy rates for each of the terms and categories obtained after a non-gamified and gamified documentation process were calculated and compared. The subsections below describe the experimental design and the main results and conclusions of our experiments.

3.1 Methodology

As a starting hypothesis, we argue that infusing gameplay and leveraging competitiveness, teamwork, emotions, and peer relationships not only facilitates the teaching of specialised translation, but it can also significantly increase learner engagement and enhance their performance. To this end, we have carried out an experiment with undergraduate students of the Bachelor's Degree in Translation and Interpreting at the University of Malaga.

A pilot study has been the method chosen to evaluate the effectiveness and usefulness of the GAs we have designed for specialised translation practice on AI terminology in the English–Spanish/Spanish–English combination. This pilot study has been carried out in order to assess the adequacy of our methodology and (re)formulate or adjust the design prior to large-scale quantitative research. As Arain et al. (2010) point out, this is precisely one of the key objectives of pilot studies. Building upon the insights of scholars like Moore et al. (2011), this pilot study has been devised as a preparatory study to ascertain the limitations of our experiment. Depending on the findings, a subsequent investigation will be formulated, rectifying the identified constraints and enabling the calculation of statistical metrics such as the Student's t-test. Thus, this preliminary study aims at encouraging the dissemination of gamification as a teaching–learning methodology and to check that it would indeed be worthwhile to carry out a larger study with a larger sample size so that the results can be judged valid and representative.

Our pilot study consisted of a two-day seminar held at the University of Malaga to facilitate the application of the proposed guided gamified approach and to gather empirical evidence of its potential. The seminar, entitled *Artificial Intelligence (AI): A burgeoning domain of expertise*, comprises two parts: Traditional Seminar (Part I) and Gamified Seminar (Part II). Each part lasted 90 minutes and took place on two different days within the same module and with the same class of the Bachelor's Degree in Translation and Interpreting. However, due to the seminar being conducted on two different days, there was a lack of consistency in student attendance. Consequently, our sample does not comprise two controlled groups. The sole aspect we could control is that they are second- and third-year students enrolled in the Bachelor's Degree in Translation and Interpreting at the University of Malaga during the academic year 2022–2023. Each part was structured into three sections, as described below.

Part I constitutes the Traditional Seminar held on Day 1, and it was divided into the following activities and tasks (see Appendix 1):

1. *Completion of the pre-task questionnaire and brief overview of the history and some key concepts of AI (30 minutes).* This questionnaire was used to collect socio-demographic data, some previous perceptions, and the translation of the Day 1 text. Table 1 shows the structure and content of the questionnaire.

Before moving on to the next two activities, the topic was briefly introduced through participatory activities, such as a word cloud generated on Mentimeter with

Table 1 Pre-task questionnaire structure

Pre-task questionnaire (Google Forms)		
Section 1	Introduction and consent	
Section 2	Socio-demographic data	(A) Age, (B) Sex, (C) Academic year of the Bachelor's Degree in Translation and Interpreting, (D) Mother tongue, (E) Level of English (CEFR)
Section 3	Specific questions	More-than-one-possible-answer questions (Questions 1 and 3)
		Yes/no questions (Questions 2, 5, and 9)
		Open-ended questions (Questions 4, 8, and 10)
		Likert scale question (Question 6)
		One-possible-answer question (Question 7)
Section 4	Translation exercise	

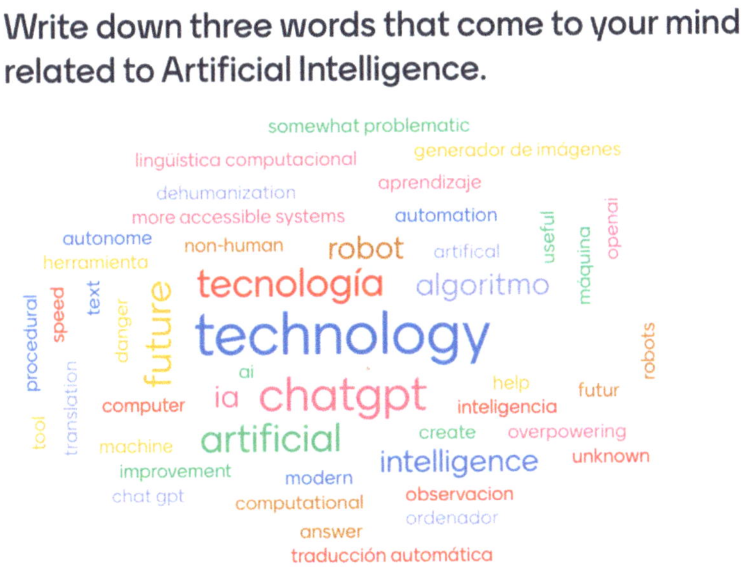

Fig. 8 Student's word cloud for the concept "artificial intelligence"

the words written by the students (see Fig. 8).[6] This activity was used as a brainstorming exercise, to enhance their level of engagement and prompt reflection on the subject matter.

2. *Traditional documentation (30 min)*. This documentation process was performed by students individually or in pairs. Beforehand, some databases were shown for the purpose of documentation, and the text to be translated was projected for 5 min on the digital whiteboard. The text was projected for only 5 min at this stage

[6] Available at https://www.mentimeter.com/app/presentation/aler6gnrrch9jc6bp1u2dpicfp652n2t.

for two reasons: (1) to stimulate students' short-term memory, and (2) to prevent trainees from starting to translate the text immediately. After the screening of the Day 1 text, the translators-to-be were given 25 min to research the AI topic in order to be able to translate the previously read text as well as possible. They were allowed to do their research using any method of their preference: reading texts on the subject, looking for glossaries or parallel texts on databases, using corpora, or even creating their own glossaries. Throughout this stage, the teachers assumed the responsibility of providing guidance to the learners, and answering any questions or doubts. Thus, the teachers took on the role of facilitators. Some caveats notwithstanding, the aim of this phase was to simulate the process of a real translation assignment.

3. *Translation exercise (30 min).* Students were explicitly informed that they were allowed to employ any digital resources or technological tools to undertake the translation of the short specialised text on AI of an informative nature in the English-Spanish direction, with the exception of machine translation and AI systems, as Large Language Models (LLMs). Regarding the proposed Day 1 text (see Appendix 1), only two adaptations were made to the original text: (1) cutting some sentences, and (2) removing the full form of terms, such as *artificial intelligence*, and *machine learning*, and replacing them with their acronyms. These modifications were made so that the text would not be too long and to check the differences in the identification/translation of the acronyms in the Traditional Seminar and the Gamified Seminar.

Part II comprises the Gamified Seminar held on Day 2, and it was split into the following activities (see Appendix 2):

1. *Implementation of four GAs (40 min).* The gamified documentation process was composed of four GAs, which were deployed in the following order: GA1. The millionaire translator, GA2. Transmissing word, GA3. AI-Transelection, and GA4. TransAIacronyms. Trainees were divided into groups of 3–4 members of their choice and in each group there was a spokesperson. Each activity took 10 min. The GAs were guided by Marta Alcaide-Martínez and played by all the students at the same time. The completion of these four GAs would be equivalent to the gamified documentation process on the AI domain prior to the Day 2 text translation.
2. *Translation exercise (30 min).* Students were asked to translate the short, specialised text on AI of an informative nature (see Appendix 2) in the English-Spanish direction. The Day 2 text has undergone the same adaptations as the Day 1 text. As in the previous case, students were allowed to use any tools and resources of their choice, except machine translation and AI systems, as LLMs.
3. *Completion of the post-task questionnaire (20 min).* This questionnaire was used to gather socio-demographic data, some further impressions, and the translation of the Day 2 text. Table 2 illustrates the structure and content of the questionnaire.

Table 2 Post-task questionnaire structure

Post-task questionnaire (Google Forms)		
Section 1	Introduction and consent	
Section 2	Socio-demographic data	(A) Age, (B) Sex, (C) Academic year of the Bachelor's Degree in Translation and Interpreting, (D) Mother tongue, (E) Level of English (CEFR)
Section 3	Translation exercise	
Section 4	Specific questions	More-than-one-possible-answer question (Question 1)
		Yes/no questions (Questions 2, 8, and 10)
		One-possible-answer questions (Questions 3, 4, and 5)
		Open-ended questions (Question 6)
		Likert scale questions (Questions 7 and 9)

As a follow-up to the two-day seminar, AI domain terminology was retrieved from the two proposed texts and split into three categories (domain-specific terminology, semi-specialised terminology, and banal terms with new meanings). Translation accuracy rates were measured for each term and all the categories, and the percentages for the Traditional Seminar and the Gamified Seminar were compared. In the next subsections, the characteristics of the two participating population groups and the conclusions drawn from the data collected are presented.

3.2 *Participants*

The pre-task and post-task questionnaires included a first section on socio-demographic items (see Appendices 1 and 2) which provided relevant data about participants in both the Traditional Seminar and the Gamified Seminar. Tables 3 and 4 summarise the main findings.

The participant cohort comprises a group of undergraduates who share certain modules, despite not being enrolled in the same academic year of the Bachelor's Degree in Translation and Interpreting at the University of Malaga. Due to time constraints, the sample size was different for the Traditional Seminar (29 participants) and the Gamified Seminar (14 participants). This is because our experiments were conducted at the end of the academic year 2022–2023, which prevented us from having access to a control group.

It is worth noting that gender issues were considered, as we have broadened beyond the traditional binary option for sex by introducing two additional options: "Prefer not to say" and "Other" (with the option to specify).

The varying socio-demographic profiles of the two participating groups have an influence on the results obtained. It is particularly relevant in this regard that not all students have Spanish as their mother tongue (only 72.4% in the Traditional Seminar and 64.3% in the Gamified Seminar). This multicultural environment has

Table 3 Socio-demographic data of the participating sample in the Traditional Seminar

Socio-demographic data	Traditional Seminar (29 participants)					
Age	**19 years**	**20 years**	**21 years**	**22 years**	**23 years**	**63 years**
	13 (44.8%)	8 (27.6%)	4 (13.8%)	2 (6.9%)	1 (3.4%)	1 (3.4%)
Sex	**Male**		**Female**		**Prefer not to say**	
	11 (37.9%)		17 (58.6%)		1 (3.4%)	
Academic year	**Second academic year**			**Third academic year**		
	23 (79.3%)			6 (20.7%)		
Mother tongue	**Spanish**		**French**		**English, Italian, Arabic, Polish, Galician, Slovak, Czech, and Catalan**[7]	
	21 (72.4%)		3 (10.3%)		8 (3.4%)	
Level of English (CEFR)	**B2 (upper intermediate)**		**C1 (advanced)**		**C2 (mastery or proficiency)**	
	14 (48.3%)		12 (41.4%)		3 (10.3%)	

Table 4 Socio-demographic data of the participating sample in the Gamified Seminar

Socio-demographic data	Gamified Seminar (14 participants)					
Age	**19**	**20**	**21**	**22**	**26**	**64**
	6 (42.9%)	3 (21.4%)	1 (7.1%)	2 (14.3%)	1 (7.1%)	1 (7.1%)
Sex	**Male**			**Female**		
	7 (50%)			7 (50%)		
Academic year	**Second academic year**			**Third academic year**		
	12 (85.7%)			2 (14.3%)		
Mother tongue	**Spanish**			**French, Italian, Danish, Polish, Czech**[8]		
	9 (64.3%)			5 (7.1%)		
Level of English (CEFR)	**B2 (upper intermediate)**		**C1 (advanced)**		**C2 (mastery or proficiency)**	
	6 (42.9%)		6 (42.9%)		2 (14.3%)	

allowed the creation of groups made up of students from different cultures who have enriched each other, especially during the GAs. Furthermore, the majority of learners have B2 (48.3% in the Traditional Seminar and 42.9% in the Gamified Seminar) and C1 (41.4% in the Traditional Seminar and 42.9% in the Gamified Seminar) levels of English. Finally, it is imperative to take into account the repercussions of the smaller size of the Gamified Seminar sample in comparison to the Traditional

[7] There is a native speaker for each of the mentioned languages.

[8] There is a native speaker for each of the mentioned languages.

Seminar sample, as five out of the 14 Gamified Seminar participants do not have Spanish as their mother tongue.

3.3 *Results and Discussion*

The triangulation of results (translation tasks versus specific questions) is presented here. For this purpose, the analysis is divided into two subsections: (1) Traditional Seminar results and (2) Gamified Seminar results. In each of these subsections, the translations submitted by the sample of undergraduate students are assessed for translation accuracy of terms (accuracy rate) classified into three categories: (i) domain-specific terminology, (ii) semi-specialised terminology, and (iii) banal terms with new meanings (see Tables 5 and 6). In order to classify the terms found in the selected texts for the two-day seminar into the aforementioned three categories, we have used the two glossaries mentioned above: *Glossary of human-centric artificial intelligence* by Estévez Almenzar et al. (2022) and the glossary on AI of the Council of Europe. After the data collection during the two-day seminar, we proceeded to analyse the terminological accuracy of the translations produced by the participants after a traditional documentation process in the Traditional Seminar (Part I) and after a gamified documentation process in the Gamified Seminar (Part II). Hence, we evaluate the effectiveness, benefits, and drawbacks of applying a protocolised gamified methodology in the specialised translation classroom.

3.3.1 Part I: Traditional Seminar

With the aim of examining the translation outcomes resulting from a traditional documentation process, this subsection presents a comparison between the responses collected through the Pre-task questionnaire and the accuracy rate of the terminology identified in the provided text on Day 1 of the seminar. Table 5 depicts the terminology organised in the three named categories, accompanied by their respective accuracy rates. The terms in each category are arranged by order of appearance in the text.

Although the average accuracy rates for each category are relatively high, a great majority of students (75.9%) indicated in both Questions 1 and 10 that terminology is the aspect they find most challenging in specialised translation. Following terminology, the second most challenging aspect for our sample is style (44.8%). Furthermore, a significant proportion of undergraduates in Questions 8 and 9 (86.2%) reported having limited familiarity with the field and the terminology of AI. In this sense, students acknowledged that their limited knowledge of the field could pose a challenge when seeking to translate a text belonging to this area of expertise (Question 10 results).

It is noteworthy that a staggering 96.6% of undergraduates reported employing digital tools and resources regularly before translating specialised texts, with the exception of a single student who indicated otherwise. This finding is hardly surprising given the pervasiveness of technology in contemporary society. Neither is it striking to notice in Question 3 that students' favourite resources for documentation are online bilingual dictionaries (96.4%) and online monolingual dictionaries (50%). However, specialised corpora in the domain involved are one of the least widely used resources by learners (7.1%). This is likely to be a contributing factor to the comparatively lower average accuracy rate spotted in the "semi-specialised terminology" category, as sometimes semi-specialised terms are multiword terms (MWTs) that are not covered by dictionaries, as in the case of *raw, written text*. In this respect, corpora are very convenient tools for analysing and understanding the actual use of a given term and, thus, for producing a more appropriate translation. It is common, though, for bilingual and monolingual online dictionaries to contain the terms listed under the categories "banal terms with new meanings" and "domain-specific terminology". A plausible explanation for the higher accuracy rate of banal terms with new meanings is that students are more acquainted with them, having encountered them in a greater variety of contexts and on more frequent occasions.

Concerning the three questions related to gamification (Questions 5, 6, and 7), it is interesting to find that, although 72.4% of respondents state in Question 5 that they have not heard of this teaching–learning methodology before, in Question 7, 58.6% (17 students) choose gamification over traditional methodology as the approach they consider would be most effective in helping them to internalise domain-specific terminology. Likewise, as can be seen in the results of Question 6, the majority of students believe that the application of game-like elements in the classroom could benefit and improve their learning and practice of specialised translation to different extents. According to the Likert scale ranging from 1 to 5 of Question 6, 3.4% of students have rated themselves at the lowest point (1), while 24.1% of students have positioned themselves at the midpoint (3), and 48.3% and 24.1% of learners have ranked themselves at the upper end of the scale (4 and 5). Finally, the socio-demographic characteristics of the participating sample (Table 3) should not be overlooked in order to comprehend the results shown in Table 5.

It is not unexpected to find that the category with the highest average accuracy rate is "banal terms with new meanings", since this category includes terms stored in bilingual and monolingual dictionaries. Moreover, students have probably read and used these terms in other contexts, so they only need to adjust their translation to the AI domain. In fact, the term having the highest accuracy rate is *computer* (96.55%) and is grouped under this category. Conversely, the two terms with the lowest accuracy rates were *raw, written text* (62.07%) from the category "semi-specialised terminology" and *Machine Learning (ML)* (62.07%) from "domain-specific terminology". These lower accuracy rates are likely due to the following reasons we inferred from the translations provided by the translators-to-be: (1) *raw, written text* is an MWT that is not found in dictionaries altogether, so it is essential to translate and adapt the two adjectives accompanying the noun, and (2) students have assumed to know the *Machine Learning (ML)* translation and have not consulted dictionaries in many cases. This has led them to produce incorrect translations.

Table 5 Translation accuracy rates of the traditional seminar text terminology

Domain-specific terminology	Accuracy rate	Semi-specialised terminology	Accuracy rate	Banal terms with new meanings	Accuracy rate
Machine Learning (ML)	62.07%	Raw, written text	62.07%	Technology	86.21%
NLP	75.86%	Statistical techniques	75.86%	Machines	79.31%
AI	93.10%	Large-scale data	72.41%	Tasks	75.86%
ML	86.21%	Algorithms	86.21%	Natural human languages	72.41%
Natural language processing	68.97%	Robotics	82.76%	Computer	96.55%
Computer vision	79.31%			Data	86.21%
				Human intervention	93.10%
				Automated processes	86.21%
				Efficiently	72%
TOTAL: 6 terms Average accuracy rate: 77.59%		TOTAL: 5 terms Average accuracy rate: 75.86%		TOTAL: 9 terms Average accuracy rate: 83,09%	

3.3.2 Part II: Gamified Seminar

For the purpose of assessing the translation performance after a gamified, guided documentation process, this subsection establishes a comparative analysis of the students' opinions gathered through the Post-task questionnaire and the accuracy rates of the terminology extracted from the Day 2 text. Table 6 follows the same organisational structure as Table 5.

In Question 1 of the Post-task questionnaire, we observe that after translating the texts on AI, terminology continues to be perceived as the most challenging factor (92.9%). Unlike the Pre-task questionnaire, in this case the second most challenging element has changed, becoming syntax (28.6%) rather than style (14.3%). The results obtained in Question 2 are noteworthy because the majority of undergraduate students (78.6%) point out that they had not experienced the gamification methodology in a translation subject before this seminar. This result corroborates the assertions made in previous sections, i.e., that the inclusion of this methodology in the syllabus of the Bachelor's Degree in Translation and Interpreting is not commonplace.

Students show a predominantly positive perception towards gamification, which correlates with the quality of their translation outputs. In Question 3, 57.1% of the

Table 6 Translation accuracy rates of the gamified seminar text terminology

Domain-specific terminology	Accuracy rate	Semi-specialised terminology	Accuracy rate	Banal terms with new meanings	Accuracy rate
AI	100%	Enterprise IT	50%	Technologies	92.86%
ML	92.86%	Algorithms	92.86%	Accurate	85.71%
DL	78.57%	Data-driven learning and decision-making	35.71%	Machines	85.71%
NLP	71.43%	Paradigm	85.71%	Interactions	85.71%
ANN	92.86%	Optimisation	85.71%	Environment	85.71%
NN	92.86%	Linguistics	85.71%	Functionality	71.43%
Reinforcement learning (RL)	85.71%				
AI system	78.57%				
Deep reinforcement learning (DRL)	85.71%				
RL	85.71%				
General AI	78.57%				
Computer science	85.71%				
TOTAL: 12 terms Average accuracy rate: 85.71%		TOTAL: 6 terms Average accuracy rate: 72.62%		TOTAL: 6 terms Average accuracy rate: 84.52%	

students state that they found the gamification methodology more useful and effective than the traditional methodology for the process of documentation in the specialised domain of AI. In Question 4, we obtained an even higher percentage (78.6%) who felt more motivated and involved in the documentation process with gamification. On the Likert scale from 1 to 5, regarding Question 7 (To what extent gamification can enhance their learning experience in the specialised translation classroom?), students placed themselves in the top three positions: Position 3 (35.7%), Position 4 (42.9%), and Position 5 (21.4%). Particularly outstanding are the results for Question 8, in which 92.9% of the students state that the application of gamification could be advantageous in other modules/subjects of the Bachelor's Degree in Translation and Interpreting. Only one student felt that it would not be beneficial.

In Question 9, we also collect data through a Likert scale graded as follows: strongly disagree, disagree, agree, and strongly agree. Participants are asked to indicate the extent to which they agree with the following statements: the gamification methodology... (1) has increased my level of motivation, (2) has helped me to be more focused, (3) has made my learning process more enjoyable, (4) has enabled me to internalise domain-specific terminology, and (5) has helped me to translate a specialised text more easily. The majority of undergraduates rated themselves in the agree and strongly agree categories, with the third statement receiving the most favourable results. In addition, this gamification training increased the learners' confidence, as 85.7% of the students stated in Question 10 that after the Gamified Seminar they feel more confident about translating a text in the specialised domain covered.

As far as the GAs in Question 5 are concerned, GA2 has been deemed most helpful by the students (35.7%), while GA1, GA3, and GA4 have had the same percentage of success among learners (21.4%). On the basis of the answers to Question 6, learners who chose GA2 as their preferred exercise reported finding it the most beneficial. They point out that this activity facilitated the comparison between the original text and its potential translation, while also aiding in the internalisation of terminology with less cognitive load (and perceived stress) than the other proposed GAs.

Bearing in mind all of the above, we observe an increase of 8.12% in the accuracy rate of domain-specific terminology after implementing a gamified documentation process. The reason why this category has the most significant improvement is explained by the fact that the GAs focus especially on this category of terms, so its effectiveness is demonstrated. The accuracy rate for banal terms with new meanings has also risen by 1.43%. While this is a minor increase, it also reinforces the impact of gamification. However, we have detected a decrease of 3.24% in the accuracy rate of semi-specialised terms in the Gamified Seminar, mainly due to the MWT *data-driven learning and decision-making*, which obtained the lowest accuracy rate (35.71%). This phenomenon can be ascribed to the frequent mistake in technical and specialised translation, where students fail to realise that the adjective premodifies both nouns, not only *learning*, in this case.

We have additionally observed a heightened accuracy rate subsequent to the application of the Gamified Seminar across multiple terms repeated on both days' texts. The ensuing examples illustrate this trend: AI (93.10% vs. 100%), ML (86.21% vs. 92.86%), algorithms (86.21% vs. 92.86%), technology/technologies (86.21% vs. 92.86%), and machines (79.31% vs. 85.71%). In conjunction with these percentage improvements, it is worth highlighting the notable increase in engagement and motivation levels witnessed in the Gamified Seminar when juxtaposed with the Traditional Seminar. This empirical evidence originates from direct classroom observations conducted by instructors, complemented by the responses given by learners to Question 4 of the Post-task questionnaire.

The results of our work are in line with the findings obtained by Hamari et al. (2014), Marín et al. (2015), Gutiérrez-Artacho and Olvera-Lobo (2016), Chen (2019), Alcalde Peñalver and Santamaría Urbieta (2020), Alcaide-Martínez and Taillefer (2022), and Meyers (2022). The advantages and benefits of gamification appear to be self-evident. Besides, our work focuses on a little-studied aspect, i.e., the application of gamification for domain-specific terminology acquisition. In this sense, the results achieved are revealing, as there has been an increase not only in students' motivation and engagement, but also in the translation accuracy rate in two of the three categories of terms.

4 Conclusions

In this research, we have developed a corpus-based gamified and technological didactic proposal consisting of four GAs geared towards the translatological practice of domain-specific terminology in the specialised field of AI. For its development and implementation, a theoretical review of the literature, a two-step protocol, and an experiment design have been conducted, which have enabled the collection of valuable and revealing data.

Although this is a pilot study and its results cannot be deemed conclusive due to its inherent limitations, we have observed an improvement in the translation accuracy rates for AI domain-specific terminology and banal terms with new meanings after the Gamified Seminar. Generally speaking, we have also noted greater coherence and cohesion in the textual compositions of the translations submitted after the gamified documentation process. Concerning the students' attitudes observed in class, we detected significant growth in the levels of motivation, engagement, and involvement in the Gamified Seminar.

Therefore, we envisage three main future lines of work. Firstly, we plan to apply this gamified approach to a larger, controlled sample that would be divided into two groups: Traditional Seminar (group A) and Gamified Seminar (group B). These groups will comprise an equivalent number of participants to facilitate the calculation of statistical metrics, such as the t-test, for the purpose of assessing significance levels. We also propose to create subgroups of samples if there is a recurrence of foreign students as participants. Furthermore, we suggest extending the duration of each seminar to 120 minutes to prevent potential technical issues from disrupting its progression and to facilitate a more thorough explanation of each activity. Secondly, we believe that it would be advisable to delve deeper into semi-specialised terms and especially into MWTs, due to their frequency in the specialised and technical spheres and their translation difficulty for students and professionals. Thirdly, we intent to exploit the AI-Cor corpus for the creation of more GAs, due to the huge importance of the field for all spheres of human life.

Notwithstanding the constraints inherent in our work, whose enhancements we propose as potential future avenues of research, gamification methodology should be given greater prominence within the framework of university education taking into account the outcomes collected through this pilot study. We are confident that our study will contribute to the scientific and academic community, expanding the scope of the teaching–learning methodology of gamification for both the training and the professional practice of translators and even interpreters.

Acknowledgements This research is funded by an FPU (Formación del Profesorado Universitario) contract, ref. no. FPU21/03104, awarded by the Spanish Ministry of Science, Innovation and Universities to Marta Alcaide-Martínez. This work has also been carried out within the framework of several research projects on linguistic technologies applied to translation and interpreting: VIP II (PID2020-112818GB-I00), Proof of Concept (PDC2021-121220-I00), GAMETRAPP (TED2021-129789B-I00), and RECOVER (ProyExcel_00540).

Appendices

Appendix 1: Pre-task Questionnaire

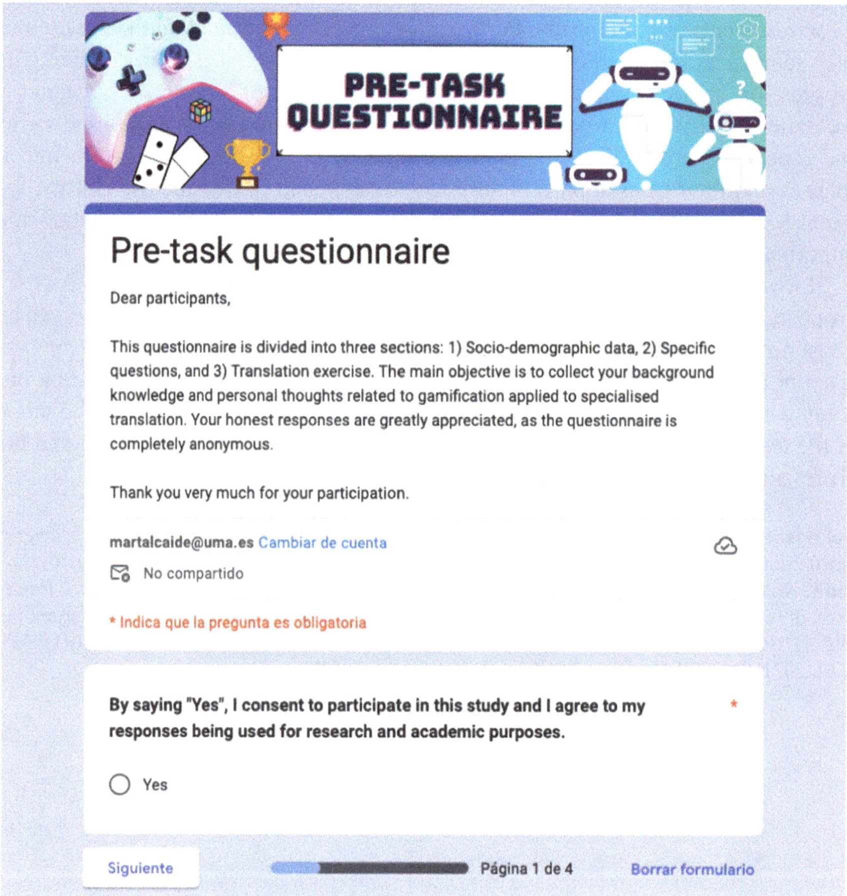
PRE-TASK QUESTIONNAIRE

Pre-task questionnaire

Dear participants,

This questionnaire is divided into three sections: 1) Socio-demographic data, 2) Specific questions, and 3) Translation exercise. The main objective is to collect your background knowledge and personal thoughts related to gamification applied to specialised translation. Your honest responses are greatly appreciated, as the questionnaire is completely anonymous.

Thank you very much for your participation.

martalcaide@uma.es Cambiar de cuenta

No compartido

* Indica que la pregunta es obligatoria

By saying "Yes", I consent to participate in this study and I agree to my responses being used for research and academic purposes. *

Yes

Siguiente Página 1 de 4 Borrar formulario

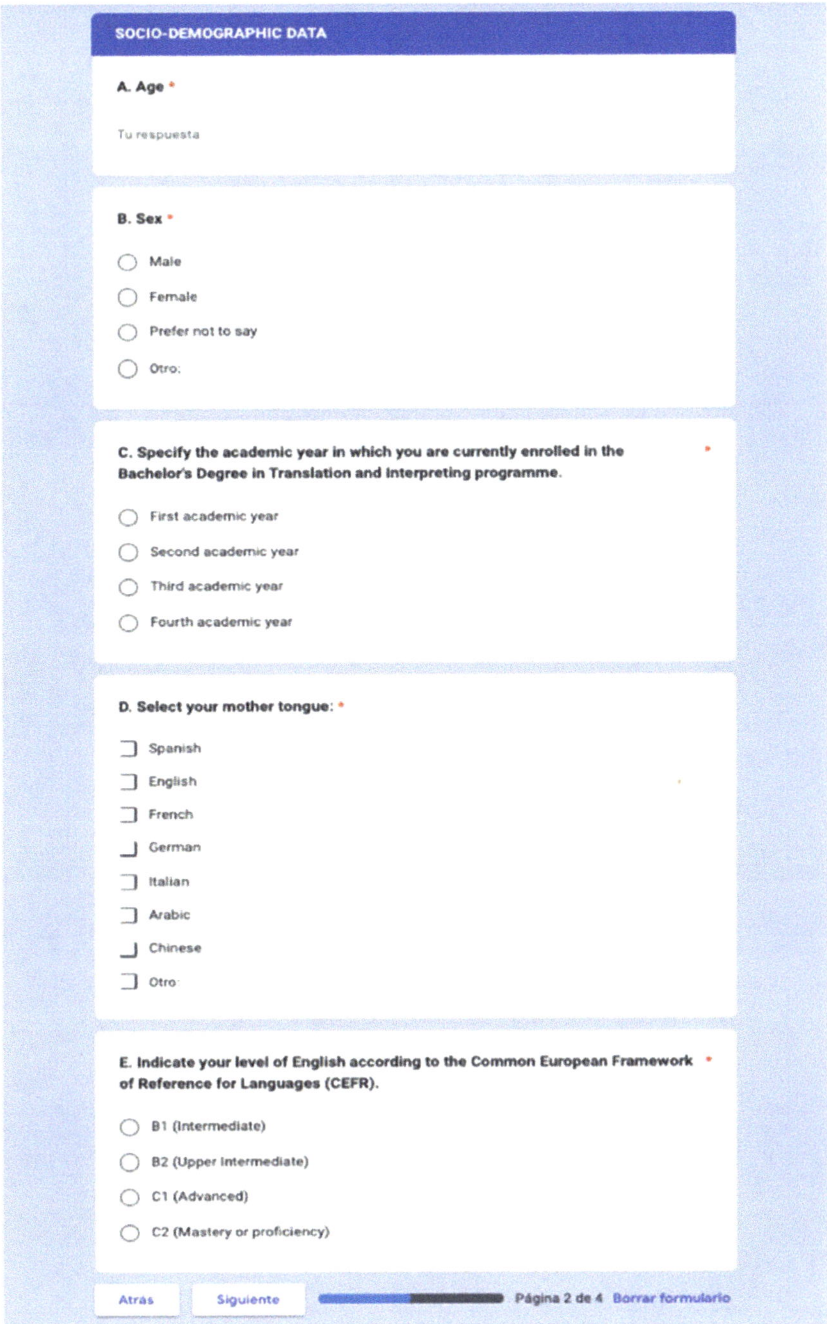

SOCIO-DEMOGRAPHIC DATA

A. Age *

Tu respuesta

B. Sex *

- ◯ Male
- ◯ Female
- ◯ Prefer not to say
- ◯ Otro:

C. Specify the academic year in which you are currently enrolled in the Bachelor's Degree in Translation and Interpreting programme. *

- ◯ First academic year
- ◯ Second academic year
- ◯ Third academic year
- ◯ Fourth academic year

D. Select your mother tongue: *

- ☐ Spanish
- ☐ English
- ☐ French
- ☐ German
- ☐ Italian
- ☐ Arabic
- ☐ Chinese
- ☐ Otro:

E. Indicate your level of English according to the Common European Framework of Reference for Languages (CEFR). *

- ◯ B1 (Intermediate)
- ◯ B2 (Upper Intermediate)
- ◯ C1 (Advanced)
- ◯ C2 (Mastery or proficiency)

Atrás Siguiente Página 2 de 4 Borrar formulario

SPECIFIC QUESTIONS

1. Mark which of the following components of specialised translation you find to be more challenging when translating a specialised text (mark no more than three options). *

- [ ] Content
- [ ] Format
- [ ] Terminology
- [ ] Syntax
- [ ] Style
- [ ] Otro:

2. Before starting to translate a specialised text, do you usually use digital tools and resources to research the subject matter concerned? *

- ○ Yes
- ○ No

3. If you answered "Yes" to the preceding question, point out which of the following tools and resources you frequently employ to the purpose of documentation.

- [ ] Monolingual online dictionaries
- [ ] Bilingual online dictionaries
- [ ] Online encyclopaedias
- [ ] Online glossaries
- [ ] Databases (Google Scholar, Scopus, Web of Science, Dialnet, etc.)
- [ ] Parallel texts
- [ ] Specialised corpora on the domain involved
- [ ] Videos on the subject
- [ ] Otro:

4. If you answered "No" to question 2, explain how you usually research a subject before you start translating.

Tu respuesta

5. Have you heard of the teaching-learning methodology known as *gamification*? *

- ○ Yes
- ○ No

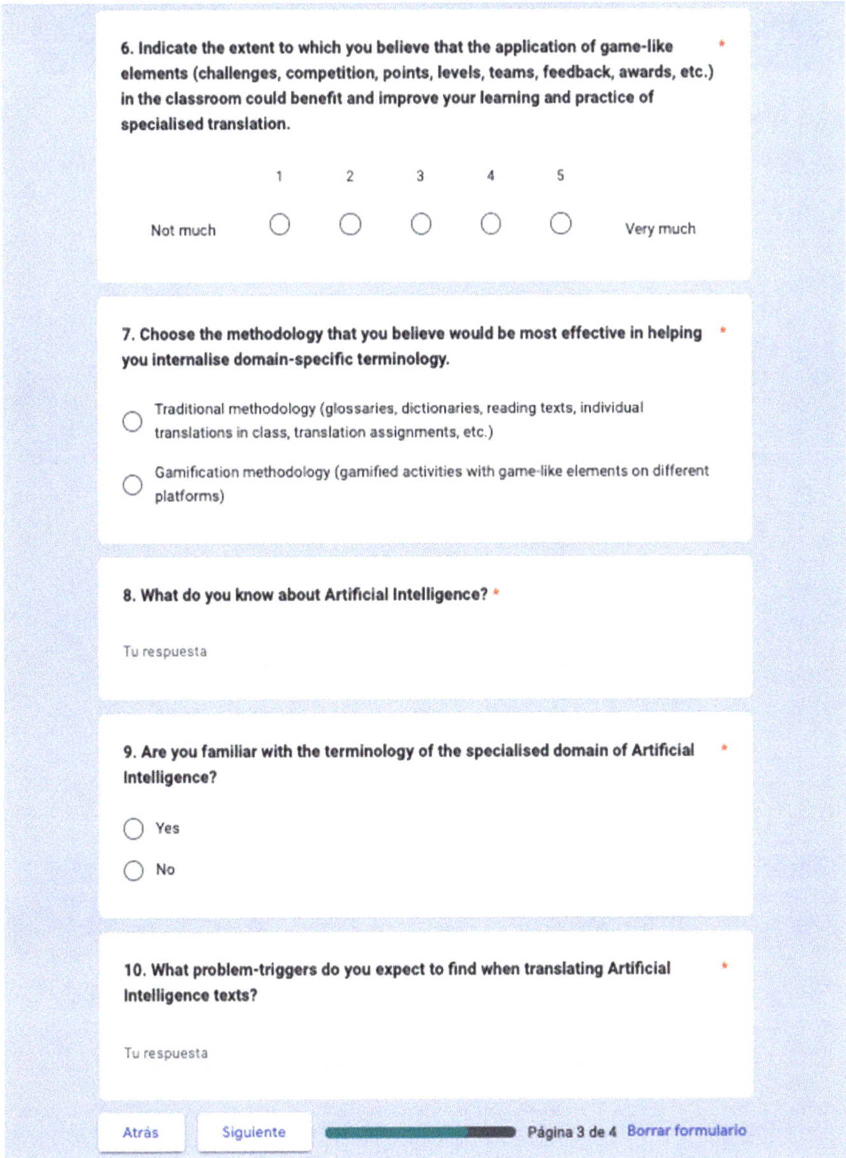

6. Indicate the extent to which you believe that the application of game-like elements (challenges, competition, points, levels, teams, feedback, awards, etc.) in the classroom could benefit and improve your learning and practice of specialised translation. *

	1	2	3	4	5	
Not much	○	○	○	○	○	Very much

7. Choose the methodology that you believe would be most effective in helping you internalise domain-specific terminology. *

○ Traditional methodology (glossaries, dictionaries, reading texts, individual translations in class, translation assignments, etc.)

○ Gamification methodology (gamified activities with game-like elements on different platforms)

8. What do you know about Artificial Intelligence? *

Tu respuesta

9. Are you familiar with the terminology of the specialised domain of Artificial Intelligence? *

○ Yes

○ No

10. What problem-triggers do you expect to find when translating Artificial Intelligence texts? *

Tu respuesta

Atrás Siguiente Página 3 de 4 Borrar formulario

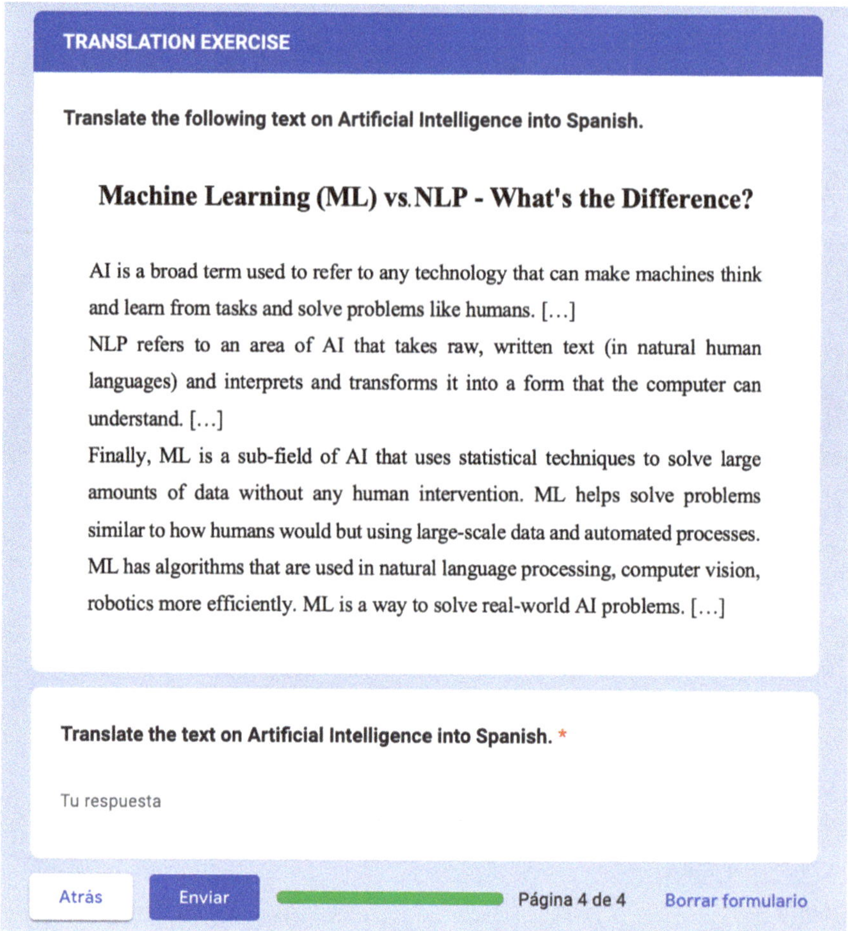

TRANSLATION EXERCISE

Translate the following text on Artificial Intelligence into Spanish.

Machine Learning (ML) vs. NLP - What's the Difference?

AI is a broad term used to refer to any technology that can make machines think and learn from tasks and solve problems like humans. [...]
NLP refers to an area of AI that takes raw, written text (in natural human languages) and interprets and transforms it into a form that the computer can understand. [...]
Finally, ML is a sub-field of AI that uses statistical techniques to solve large amounts of data without any human intervention. ML helps solve problems similar to how humans would but using large-scale data and automated processes. ML has algorithms that are used in natural language processing, computer vision, robotics more efficiently. ML is a way to solve real-world AI problems. [...]

Translate the text on Artificial Intelligence into Spanish. *

Tu respuesta

Atrás | Enviar | Página 4 de 4 | Borrar formulario

Appendix 2: Post-task Questionnaire

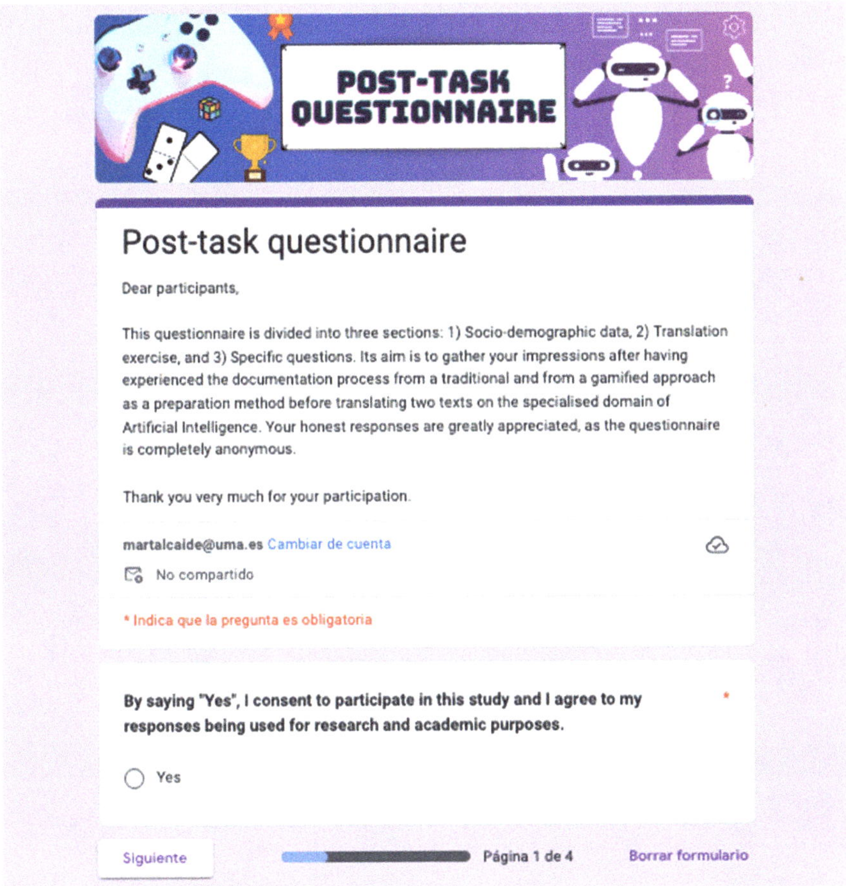

POST-TASK QUESTIONNAIRE

Post-task questionnaire

Dear participants,

This questionnaire is divided into three sections: 1) Socio-demographic data, 2) Translation exercise, and 3) Specific questions. Its aim is to gather your impressions after having experienced the documentation process from a traditional and from a gamified approach as a preparation method before translating two texts on the specialised domain of Artificial Intelligence. Your honest responses are greatly appreciated, as the questionnaire is completely anonymous.

Thank you very much for your participation.

martalcaide@uma.es Cambiar de cuenta

No compartido

* Indica que la pregunta es obligatoria

By saying "Yes", I consent to participate in this study and I agree to my responses being used for research and academic purposes. *

Yes

Siguiente Página 1 de 4 Borrar formulario

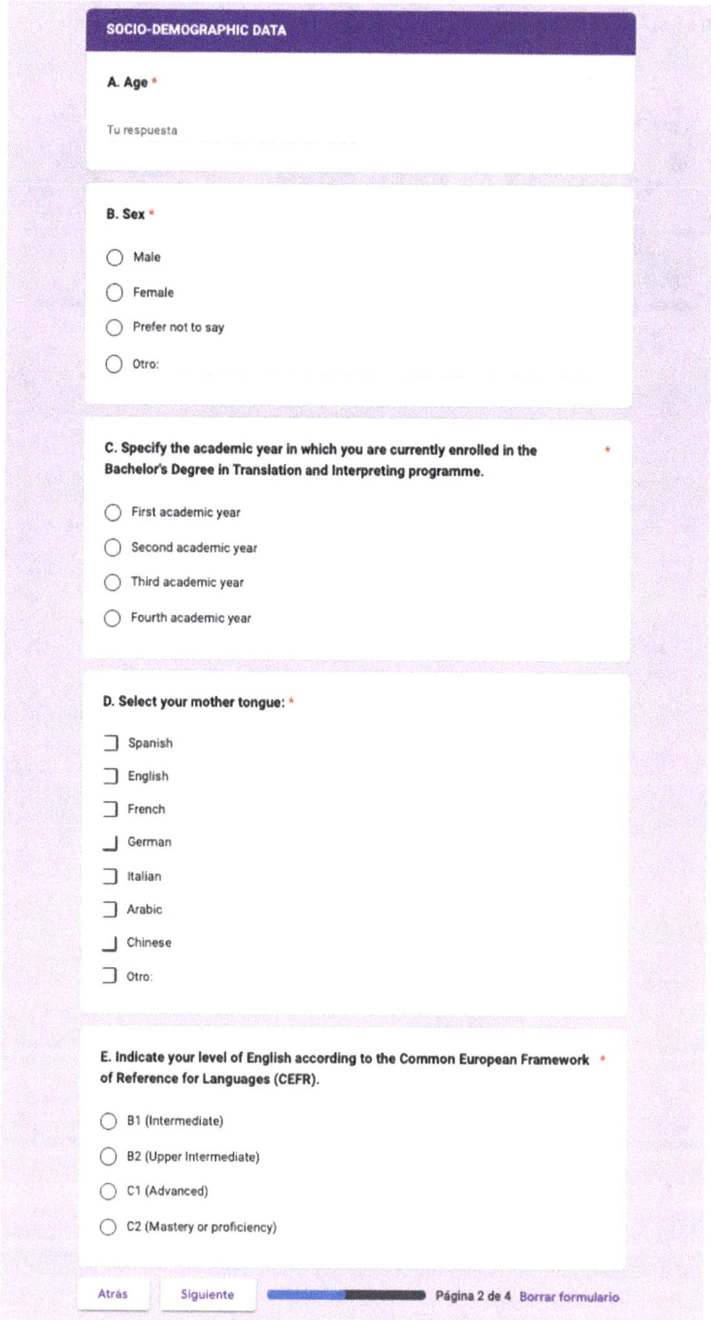

SOCIO-DEMOGRAPHIC DATA

A. Age *

Tu respuesta

B. Sex *

- Male
- Female
- Prefer not to say
- Otro:

C. Specify the academic year in which you are currently enrolled in the Bachelor's Degree in Translation and Interpreting programme. *

- First academic year
- Second academic year
- Third academic year
- Fourth academic year

D. Select your mother tongue: *

- Spanish
- English
- French
- German
- Italian
- Arabic
- Chinese
- Otro:

E. Indicate your level of English according to the Common European Framework of Reference for Languages (CEFR). *

- B1 (Intermediate)
- B2 (Upper Intermediate)
- C1 (Advanced)
- C2 (Mastery or proficiency)

Atrás Siguiente Página 2 de 4 Borrar formulario

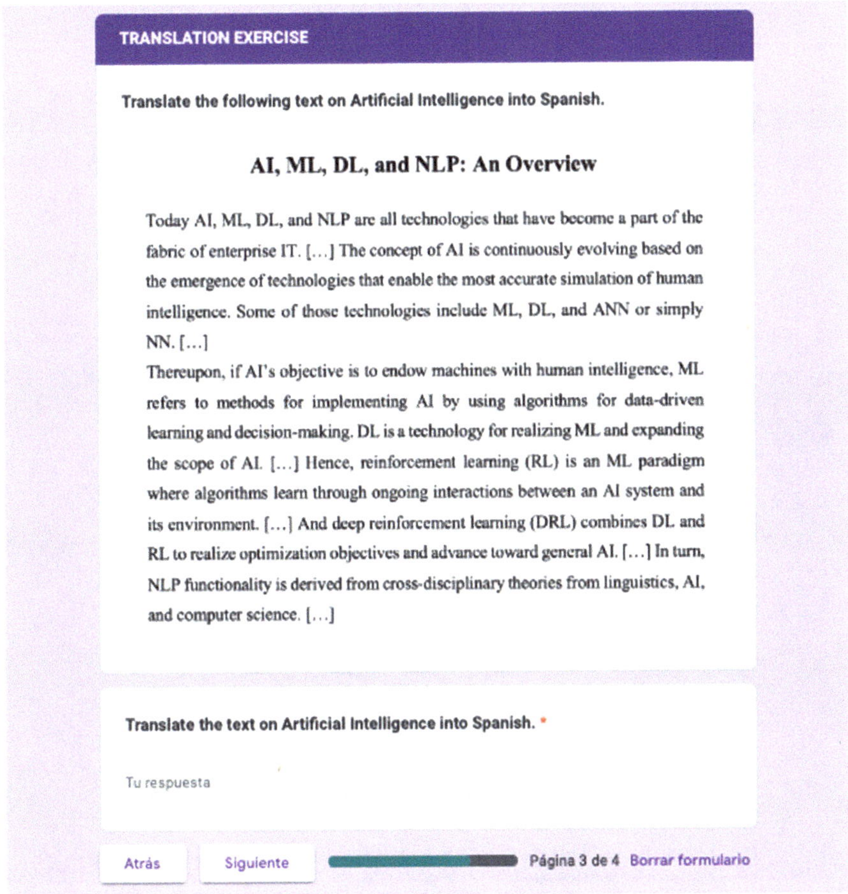

TRANSLATION EXERCISE

Translate the following text on Artificial Intelligence into Spanish.

AI, ML, DL, and NLP: An Overview

Today AI, ML, DL, and NLP are all technologies that have become a part of the fabric of enterprise IT. […] The concept of AI is continuously evolving based on the emergence of technologies that enable the most accurate simulation of human intelligence. Some of those technologies include ML, DL, and ANN or simply NN. […]

Thereupon, if AI's objective is to endow machines with human intelligence, ML refers to methods for implementing AI by using algorithms for data-driven learning and decision-making. DL is a technology for realizing ML and expanding the scope of AI. […] Hence, reinforcement learning (RL) is an ML paradigm where algorithms learn through ongoing interactions between an AI system and its environment. […] And deep reinforcement learning (DRL) combines DL and RL to realize optimization objectives and advance toward general AI. […] In turn, NLP functionality is derived from cross-disciplinary theories from linguistics, AI, and computer science. […]

Translate the text on Artificial Intelligence into Spanish. *

Tu respuesta

Atrás Siguiente Página 3 de 4 Borrar formulario

SPECIFIC QUESTIONS

1. Mark which of the following components of specialised translation you found most challenging when translating the two texts on Artificial Intelligence. *

- [ ] Content
- [ ] Format
- [ ] Terminology
- [ ] Syntax
- [ ] Style
- [ ] Otro:

2. Had you experienced the gamification methodology in a translation subject before this seminar? *

- ○ Yes
- ○ No

3. Specify which methodology you have found most useful and effective for the process of documentation on the specialised domain of Artificial Intelligence. *

- ○ Traditional methodology
- ○ Gamification methodology

4. Select the methodology with which you felt most motivated and involved in the documentation process. *

- ○ Traditional methodology
- ○ Gamification methodology

5. Which gamified activity have you found most helpful for the documentation process and the translation practice on Artificial Intelligence? Please, tick as appropriate. *

- ○ GA1: The millionaire translator
- ○ GA2: Transmissing word
- ○ GA3: AI-Transelection
- ○ GA4: TransAIacronyms

6. Justify your answer to the previous question. *

Tu respuesta

7. To what extent can gamification enhance your learning experience in the specialised translation classroom? *

	1	2	3	4	5	
Not much	○	○	○	○	○	Very much

8. Do you think that the application of gamification methodology could be advantageous in other subjects of the Bachelor's Degree in Translation and Interpreting (languages, interpreting, etc.)? *

○ Yes

○ No

9. Mark the extent to which you agree with the following statements: *
The gamification methodology...

	Strongly disagree	Disagree	Agree	Strongly agree
has increased my level of motivation.	○	○	○	○
has helped me to be more focused.	○	○	○	○
has made my learning process more enjoyable.	○	○	○	○
has enabled me to internalise domain-specific terminology.	○	○	○	○
has helped me to translate a specialised text more easily.	○	○	○	○

10. After this gamification seminar, do you feel more confident about translating texts on the specialised field of Artificial Intelligence? *

○ Yes

○ No

Atrás Enviar Página 4 de 4 Borrar formulario

References

Aggarwal, K., M. M. Mijwil, Sonia, A.-H. Al-Mistarehi, S. Alomari, M. Gök, A. M. Z. Alaabdin, and S. H. Abdulrhman. 2022. Has the future started? The current growth of artificial intelligence, machine learning, and deep learning. *Iraqi Journal for Computer Science and Mathematics* 3(1): 115–123.

Alcaide-Martínez, M., and L. Taillefer. 2022. Gamification for English language teaching: A case study in translation and interpreting. *Lebende Sprachen* 67 (2): 283–310.

Alcalde Peñalver, E., and A. Santamaría Urbieta. 2020. Enhancing medical translation skills through a gamified experience. Failure or success? *Panace@* 21(51): 4–12.

Arain, M., M.J. Campbell, C.L. Cooper, and G.A. Lancaster. 2010. What is a pilot or feasibility study? A review of current practice and editorial policy. *BMC Medical Research Methodology* 10 (1): 1–7.

Baker, M. 2018. *In other words: A coursebook on Translation*. Oxon, New York: Routledge.

Chaiyo, Y., and R. Nokham. 2017. The effect of Kahoot, Quizizz and Google forms on the student's perception in the classrooms response system. In *2017 International Conference on Digital Arts, Media and Technology (ICDAMT)*, ed. Institute of Electrical and Electronics Engineers (IEEE), 178–182. Red Hook, NY: Curran Associates, Inc Chiang Mai, Thailand.

Chen, Y.-M. 2019. Motivational design in translation crowdsourcing: A gamification approach to Facebook community translation. *Compilation and Translation Review* 12 (1): 141–176.

Corpas Pastor, G. 2004. Localización de recursos y compilación de corpus vía Internet: aplicaciones para la didáctica de la traducción médica especializada. In *Manual de documentación y terminología para la traducción especializada*, ed. C. Gonzalo García, and V. García Yebra, 223–257. Madrid: Arco/libros, S. L.

Corpas Pastor, G. 2008. *Investigar con corpus en traducción: Los retos de un nuevo paradigma*, vol. 49. Frankfurt: Peter Lang.

Corpas Pastor, G., and M. Seghiri Domínguez, eds. 2016. *Corpus-based approaches to translation and interpreting: From theory to applications (Studien zur romanischen Sprachwissenschaft und interkulturellen Kommunikation, 106)*. Frankfurt: Peter Lang.

Council of Europe. n.d. *Glossary*. Council of Europe Portal. https://www.coe.int/en/web/artificial-intelligence/glossary.

Deterding, S., D. Dixon, R. Khaled, and L. Nacke. 2011a. From game design elements to gamefulness: Defining "gamification". In *Proceedings of the 15th International Academic MindTrek Conference: Envisioning Future Media Environments*, 9–15. ACM.

Deterding, S., R. Khaled, L. E. Nacke, & D. Dixon. 2011b. Gamification: Toward a definition. *CHI 2011 Gamification Workshop Proceedings*. Vancouver BC, 1–4.

Estévez Almenzar, M., D. Fernández Llorca, E. Gómez, and F. Martínez Plumed. 2022. *Glossary of human-centric artificial intelligence* (No. JRC129614). Luxembourg: Publications Office of the European Union.

Faber Benítez, P. 2009. The cognitive shift in terminology and specialized translation. *MonTI. Monografías De Traducción e Interpretación* 1: 107–134.

Fiola, M.A. 2013. Should the market dictate the content of specialized translation curricula? *Connexions International Professional Communication Journal* 1 (1): 59–63.

Ghenţulescu, R. 2017. Cultural challenges in specialized translations. *ФИЛКО/FILKO*, 91–99.

Grewal, D.S. 2014. A critical conceptual analysis of definitions of artificial intelligence as applicable to computer engineering. *IOSR Journal of Computer Engineering* 16 (2): 9–13.

Gutiérrez-Artacho, J., and M. D. Olvera-Lobo. 2016. Gamification in the translation and interpreting degree: A new methodological perspective in the classroom. *Proceeding of EDULEARN16. 8th Annual International Conference on Education and New Learning Technologies*, 50–58. Barcelona: IATED.

Haenlein, M., and A. Kaplan. 2019. A brief history of artificial intelligence: On the past, present, and future of artificial intelligence. *California Management Review* 61 (4): 5–14.

Hamari, J., J. Koivisto, and H. Sarsa. 2014. Does gamification work? A literature review of empirical studies on gamification. In *Proceedings of the 47th Hawaii International Conference on System Sciences*, 3025–3034. IEEE.

Kapp, K.M. 2012. *The gamification of learning and instruction: Game-based methods and strategies for training and education.* San Francisco, CA: Wiley.

Marín, V., M. López Pérez, and G.A. Maldonado Berea. 2015. Can gamification be introduced within primary classes? *Digital Education Review* 27 (27): 55–68.

McCarthy, J. 2007. *What is artificial intelligence?* [PDF document], 1–15, Nov 12. https://www.diochnos.com/about/McCarthyWhatisAI.pdf.

Meyers, C. 2022. The translation duel as a gamified hybrid learning activity. *Journal of Research in Higher Education* 6 (2): 88–112.

Moore, C.G., R.E. Carter, P.J. Nietert, and P.W. Stewart. 2011. Recommendations for planning pilot studies in clinical and translational research. *Clinical and Translational Science* 4 (5): 332–337.

Octaberlina, L.R. 2023. EFL learning gamification: Exploring high school learners' vocabulary acquisition through experimentation. *Salience Journal: English Language, Literature, and Education* 3 (1): 12–22.

Postolea, S. 2016. Translating in a specialised context: Challenges and risks. In *Buletinul Institutului Politehnic din Iasi/Bulletin of the Polytechnic Institute of Iasi.* LXII(LXVI), f.1 2016. Section: Social Sciences, 51–66. Iasi: "Gheorghe Asachi" Technical University of Iasi. Politehnium.

Puaschunder, J.M. 2019. Artificial Intelligence evolution: On the virtue of killing in the artificial age. *Scientia Moralitas-International Journal of Multidisciplinary Research* 4 (1): 51–72.

Rogers, M. 2015. Terminology and specialised translation: A historical perspective. In *Specialised translation. Palgrave studies in translating and interpreting*, ed. M. Rogers, 81–109. London: Palgrave Macmillan.

Soyoof, A., B. L. Reynolds, R. Shadiev, and B. Vazquez-Calvo. 2022. A mixed-methods study of the incidental acquisition of foreign language vocabulary and healthcare knowledge through serious game play. *Computer Assisted Language Learning* 1–34.

Steurs, F., K. De Wachter, and E. De Malsche. 2015. Terminology tools. In *Handbook of terminology*, vol. 1, ed. H.J. Kockaert and F. Steurs, 222–249. Amsterdam/Philadelphia: John Benjamins Publishing Company.

Varela Vila, T. 2009. Córpora ad hoc en la práctica traductora especializada: Aplicación al ámbito de las enfermedades neuromusculares. In *A survey of corpus-based research* [Recurso electrónico], ed. P. Cantos Gómez, and A. Sánchez Pérez, 814–831. Murcia, España: Asociación Española de Lingüística del Corpus.

Werbach, K., and D. Hunter. 2012. *For the win: How game thinking can revolutionize your business.* Philadelphia: Wharton Digital Press.

Yang, X., Y. Wang, R. Byrne, G. Schneider, and S. Yang. 2019. Concepts of artificial intelligence for computer-assisted drug discovery. *Chemical Reviews* 119 (18): 10520–10594.

Zhuang, Y., M. Cai, X. Li, X. Luo, Q. Yang, and F. Wu. 2020. The next breakthroughs of artificial intelligence: The interdisciplinary nature of AI. *Engineering* 6 (3): 245–247.

Gloria Corpas Pastor is Professor in Translation and Interpreting at the University of Malaga, Spain (since 2008), and honorary Adjunct Professor at Xi'an Jiaotong-Liverpool University, China (since 2020). She is currently Director of the Research Institute in Multilingual Language Technologies (IUITLM). Her research interests cover translation technology, interpreting technology, NLP, corpus linguistics, and phraseology.

Marta Alcaide-Martínez is Lecturer in Translation and Interpreting at the University of Malaga, Spain (since 2020). She is currently a Trainee Researcher, thanks to an FPU contract (ref. FPU21/03104) awarded by the Spanish Ministry of Science, Innovation and Universities. Her research interests include gamification, translation and interpreting technologies, AI, corpus linguistics, and phraseology.

Things to Do in the Translation Class When Technologies Change: The Case of Generative AI

Nune Ayvazyan, Yu Hao, and Anthony Pym

Abstract The rapid evolution of translation technologies, especially the emergence of generative artificial intelligence, presents major pedagogical challenges to the extent that stable knowledge and skills are in flux. This makes it difficult to know what to teach and how to teach it. These challenges can be addressed through student-led discovery activities, the fostering of a critical comparative attitude towards technologies, awareness of an extended range of aids, and emphasizing both foundational skills and AI literacy. Some 18 group activities have been developed on those bases and are presented here. All are designed to engage students in a dynamic learning process. Some activities involve making comparisons between unaided human translation, AI-generated text, and post-edited outputs; others venture into pre-editing, different workflows, and literary translation. These activities aim to cultivate an understanding of the strengths and limitations of various technologies while promoting critical thinking and practical translation skills.

At the time of writing, translation technology is not the same as it is for you when you are reading this. That is the only prediction we can be sure of. As we write, translators are still mostly typing rather than speaking to computers, despite vast improvements in speech-to-text tools. Translators are still post-editing neural machine translation, despite the free availability of artificial intelligence (AI) feeds in Trados Studio and MateCat. And there is still a lot of background chatter about large language models (LLMs) and generative pre-trained transformer (GPT) technologies—the names are not yet stable, but we will call them "generative AI"—that are variously said to be destroying jobs, spreading lies, consuming vast amounts of energy, threatening

N. Ayvazyan (✉) · A. Pym
Universitat Rovira i Virgili, Tarragona, Spain
e-mail: nune.ayvazyan@urv.cat

A. Pym
e-mail: anthony.pym@urv.cat

Y. Hao
The University of Melbourne, Melbourne, VIC, Australia
e-mail: haoyh2@unimelb.edu.au

Y. Peng et al. (eds.), *New Advances in Translation Technology*, New Frontiers in Translation Studies, https://doi.org/10.1007/978-981-97-2958-6_11

humanity, curtailing creativity, and incidentally helping students cheat on their homework (cf., for example Bender et al. 2021). In short, there is much talk of technological change happening on several fronts, and the only thing we really know is that we do not know much about it. On balance, most of the current discourses predict benefits that do not outweigh the risks. At the same time, common sense suggests the technologies are not going away.

When we try to teach translation technologies in such a situation of fundamental change, the practical problem is not so much with grasping the general tendencies as it is the speed of change. It takes time to assess innovations and make them teachable. Our main concern here is thus with the appearance of generative AI capacities based on large language models, where there are many questions to be asked and answered. One such query pertains to the positioning of the new technologies relative to established neural machine translation systems (Google Translate, DeepL, and the like). A related question is what impact these developments will have on job prospects for translators and interpreters. Both those questions directly concern how we teach students about emerging technologies.

In this kind of situation, several basic alternatives are available. We could go back and teach the technologies we are sure about, hoping that the old skills and models will serve our students in the future—just as we teach handwriting because it is somehow presumed to help students learn to type. Alternatively, we could wait until we have firm data on the capacities and risks of each new technology—just as one might teach about climate change only when the climate has changed. Between those two extremes, however, we propose that it is possible to teach in a way that is based on in-class experiments, setting up a dynamic of shared discovery in which students are trained not in any one fixed state of play but in how to cope with technological change itself.

What might that mean in the actual space of the classroom? Here we seek some general guidelines from previous or neighbouring research, then we advance a few suggestions that will hopefully be of use to anyone asking our questions.

1 How Does Generative AI Affect Translation?

Research on generative AI is so far almost exclusively on various avatars of ChatGPT, which has been free online since November 2022. Most of the studies have been focused on assessing the quality of its output. With respect to how well the technology translates between languages, the general finding is that it does not perform significantly better than the neural machine translation systems we have been working with since 2016. To that extent, we can afford to stay calm, perhaps calmer than professionals in many other fields. There are, however, some important nuances.

Jiao et al. (2023) find that GPT-3 and GPT-4 are basically on par with neural machine translation systems for work with high-resource European languages but perform significantly more poorly with low-resource languages. Hendy et al. (2023) examine the performance of three GPT models when translating in 18 directions, including both high- and low-resource languages as well as non-English-centric translations. They similarly find that GPT models produce competitive translation quality for high-resource languages but are less effective for low-resource languages. Ghosh and Caliskan (2023) look at GPT's performance when translating between English and Bengali, Farsi, Malay, Tagalog, Thai, and Turkish. They find not only that the low-resource languages fare worse but also that "ChatGPT perpetuates gender defaults and stereotypes assigned to certain occupations (e.g., man = doctor, woman = nurse) or actions (e.g., woman = cook, man = go to work)" (2023, 1). Peng et al. (2023) consider variables such as the relative creativity ("temperature") of a text, task information, domain information, and prompts that are task-specific or domain-specific. They report that GPT performs best when task information is emphasized in the prompt and the text is relatively standardized. It also produces hallucinations for translation tasks involving low-resource languages, and ostensibly powerful chain-of-thought prompts tend to have a negative impact.

From these studies, we conclude that any pedagogy for teaching the use of generative AI will have to pay careful attention to the status of the languages being dealt with (where the main variable is what kind of electronic assets are available), the text types used (less standardized discourse creates more problems, as with machine translation), the tendency to reproduce stereotypes (since the algorithms tend to opt for high-probability, middle-of-the-road solutions, again as in neural machine translation), and the prompts used to instruct the technologies (which would be a relatively new set of skills). Those are all useful guidelines that could have a relatively long shelf-life.

From our own experience, we further propose that the impact of AI technology is not so much in straight translation tasks but in assisting a wide range of language-processing and transcreation tasks, to which we return below.

2 How Do We Teach Translation Technologies in General?

Discussions regarding the integration of translation technologies into classroom activities have been ongoing ever since machine translation became available online. Some advocate for students to gain strong language skills before they interact with technologies (Bowker 2015); others believe that technologies should be introduced as early as possible (e.g., Somers 1997; O'Brien 2002). Our standpoint here is that, while acquiring foundational translation skills is undeniably important, we must also acknowledge that students are already using many translation technologies in their daily lives. For that simple reason, it is no longer practical to keep technology for the end of a program of study because it is considered "hard", just as it makes increasingly less sense to relegate technologies to just one special course, as if they were not of use in translation activities in all courses. Those general principles also concern generative AI, which students are already using, whether we like it or not (see, for example, von Garrel and Mayer 2023).

Due to the recent emergence of generative AI, we have been unable to locate any serious empirical research specifically on its use in translator training, although there is no real shortage of anecdotal observations (as in Xiao and Zhi 2023; Pym and Hao 2024). Here we mainly draw on our own teaching practices, in many cases adapting or extending activities we have used when teaching the post-editing of neural machine translation.

What follows from the existing research is that, even though technologies keep evolving, AI-generated output still needs some human intervention. Post-editing, in its turn, requires not only knowledge of the subject matter, but also professional MT literacy, defined as "the full range of MT-related competences professional translators (and other language professionals) may require in order to participate successfully in the various phases of the MT-assisted professional translation process" (Krüger and Hackenbuchner 2022, p. 384). Krüger and Hackenbuchner argue that professional machine-translation literacy encompasses various skills and knowledge areas, including technical, linguistic, economic, societal, and cognitive aspects. Among these, having expertise in the technical aspects of neural machine translation is crucial because it equips translators with the necessary understanding of both the advantages and dangers of automation (Krüger and Hackenbuchner 2022, p. 389). As such, MT literacy blends into AI literacy, which can be seen as "a set of competencies that enables individuals to critically evaluate AI technologies; communicate and collaborate effectively with AI; and use AI as a tool online, at home, and in the workplace" (Long and Magerko 2020). Assuming that all these technologies are here to stay, it becomes evident that equipping our students to confront present-day challenges and any forthcoming obstacles is the logical course of action.

Back in the days of statistical machine translation, Pym (2013) proposed a list of ten skills that translators should acquire when learning to work with the technology. The skills came under three general heads: (1) learn to learn, (2) learn to trust and distrust data, and (3) learn to revise translations as texts. How many of those skills are still required in the age of generative AI? What new skills should be added to the list?

3 Principles for a Pedagogy of Technological Change

Here we propose a pedagogy based on awareness of the constant imperfection of current knowledge. This means that we, as teachers, never know all the technologies available; we do not know all the capacities, advantages, and disadvantages; and we certainly do not know which technologies our students will be using five or ten years after our classes. This basic awareness of relative ignorance has several clear consequences for the way learning outcomes can be formulated:

- *Student-led discovery*: Rather than attempt to convey fixed knowledge, our role is to organize activities in which students discover knowledge for themselves. This can be done as a series of group experiments (Pym 2009).

- *Critical evaluation of technologies*: Even when we choose to focus on one technology in depth, we must encourage students to make critical comparisons *between* technologies. They should thus know how to assess future technologies that we do not yet know about.

At the same time, any teaching must work from the initial capacities and expectations of learners. In the case of translation technologies, this can often mean negotiating both inflated expectations of automated output and, from other students, significant initial resistance, and preconceptions about the inferiority of any automated solution. This means that initial exploratory activities should be designed to challenge such preconceptions, especially in two respects:

- *Exploration of the aided human*: Most translators with strong language skills will start from the supposition that a human translator will always work better than automation ("I can translate better than any machine!"). The basic comparison nevertheless should be between the aided and unaided human ("Can I translate better with the help of automation?").
- *An extended range of aids*: Most beginners also start from the supposition that automation only replaces the translator's decision-making while translating. Time must therefore be taken to explore the many other ways in which generative AI can help translators. Here is a short list of things that AI technologies can do to one degree or another:

  - Give alternative translations to choose between
  - Answer questions about comparative grammar
  - Provide contextualized bilingual dictionary definitions
  - Give background information on a word, phrase, citation, or topic
  - Align previous translations
  - Pre-edit the start text
  - Adapt the translation to specific readerships and/or purposes
  - Write your translation as you speak it
  - Read your translation back to you
  - Revise your translation for spelling
  - Revise your translation for punctuation
  - Revise your translation for grammar
  - Revise your translation for readability
  - Revise your translation to suit a specific register
  - Extract terminology
  - Manage terminology
  - Check for consistency in numbers, terms, and formatting,

and certainly much else as well. It is simply a question of exploring the possibilities.

4 Suggested Activities

The following activities involve the use of generative AI to carry out translation activities, either in a language class or as a part of translator training. They are at various levels of difficulty: some should work in secondary education; others are better for postgraduate level. Our purpose here is simply to give examples of what can be done: we address only a few of the extended capacities listed above. Similar activities can be found in Pym (2009, 2019) and Koponen (2015), while fuller explanations of most of these activities can be found in Pym and Hao (2024)—to which we also offer a few alternatives.

4.1 Beginners' Mistake: What not to Do

If you give your whole class a translation to do and you allow them to use any kind of automation to do it, do not be surprised when all the students send you virtually the same translation.

There are two main ways to avoid this happening. Either you have the students do an unaided translation first, which they then compare with the generative AI version (and will usually learn from it) or you select a text that is full of traps for automation: gendered pronouns, neologisms, long sentences, incomplete sentences, and non-standard language, forcing the students to correct ("post-edit") whatever output they get.

Whatever you do, it is best to not let anyone start from the generative AI translation of a straightforward text. No one will learn anything.

4.2 Compare Unaided and Automated

Here is how to correct the beginners' mistake: Have students translate a text into their first language (L1) without any use of automation (hence "unaided"), then compare the result with what generative AI produces. This should ideally be done using a text that has opaque technical terms (where AI will probably do better than the human) and long sentences with pronouns, as gendered as possible (where the humans will probably do better).

It is important that this exercise be done in the students' L1, even in a mixed-language class. If the translation is into L2, students are likely to lack the required skills to spot syntactic errors and will be inclined to trust the output. That said, a useful variant is to have mixed-language groups compare the results, bringing together critical awareness in both L1 and L2.

The risk of this activity is that it may reinforce initial prejudices *against* automation. In most cases, though, students increasingly express surprise at the improving quality of raw outputs.

4.3 Compare Generative AI Solutions

One of the saving graces of current automation systems is that they allow for numerous retranslations. In most generative AI systems (except Microsoft Copilot on this occasion), you can ask for a translation into a language ("Translate into Chinese"), then use exactly the same prompt again, with the same system, and you will get a slightly different translation. Then use the prompt again, and a third translation is given. Whatever the logic behind this may be (do the algorithms assume that if you want a second helping, you were not satisfied by the first?), the inherent variability of translation becomes immediately obvious. For anyone given to believe that there is only one correct translation for each sentence, this discovery can be pedagogically liberating (for students) or existentially confusing (for some lay users). Used in this way, generative AI can become more interactive than most neural machine translation systems except DeepL.

When these retranslations are produced in the students' L1 as far as possible, students can be invited to make the comparisons and pick up the limitations. They will often find that the variants are fairly minor, but they will at least have learned that there are always alternative translations.

Google Gemini is particularly good at proposing alternatives when asked to translate repeatedly. Here is what it offers for a sentence from the Catalan public health website (see Pym et al. 2022):

ST: Fes gestions de forma no presencial amb el sistema sanitari

TT1: Carry out procedures non-face-to-face with the health system.

TT2: Do your paperwork remotely with the healthcare system.

TT3: Connect with your doctor or nurse virtually.

TT4: Handle your healthcare affairs remotely!

TT5: Schedule appointments online.

TT6: Get your test results electronically.

TT7: Refill prescriptions online or by phone.

The more you ask, the more the proposals move away from the original text, and the more ideas we have for various modes of transcreation.

A further variation is to line up four or five candidate translations, discuss their shortcomings and virtues, and then have students vote for the best one. As far as we know, this kind of democratic translation quality came to the fore when Facebook launched its now-defunct crowd translation platform.

4.4 Compare AI and Machine Translation

An obvious variation on the above activity is to invite comparisons with a few machine translation systems, if only to see what the differences might be. Sometimes this produces little interest. The above Catalan example gives the following suggestions, which are neither better nor worse than the AI versions, and they are both reasonably creative:

Google Translate: Make arrangements in person with the health system.

Microsoft Translator: Carry out procedures remotely with the health system.

How can we explain the variability of these retranslations? A possible explanation is that there are many different kinds of algorithms working in generative AI, which means that they generally draw on monolingual databases but also appear to move in and out of the kinds of databases that machine translation systems use.

One way to test this in class is to take a perennial translation problem and ask for generative AI for advice. We did this for the Spanish past subjunctive, which has no equivalent form in English but is not especially problematic when used for unreal conditionals. GPT told us that the past subjuctive “tuviera” could be rendered as follows:

ST: Si yo tuviera más dinero, viajaría por el mundo.

GPT: If I had more money, I would travel the world.

ST: Me habría gustado que ella tuviera más tiempo para venir.

GPT: I would have liked her to have had more time to come.

These are straight translations; the grammar lesson is clear enough. But watch what happens when these same sentences are run through the neural machine translation system DeepL and we select the top two suggestions:

DeepL 1: If *only* I had more money, I would travel the world (italics ours).

DeepL 2: I *wish* she had had more time to come (italics ours).

Why do the machine translations seem to be more idiomatic? One reason could be that they have been generated from a database of human translations. That is, if you ask generative AI for a translation lesson, you often get a good lesson in comparative grammar and semantics. But if you want something closer to a human translation, your students might decide to work from machine translations.

4.5 Spot the Automation

For a fairly complex text, not necessarily technical, give students two unaided translations and a translation done by generative AI. Then ask them to spot the AI version, as in a simple Turing test—Turing (1950) proposed that a machine successfully imitates thought when users cannot distinguish its answers from those of a human.

Why *two* human translations? In theory, it should provide some clues: if two translations give X and one gives Y, and X and Y are mutually exclusive, the mistake is likely to be in Y. This particularly concerns the strategic omissions that some AI systems are prone to make. The omission may seem trivial, but once you begin to doubt parts of a translation, distrust can spread to the rest.

Here is an example from COVID information in Catalan, which is a language with only moderate electronic resources—so language mistakes do occur:

> TT1: If you already have your first COVID-19 shot, find out how to get your second COVID-19 shot.
>
> TT2: If you have already been given a first dose of the COVID-19 vaccine, find out how the second dose is called up.
>
> TT3: If you already have your first dose of the COVID-19 vaccine, find out about the scheduling of your booster shot.

Can you pick the AI translation? The first version is unaided, the second is from Google Gemini, and the third is unaided.

In principle, this activity should not show the original text while the guessing game is happening, but it can be shown later. Here is the original Catalan:

> ST: Si ja tens administrada una primera dosi de la vacuna contra la COVID-19, descobreix com es duu a terme *la convocatòria* de la segona dosi (italics ours).

The AI version stumbled over the expression "convocatòria", which is generally a "call" but not in this context—it refers to the scheduling of the booster shots.

The game implicitly assumes that the AI version is likely to have an error somewhere. However, if it is played with some of the more creative or difficult literary texts (we do it for historical versions of the opening sentences of *Don Quijote*), the opposite can also hold: the AI version is the one closest to the text, while the unaided translations tend to use omission for the unknown values, as well as occasional flights of fantasy as appeals to literariness.

The more interesting discussions then come when students sometimes recognize the syntactic structures that give a specific voice to different AI systems. The regular sentence lengths and balanced non-committal judgements of GPT become familiar after a while, over and above questions of specific translation mistakes. And once students get to that level of forensic linguistics, they might be able to appreciate how teachers can tell when their essays lean on AI.

4.6 Compare Generative AI, Neural Machine Translation, and Post-editing

The same comparisons can be extended to include a human correction of MT and AI outputs, the most common term for which is still "post-editing". That is, students not only spot the errors, but they correct them at the same time. Of course, they might have been doing this already in the previous comparative activity. If they use Track

Changes (teach them to use it!), they can quickly have a numerical score of how many changes are made, which can be used as a very rough evaluation of how well the technologies performed.

In cases where the comparison is based on producing translations in class, it is important to have students keep track of *how long* they spend post-editing the different outputs. The measuring of time is important for several reasons.

First, some students (and thus some groups) will typically spend about twice as long as others, in our experience. This sets up an empirical basis for discussions of how much post-editing is required, the distinction between "light" and "heavy" post-editing, and the various scenarios in which quicker post-editing can be entirely acceptable.

Second, more obviously, it is possible to compare the time spent on post-editing with the time spent on translating the text unaided.

4.7 Compare Post-editing with Unaided Translation

The key to combatting initial prejudices against technology should be the time saved. Yet the calculation of that time only makes sense once the group has a clear understanding of the nature of post-editing and its various degrees. If not, one simply finishes up with a wide range of different times and translation practices.

One way to carry out the activity is to divide each group of four into two, then have one pair translate a 200-word text without MT or AI (but with other Internet resources) while the other pair puts the same text through AI and post-edits the result. Both groups keep track of the time spent on the entire task. The result one is looking for is a significant time advantage for AI. The interesting thing is that this does not always happen: there are some brilliant translators who work fast unaided, and there are nit-picking perfectionists who will spend forever finding and correcting and re-correcting errors in the outputs of AI. That is the point where the discussion has to go back to the different kinds of post-editing and their different reasons. The discussion of time savings might be attributed to financial consequences: if one workflow gives a time saving of 25%, then that is perhaps 25% more income for the translator over the course of their entire professional career.

Objections will be raised, of course, since quality is also a variable. But that can also be measured in an admittedly rough way. Have each translation (whether unaided or aided) revised, using Track Changes, by a student who has just rendered the same text into the same language. Those revised texts are then sent back to the translator or post-editor, who can choose to accept or reject the proposed changes. The number of accepted changes is then an approximate measure of the quality of the text. In the process, the students find numerous issues to discuss with each other—which is where much of the actual learning happens.

The various groups then present their results to the whole class, highlighting how much time was gained and the relative quality of the outputs (see Pym 2009). There will always be exceptions, but the ideal general result should be a significant time gain from automation with approximately the same quality. If the time gain is not significant and the quality is higher for the unaided translations, the text probably did not have enough culture-specific terms, long sentences, or implicatures. There is room for experimentation.

An additional step, of course, would be for the teacher to grade all the outputs and then show the average grades to the whole class. Such solutions are possibly for teachers who love hard work or institutionally need numerous numerical grades.

An extension of this basic time-based activity is to explore the hypothesis that a text that is produced quickly will take more time for receivers to process. This could be tested in class, especially in a multilingual class where some readers do not have access to the start language of some texts. The greater reading ease of AI-generated texts would seem to give them a significant advantage here.

4.8 Compare Time-On-Task in Post-editing with Unaided Translation

An extension of the previous activity is to have the students screen-record their performances then play back the recordings (at a fast speed) and keep track of how they spent their time. Students' first discovery tends to be how much time they spend correcting typos (they should learn to touch-type or use a speech-to-text tool). Some are then surprised by how often they change from A to B and then back to A (they need more confidence in their intuitions).

The way the tasks are divided must depend on the hypotheses to be tested. The simplest and easiest taxonomy is perhaps (1) pre-translation (time spent prior to typing the first word of the translation), (2) documentation (all the time spent outside of the program in which the translation is written), (3) revision (all the time spent after typing the last word of the translation), and (4) drafting (all the remaining time).

Perhaps the most interesting hypothesis to test is the claim that automation enables translators to spend more time solving important problems that machines are not yet able to solve. This should appear in different distributions of documentation activities—so the class might want to focus on that analysis.

4.9 Compare Pre-editing with Unaided Translation

When errors are found in AI output, they can be corrected in the translation ("post-editing") or they can be avoided by re-writing the start text ("pre-editing").

The easiest way to explore pre-editing is to have students translate a text online in DeepL, Google Translate, Youdao, Baidou, or Sougou then use the same interface to change the start text and see how the translation adjusts accordingly. Unfortunately, the AI interfaces do not allow you to do this.

Good examples here are the cases of gender bias:

ST: Seek medical advice from your local doctor or Nurse-On-Call at 1300 60 60 24.

GPT 4: Consulte a su médico local o a la Enfermera de Guardia llamando al 1300 60 60 24.

[Consult your local MALE doctor or FEMALE Nurse on Call by phoning 1300 60 60 24.]

How can we stop Spanish (and many other languages with gendered nouns and adjectives) from making the doctor a man and the nurse a woman? Clever students will find clever solutions. One of the possible strategies is to ask GPT to repeat the translation avoiding gendered professions. This gave: "Busque asesoramiento médico de su profesional local o del servicio de enfermería de guardia llamando al 1300 60 60 24." If we translate that back into English, we have a successful pre-edit, designed to remove sexist bias from almost any language you want to translate into:

Seek advice from your local medical professional or phone the emergency nursing service at 1300 60 60 24.

Problem solved, more or less?

Pre-editing is a skill set that was always intended for machine translation and is perhaps limited to it, given that AI can solve these problems when instructed to do so. The reason why pre-editing is still worth teaching is that a well-written start text can avoid myriad thorny problems before they occur, both for machine translation and for AI. That is, pre-editing remains useful whenever one text has to go into more than one language, and the more target languages the text goes into, the greater the relative benefits of pre-editing.

4.10 *Translate from a Language You don't Know*

We calculate that much less than one per cent of the words translated in the world are done by professional translators (Pym and Torres-Simon 2021). That means that most of the world is using automation to translate, and most users are probably translating from languages they do not know, or do not know well. It can be instructive for translation students to put themselves in the shoes of those everyday users, to experience the benefits and risks involved.

Find a few restaurant menus in languages that your students do not know. Then ask the students to use generative AI to select three dishes that they think they would like, and then three that they would not order because they have no idea what they are. Is it still possible to eat in the restaurant? Probably, given that most of us can sort out the risks in a pragmatic way: check and learn the things you like, and don't trust anything you don't understand.

The instructive part comes in when you include languages with reduced electronic resources. Everyone can find something to eat when the menu is in a hegemonic language with abundant electronic databases for generative AI to draw on. But when you get to a menu in Armenian or Hausa, eating can become a far more adventurous affair.

4.11 Check Terminology

Some of the most useful questions to ask generative AI concern terminology, especially the use of a term in a specified context. This is the function that can be found in the free online translation memory suite MateCat, and the responses can fruitfully be used when clarifying terms in the translation. Similar definition functions are also found in free online machine translation, but the output tends not to be so context-specific.

In class, a basic activity is to compare the terminology used by machine translation, AI, and unaided translation for the straight translation of a highly technical text—automated solutions tend to be remarkably exact. A more focused exercise is to compare the various ways of *checking* terminology: online dictionaries, specialized glossaries, and parallel texts, all versus questions to AI systems.

4.12 Create a Term Base

Translators need to know at least the basics of terminology, and a good way to practice the basics is to extract terms from a text manually. The lesson is straightforward: explain what a term is, then get groups to go through a text and draw up a list of terms, perhaps with short descriptors. They can then go through a parallel text in another language and extract corresponding terms, thus compiling a bilingual term base or glossary. It is important that this be done manually at first, to demonstrate how hard the task can be. It is also a good way to get students to argue about what is or is not a term.

Once they have done that, invite student groups to discover how to do the same task with generative AI. And when they have worked out the prompts for that, they can invent prompts for bilingual term extraction based on texts in different languages.

When comparisons are made between the manually created term bases and those that are generated automatically, what happens? So far, we are finding that the automated compilation saves a lot of time but includes items that are not really terms. Of course, the performance could be better next week.

These results can also be compared with those given by Sketch Engine or a number of other solutions available online.

4.13 Play with Prompts

The art of term extraction leads directly to the importance of prompts. Generative AI will translate when you tell it to do so: "Translate this text into Spanish". With this prompt, the kind of translation you get is usually straightforward, although not necessarily literalist. Additions to the prompt can then adapt the translation in several useful ways.

One of the problems in behaviour-change messaging is the use of the second person ("you"). The pronoun is recommended in most of the manuals for this kind of writing since it involves the receiver directly and can convey a sense of urgent personal action. Unfortunately, the second person is unmarked in English but has rival formal and informal translations in many other languages, so the algorithms have to decide between the two. Machine translation can often decide well for one or two sentences, based on the context, but not for a whole text: in Spanish, the outputs tend to switch between the informal ("tú") and the formal ("usted") from paragraph to paragraph.

Invite your students to find a way to solve this problem using AI. With luck, they will come up with a solution that specifies something about the receiver: "Translate this text with a formal register" or "Translate this text for an older person". And if they keep experimenting, they might find that the algorithms know a bit about linguistics: "Translate this text using the formal second person". The problem is thereby solved for the whole text, we hope.

Students should be encouraged to experiment with prompts to see how far the results are useful. Texts can be translated for different levels of literacy ("Translate for a reader with six years of schooling") or for different backgrounds (in the case of bushfires, "Translate for a reader who has just come to Australia"). They can go further: ask for images to accompany the text to give it more impact; ask for ideas about how to turn the written text into an audiovisual presentation. When asked to do this, Gemini gave a dialogue between a mother and child about what to do as a bushfire approached. At that level, AI throws out creative ideas that creative students should be able to play with and build on.

4.14 Assess the Risks of Adaptation

In all these cases, examples should be used that show the extent to which creative adaptation is risk-laden—it can go wrong and needs to be checked by humans. Generative AI technologies are very smooth talkers. They can sound convincing even when producing outright lies, or more commonly half-lies or white lies. They can lull the user, and indeed the translator, into trusting everything they produce, since it all flows in neat accessible sentences. That deceptive claim to trustworthiness is interestingly opposed to the other capacity that students should soon pick up: the ability of generative AI to produce different retranslations. The more different translations the lay user sees, the less likely they are to trust each one. And yet the voice of generative AI appeals to facile trust. What students have to grasp, therefore, is that a particularly active kind of *distrust* is needed in order to critically compare the retranslations and thereby use the technologies productively and creatively.

One way of pointing towards that distrust—"critical thinking" is the more traditional term—is to track the ways generative AI can adapt a text when asked to do so, and then note when it falls into error precisely because it is seeking to adapt. For example, this is from a text about a former Australian prime minister:

ST: Born in July 1928...

GPT ("adapt for 12-year-old"): Born in the summer of 1928...

The reference to summer certainly makes the text more real, more lived, and perhaps closer to the young reader. But the smooth talker somehow forgot that July is a *winter* month in Australia, where the prime minister was born.

The class activity should start by inviting students to use prompts requesting increasing degrees of adaptation, so they should be on the lookout for increasing number of errors. All adaptation requires a certain amount of guesswork, and all guesses can be wrong.

4.15 Use AI for Summaries or Gist Translation

Generative AI can summarize texts in a given number of words, but does it do a good job? An easy way to test this is to have students write unaided summaries of texts that they know fairly well, perhaps because they have written them themselves or studied them in a different course. They then compare the unaided summaries with the ones produced by AI.

When doing this activity, it is important to specify what the summary is for. If it is an academic abstract, then certain rules need to be applied, and AI tends not to apply them very well—it prefers reported speech. On the other hand, if the purpose is to enable a client to identify which key passages are worth translating professionally, then AI tends to provide summaries that are as specific as the prompts that ask for them. That is, it does what it is told.

4.16 Use Technologies for Literary Translation

When we do the basic comparative activities, students can see that post-editing of various kinds can be advantageous in terms of both time and quality. However, when we then ask the class if they will use the technologies in all their future translations, a frequent answer is that the technologies will certainly be used but *never* for literature (Hao et al. 2024). Literature is somehow sacred.

What can we do? You can force students to use AI to translate a few excerpts from literary texts, to see what it gives. Much will depend, of course, on what kind of text you count as literature. An unrhymed verse often comes through automation marvellously well, to the extent that the odd mistake can sometimes add to the pleasure of the text. Of course, as soon as you get into long sentences, archaic diction, and playful implicatures, the difficulty increases and the technologies falter. But there is no particular reason why those specific linguistic features are or should be exclusively literary. The ideologies of literary exceptionalism deserve to be tested at every turn.

We note in passing the existence of platforms where readers can post-edit web novels online. The Chinese-to-English platform "Light Novel Machine Translation" (LNMTL) amazingly invites users to make sense of some rather impenetrable machine translations, like the following sentence, selected almost at random:

> Just, these dragonet dragon horn have not lived, scales cannot form, the claw has not appeared, is the dragon, is more like the snake on the contrary (https://lnmtl.com/chapter/nine-star-hegemon-body-art-book-12-chapter-5949).

If some people enjoy making sense of that kind of automation, good luck to them! Our classes will hopefully fare well on the much better post-edit offered by Google Gemini, working from the above English version:

> However, these dragonets lack horns, cannot yet form scales, and haven't developed claws. While not yet true dragons, they currently resemble snakes more than anything else.

Then again, for some, the better the output, the less pleasure can be taken in resolving cryptic clues.

4.17 Explain Translation Technologies to Clients

It is not enough to know how to use technologies; we must also *explain* what we are doing to our clients, who ultimately should trust us. This is thus an activity on translator-client relations, which can be done with or without technology and is well suited to a multilingual classroom (cf. Pym 2019). We allocate two weeks to it every year.

The class groups become translation companies, with students having different roles (translators, revisers, terminologists, project managers, and presentation designers). Half the groups will compete to win a specified translation contract; the other half compete for a different contract. The contracts might concern missions like the promotion of a film from Culture A in Culture B, the export of a culture-specific sport (Australian football is marketed in China), the opening of new branches of a restaurant chain, and so on. Let each group pick its preferred film, sport, or restaurant chain.

Each group prepares a ten-minute pitch of its company, including sample translations of a webpage and subtitles for some audiovisual material. The presentation must also explain how the company uses technologies to improve their work—their ability to work with technologies will be a point of prestige for the company. The main aim is to make the technology understandable, trusted, and potentially profitable for the client.

In the first week, half the companies do their presentations (for instance, Australian films to be promoted in China) and the other companies act as clients, asking questions following the pitches, evaluating the proposals, and awarding the contract to the winner. The next week, the roles are reversed (for example, extending Chinese restaurant chains to Australia) (Whether or not you have winners and losers might depend on each student's culture.).

4.18 Triage Translations in Different Situations

The term "triage" is from French, where it means "sorting". It usually refers to the prioritization of patients when they are brought to a hospital in a situation of emergency (Pym 2023). Applied to translations, it can mean prioritizing texts in terms of relative urgency, which may in turn determine which technologies should be used. This mostly concerns simple trade-offs between speed and quality: where speed is necessary, a certain loss of quality can be accepted; when not, then not. Questions of costs and available expertise can also be entered into the calculation.

The obvious classroom activity here is to present a list of situated translation purposes in one column and then a list of translation workflows in another. Student groups then have to discuss how to match the workflows with the situated purposes. For example, a survey of bushfire-related documents in Australia gives the following situations (which can be deduced from the nature of the texts themselves):

- Urgent messaging ("it's too late to leave")
- Templates for the urgent messaging (since bushfires come every year)
- Instructions on how to make insurance claims after a fire
- Instructions on how to maintain and check fire alarms.

Much as one might think that everything related to fire is urgent, only the first item in this list has time as a make-or-break factor, although the insurance claim instructions can also be context-specific and thus have a certain limited timeframe.

The workflows can include everything from unchecked automation through to various degrees of post-editing and pre-editing, and then unaided translation if and when the necessary human resources are available (and they should be!).

4.19 Speed Trials

Building on the idea of triage, some fun can be had with the translation of short messages on SMS, WeChat, or X (formerly Twitter). Since the messages typically have a very short shelf-life, it makes sense for them to be translated fast. But how fast can students go? Translation races can be organized (as suggested in Desjardins 2011, 185).

5 A Conclusion Against Overreaction

In any technical field that is surrounded by profuse public discussion, it is easy to be misled by facile causes based on anecdotal examples. Students (and teachers) will come into the classroom with many preconceived notions of what is good and bad in new technologies. Many of those ideas must be tempered, and the only way to do this is by having students experiment with the technologies, and then drawing their own conclusions.

In these general discussions, it should be clear to students that they have to know about the technologies and how to use them, whether they like them or not. A further important consideration is the extent to which awareness of technological change will be our students' generational advantage in the job market. Established translators rose in the profession, thanks to older technologies, which is one very good reason why they tend to downplay the advantages of the newer technologies. Faced with the eternal dilemma that all employers require experience, but new graduates have very little, our students should be prepared to emphasize their command of machine translation and generative AI, their ability to get the most out of the technologies, and their capacity to convince employers and future clients that there is good and bad to be discovered, if you can get beyond the hype.

References

Bender, Emily M., Timnit Gebru, Angelina McMillan-Major, and Shmargaret Shmitchell. 2021. On the dangers of stochastic parrots: Can language models be too big? In *Conference on Fairness, Accountability, and Transparency (FAccT '21)*, 610–623. https://doi.org/10.1145/3442188.3445922.

Bowker, Lynne. 2015. Computer-aided translation: Translator training. In *Routledge Encyclopedia of Translation Technology*, ed. S.W. Chan, 88–104. Routledge.

Desjardins, Renée. 2011. Facebook me! Initial insights in favour of using social networking as a tool for translator training. *Linguistica Antverpiensia* 10: 175–193.

Ghosh, Sourojit, and Aylin Caliskan. 2023. ChatGPT Perpetuates gender bias in machine translation and ignores non-gendered pronouns: Findings across Bengali and five other low-resource languages. https://arxiv.org/abs/2305.10510.

Hao, Yu, Ke Hu, and Anthony Pym. 2024. Who's afraid of literary post-editing? Performances and reflections of student translators. Unpublished manuscript.

Hendy, Amr, Mohamed Abdelrehim, Amr Sharaf, Vikas Raunak, Mohamed Gabr, Hitokazu Matsushita, Young Jin Kim, Mohamed Afify, and Hany Hassan Awadalla. 2023. How good are GPT models at machine translation? A comprehensive evaluation. https://arxiv.org/abs/2302.09210.

Jiao, Wenxiang, Wenxuan Wang, Jen-tse Huang, Xing Wang, and Zhaopeng Tu. 2023. Is ChatGPT a good translator? Yes with GPT-4 as the engine. https://arxiv.org/abs/2301.08745.

Koponen, Maarit. 2015. How to teach machine translation post-editing? Experiences from a post-editing course. In *4th Workshop on Post-Editing Technology and Practice (WPTP4)*, ed. Sharon O'Brien, and M. Simard, 2–15. Association for Machine Translation in the Americas. https://aclanthology.org/2015.mtsummit-wptp.1.pdf.

Krüger, Ralph, and Janiça Hackenbuchner. 2022. Outline of a didactic framework for combined data literacy and machine translation literacy teaching. *Current Trends in Translation Teaching and Learning*, E.375–432. https://doi.org/10.51287/cttl202211.

Long, Duri, and Brian Magerko. 2020. What is AI literacy? competencies and design considerations. In *Proceedings of the 2020 CHI Conference on Human Factors in Computing Systems.*

O'Brien, Sharon. 2002. Teaching post-editing: A proposal for course content. In *6th EAMT Workshop Teaching Machine Translation.* https://aclanthology.org/2002.eamt-1.11.

Peng, Kegin, Liang Ding, Qihuang Zhong, Li Shen, Xuebo Liu, Min Zhang, Yuanxin Ouyang, and Dacheng Tao. 2023. Towards making the most of ChatGPT for machine translation. https://arxiv.org/abs/2303.13780.

Pym, Anthony. 2009. Using process studies in translator training. Self-discovery through lousy experiments. In *Methodology, Technology and Innovation in Translation Process Research*, ed. S. Göpferich, F. Alves, and I. M. Mees, 135–156. Copenhagen: Samfundslitteratur.

Pym, Anthony. 2013. Translation skill-sets in a machine-translation age. *Meta* 58 (3): 487–503.

Pym, Anthony. 2019. Teaching translation in a multilingual practice class. In *Translator Education: The Evolving Curriculum*, ed. David Sawyer, Frank Austermühl, and Vanessa Enríquez Raído, 75–79. Amsterdam and Philadelphia: Benjamins.

Pym, Anthony. 2023. Triage and technology in healthcare translation. In *What's Special about Specialised Translation? Essays in Honour of Federica Scarpa*, ed. G. Palumbo, K. Peruzzo, and G. Pontrandolfo, 247–268. Peter Lang.

Pym, Anthony, and Ester Torres-Simón. 2021. Is automation changing the translation profession? *International Journal of the Sociology of Language* 270: 39–57. https://doi.org/10.1515/ijsl-2020-0015.

Pym, Anthony, and Yu Hao. 2024. *How to Augment Language Skills. Generative AI and Machine Translation in Language Learning and Translator Training.* Routledge.

Pym, Anthony, Nune Ayvazyan, and Jonathan Prioleau. 2022. Should raw machine translation be used for public-health information? Suggestions for a multilingual communication policy in Catalonia. In *Linguistic Policies for Social Justice*, ed. Ester Monzó-Nebot, and Chris D. Mellinger; Special issue of *Just. Journal of Language Rights & Minorities, Revista de Drets Lingüístics i Minories* 1(1): 71–99. https://doi.org/10.7203/Just.1.24880.

Somers, Harold. 1997. A practical approach to using machine translation software. *The Translator* 3: 193–212.

Turing, Alan M. 1950. Computing machinery and intelligence. *Mind* 59 (236): 433–460.

Von Garrel, Jörg, and Jana Mayer. 2023. Artificial Intelligence in studies—use of ChatGPT and AI-based tools among students in Germany. *Humanities and Social Sciences Communications* 10(799). https://doi.org/10.1057/s41599-023-02304-7

Xiao, Yangyu, and Yuying Zhi. 2023. An exploratory study of EFL learners' use of ChatGPT for language learning tasks: Experience and perceptions. *Languages* 8: 212. https://doi.org/10.3390/languages8030212.

Nune Ayvazyan is a Lecturer in Translation at Universitat Rovira i Virgili in Tarragona, Spain. She holds a Ph.D. in Translation and Intercultural Studies from the Universitat Rovira i Virgili. Her current research interests are in the use of new technologies in teaching translation and languages, and in multilingual policies.

Yu Hao is Lecturer in Translation Studies at the University of Melbourne in Australia. Her research interests are in translation curriculum development, translation-technology teaching, and international education studies.

Anthony Pym is Distinguished Professor of Translation and Intercultural Studies at the Rovira i Virgili in Tarragona, Spain, and Extra-ordinary Professor at Stellenbosch University, South Africa. His research interests are in sociological approaches to intercultural communication.

Students' Attitudes Towards Interactive and Adaptive Translation Technology: Four years of Working with Lilt

Joke Daems

Abstract Surveys with professional translators show that there is still a lot of frustration with translation tools, especially when it comes to the integration with machine translation (MT) in classic environments. As new MT integrations are developed, it becomes important to study user experience of a variety of users. During the final assignment for a postgraduate course on machine translation and post-editing, I let students reflect on features in different translation environments. Students are introduced to Lilt, currently the only translation environment to offer interactive and adaptive MT, and are asked to compare its features to those of other environments they are familiar with. Since the integration of interactive and adaptive MT are integral to the tool, students are explicitly asked to reflect on the quality of the MT output and the perceived usefulness of these features. To better assess the adaptivity of the system, students translated two texts using Lilt: one where the MT system is additionally trained on a relevant translation memory, one with the generic MT system. In this chapter, I analyse student reports from four academic years. Results show that Lilt's minimalist interface and particularly the interactive and adaptive elements are received positively by the students, and that Lilt could be a good tool to include in future translation technology courses, perhaps especially for students less experienced with translation technology.

1 Introduction

Given the ubiquity of translation technology and machine translation, translation technology teaching has now become an integral part of translator training. It is therefore not surprising that networks such as the European Master's in Translation—of which Ghent University is a member—list 'Technology' as one of the five main areas of competence (EMT Competence Framework 2022). According to this framework, the technology competence 'includes all the knowledge and skills used to implement and advise on the use of present and future translation technologies

J. Daems (✉)
Ghent University, Ghent, Belgium
e-mail: joke.daems@ugent.be

Y. Peng et al. (eds.), *New Advances in Translation Technology*, New Frontiers in Translation Studies, https://doi.org/10.1007/978-981-97-2958-6_12

within the translation process. It also includes basic knowledge of machine translation technologies and the ability to implement machine translation according to potential needs' (p. 9).

The term 'translation technologies' can cover quite a diverse range of tools and software, and it is sadly impossible to cover every form of translation technology within the span of a one or two year master's programme in which students are also expected to master the art of translation itself. When choosing which forms of technology to teach, most educators (myself included) therefore tend to default to the market leader(s). In the EMT 2017 survey report on translation tools, Trados Studio was shown to be compulsory in no less than 82% of EMT programmes, after having been the dominant tool in translator education for at least five years since the previous survey in 2012 (Rothwell and Svoboda 2019). According to the EMT annual report (2022), a new EMT survey was planned for 2022, but has been postponed until 2023 so the results were not available at the time of writing.

While it is undoubtedly important to teach students how to work with the tool that is currently preferred in the industry (ELIS Research 2023), anecdotal evidence from my decade of teaching suggests that students are often overwhelmed by the many functionalities and interface of Trados Studio. This is supported by findings from Sun (2021), who compared students' user experience for four different CAT tools and found that Trados scored worst on usability, and O'Brien et al. (2017), who found that complexity of CAT tool interfaces is the most irritating feature, even according to professional translators. This becomes particularly problematic when we consider the rising importance of machine translation and its integration in existing translation technologies. Moorkens and O'Brien (2017) studied the specific user interface needs for post-editing 'with a view to making the task less boring, repetitive and edit-intensive for the human translator' (p. 127) and found that participants felt that there was a 'lack of development within existing translation interfaces' (p. 144).

Since then, the so-called 'automation age' has seen the development of adaptive neural MT and interactive MT, but researchers bemoan the lack of studies exploring how users experience interacting with such systems (Briva-Iglesias 2023). In a pilot study, we asked professional translators about their experience working with Lilt, the only translation environment to offer interactive and adaptive machine translation (Daems and Macken 2019). Most translators in this study felt that Lilt indeed offered more support than their familiar tools, with five out of eight translators even willing to consider exchanging their current CAT tool for Lilt in the future. Based on these findings, I decided to introduce Lilt in the postgraduate course on Machine Translation and Post-editing at the Department of Translation, Interpreting and Communication at Ghent University (Belgium) in 2019. Working with Lilt and reflecting on features of translation technology in general has become a core assignment in the course since then. In this chapter, I report on student attitudes towards working with Lilt and other translation tools, based on student reports collected over four academic years (2019–2022). In the following sections, I discuss relevant related research on the integration of machine translation in translation environments, the search for the optimal level of human–computer interaction (HCI) and the importance of translation technology teaching. I then present the methodology, introducing the course goals and the data collection in more detail. This section is followed by the analysis and discussion of results. While the assignment was not developed with this chapter in mind, the student reports contain valuable insights into attitudes and experiences towards modern translation technologies. More specifically, I will use the reports to answer the following research questions:

- RQ1: What are students' attitudes towards interactivity and adaptivity in a translation environment?
- RQ2: Which features do students like or dislike in a translation environment?
- RQ3: Which additional features would students like to see in a translation environment?
- RQ4: What do students think about the MT quality of Lilt? Do they perceive a difference in quality between the generic MT output and the MT output adapted to a translation memory?

Where possible, the comparison is made with existing research in the field (be it from a HCI perspective or a translation teaching perspective). The main takeaways and directions for future research are presented in the conclusion of this chapter.

2 Related Research

An overview of the literature on translation technology makes apparent that there has always been a mismatch between what users want and what is actually being developed (Lagoudaki 2006). Machine translation, for example, was quite rapidly introduced in commercial translation tools, yet in 2004, 75% of translators were not familiar with MT, and not even convinced of CAT tools as a whole (Fulford and Granell-Zafra 2005). A decade later, about a third of translators was still not aware whether or not their CAT tool offered MT support, with only half of the respondents thinking of MT as (potentially) useful (Zaretskaya et al. 2015). The authors suggested that 'making MT integration into CAT tools more accessible and user-friendly might improve the situation' (p. 84).

2.1 The Integration of Machine Translation in Translation Technology

The question about how to best integrate MT into CAT tools to make it more user-friendly is not a new one, however. Historical overviews demonstrate how the development of CAT tools and machine translation intertwined (Briva-Iglesias 2023; Chan 2023). Focusing specifically on human–computer interaction, Läubli and Green's overview (2019) starts with the 'theorized' systems from the 1960s to 1980s, with a clear division between the work a human would be responsible for and the more routine work that could be entrusted to a machine translation system, and ends with the more recently developed interactive MT systems. As the name suggests, these are systems that continuously interact with the user. An example of such a system was *TransType2*, which offered new likely MT suggestions based on what the user was typing. While this interactivity had the potential to greatly enhance productivity, especially after using the tool for a while, translators were particularly annoyed by the fact that the system did not seem to learn from their edits, and that it did not adapt future suggestions accordingly (Macklovitch 2006). A seemingly logical next step was therefore the development of adaptive tools. An adaptive system picks up on the changes a post-editor makes and then uses those to retrain the system, which leads to less mechanical effort for the user (fewer keystrokes to make changes) and seems to be preferred by translators (Denkowski 2015).

There has been a variety of research projects aiming to develop translation interfaces, testing different aspects of interaction with machine translation and the integration of adaptivity (e.g. Koehn 2009; Alabau et al. 2014; Coppers et al. 2018). Some common issues with these projects, however, are that they look too different from familiar translation environments for translators to confidently work with them, and that there is limited or no funding available to maintain them after the research project ends. On the other hand, most commercial tools have to date only integrated adaptive MT, e.g. via ModernMT (Bertoldi et al. 2018). Despite the potential of interactive post-editing (IPE), 'no adoption of IPE has been seen in the translation industry besides that of Lilt' (Briva-Iglesias et al. 2023, p. 63). Lilt is the only commercial system currently available that combines interactivity with adaptivity of an NMT system in real time (Läubli and Green 2019). Despite it being a commercial system, the development is research-based, with the developers first researching how best to integrate interactivity (Green et al. 2014), then how to measure and improve immediate adaptation performance of the MT system (Simianer et al. 2019), and even how to best present the text to the translators (Läubli et al. 2020). However, the focus in these analyses is primarily on improving the performance of either the MT system (responsiveness, quality) or the translator (speed, accuracy), and to a far lesser degree on improving the user interface (UI) based on translator needs.

2.2 *From User Interface Needs to User Experience*

Reporting on a survey and interviews conducted in 2013, Moorkens and O'Brien (2017) established a 'UI wish list' for post-editors of machine translation. At the time, MT 'tended to be appended as an afterthought' (p. 127) in existing translation environments and the authors were the first to explore which features specifically developed for post-editing users would like to see in a translation environment. While the focus was on features for MTPE, their findings show that respondents were often unhappy with the user interface of their translation environment in general, and that they would prefer to have more customisation options as well as a clean and uncluttered user interface. For features specific to MTPE, Moorkens and O'Brien

(2017) found that translators would like to have confidence scores as they did not trust MT output, and that they were mostly enthusiastic about the idea of adaptive MT, where a system gets retrained in real time. Attitudes towards interactive MT, where the MT suggestions dynamically change depending on user typing activity and edits, were more mixed, with about half of the participants in favour of this suggestion. Another feature translators would like according to this survey was a dynamic productivity report expressed as a percentage or as words per hour.

While Moorkens and O'Brien (2017) envisioned that features for MTPE could be integrated into existing translation environments, it was a newly developed translation environment that first integrated both adaptive and interactive machine translation. Described as a 'translation environment tool of a different kind', the reception of Lilt when it was first revealed was very positive (Zetzsche 2015). Lilt was developed as a human-in-the-loop system from the start, setting it apart from more traditional translation environments. In addition to adaptivity and interactivity, Lilt mostly delivers on the 'uncluttered user interface' requirement identified in the UI wish list for post-editors, and it also offers a dynamic productivity report. Lilt does not offer any customisation options or confidence scores, however. Given the nature of MT integration in Lilt and the industry shift to neural machine translation since the survey by Moorkens and O'Brien (2017), it is not entirely clear whether confidence scores would still be a requirement of translators today. In a pilot study with professional translators working with Lilt, we found that translators preferred starting from NMT output rather than SMT output for post-editing (Daems and Macken 2019), which suggests that user experience has improved with the introduction of NMT. Overall, participants in this pilot study found Lilt user-friendly and they enjoyed working with it, although some mentioned that they were annoyed by the persistent QA checks and wrong translations of product names. More recently, Briva-Iglesias et al. (2023) compared the user experience of professional translators working with Lilt in a traditional post-editing and an interactive post-editing modality, arguing that this is an aspect of human–computer interaction that has not been studied yet. They found that, while quality and productivity were similar, translators actually preferred the interactive modality, perceiving it as faster, less effortful, more exciting and feeling more in control than in the traditional modality. The authors further advocate for more research into Machine Translation User Experience (MTUX) in general, which they describe as '[a] person's perceptions and responses resulting from the use and/or anticipated use of MT' (Briva-Iglesias et al. 2023, p. 65).

The limited number of user experience studies is particularly striking given that Lilt has become a preferred tool for translators working with MT according to a relatively recent CSA Report (Pielmeier and O'Mara 2020). On the other hand, the tool does not appear in the 'preferred tools' overview in the European Language Industry Survey (ELIS Research 2023). This discrepancy might be explained by the tool being lesser known in Europe, or the fact that it is not actively included in translator training (yet) (Rothwell and Svoboda 2019). Awareness and training are indeed key elements for technology acceptance (Dillon 2001; Dillon and Fraser 2007) and in our pilot study, we found that translators had chosen their current translation environment (not Lilt) based on familiarity, either through training or colleagues, or based on client and market expectations (Daems and Macken 2019).

2.3 Translation Technology Teaching and Student Perceptions

The role of training with regard to technology acceptance cannot be overestimated (Chan and Shuttleworth 2023). Research shows that students who received translation technology training have a positive attitude towards MT (Pastor 2021), and that attitudes towards translation technology in general can be improved by taking translation technology courses (Su and Li 2023) or by teachers encouraging students to adopt a growth mindset (Tian et al. 2023). While some work has been conducted on student perceptions towards MT quality and the efficiency of MTPE in the classroom (Yang et al. 2021; Wang et al. 2021; Cui et al. 2023), this is often combined with a process and product study. These studies require the use of logging tools like Translog-II (Carl 2012), and therefore do not tell us much about user experience or student perceptions specifically related to the integration of machine translation in existing translation environments.

Sun (2021) did focus on user experience and let translation students compare four different CAT tools (SDL Trados Studio, memoQ, Snowman CAT and YiCAT). Perhaps surprisingly, the international market leaders (Trados and memoQ) performed worse in this analysis than the Chinese market systems (Snowman Cat and YiCAT). While the first two were seen as offering the most functionality, students found them complex to use and found certain features difficult to find (Sun 2021). To the best of my knowledge, only two studies to date looked at student perceptions of the Lilt interface. Kappus and Ehrensberger-Dow (2020) let master students work with both Trados and Lilt and found that Lilt was more ergonomic and easier to use. The authors suggest that a tool with a less complicated interface (Lilt) might be an ideal way to introduce students to translation technology before overwhelming them with the many features of a complicated interface like Trados. Martikainen (2022) conducted a study with translation students working only with Lilt and found that they generally liked the adaptivity and interactivity, particularly because it reduced typing effort, it worked intuitively, and students felt like they were less constrained by the MT than in static systems. On the other hand, MT quality seemed to be an even more important factor for the perceived usability of the tool than adaptivity and interactivity, with large differences across language combinations (Martikainen 2022).

Overall, it seems that Lilt is a promising translation environment when working with machine translation, as it offers a minimalist interface with adaptive and interactive MT. Using Lilt could also offer a less overwhelming introduction to translation technology for certain students. In this chapter, I analyse postgraduate student attitudes towards Lilt, as collected in four years of student reports, to see if their comments are in line with some of the previous findings detailed above. Given that adaptivity and interactivity were still hypothetical features when Moorkens and O'Brien (2017) conducted their survey, it becomes crucial to now observe how these features are perceived in practice (RQ1). In addition to these relatively novel features, it remains relevant to understand which other features contribute to a positive or negative user experience (RQ2) and which features users currently still miss (RQ3). Particular focus will be on the (perceived) differences in quality between a project with and without additional TM training data (RQ4), something that—to the best of my knowledge—has not been explored before.

3 Methodology

3.1 Data Collection

Data was collected during the Machine Translation and Post-Editing (MTPE) course at Ghent University, originally offered as part of the Postgraduate in Computer-Assisted Language Mediation (CALM), but from 2021 onwards also available for students from the European Master's in Technology for Translation and Interpreting (EMTTI). For the postgraduate, students select 8 modules out of a total of 14 available modules. The MTPE course is a one-semester course worth 5 credits and gives students a solid background in MT and PE. Some of the topics covered are challenges for MT, different MT architectures, evaluation of MT output, post-editing (tools) and the integration of MT in interactive and/or adaptive translation environments. This last topic forms the focus of one of the course assignments, in which students need to reflect on the integration of MT in translation environments and on the usefulness of certain features. In this chapter, I analyse the student reports for this particular assignment across four academic years (2019–2022). In total, 37 student reports were analysed. Especially in the earlier years, most students signed up for the postgraduate after completing their master's in translation studies, but the postgraduate is open to students with more diverse backgrounds, so not all students had experience translating before attending the course.

3.2 Course Content and Student Reports

During the class on MT integration in translation environments, students were introduced to two translation environments: Intellingo (Coppers et al. 2018), the result of the SCATE research project to create a more intelligible translation environment, and Lilt,[1] a commercial translation environment. The main motivation for selecting these

[1] https://lilt.com/.

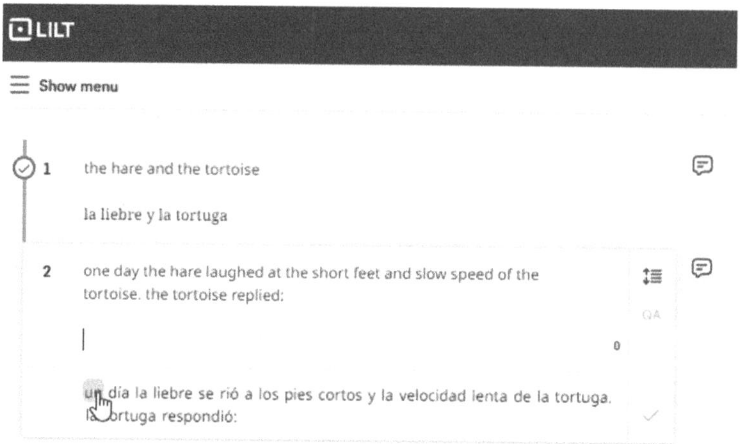

Fig. 1 The Lilt Translate editor. Screenshot taken from https://support.lilt.com/kb/translating-documents

tools was that they both integrate MT in an interactive way (predictive typing), but that their UIs showcase different priorities. The focus of Intellingo is on providing additional information to the translator, such as confidence scores for terminology, TM and MT suggestions; whereas the focus of Lilt is on offering an uncluttered and minimalist interface (see Fig. 1). As both the 'improved display of provenance data' and 'a clean and uncluttered UI' were elements on translators' UI wish list for post-editing (Moorkens and O'Brien 2017), we were curious to find out how students experienced these elements in practice, particularly as they seem potentially at odds with each other (as more information almost invariably leads to more clutter).

In 2019 and 2020, students had to translate a patient information leaflet from English into Dutch using the Intellingo demo that was online available. In 2021 and 2022, Intellingo was still shown as an example of how translation environments can integrate MT in different ways, but since the demo was only available for Dutch and the student cohort became more diverse, its role in the assignment was reduced significantly. Students in all years performed two translation tasks with Lilt: one where no additional information was provided (generic MT), and one where a relevant translation memory was uploaded as additional training data for the Lilt MT system (trained MT).

In addition to working with Lilt and Intellingo, students had to read two research papers in which interactions of professional translators with Lilt and/or Intellingo were studied (Daems and Macken 2019; Vandeghinste et al. 2019). They were also encouraged to look up additional research papers themselves and to consult online reference material on modern translation environments. Based on their personal experience and background reading, they then had to write a report containing an answer to the following questions:

- Explain in your own words: What is adaptivity? What is interactivity? How useful do you think these are in a translation tool (RQ1)? Clarify.
- Which features do you find useful in the different translation environments (RQ2)? Which additional features would be on your UI wish list (RQ3)?
- Which differences (if any) did you notice between the generic and trained version of Lilt (RQ4)?

The overarching goal of this assignment was kept constant, although the exact questions students needed to answer evolved through the years (in the first two years, students had to compare Lilt with Intellingo specifically, in the later years, students had to compare Lilt to at least one other translation environment of their choice). For the assignment with Lilt, the text type evolved through the years as well, influenced by a mix of practical considerations, student questions, and my personal research focus at the time. An overview of the data collected can be seen in Table 1, followed by a description and motivation of the changing Lilt assignment.

To more accurately mimic the Intellingo data in the first year, students translated two information leaflets (±200 words each) using Lilt, one with the generic MT system without additional training data, and one where an additional TM and glossary was provided. The TM was the English-and-Dutch EMEA TM as available through OPUS (Tiedemann 2009), which was also used in Intellingo. This TM contained 198k segments, and the corresponding manually created list of medical terms consisted of 360 instances.

From 2020 onwards, literary texts were used for the Lilt assignment. This was in part motivated by my own research focus at the time (the potential of MT for literary translation), but also by the desire of the students to test the medium to its limits. In 2020, the text to translate was the last chapter of *the Memoirs of Sherlock Holmes* by Sir Arthur Conan Doyle (Adventure XI: The Final Problem). Each student had to

Table 1 Overview of data collected

Academic year	Student groups	Number of reports	Intellingo used	Lilt used	Lilt source text	Target languages
2019–2020	CALM	6	Yes	Yes	Patient information leaflet	NL
2020–2021	CALM	10	Yes	Yes	*Memoirs of Sherlock Holmes* by Sir Arthur Conan Doyle	NL
2021–2022	CALM + EMTTI	5	No	Yes	Detective novel (NL) & *the Boy in the Striped Pajamas* by John Boyne (RU & PT-br)	NL(1), PT-br(1), RU(3),
2022–2023	CALM + EMTTI	17	No	Yes	*The Boy in the Striped Pajamas* by John Boyne	FR(1), NL(5), PT-br(2), RO(1), RU(5), TR(3)

translate an excerpt of approximately 300 words using the generic Lilt system, and the subsequent excerpt of similar length using Lilt with additional training data. The translation memory that was used as additional training data was the official Dutch translation of the first ten chapters of the book (4896 segments).

In 2021, students had to translate two fragments of approximately 400 words with Lilt, as the student group became more diverse and Intellingo could no longer be used. The Dutch-speaking student translated the first section of a detective novel (*Ellen Holms*), whereas the Russian (3) and Brazilian (1) students translated the first chapter of *the Boy in the Striped Pajamas* by John Boyne. To train the MT system, a translation memory was created containing the translation for the rest of the respective novels (4164 segments for *Ellen Holms*, and 2322 and 2696 segments for *the Boy in the Striped Pajamas*, for Russian and Portuguese, respectively). The detective novel was selected because it was part of an exploratory research study into adaptive MT, *the Boy in the Striped Pajamas* was chosen because it is one of the novels published since 2000 with the highest number of translations.[2] In 2022, all students translated sections from *the Boy in the Striped Pajamas* by John Boyne. Translation memory size was 2335 segments for Dutch, 2530 for Turkish, 2615 for French, and 2677 for Romanian.

3.3 Data Selection and Coding

Since the information is based on student reports, this naturally means that there is a great discrepancy between the different reports. Some students took the time to answer the questions in great detail, adding specific examples or commenting on a wide variety of features, whereas other students only offered minimal feedback. To keep the analysis true to the data, however, I did not filter out any of the shorter student reports in the analysis. The only instances where I did not include student answers was when they clearly misunderstood the question (when they discussed features of 'interactivity' or 'adaptivity' but described something completely different), or when it was not entirely clear whether their comment was an expression of their personal attitude (which is what I am interested in for this chapter) or rather a conclusion drawn from a research paper they read on the topic. While I definitely encourage students to connect their thoughts to related research whenever possible and to reflect on what they read, it is important to limit this particular analysis to personal attitudes. So, for example, a comment like 'Just like Author X, who found that translators working with adaptive MT worked faster, I also think adaptive MT would be good because it can save you time if you don't have to change the same error all the time' would be included in the analysis (the 'I also think' implies a personal attitude), but a comment like 'Adaptive MT leads to faster translation (Author X)' would not be included, because it is not obvious from this statement that the student personally feels the same way.

[2] https://en.wikipedia.org/wiki/list_of_literary_works_by_number_of_translations.

I performed a thematic analysis by first carefully reading each student report and highlighting all statements that contained an answer to the research questions. More specifically, I highlighted statements that alluded to student attitudes towards interactivity and adaptivity (RQ1), mentions of features they liked or disliked in specific translation environments (RQ2), comments related to a feature wish or improvement (RQ3) and comments related to the MT quality of Lilt (RQ4). I then made an overview in Microsoft Excel, where each comment was kept in one row, followed by the corresponding class year, student name (anonymised), a label for the research question it belonged to, an indication of the nature of the comment where relevant (positive/negative), and a shortened version of the comment. I then went over these shortened comments to ensure they were all uniformly coded and tried to identify higher-level codes whenever possible (e.g. comments like 'time-saving', 'speeds things up' and 'I work much faster' were all grouped together into one 'speed' code). After coding everything, I went through the reports and the overview once more, to double-check that I had included all relevant statements and coded them consistently throughout.

4 Analysis

4.1 Student Attitudes Towards Interactivity and Adaptivity

The responses to the question how useful students thought interactivity and adaptivity were in a translation tool (RQ1) were overwhelmingly positive. Of all the comments collected throughout the years, 53 out of 57 were positive for both adaptivity and interactivity, as can be seen in Table 2.

Out of the four negative responses for adaptivity, two indicated that the system does not adapt quickly enough, one student preferred to start without MT altogether, and another indicated that the loss of rich vocabulary made it unsuited for literary translation (which was the genre of text they were working on). For interactivity, two of the negative responses indicated that the constantly changing text was chaotic and negatively influenced the translator's focus: 'it can be hard to keep track of both

Table 2 Number of positive (+) and negative (−) comments made about the usefulness of adaptivity and interactivity in a translation environment per academic year

Academic year	Adaptivity		Interactivity	
	−	+	−	+
2019–2020	1	9	0	10
2020–2021	2	24	3	19
2021–2022	0	4	0	7
2022–2023	1	16	1	17
Total	4	53	4	53

Table 3 Number of comments related to each of the perceived benefits of adaptivity and interactivity

Perceived benefits	Adaptivity	Interactivity
Increased speed	12	19
More efficient	12	3
Improved user experience	6	17
Improved translation quality	6	5
Useful feature	6	4
Improved consistency	4	2
Makes the process easier	2	2
Improved MT quality	4	0
User-friendly	1	1

the suggestions MT gives and the translation your mind is making' and 'The fact that it changes constantly can be overwhelming, because sometimes you absolutely do not want to use anything the MT has to offer, but it does keep bombarding you with its suggestion as you type'. One student again indicated that they preferred to start without MT, and another that they did not understand the advantage of the interactivity.

With regard to positive comments, different aspects were stressed when students discussed adaptivity versus when they discussed interactivity. For adaptivity, the main perceived benefits were increased efficiency (mentioned 12 times), because translators no longer have to correct the same error over and over again, and speed (also mentioned 12 times). For interactivity, speed was also seen as a key benefit (mentioned 19 times), but here students introduced a lot more comments related to how they experienced the post-editing process itself (17 mentions). For example, students indicated that they did not feel so alone when working with an interactive system, that it felt like they collaborated with the system, that they felt in control, and that it made the process more fun and interesting. Other comments covered topics ranging from improved (MT) quality to user-friendliness, and can be seen in Table 3.

4.2 Positive and Negative Perceptions of Translation Tool Features

Since a main focus of the assignment was to compare Lilt to other translation tools students were familiar with, all students commented on positive and negative features in the Lilt tool. The second most mentioned translation tool was the SCATE Intellingo environment, as this was also explicitly mentioned in class (and was a fixed reference point for the assignment in the earlier years of the course). Other tools that were mentioned (sorted by number of comments made) were Matecat, Trados, Smartcat, Multimodal Post-editing (MMPE) tool (briefly introduced during class), memoQ, Phrase, ModernMT, Casmacat, Wordfast and Transit.

When comparing features in translation tools (RQ2), students mostly focus on the positive features of a tool, as can be seen in Fig. 2. The only exception is Trados, which received somewhat more negative remarks (12) than positive (7).

The features that were commented on most frequently overall were the interface, the availability of different resources and the user-friendliness of the tool (an overview of all features mentioned at least 10 times can be seen in Table 4). It can be assumed that these are all features translators find most important, or features that struck them as being particularly different across translation environments. Of these, the time or progress tracker struck me the most, as I did not consider this a core feature of a translation tool, but it does seem to be something students care about from a motivational perspective: 'Being able to visualise the beginning and end of a task does wonders for my motivation.'

Not surprisingly, given the nature of the assignment, the highest number of comments was made about the Lilt environment. Of the total of 239 comments received, 72% were positive, and 28% were negative. The feature that was mentioned most commonly in a positive way (37 times) was the interface. Students specifically mentioned the fact that it is minimalist and uncluttered and that it presents the texts vertically instead of horizontally—like many translation tools they are familiar with—as the main benefits of the Lilt interface. Not everyone perceived the interface positively, however, with some students commenting that the interface lacks professionalism, or that the layout makes it hard to find features they are used to seeing on screen (8 comments total). Other positive features that were mentioned at least five times were the interactivity (17 mentions), user-friendliness (16 mentions), adaptivity (14 mentions), speed (14 mentions), QA check (8 mentions), keyboard shortcuts (7 mentions), concordance search (6 mentions), availability of different sources (6 mentions), time tracker (6 mentions) and find/replace (5 mentions). Interactivity was sometimes perceived negatively as well (8 mentions), because the changing suggestions were seen as distracting or annoying when useful fragments disappeared during the editing process. Other negative features mentioned at least five times were adaptivity, particularly with respect to its being too slow (7 mentions), the lack of synonyms or alternative sources (7 mentions), MT quality (6 mentions of bad MT

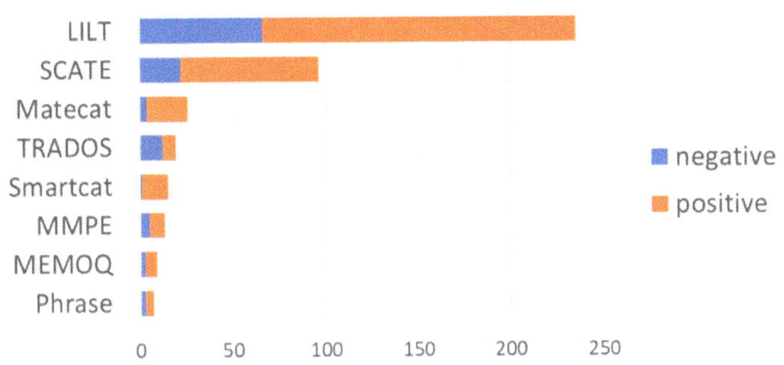

Fig. 2 Number of positive and negative remarks about different features per translation tool (only tools with more than 5 mentions included)

Table 4 Overview of features mentioned at least 10 times, and the number of positive (+) and negative (-) comments related to this feature for each of the eight most commented on tools. Totals represent total mentions across all tools (including tools not presented in the table)

Feature	LILT		SCATE		Matecat		Trados		Smartcat		MMPE		memoQ		Phrase		TOT
	–	+	–	+	–	+	–	+	–	+	–	+	–	+	–	+	
Interface	8	37	7	19	1	2	4			1			2			1	82
Different sources	7	6	4	20		5											43
User-friendly	3	16		3		2	3			3	1			1		1	33
Interactivity	8	17					1										27
Speed		14	1	7							1						23
Compatibility	2	3			1	4	1	2		2	1	4			1	1	22
Adaptivity	7	14	1														22
Feature-rich	5	1	3	1		1		3			1	2		2			19
QA check	5	8										1					15
MT quality	6	3	2	2													13
Time tracker	1	6		3		2				1							13
Shortcuts	1	7		1				1				1					11
Preview	3	3												3		1	10

quality—compared to 3 students who explicitly mentioned that the MT quality was good/fluent), the overwhelming or limiting features (5 mentions) and the persistent QA check (5 mentions).

For the SCATE Intellingo environment, the main benefits according to students were the availability of different sources of information (20 mentions), and the interface (19 mentions). Students commented specifically on the central positioning of the current segment and the fact that additional information was presented under the sentence rather than hidden away in different toolbars. As they did with Lilt, they again seemed to prefer the vertical presentation of the text.

When it comes to Trados, students appreciated the many features, although these were often perceived as too overwhelming, leading to a cluttered interface.

4.3 Features to Be Added or Improved

While most students seemed to enjoy the Lilt interface and preferred it over the—generally more cluttered—interfaces of other translation environments they are familiar with, they still had thoughts on which features were needed to create their ideal translation environment (RQ3). Not all students answered this question separately, as some of them covered their 'wish list' features when discussing what they liked and disliked about Lilt and other translation environments in general.

From the comments, it seems that students would enjoy a mix of the features Lilt and Intellingo have to offer: 'A happy medium between these two ways would be better. For example, showing the possible translations of words directly below the active sentence, but initially hiding the sentence they appear in until the translator specifically clicks on a suggested translation or searches for it in a concordance search.' While some found the information in Intellingo too overwhelming, the idea of having multiple suggestions and sources did seem to appeal to them (18 mentions), along with having more information about the provenance of (MT) suggestions (6 mentions) and maybe even a quality estimation score (2 mentions). While the basic idea of quality estimation scores appealed to some students ('It might be useful for translators to start by translating the easy segments first and feel like they have already accomplished some work.'), others were more sceptical and commented on the potential risks of quality estimation scores, especially when they are incorrect: 'If it is green, the translator might be tempted to accept the translation more easily than they should and if it is red they might dwell more and overthink due to it supposedly being difficult. If the colour is then wrong, this could lead to distrust towards the translation tool or confusion on behalf of the translator.'

Specifically for Lilt, instead of having just the one MT system suggestion, students suggested that it could be interesting to have a 'generate alternative MT suggestion' function, or that it could be interesting to include other resources more easily. Instead of navigating to separate webpages for each resource (dictionary, synonym search), it would be helpful to have those integrated into the environment somehow, with the necessary level of customisability (translators could select the dictionaries and resources most relevant for their projects).

Customisability in general was frequently mentioned (10 times). Not just customisation of the interface itself (although this was mentioned a few times, including the desire to choose custom colours), but also the customisation of the levels of interactivity, visibility of alternative suggestions and the degree of QA checks. Some students would prefer to disable QA checks altogether: 'I do not find QE or QA systems useful in any translation environment that I worked with so far. I find them bothersome and I feel like they waste my time and make me enjoy translation less.'

Interactivity and adaptivity were liked by most students, but the performance of both could still be improved. For interactivity, some students commented that they didn't like when the initial MT suggestion disappeared, especially when they wanted to return to a previous version of their sentence: 'In a long sentence, I altered one word, but I liked the clause that was at the end of the sentence. However, the introduced change has influenced all the further suggestions of the sentence, and I could not remember exactly what the initial suggestion of that clause was, and had to invent it on my own.' Potential suggested solutions were the creation of an 'undo' function, which would undo the last edits (and also return the previous MT suggestion) or a report with edit information that keeps tracks of all edits made (comparable to what is available in the report in, e.g. Matecat). For adaptivity, the main issue for students was that it didn't always adapt quickly enough. One student wondered if interactivity and adaptivity could not be combined even more, so that a system could, for example, learn what a translator's favourite sentence structures are. Another student wanted the element of adaptivity integrated in their favourite translation tool (Phrase).

In addition to some comments on typical translation tool features (easy and custom shortcuts, integration of termbases, improved automated tag handling, split/merge functionalities), a variety of comments related to compatibility and accessibility of the tool as a whole. While in 2019, a student commented that they would prefer to also have an offline tool so they were not dependent on internet access all the time, students in 2022 indicated that they would prefer to have a mobile app or a tool that is compatible with a tablet, because they often work while travelling: 'An adapted use of the MMPE approach for a tablet would not only represent more workspace flexibility, but it would also mean I could perform more jobs in several other situations that are not so practical, such as during commuting'. Modalities like speech-to-text or the use of a stylus or touch were mentioned by some students, although one student explicitly wondered how those would then be combined with the existing interactivity offered by Lilt. Some comments were related to very specific language or region-related issues (compatibility of different keyboard layouts, and the visualisation of special characters like diacritics).

4.4 Machine Translation Quality

When asked to compare the suggestions made by Lilt in a project with and without an additional translation memory as training data (RQ4), about 60% of students indicated that they could not identify a clear overall difference in quality or post-editing effort reduction. The other 40% indicated that the trained version performed better, although here as well some students indicated that it performed 'only marginally' better. Some explained that the text fragment they had to translate was simply too short to make an accurate comparison ('I do not think the differences were so great that perhaps creating a trained version would be worth the work for such a small translation task—maybe I would have experienced this differently if it were a larger task'), or that the fact that they translated two different fragments could influence the experience as well (some fragments contained more dialogue or shorter sentences than others, for example). The text type was also mentioned as a potential influencing factor: 'The lack of noticeable differences (in my case) may be due to the source text already being complex because of its genre and because of the long sentences'. Additionally, some students found it hard to tease apart the effect of the training data and the effect of the adaptivity of the tool itself: 'As the translating process went on, however, this gap became less noticeable, as the adaptive component of Lilt started taking into account my previous translations which allowed for better suggestions.'

This overall comparison was, in some cases, supplemented by a detailed error analysis. It is impossible to include all those analyses here, so I will limit the discussion to a few key components that were brought up by more than one student.

The students who found the trained system better often described it as 'feeling' more fluent and idiomatic or more 'literary', which is of course hard to quantify. An argument that was frequently made was that the trained system allowed them to keep more of the MT output and that fewer sentences had to be translated completely from scratch compared to the untrained system. Students also felt that this allowed them to work faster. Error types that were mentioned as less problematic in the trained version were morphological issues, word order issues and mistranslations. Some more specific instances of the trained system performing better were often related to seemingly small changes. For the literary texts, students were surprised that it picked up on the—sometimes rather complicated—markers for dialogue such as specific punctuation marks or spaces. Given names were also translated more accurately by the trained system: 'In the untrained version, the name *Fury* was simply transliterated (*Фури*), which does not mean anything in Russian; however, since it is a pun ("Fury" sounds similar to "Führer"), it should also be preserved in translation. The translation I came up with was *Фурор* (meaning "furor" in English), which was probably also used in the official translation of the book, as the trained version rendered it in the same way. The generic version also simply transliterated the word Cook (Кук), but the trained one translated it as повар (which is correct).'

Not everyone perceived the improved quality as a benefit, however. As one student explained: 'Because the suggestions provided by the trained system are good, you tend to follow its example. Because the untrained system makes some mistakes your creativity comes in play a bit more.' Someone else offered caution related to the types of errors: 'Ultimately, the trained MT system generated less errors and a more fluent text but the type of errors seriously undermined the meaning and accuracy of the text.'

5 Discussion

Overall, students enrolled in the postgraduate course seemed to enjoy working with Lilt. They particularly appreciated the minimalist interface with vertical text presentation, and the interactivity and adaptivity of the machine translation, which made them feel like they collaborated with the system. This seems in line with findings from a user experience study with professional translators (Briva-Iglesias et al. 2023). While some students explicitly stated that they would like to work with Lilt for future translation assignments, others saw quite a bit of room for improvement, either by adding certain features to Lilt, or by adding features from Lilt (such as interactivity and adaptivity) to their more familiar translation environment. Limitations of this particular study are of course the fact that there were only a few student reports for some years, and that the text genre changed throughout the years, making it hard to make a meaningful diachronic comparison. That being said, I would like to raise a few points for discussion, both with regard to future development or improvement of translation environments, and with regard to translation technology teaching.

5.1 Improving Translation Environments

Unsurprisingly—yet frustratingly, given how long this has been a known issue with translation tool design (see, e.g. Moorkens and O'Brien 2017)—the need for customisation is mentioned quite frequently. All translators are different, and they have different needs for their translation environment, both on a personal level (personal preference for certain colours or features), and on a project or client basis. Students wanted to turn features on or off and toggle the level of support and interactivity offered by the MT system, as well as the type and persistence level of any QA checks. Unfortunately, I do not expect this level of customisability to be available anytime soon. From an industry perspective, 'the design of these tools is unlikely to change until measurements show that alternative designs speed translators up or cause them to make fewer mistakes' (Läubli et al. 2020). The question is how reasonable it is to keep expecting those speed and quality gains, and whether ergonomics should not be a goal in and of itself, a point that has also been raised before (Teixeira and O'Brien 2017). This same perspective can be found in the recently launched call for research into MTUX (Briva-Iglesias et al. 2023). In future work, it would be good to validate the findings from the present qualitative study with more controlled studies employing the MTUX questionnaire.

In contrast with Läubli and Green (2019), who claimed that 'showing more than one suggestion at a time is not useful', it does seem that students are not entirely convinced that the one MT suggestion (even an interactive, adaptive one) is sufficient for their needs. They indicated they like the multiple suggestions they get from a system like Intellingo, although some students commented they found these too overwhelming. Here as well, customisation to a user's needs could offer a solution: how much additional information do they want to get? Do they want to add their own dictionaries or links to common websites? Do these suggestions need to be visible all the time or hidden in a sidebar or shown after a user clicks on a word? All these elements could (should?) be customisable to create the best user experience at a given time.

Since Lilt was developed around an MT system, I expected the concerns raised by Moorkens and O'Brien (2017) with regard to user interfaces for post-editing to have become less valid for this particular tool. Although Lilt indeed offers the requested minimalist and intuitive interface, and the interactive and adaptive MT system makes certain mechanical post-editing operations less tedious (changing cases or number, word order issues, etc.), students still commented on the lack of customisability, the fact that they want to see provenance data (which was found particularly tricky in Lilt, where all the information is used to improve the MT system, and there is no longer a classic 'terminology-TM-MT' paradigm), and the need for formatting support, particularly for previews of the final document. For certain language combinations, students were disappointed with the MT quality, and a few even indicated that they would still like to have shortcuts for operations like word reordering—this despite the interactive and adaptive nature of the MT system. In conclusion, while certain issues identified years ago have been addressed with this different translation environment, there is still a lot of room for improvement (particularly with regard to customisation). In addition to known issues, some comments from students indicated that future translation technology developments should consider accessibility and compatibility with different devices (e.g. phones, tablets), and the potential of combining interactivity with different modalities (e.g. touch, speech).

5.2 Improving Translation Technology Teaching

I personally tend to introduce Lilt towards the end of a course, precisely because it handles MT so differently from classic translation environments and I want my students to understand the difference between terminology, translation memory and machine translation. I also teach a master's course on translation technology, where students first learn to work with Trados. I only introduce Lilt if there is time left at the end. From the student feedback in these reports and in line with the suggestions from other researchers (Kappus and Ehrensberger-Dow 2020), it seems like it could make more sense to introduce Lilt at the start of a translation technology course: 'Lilt felt like a more accessible tool to use, especially for people like me who are not too familiar with translation activities and its accompanying tools.' Another student confirmed this idea: 'For novice translators or for people with moderate computer literacy, this may be an advantage. On the other hand, for experienced translators, Lilt may feel limiting.'

When working with machine translation, special attention should be given to the potential impact of quality/difficulty estimation scores (if available), the role of QA checks, and the benefits and dangers of machine translation quality in general. While quality estimation scores were seen as a potentially useful feature, some students rightfully raised concerns about the accuracy and negative impact on their process (not being critical enough, or being too critical), which is a known concern in the field (Vandeghinste et al. 2019). A similar issue can be seen with MT quality, particularly when working with additionally trained systems, where some students indicated that the seemingly fluent suggestions caused them to overlook errors. The problem with the invisibility of errors in NMT systems has been established before (Van Brussel et al. 2018), and it seems that this will only get worse with adaptive systems. This raises issues for educators, who need to find ways to give students the right levels of trust and critical thinking when working with MT.

6 Conclusion

In this chapter, I analysed student reports of a postgraduate course in machine translation post-editing, where students had to reflect on their experience working with Lilt, a translation environment with a minimalist interface and optimal MT integration via interactivity and adaptivity. Students were asked to comment on interactivity and adaptivity, additional features they like or dislike, features they currently still miss in existing translation environments, and the perceived differences in MT quality between the generic Lilt system and a system that was additionally trained on a relevant translation memory.

Attitude analysis shows that a large majority of students think very positively about the elements of interactivity and adaptivity, although some found the constantly changing suggestions distracting, particularly for longer sentences, and others commented on the fact that adaptivity was not always noticeable or fast enough.

When asked about positive or negative translation environment features, the interface was commented on the most (more than twice as frequently than any other category). The other most important features were the availability of different sources and the user-friendliness of a tool. When describing Lilt, the majority of comments were positive (72%), and many of them related to the minimalist interface, user-friendliness of the tool and the interactive and adaptive machine translation. Features students preferred in other tools were the better integration of alternative suggestions and termbases. A vertical layout with a central positioning of the active segments seems to be the preferred way of visualising a translation task.

If students could describe their ideal translation environment, many would prefer a mix of what Lilt has to offer with what Intellingo or other known translation environments have to offer. For some, Lilt felt too minimalist, and they would like to have access to alternative translations or resources. Customisation is a key desire, as this would allow translators to pick and choose the relevant features for a given task or their personal preference. The multitude of features that is visible by default in Trados, for example, is seen as too overwhelming.

The trained MT system was not always perceived as markedly better than the untrained system, although some students felt they could work a little faster and keep more of the initial MT suggestion than with the untrained system.

In light of these findings, the discussion section contains some ideas for the improvement of translation environments and some challenges for modern translation technology teaching.

References

Alabau, Vicent, Christian Buck, Michael Carl, Francisco Casacuberta, Mercedes García-Martínez, Ulrich Germann, and Jesús González-Rubio, et al. 2014. 'CASMACAT: A Computer-Assisted Translation Workbench'. In *Proceedings of the Demonstrations at the 14th Conference of the European Chapter of the Association for Computational Linguistics*, 25–28. Gothenburg, Sweden: Association for Computational Linguistics. https://doi.org/10.3115/v1/E14-2007.

Bertoldi, Nicola, Davide Caroselli, and Marcello Federico. 2018. The ModernMT project. In *Proceedings of the 21st Annual Conference of the European Association for Machine Translation*, ed. Juan Antonio Pérez-Ortiz, Felipe Sánchez-Martínez, Miquel Esplà-Gomis, Maja Popović, Celia Rico, André Martins, Joachim Van den Bogaert, and Mikel L. Forcada, 365. Alicante, Spain. https://aclanthology.org/2018.eamt-main.46.

Briva-Iglesias, Vicent. 2023. *Translation Technologies Advancements: From Inception to the Automation Age*, 137–152.

Briva-Iglesias, Vicent, Sharon O'Brien, and Benjamin R. Cowan. 2023. The impact of traditional and interactive post-editing on machine translation user experience, quality, and productivity. *Translation, Cognition & Behavior* 6 (1): 60–86. https://doi.org/10.1075/tcb.00077.bri.

Carl, Michael. 2012. Translog-II: A program for recording user activity data for empirical reading and writing research. In *Proceedings of the Eighth International Conference on Language Resources and Evaluation (LREC'12)*, ed. Nicoletta Calzolari, Khalid Choukri, Thierry Declerck, Mehmet Uğur Doğan, Bente Maegaard, Joseph Mariani, Asuncion Moreno, Jan Odijk, and Stelios Piperidis, 4108–4112. Istanbul, Turkey: European Language Resources Association (ELRA). http://www.lrec-conf.org/proceedings/lrec2012/pdf/614_Paper.pdf.

Chan, Sin-wai. 2023. The development of translation technology: 1967–2023. In *Routledge Encyclopedia of Translation Technology*, 2nd ed. Routledge.

Chan, Venus, and Mark Shuttleworth. 2023. Teaching translation technology. In *Routledge Encyclopedia of Translation Technology*, 2nd ed. Routledge.

Coppers, Sven, Jan Van Den Bergh, Kris Luyten, Karin Coninx, Iulianna Van Der Lek-Ciudin, Tom Vanallemeersch, and Vincent Vandeghinste. 2018. Intellingo: An intelligible translation environment. In *Proceedings of the 2018 CHI Conference on Human Factors in Computing Systems*, 1–13. Montreal QC Canada: ACM. https://doi.org/10.1145/3173574.3174098.

Cui, Ying, Xiao Liu, and Yuqin Cheng. 2023. A comparative study on the effort of human translation and post-editing in relation to text types: An eye-tracking and key-logging experiment. *SAGE Open* 13 (1): 21582440231155850. https://doi.org/10.1177/21582440231155849.

Daems, Joke, and Lieve Macken. 2019. Interactive adaptive SMT versus interactive adaptive NMT: A user experience evaluation. *Machine Translation* 33 (1): 117–134. https://doi.org/10.1007/s10590-019-09230-z.

Denkowski, Michael. 2015. *Machine translation for human translators*. Thesis, Carnegie Mellon University. https://doi.org/10.1184/R1/21671609.v1.

Dillon, Andrew. 2001. User acceptance of information technology.

Dillon, Sarah, and Janet Fraser. 2007. Translators and TM: An investigation of translators' perceptions of translation memory adoption. *Machine Translation* 20 (2): 67.

ELIS Research. 2023. European language industry survey 2023.

EMT Competence Framework. 2022 https://commission.europa.eu/document/download/b482a2c0-42df-4291-8bf8-923922ddc6e1_en?filename=emt_competence_fwk_2022_en.pdf. Info on publication: https://commission.europa.eu/news/updated-version-emt-competence-framework-now-available-2022-10-21_en

European Master's in Translation. 2022. EMT annual report 2022.

Fulford, Heather, and Joaquín Granell-Zafra. 2005. Translation and technology: A study of UK freelance translators. *The Journal of Specialised Translation* 4 (1): 2–17.

Green, Spence, Jason Chuang, Jeffrey Heer, and Christopher D. Manning. 2014. Predictive translation memory: A mixed-initiative system for human language translation. In *Proceedings of the 27th Annual ACM Symposium on User Interface Software and Technology*, 177–187. Honolulu Hawaii USA: ACM. https://doi.org/10.1145/2642918.2647408.

Kappus, Martin, and Maureen Ehrensberger-Dow. 2020. The ergonomics of translation tools: Understanding when less is actually more. *The Interpreter and Translator Trainer* 14 (4): 386–404. https://doi.org/10.1080/1750399X.2020.1839998.

Koehn, Philipp. 2009. A web-based interactive computer aided translation tool. In *Proceedings of the ACL-IJCNLP 2009 Software Demonstrations*, 17–20. Suntec, Singapore: Association for Computational Linguistics. https://aclanthology.org/P09-4005.

Lagoudaki, Elina. 2006. Translation memories survey 2006: User's perceptions around TM usage. In *Proceedings of Translating and the Computer*, 28. London, UK: Aslib. https://aclanthology.org/2006.tc-1.2.

Läubli, Samuel, and Spence Green. 2019. Translation technology research and Human–Computer Interaction (HCI). In *The Routledge Handbook of Translation and Technology*, ed. Minako O'Hagan, 1st ed., 370–83. Abingdon, Oxon; New York, NY: Routledge (2020). https://doi.org/10.4324/9781315311258-22.

Läubli, Samuel, Patrick Simianer, Joern Wuebker, Geza Kovacs, Rico Sennrich, and Spence Green. 2020. The impact of text presentation on translator performance. http://arxiv.org/abs/2011.05978.

Macklovitch, Elliott. 2006. TransType2: The last word.

Martikainen, Hanna. 2022. Ghosts in the machine: Can adaptive MT help reclaim a place for the human in the loop?

Moorkens, Joss, and Sharon O'Brien. 2017. Assessing user interface needs of post-editors of machine translation. In *Human Issues in Translation Technology*, 127–148. The IATIS Yearbook. Routledge.

O'Brien, Sharon, Maureen Ehrensberger-Dow, Megan Connolly, and Marcel Hasler. 2017. Irritating CAT tool features that matter to translators. *HERMES—Journal of Language and Communication in Business*, 56: 145–162. https://doi.org/10.7146/hjlcb.v0i56.97229.

Pastor, Diana González. 2021. Introducing machine translation in the translation classroom: A survey on students' attitudes and perceptions. *Revista Tradumàtica. Tecnologies De La Traducció* 19: 47–65. https://doi.org/10.5565/rev/tradumatica.273.

Pielmeier, Hélène, and Paul O'Mara. 2020. The state of the linguist supply chain.

Rothwell, Andrew, and Tomáš Svoboda. 2019. Tracking translator training in tools and technologies: Findings of the EMT survey 2017. *Journal of Specialised Translation* 32: 26.

Simianer, Patrick, Joern Wuebker, and John DeNero. 2019. Measuring immediate adaptation performance for neural machine translation. In *Proceedings of the 2019 Conference of the North American Chapter of the Association for Computational Linguistics: Human Language Technologies*, vol 1. Long and Short Papers, 2038–2046. Minneapolis, Minnesota: Association for Computational Linguistics. https://doi.org/10.18653/v1/N19-1206.

Su, Wenchao, and Defeng Li. 2023. The effectiveness of translation technology training: A mixed methods study. *Humanities and Social Sciences Communications* 10 (1): 1–12. https://doi.org/10.1057/s41599-023-02066-2.

Sun, Sanjun. 2021. Measuring the user experience of computer-aided translation systems: A comparative study. In *Advances in Cognitive Translation Studies*, ed. Ricardo Muñoz Martín, Sanjun Sun, and Defeng Li, 67–88. New Frontiers in Translation Studies. Singapore: Springer. https://doi.org/10.1007/978-981-16-2070-6_4.

Teixeira, Carlos, and Sharon O'Brien. 2017. Investigating the cognitive ergonomic aspects of translation tools in a workplace setting. *Translation Spaces* 6: 79–103. https://doi.org/10.1075/ts.6.1.05tei.

Tian, Sha, Lingxiao Jia, and Zhining Zhang. 2023. Investigating students' attitudes towards translation technology: The status quo and structural relations with translation mindsets and future work self. *Frontiers in Psychology* 14: 1122612. https://doi.org/10.3389/fpsyg.2023.1122612.

Tiedemann, Jörg. 2009. News from OPUS—a collection of multilingual parallel corpora with tools and interfaces. In *Recent Advances in Natural Language Processing V: Selected Papers from RANLP 2007*, ed. Nicolas Nicolov, Galia Angelova, and Ruslan Mitkov, 237–248. Current Issues in Linguistic Theory. John Benjamins Publishing Company. https://doi.org/10.1075/cilt.309.19tie.

Van Brussel, Laura, Arda Tezcan, and Lieve Macken. 2018. 'A fine-grained error analysis of NMT, SMT and RBMT Output for English-to-Dutch'. In *Proceedings of the Eleventh International Conference on Language Resources and Evaluation (LREC 2018)*. Miyazaki, Japan: European Language Resources Association (ELRA). https://aclanthology.org/L18-1600.

Vandeghinste, Vincent, Tom Vanallemeersch, Liesbeth Augustinus, Bram Bulté, Frank Van Eynde, Joris Pelemans, Lyan Verwimp, et al. 2019. Improving the translation environment for professional translators. *Informatics* 6 (2): 24. https://doi.org/10.3390/informatics6020024.

Wang, Xiangling, Tingting Wang, Ricardo Muñoz Martín, and Yanfang Jia. 2021. Investigating usability in postediting neural machine translation: Evidence from translation trainees. *Self-Perception and Performance:' across Languages and Cultures* 22 (1): 100–123. https://doi.org/10.1556/084.2021.00006.

Yang, Yanxia, Xiangling Wang, and Qingqing Yuan. 2021. Measuring the usability of machine translation in the classroom context. *Translation and Interpreting Studies* 16 (1): 101–123. https://doi.org/10.1075/tis.18047.yan.

Zaretskaya, Anna, Gloria Corpas Pastor, and Miriam Seghiri. 2015. Integration of machine translation in CAT tools: state of the art, evaluation and user attitudes. *SKASE Journal of Translation and Interpretation* 8(1).

Zetzsche, Jost. 2015. 'Lilt'. MultiLingual, Dec 15. https://multilingual.com/articles/lilt-2/.

Joke Daems is assistant professor human–computer interaction at Ghent University. Their 2016 PhD thesis on differences between human translation and post-editing received the CIUTI PhD Award. Their research focuses on the impact of translation technology on translation, translators and society (e.g. gender bias). Although mainly involved in research, they have taught numerous classes on translation technology and MTPE.

Who's afraid of literary post-editing? Performances and Reflections of Student Translators

Yu Hao, Ke Hu, and Anthony Pym

Abstract Despite the advances in the automation of translation processes, several discourses insist that there is still a privileged status for the non-automated human, especially in idealized conceptualisations of literary translation. Empirical data from experiments with 141 students show general awareness of trade-offs between the advantages and disadvantages of post-editing texts by Agatha Christie. Although machine translation was assumed to suffer from excessive literalism, it was also criticized for being deceptively fluent. Comparison of work by post-editors and from-scratch translators shows that the former tends to use risk transfer, trusting machine translation in situations of uncertainty, while the latter are more prone to risk taking. The two strategies lead to errors of different kinds, with the from-scratch translations having significantly fewer errors than the results of post-editing, with the exception of the "deviations" resulting from excessive risk taking.

1 Introduction

The impact of automation on translation practices has led to deep changes in attitudes over the years. For decades, professional translators and translator trainers assured the world that "machine translation will never work", assuming that the complex nature of the task, and indeed of language itself, would ensure long-term resistance.

With the improvement of machine translation systems that entrenched belief has given way to recognition that some translation tasks can be assisted by technology. The concept of "computer aided translation" was quickly enshrined for translation

Y. Hao (✉) · K. Hu · A. Pym
The University of Melbourne, Melbourne, VIC, Australia
e-mail: haoyh2@unimelb.edu.au

K. Hu
e-mail: ke.hu@unimelb.edu.au

A. Pym
e-mail: anthony.pym@urv.cat

Y. Peng et al. (eds.), *New Advances in Translation Technology*, New Frontiers in Translation Studies, https://doi.org/10.1007/978-981-97-2958-6_13

memory software. That change to "working with" technology has in turn called for new conceptual work on the exact role and agency of the human translator.

Of very particular interest here is the exceptional status accorded to *literary* translation, which in many respects represents the ultimate stronghold of human agency. Even when automation provides benefits for the productivity, coherence, and terminology for all kinds of pragmatic texts, the field of the literary is supposed to be ruled by quite different values. Here we ask whether there are changes on that front. One might expect continued discursive resistance from entrenched translators and translator trainers, who climbed to the top of their professions using one set of technologies and thus have an active interest in casting doubt on more recent technologies. But are younger translators—in this case postgraduate students—still against the use of post-editing machine translations of literary texts? If so, why? And then, when they post-edit machine translation for literature, are the results really so bad? Do their opinions about literary post-editing correspond to what they actually do?

2 Literature Review

There have been numerous studies on resistance to translation technology. The early ALPAC report included an experiment where "most of the translators found postediting tedious and even frustrating" (1966, p. 96). Later complaints concerned translation memories losing the translator's unique voice (Bédard 2000), a criticism later repeated with respect to post-editing literary texts (Kenny and Winters 2020). O'Brien (2012) and Ehrensberger-Dow and O'Brien 2015) explored the "cognitive friction" produced when technologies interrupt the translator's immersion while translating, producing frustration. That frustration might then underlie reports of generally negative views of technology held by translators, translation students, and translation teachers across the board. Possible changes in attitudes might nevertheless be indicated by Vieira (2020), who reports that translators are against not so much the technologies themselves as the economic effects that might ensue, and Rico and González Pastor (2022, p. 190), who find that translation teachers are starting to express more positive values albeit still emphasizing the centrality of human agency. Torres-Simón and Pym (2021) nevertheless find that translation students still maintain negative opinions of post-editing even when it increases their productivity and terminology—empirical results need not change inherited presuppositions.

With respect to specifically literary translation, a long position paper by the Association pour la promotion de la traduction littéraire (2023) denounces translation technologies as dehumanizing the emotional and creative role of literary translators, at the same time as algorithms are "plundering what humans have created" (p. 4) and cannot actually translate, since only humans translate. This radical critique is unfortunately only supported by a trivial example of what is called "anchoring bias" (p. 7), where five students all gave the same translation because it was suggested by machine translation, whereas five students who did not have machine translation gave varied renditions. This kind of result merits more serious testing—we return to it below.

Stimulated by advances in neural machine translation, there has emerged a body of empirical research on literary machine translation. Most studies focus on the quality of raw machine translations of poetry (Greene et al. 2010; Genzel et al. 2010; Almahasees 2017; Humblé 2019; Seljan et al. 2020) and prose (Voigt and Jurafsky 2012; Jones and Irvine 2013; Toral and Way 2015a, b; Kuzman et al. 2019; Matusov 2019; Tezcan et al. 2019; Webster et al. 2020; Jiang and Niu 2022). In comparison, the *post-editing* of literary machine translation remains underexplored. While a few studies look at the reception of post-edited literary machine translations (Besacier and Schwartz 2015; Guerberof-Arenas and Toral 2020, 2022b; Hu 2022), other researchers examine the creativity of post-edited machine translation, understood by Şahin and Gürses (2019, 2021) to be the ability to generate non-literal translation, and as novelty (measured by the number of creative shifts) and acceptability (measured by the number of errors) in Guerberof-Arenas and Toral (2020, 2022a).

Only a few studies tap into attitudes to post-editing literary machine translations. Toral et al. (2018) compared the six professional literary translators' temporal, technical, and cognitive efforts when translating an English novel into Catalan from scratch and by post-editing machine translations generated by previously trained machine translation systems. They found that, in comparison with from-scratch translation, post-editing had less production time, fewer keystrokes, and fewer but longer pauses in the translation process. In a follow-up study, Moorkens et al. (2018) examined professional literary translators' attitudes to post-editing. All translators preferred translating from scratch to post-editing, even when they achieved an average productivity gain of 36% by post-editing. This dislike was attributed to the priming effect of the MT output, which conditioned them to translate less creatively.

Şahin and Gürses (2019) asked 21 translation students to post-edit a Turkish machine translation of excerpts from an English novel. They found that the post-editing was more literal than the published professional translations. They also found that most students preferred translating from scratch, arguing that post-editing was more difficult. Şahin and Gürses (2021) then analyzed nine professional translators' and eleven translation students' post-editing of passages from another English novel. Both groups expressed negative attitudes to post-editing, arguing that machine translation was "not yet able to contribute to literary translation from English into Turkish" (p. 197).

Guerberof-Arenas and Toral investigated the creativity of Catalan (2020, 2022) and Dutch (2022) translations in three modalities: raw machine translation, post-edited machine translation, and fully human translation by professionals. They report that, although post-editing increased the creativity of raw machine translations, the post-edited versions were of poorer quality and often not fit for publication. Post-hoc interviews showed that the translators believed that "MT can only be partially useful in literary translation" and that the MT outputs "act as a constraint to creativity" (pp. 204–205).

Hu (2022) tested the receptions of machine-translated prose and poetry by more than 130 readers and found that an initial distrust of literary machine translation contrasted with the readers' relative success in working with actual machine translations.

The studies thus show general agreement among both professional translators and students that post-editing has negative effects on literary translation, despite some clear productivity gains.

3 Methods

Here we are interested in whether the generally negative views found in the previous research are held by a younger generation of translation students. We are also concerned with the relation between students' opinions about literary machine translation and their actual performance when doing it, especially with respect to various kinds of "anchoring" in machine translation.

The participants in this study were students (n = 141) in the postgraduate course *Translation and Interpreting as Process* offered at the University of Melbourne for three consecutive years (2020, n = 58; 2021, n = 54; 2022, n = 29).[1] More than 90% of the participants were international students who used Chinese as their primary language. Despite adopting machine translation in assignments or for non-academic purposes, they had not had any formal training in post-editing, understood as the process whereby a human corrects machine-generated translations.

This was an elective course that focused on the central issues in process-based translation studies. The students were allowed to take this course at any stage of their postgraduate studies, without prerequisites. In this course, students experimented with the main variables in translation processes (e.g., directionality, speed, and revision) so as to reflect on efficiency and quality. One third of the course was dedicated to work with machine translation, translation memory suites, and other tools.

The data reported on in this study were collected through a classroom experiment completed in the post-editing module. The experiment was "lousy" (Pym 2009) in that it was only loosely controlled, the subjects were whichever students had enrolled, two different texts were used, machine translation evolved over the three years, and each experiment was completed in a class of about 90 min (leaving 20 min for in-class reports).

Students were invited to work in groups of four to render into Chinese an excerpt from Agatha Christie's *The Mysterious Affair at Styles* (177 words, used in 2020) or *Murder on the Orient Express* (207 words, used in 2021 and 2022).[2] In each group, half the members translated from scratch in Microsoft Word (hereafter called

[1] Ethics clearance was received from the Human Research Ethics Committees, Faculty of Arts, University of Melbourne (Ethics Authorization Number 21607). We thank all the students who gave individual permission for their translations and reflections to be used in this research.

[2] Receptions of machine translations into Dutch of the first chapter have been studied by Tezcan et al. (2019), Fonteyne et al. (2020), Webster et al. (2020), Colman et al. (2022), and into Chinese by Hu

"translators"), while the other half were asked to use Microsoft Word to post-edit MT output from DeepL ("post-editors"). Those who worked as translators could only use machine translation as a bilingual dictionary; all students were permitted to consult any web-based resources they liked.

Once completed, the translators and post-editors were asked to exchange their translations within their group and revise each other's work, using track changes and adding comments. That is, post-editors revised the from-scratch translations produced by their group members, and vice-versa. After the revisions, they were encouraged to compare the translations in terms of time taken and difficulties encountered, then collaboratively reflect on whether post-editing is suitable for literary texts. The students submitted their Chinese translations and individual reflective notes in English.

We divided the notes into two categories: for or against literary machine translation. An inductive thematic analysis then coded the data for perceived productivity and quality gains or losses; perceived human irreplaceability in literary translation: mention of emotions, creativity, or context-detection; use of rhetorical devices; and discursive presence of the translator. These bottom-up codes were organized around three recurring themes: speed, quality, and human centrality. These three themes were not mutually exclusive: one reflective note could address more than one theme.

The times taken were measured by seconds per word and an unpaired t-test, with the alpha value at 0.05. Quality was assessed by a NAATI-credited translator for Chinese-English. A bottom-up approach was then used to categorize inappropriate renditions at various levels with respect to both content and form.

4 Results

4.1 *Perceptions: For and Against Literary Machine Translation*

After their translation activity, we asked the students, "Do you think translators should render literary texts by post-editing machine translation? Why or why not?". Over two-thirds of the students (N = 98, 69.5%) expressed negative attitudes towards literary machine translation, while the rest (N = 43, 30.5%) believed post-editing *could* be used for literary texts. Slightly more post-editors (N = 24, 33.3%) demonstrated a positive attitude than did translators (N = 19, 27.5%) (Table 1).

We organized the responses around three recurring themes: speed, quality, and human centrality (Table 2). The positive and negative values were often expressed as trade-offs (Pym and Hu 2023), as in "MT is fast but of poor quality". Here we have categorized such cases under the value accorded the more weight. While speed and

(2022). The second text contains a dialogue where contextual cues became especially important to understand the intended meaning. This text was used from 2021 to test the performance of machine translation.

Table 1 Attitudes towards literary machine translation

	Positive	Negative	Total
Post-editors	24 (33.3%)	48 (66.7%)	72
Translators	19 (27.5%)	50 (72.5%)	69
Total	43 (30.5%)	98 (69.5%)	141

Table 2 Comments for and against literary machine translation by theme and value (N = 141)

Themes	N	Feedback category			
		Positive value	%	Negative value	%
T1 speed	34	29	66	15	34
T2 quality	57	23	40	34	60
T3 human centrality	124	–	–	–	–

quality were discussed with both positive and negative values, opinions on human centrality were uniformly against machine translation.

With respect to speed, some saw post-editing as counterproductive (N = 15): "*post-editing is time-consuming as the machine tends to produce literal and decontextualised translations.*" It was perceived to be no faster than translating from scratch, as the translator must work constantly to fix "*various types of errors such as omissions and mismatches of names or pronouns*". That said, more (N = 29) believed post-editing could speed up the process: "*MT can provide a gist of meaning in no time*", allowing one to concentrate on the important problems.

The "quality" comments mostly saw machine translations as "unnatural", "stiff", "unreadable", and "losing literariness". However, some students expressed an opposite concern: "*MT output sometimes sounds so fluent but is actually misleading and inaccurate*". Fluency can thus be negative. Machine translation was also seen as enhancing quality: "*MT helps translators easily grasp the big picture of what the original text is about*", providing a "*good place to start*".

The theme of human centrality emerged from 124 comments. Even those in favor of post-editing insisted that literary translation required human cognition. The various reasons can be organized around five features: voice (N = 19), creativity (N = 40), context detection (N = 25), rhetoric (N = 23), and emotions (N = 17).

4.1.1 Human as Voice

Literary translators sometimes say they listen to the author's voice through a close analysis of stylistic features (Jansen 2019). Several students said post-editing interfered with this:

> My team members were all against using post-editing. We felt it made us do endless error picking and corrections of the MT [machine translation] output. We should have spent more time sensing the writing style of Christie and reflecting it in our translation.

> The "spirit" of a literary text is the tone and diction of the author. To reproduce this style is not something that can be accomplished by automation. Working from the MT to produce a stylistically appropriate translation is very counter-productive.

Others expressed concern that *translators* might lose their voice through post-editing. They emphasized that different translators' styles were homogenized when they worked from the same raw MT output[3]:

> And I'm concerned that [post-editing machine translation] will lead to a similarity in style. Machine translation had already translated everything. And we found that despite the minor adjustments made during the post-editing, the final texts all looked the same.

> For those translators who prioritise their own characteristics and styles, I think they are more inclined to translate on their own, that is without the help of machine translation. When using MT, their own style is largely erased. For the time being, I still believe human translators could do a better job in translating literary texts like novels and poems. A human translator can give their translation a "soul".

Some of the students further discussed the voice of "the machine", seen as unpleasant and inaesthetic noise: "*it is nearly inevitable for translators to be affected by the wording and writing style of the literal MT output, and therefore they will not be able to preserve the authentic beauty of the original text.*"

4.1.2 Human as Creativity

In opposition to machine translation, humans were assumed to use more unconventional language and make more creative changes: "*machines produce translations that could be limited to the literal meaning of the text, which hinders the purpose of most literary texts that require nuance and imagination in their translations.*" Post-editors were thus assumed to be "constrained by" and "locked into" the options offered by automation:

> Literary translation pays attention to artistry, which requires rich imagination and creativity. In my experience, when post-editing a text I only change some expressions and certain sentence structures to avoid mistakes instead of trying to recreate it. No matter how hard we post-edit it, we have the previous translation stuck in our mind, which limits our imagination.

Quite a few students believed post-editing disrupted the creative process, since it always gave a "standard answer" and made translators distrust their own intuitions.

---

[3] Here again an intriguing comparison can be made with early criticisms of translation-memory suites, which were criticized for including the voices of many translators, producing a "sentence salad" (Bédard 2000). The students' opposed assumption of *homogeneity* refers to the similarities between the students' translations, not to the many human translations that have been fed into the machine-translation database.

4.1.3 Human as Context-Awareness

Many students underscored the priority of context. Literary language was assumed to be self-referential, implicit, and thus reliant on literary context. Some related this to the style of Agatha Christie, who often uses dialogues that are highly context-dependent and full of pronouns. This means that translators have to lean on the setting to make sense of many references. Machine translation, on the other hand, was seen "decontextualised", failing to detect the "tone" and "between-the-lines meanings":

> In literary translation, we've seen many long, complicated, or ambiguous sentences, but the machine cannot make good use of context and is not able to catch the implied meaning as accurately as a human can.

Some students further asserted the importance of the historical and cultural context. Societal influences and the author's background provide clues to the intended meaning of the text.

4.1.4 Human as Rhetoric and Beauty

Literature was perceived as being distinguished by formal properties: "*we often encounter rhetoric and special writing techniques in literature, such as metaphor, metonymy, simile and so forth*". Literary writers were thus portrayed as gifted users of language, requiring their translators to have "*an excellent command of the target language*". This was seen as being beyond the capabilities of machine translation, which therefore "*spoils the beauty of the literary text*" and generates "*stiff and boring*" texts.

4.1.5 Human as Emotion

There was a strong belief that "*MT can understand neither the meaning nor the emotions behind the words in literature*". Literary language was perceived to be affect-eliciting and emotionally dense:

> Literary translation is a process that requires human involvement, human beings' emotions, sentiments, knowledge and common sense, etc. The machine translates mechanically, it can only translate the sentence and would fail to translate the emotions behind the text.

Some students further highlighted the risk of literary MT sending readers away: "*If I were the reader, I would not be interested in reading a text like this.*"

4.2 Are There Any Gains?

We now turn to students' performances. Did the use of post-editing enhance their productivity? The two modes were first compared for speed (Fig. 1).

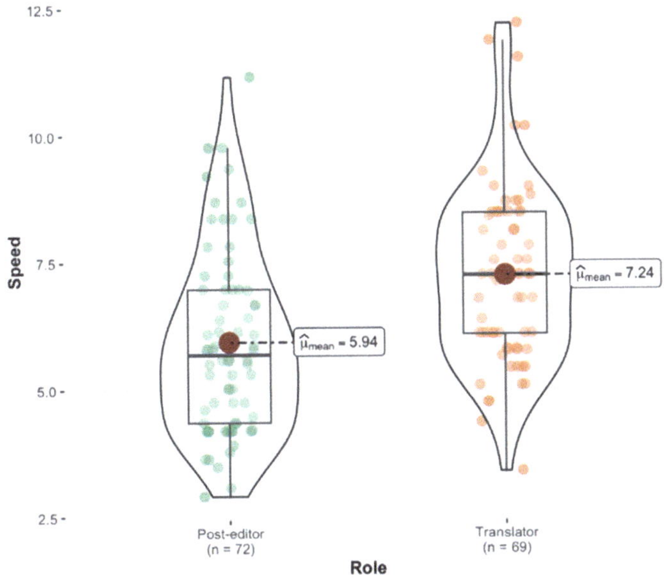

Fig. 1 Seconds per word by post-editors and translators

On average, it took post-editors 5.95 s to produce a word, whereas translators needed 7.24. The t-test shows a significant effect ($p < 0.001$): post-editing was faster than translating from scratch by about 18%.

As for quality of style (Fig. 2), we observed 2.06 ($SD = 0.85$) errors per 100 words by the post-editors and 1.28 errors by translators ($SD = 0.70$), which a t-test indicated was statistically significant ($p < 0.001$): post-editors tended to have more stylistic errors. As for semantics (Fig. 3), the post-editors made on average 1.27 errors ($SD = 0.68$) per 100 words, whereas the translators had 1.30 ($SD = 0.70$), which was not statistically significant ($p = 0.873$).

This means post-editing was advantageous for speed but disadvantageous for style and neutral for semantics. However, that broad analysis means little until we look at the kinds of problems involved, especially with respect to the possibly negative effects of MT anchoring and the kinds of creativity that involve more than error-avoidance.

As mentioned, we used a bottom-up approach to categorize inappropriate renditions at various levels. This grouped semantic errors as "distortions", "additions", "omissions", or "indecision" (where more than one rendition was provided). Stylistic errors were then grouped under "punctuation", "spelling", and "grammar", as well as renditions that sounded wrong even though they did not violate any rules overtly.

Comparison of the types of errors by each group (Table 3) shows that the translators scored better in all categories except "distortion", where they did considerably worse.

We now discuss examples of each kind of error and the creative solutions that some students found.

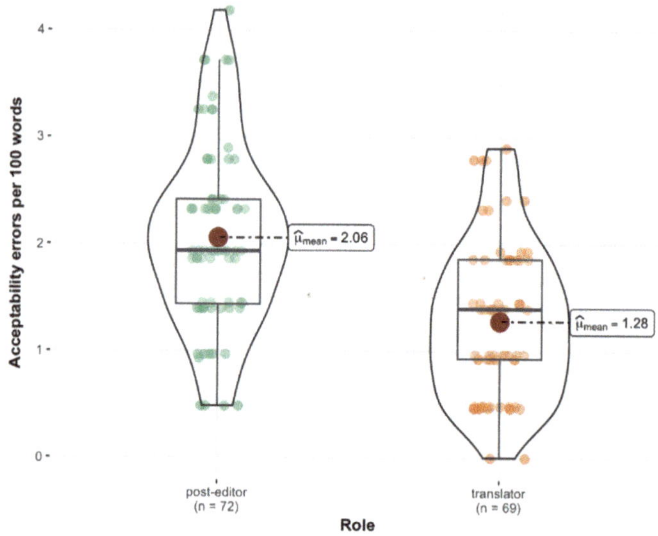

Fig. 2 Stylistic errors by post-editors and translators

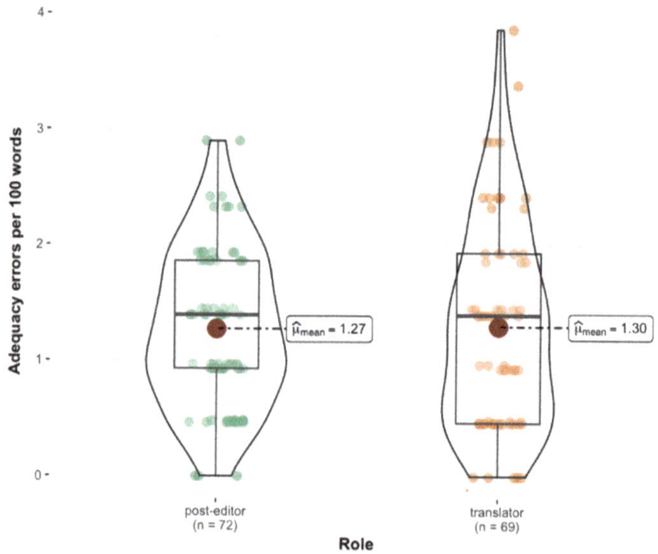

Fig. 3 Semantic errors by post-editors and translators

Table 3 Types of errors per person in post-edited and from-scratch translations

Type	Subtype	Post-editors		Translators	
		Raw	Per person	Raw	Per person
Semantic errors	Distortion	105 (16%)	1.46	123 (29%)	1.78
	Addition	63 (9%)	0.87	35 (8%)	0.50
	Omission	53 (8%)	0.74	45 (11%)	0.65
	Indecision	10 (1%)	0.14	1 (0%)	0.01
Stylistic errors	Punctuation	103 (15%)	1.43	48 (11%)	0.69
	Characters	44 (7%)	0.61	15 (4%)	0.21
	Grammar	46 (7%)	0.64	13 (3%)	0.19
	Idiomatic use	182 (27%)	2.53	96 (23%)	1.40
	Names and terms	67 (8%)	0.94	44 (8%)	0.63

4.2.1 Semantic Errors

Distortion

Although there were many distortions of meaning in both groups, the from-scratch translators strangely had 18% more. The post-editors generally picked up distortions from the MT output, whereas the translators were more prone to creative guessing:

ST[4]: I came out this way two years ago and spent three days in Istanbul then.

MT/PEMT1: 我两年前就这样出来了,然后在[伊]斯坦布尔呆[待]了三天 [I came out like this two years ago and then stayed in Istanbul for three days.]

PEMT2: "两年前出来时就坐的这辆火车" [When I came out two years ago, I took this same train.]

HT1: 我两年前出来时就坐的这辆车" [When I came out two years ago, I took this same car.]

HT2: "我两年前就出发了" [I set off two years ago.]

Here Miss Debenham mentions she had followed the same route previously and spent time in Istanbul, implying she was now going directly to England. The phrase "came out this way" means following a specific route. However, the literal proposal by DeepL as "就这样出来了" [came out like this] is less specific, even suggesting release from prison. Many post-editors did not make changes here and thus failed to nail down the meaning. Others tried to improve the MT and thereby introduced slight distortions. Quite a few gave "两年前出来时就坐的这辆火车" [when I came out two years ago, I took the same train] (PEMT 2). This risks inaccuracy since it shifts the focus from the route to the train, although it is not wholly wrong.

[4] ST = start text; MT = machine translation; PEMT = post-edited machine translation; HT = from-scratch human translation.

As the numbers suggest, the translators tended to be wider of the mark. Some did not realize this conversation was on the Orient Express and rendered the reference as "我两年前就做过这辆车" [I took this *car* two years ago] (HT1) or as "我两年前就出发了" [I embarked two years ago] (HT2), suggesting an ongoing journey of two years or more.

This is a case where post-editors could resolve uncertainty in a risk-averse way by trusting the machine translation ("I'm not sure what this means, but the machine might") whereas the from-scratch translators did not have this option and were obliged to take greater risks, with rather unhappier results. This logic seems to hold for most of the errors in this category.

Addition

Addition errors involve superfluous elements that change the meaning. The post-editors actually made more additions, which must be surprising if one believes machine translations are literal. Here is an example:

> ST: We had a good yarn about old times…
>
> MT, PEMT: 我们聊了一聊过去的趣事 [We had a chat about past amusing anecdotes.]
>
> HT1: 我们对于过去的事情谈天说地，旧时的岁月充满着令人惊奇的又刺激的故事 [We talked extensively about the past, which was filled with astonishing and thrilling stories.]
>
> HT2: 我们谈论了很多过去那些美好的时光 [We discussed many of those beautiful moments from the past.]

The reference is to a pleasant conversation about the past. Most post-editors retained the MT output "聊了一聊过去的趣事" [had a chat about past amusing anecdotes]. While "过去的趣事" [past amusing anecdotes] is semantically similar to "往事" [the past], the original refers to shared past experiences in general, making "趣事" [past amusing anecdotes] an unnecessary specification.

On the other hand, some translators misinterpreted "good" as a modifier of "old times," resulting in added specifications such as "令人惊奇的又刺激的故事" [astonishing and thrilling stories] (HT1) or "过去美好的时光" [beautiful moments from the past] (HT2).

In this way, the additions by the post-editors were generally closer to the text than those made by the from-scratch translators, who were more prone to be creatively wrong.

Omission

Unjustified omission occurred when missing content affected the overall meaning. The post-editors made slightly more omissions, which is once again surprising if one considers that machine translation is literal. But there is a catch here:

ST: They discussed old Tommy Somebody and old Reggie Someone Else.

MT: 他们讨论了老汤米某人和老雷吉某人 (literal translation)

The terms "Somebody" and "Somebody Else" are used as comical surnames. Although DeepL provided reasonable renditions, most post-editors opted to *abandon* them, rendering "Someone Else" as "等人" [and others] or "还有其他一些老伙计" [and other old buddies]. That is, the ST was so creative that, when the MT followed it literally, the post-editors decided not to trust it and took a stab in the dark. On the other hand, some translators legitimately omitted both "Someone" and "Someone Else" since the phrase "老汤米和老雷吉" [good mate Tommy and Reggie] adequately conveys the meaning.

ST: Colonel Arbuthnot talked of the Punjab and occasionally asked the girl a few questions about Baghdad *where*, it became clear, she had been in a post as governess.

PEMT: 上校谈到旁遮普邦,并且偶尔会问这个女孩一些关于巴格达的问题,很明显,她曾担任过家庭教师 [The colonel talked about Punjab and occasionally asked the girl some questions about Baghdad. It was evident that she had served as a governess.]

HT: 阿巴斯诺特上校谈到旁遮普(印度西北部的一地方), 时不时询问那个女孩几个关于巴格达 (伊拉克)的问题, 原来她曾做过一段时间的家庭教师 [Colonel Arbuthnot talked about Punjab (a region in northwest India) and occasionally asked the girl a few questions about Baghdad (Iraq). It turned out she had been a governess for a period of time.]

Here the relative adverb "where" has disappeared from most of the post-edited translations and some of the from-scratch translations. It provides information about where Miss Debenham had been working. Its omission thus obscures the reason why she and Colonel Arbuthnot have shared friends in Baghdad (mentioned in the following sentences). In the Chinese translation, "在那里" [there] should thus be explicitly mentioned.

This was problematic for all students. The machine translation omitted "where", so most post-editors followed suit: in situations of uncertainty, follow the one lead you have. The from-scratch translators, on the other hand, seem to have used omission as a more clearly risk-averse strategy: when in doubt, leave it out.

Indecision

In some cases, more than one rendition is provided for the one translation unit. This occurred much more frequently among post-editors (n = 10) than from-scratch translators (n = 1). Some post-editors put their alternative renditions in brackets, indicating a lack of confidence in the MT suggestions. In some cases, both options could be considered acceptable, such as the raw MT "问" [ask] and its edited version "(询)问" [ask or inquire]. On the other hand, the post-editors ought to have confidently changed "(另外)两人" [(The other) two people] into the accurate rendition "两人" [These two people].

4.2.2 Stylistic Errors

Punctuation

Numerous punctuation errors were found in both modes, although most were by post-editors. En-dashes and em-dashes were directly copied to the Chinese renditions, which is not in accordance with Chinese punctuation rules. All students experienced difficulties with the usage of commas and full stops.

In Chinese, translations of English names usually often have a "·" inserted between the two parts. It is unacceptable to replace "·" with a space, as many translators did. Fortunately, this issue did not appear in post-edited translations as it was handled well by DeepL.

Chinese Characters

The post-editors were significantly more prone to use incorrect characters than were the translators. Most of their errors were initially in the machine translation. For example, the verb "待" [to stay] was misspelled as one of its homophones "呆" [dazed or bewildered]. This mistake was not corrected by many post-editors, whereas the from-scratch translators were much less likely to make this kind of error.

Grammar

The following examples illustrate grammatical errors that were consistently made by post-editors but were not found in the translations created from scratch.

ST: …thought Hercule Poirot to himself with some amusement.

MT/PEMT: …赫尔克里·波洛有些好笑地暗自想道 [Hercule Poirot amusedly thought to himself.]

Here "有些好笑地" [with some amusement] is an adverbial phrase modifying "暗自想道" [thought to himself] and conveys the nuance of amusement felt by the subject when performing this action. A better rendition would be "赫尔克里·波洛暗自想到, 感到有些好笑" [Hercule Poirot thought to himself, feeling amused]. The explicitation "感到" avoids the possible reading where Poirot appeared funny or ridiculous to others.

ST: He made a kind of clumsy little bow.

MT/PEMT: 他做了一个笨拙的小鞠躬 (literal translation)

Here most post-editors used the literal translation provided by the machine translation: "make a" + "bow." However, in Chinese this action should be expressed by a verb. A more appropriate translation would be "笨拙地鞠了一躬" [took a bow clumsily].

These are both cases where the post-editors relied too heavily on the machine translation.

Idiomatic Usage

Some errors were grammatically correct but inappropriate. They often occurred when post-editors did not shift from the literal MT output or when some translators similarly copied the original sentence structure:

> ST: I will therefore briefly set down the circumstances which led to my being connected with the affair.
>
> MT/PEMT: 于是,我要简单地叙述一下使我与这件事有牵连的情况 (literal translation)

In Chinese, it is more idiomatic to switch the perspective to something like "我是如何与这件事产生关联的" [how I got to be connected with this affair]. Once again, the post-editors followed a relatively literal MT suggestion.

Names

Most renditions of names do not explicitly violate any grammar rules but may deviate from general norms. The post-editors unanimously followed DeepL's rendition of Hercule Poirot as 白罗 (Bai Luo), whereas published translations give 大侦探波洛 (Buo Luo, the grand detective). Certain names of people (Arbuthnot and Hercule Poirot) and locations (Punjab and Baghdad) were transcribed in English in the MT output and were similarly not translated by both groups. A more normal approach is to translate these names phonetically, perhaps with the original name in parentheses.

The errors identified in from-scratch translations were less unanimous. Some translators did not adhere to the existing Chinese translation of Punjab, 旁遮普, but created their own translation by copying the original sounds, e.g., 庞佳普. Additionally, some translators assigned characters with feminine connotations to the names of men. For example, "old Tommy" was rendered as "老汤美", where the last character "美" (beauty) is often associated with women.

5 Discussion

Our finding that post-editing increases speed by some 18% is no news—it is much lower than the 36% reported by Moorkens et al. (2018), and any result will depend very much on the nature of the text chosen.

Similarly unsurprising would seem the range of opinions expressed by the students with respect to human centrality in literary translation: the exceptionalism of the literary text seems to be very much intact. The students also picked up the negative effects of machine-translation anchoring (Sect. 4.1.2 above) and related it to the greater creativity of human translators—machine translation was supposed to be literal, whereas humans were not, much in line with the general tenor of previous studies. That said, just under a third of the students allowed that machine translation *could* be used for literature (Table 1), indicating a positive attitude that is much higher than reports in previous studies (especially Şahin and Gürses 2019). This could indicate a changing of outlooks, as picked up in some of the recent literature (Nunes Vieira 2020; Rico and González Pastor 2022). Further, that percentage was 33.3% among those who had actually just done literary post-editing before answering the question, as opposed to 27.5% of those who had not, which suggests that use of machine translation can improve attitudes towards it—contradicting Torres-Simón and Pym (2021), who found that students were opposed to post-editing even when they objectively gained from it.

Possible novelty might also lie in the students' criticism of the "deceptive fluency" of machine translation (Sect. 4.1 above), which would seem to contradict assumptions of literalness. This could be attributed to the improving quality of machine translation. In the days of rule-based machine translation, the extreme nature of the errors was a cognitive advantage when compared with the fuzzy matches produced by translation memory suites. The former could be identified immediately, whereas the latter required careful attention to spot the differences. These days, mistranslations read so well that they require serious cognitive effort to correct—a phenomenon that is being further enhanced by AI-based text generation systems.

This deceptive fluency of machine translation would then explain why some students complained that post-editing made them distrust their own intuitions (Sect. 4.1.2), which in turn explains not only the traces of indecision (Sect. 4.2.1.4) but also the many cases where error ensued from excessive trust in an MT suggestion.

These differences can be understood in terms of risk management, which may require a short explanation. When a French literary translators' manifesto against AI decries the "anchoring bias" of post-editing (2023, p. 7), they refer to a study where, in Hemingway's "A Very Short Story", the phrase "Luz sat on the bed" was translated differently by from-scratch translators (it could mean "Luz sat down" or "Luz was sitting") but the same way by student post-editors (Kolb 2010). This is supposedly proof that machine translation kills creativity. However, in this particular case, there is nothing to be gained or lost by either of the two ways of rendering the verb: nothing else in the story depends on whether she was sitting or sat down, so there is nothing at stake—if there were, Hemingway would have written "sat down" or "was sitting". In terms of game theory (Levý 1967/2000), no other move depended on this one. In that case, it is rational for a translator to follow the path of least effort and copy the machine translation proposal. Why vary for the sake of variation?

In contradistinction, all the examples we have presented here involve choices where there *is* something at stake, either in other parts of the text (Sect. 4.2.1) or in relation to grammatical and stylistic conventions (Sect. 4.2.2), where the translator's credibility is at risk. In the instances of uncertainty and hence variation in solutions, the post-editors and translators seem to have behaved quite differently, even when the outcomes are quantitatively similar. In the cases we have called "distortion", translators often appear to have felt obliged to risk a creative interpretation, resulting in higher percentages of error in this category (Sect. 4.2.1.1), whereas the post-editors could transfer that risk to the machine translation proposal, which presumably sounded plausible. This risk transfer in post-editing is what others criticize as "anchoring": sometimes it was successful, not just in significantly limiting distortions but also in the use of additions (Sect. 4.2.1.2) and the punctuation of names (Sect. 4.2.2.5); other times it was unsuccessful, as in the use of dashes (Sect. 4.2.2.1), Chinese characters (Sect. 4.2.2.2) and the transcription of names (Sect. 4.2.2.5). Post-editing also limited the successful use of omission as a risk-averse strategy (Sect. 4.2.1.3), basically because omission did not enter into the machine-translation algorithms used at the time—although it does figure in the algorithms of AI-based automatic text generation.

We thus find that the students' relative distrust of machine translation in their commentaries broadly corresponds to something of what happened in their performances: there is empirical justification for a reasoned, focused distrust of machine translation, and a significant number of errors did indeed ensue from excessive risk transfer to an automatic system. At the same time, it cannot be assumed that machine translations are limited to literal renditions, just as it cannot be supposed that all risk-taking by from-scratch translators resulted in successful literary translation. At the end of the day, as has long been known (ALPAC 1966), post-editing is of most assistance to the translators who need the most help.

6 Concluding Remarks

We have found indications that attitudes to the post-editing of literary texts may be becoming more positive among students, even while the centrality of human agency remains ideologically absolute. The post-editors in this study frequently adopted a risk-transfer strategy, choosing to trust machine-translation proposals in situations of uncertainty, as opposed to the more risk-taking strategies evident among the from-scratch translators. In some respects, the trust placed in machine-translation proposals had positive effects, especially in limiting the number of distortions due to unjustified guessing—risk taking always involves greater exposure to failure. In most other respects, however, the quality of the post-editing was inferior to that of from-scratch translations, justifying the students' insistence on human centrality.

Our conclusions here might nevertheless be considered temporary to the extent that they are based on a post-editing practice that started from just one machine-translation solution for each problem. This is the kind of machine translation that literary translators claim can "intoxicate your brain" or restrain like a "corset" (Guerberof-Arenas and Toral 2022b, pp. 21, 22). Our technologies are becoming more interactive and less restrictive. Systems including DeepL and Lilt increasingly offer the translator a range of alternative solutions to choose from (as indeed dictionaries have always done), adjusting the sentence as selections are made. These more interactive post-editing processes necessarily reduce the temptation to trust just one machine-translation proposal; they thereby increase the role of human agency in post-editing. These effects have been tested in the field of legal translation (Briva-Iglesias et al. 2023) but remain to be explored for the translation of literature.

References

Almahasees, Z.M. 2017. Machine translation quality of Khalil Gibran's The Prophet. *Arab World English Journal* 1 (4): 151–159.

ALPAC. 1966. *Languages and machines: computers in translation and linguistics. A report by the Automatic Language Processing Advisory Committee, Division of Behavioral Sciences.* Washington DC: National Academy of Sciences, National Research Council.

Association pour la promotion de la traduction littéraire. 2023. AI and literary translation: translators call for transparency, trans. Shaun Whiteside. https://www.atlas-citl.org/tribune-ia.

Bédard, Claude. 2000. Mémoire de traduction cherche traducteur de phrases. *Traduire* 186: 41–49.

Besacier, L., and L. Schwartz. 2015. Automated translation of a literary work: a pilot study. In *Proceedings of the Fourth Workshop on Computational Linguistics for Literature*, 114–122. Association for Computational Linguistics.

Briva-Iglesias, V., S. O'Brien, and B. R. Cowan. 2023. The impact of traditional and interactive post-editing on machine translation user experience, quality, and productivity. *Translation, Cognition & Behavior*. https://doi.org/10.1075/tcb.00077.bri.

Colman, T., M. Fonteyne, J. Daems, N. Dirix, and L. Macken. 2022. GECO-MT: The Ghent Eye-tracking Corpus of Machine Translation. In *Proceedings of the 13th International Conference on Language Resources and Evaluation (LREC 2022)*, 29–38. ELRA.

Dunđer, I., S. Seljan, and M. Pavlovski. 2020. Automatic machine translation of poetry and a low-resource language pair. In *2020 43rd International Convention on Information, Communication and Electronic Technology (MIPRO)*, 1034–1039. IEEE.

Ehrensberger-Dow, M., and S. O'Brien. 2015. Ergonomics of the translation workplace: Potential for cognitive friction. *Translation Spaces* 4 (1): 98–118.

Fonteyne, M., A. Tezcan, and L. Macken. 2020. Literary MT under the magnifying glass: assessing the quality of an NMT-translated Agatha Christie novel. In *Proceedings of the Twelfth Language Resources and Evaluation Conference*, 3790–3798. ELRA.

Genzel, D., J. Uszkoreit, and F. Och. 2010. "Poetic" statistical machine translation: rhyme and meter. In *Proceedings of the 2010 Conference on Empirical Methods in Natural Language Processing*, 158–166. Association for Computational Linguistics.

Greene, E., T. Bodrumlu, and K. Knight. 2010. Automatic analysis of rhythmic poetry with applications to generation and translation. In *Proceedings of the 2010 Conference on Empirical Methods in Natural Language Processing*, 524–533. Association for Computational Linguistics.

Guerberof-Arenas, A., and A. Toral. 2020. The impact of post-editing and machine translation on creativity and reading experience. *Translation Spaces* 9 (2): 255–282.

Guerberof-Arenas, A., and A. Toral. 2022a. CREAMT: Creativity and narrative engagement of literary texts translated by translators and NMT. In *Proceedings of the 23rd Annual Conference of the European Association for Machine Translation*, 355–356.

Guerberof-Arenas, A., and A. Toral. 2022b. Creativity in translation: machine translation as a constraint for literary texts. *Translation Spaces* 11 (2): 184–212.

Hu, K. 2022. *Can machine translation be used for literary texts? Evidence from a reception study.* Doctoral diss., The University of Melbourne.

Humblé, P. 2019. Machine translation and poetry. The case of English and Portuguese. *Ilha Do Desterro* 72: 41–56.

Jansen, H. 2019. I'm a translator and I'm proud: How literary translators view authors and authorship. *Perspectives* 27 (5): 675–688. https://doi.org/10.1080/0907676X.2018.1530268.
Jiang, Y., and J. Niu. 2022. How are neural machine-translated Chinese-to-English short stories constructed and cohered? An exploratory study based on theme-rheme structure. *Lingua* 273: 103318.
Jones, R., and A. Irvine. 2013. The (un) faithful machine translator. In *Proceedings of the 7th Workshop on Language Technology for Cultural Heritage, Social Sciences, and Humanities*. Association for Computational Linguistics.
Kenny, D., and M. Winters. 2020. Machine translation, ethics and the literary translator's voice. *Translation Spaces* 9 (1): 123–149.
Kolb, W. 2010. 'Who are they?' Decision-making in literary translation. In *Tracks and Treks in Translation Studies*, ed. C. Way et al., 207–221. Benjamins.
Kuzman, T., Š. Vintar, and M. Arcan. 2019. Neural machine translation of literary texts from English to Slovene. In *Proceedings of the Qualities of Literary Machine Translation*, 1–9, August. European Association for Machine Translation.
Levý, J. 1967/2000. Translation as a decision process. In *The Translation Studies Reader*, ed. L. Venuti, 148–159. Routledge.
Matusov, E. 2019. The challenges of using neural machine translation for literature. In *Proceedings of the Qualities of Literary Machine Translation*, 10–19. European Association for Machine Translation.
Moorkens, J., A. Toral, S. Castilho, and A. Way. 2018. Translators' perceptions of literary post-editing using statistical and neural machine translation. *Translation Spaces* 7 (2): 240–262.
O'Brien, S. 2012. Translation as human–computer interaction. *Translation Spaces* 1 (1): 101–122.
Pym, A. 2009. Using process studies in translator training. Self-discovery through lousy experiments. In *Methodology, Technology and Innovation in Translation Process Research*, ed. S. Göpferich, F. Alves, and I. M. Mees, 135–156. Copenhagen: Samfundslitteratur.
Pym, A., and K. Hu. 2023. Trade-offs in translation effects. Illustrations and methodological concerns. Unpublished manuscript.
Rico, C., and D. González Pastor. 2022. The role of machine translation in translation education: A thematic analysis of translator educators' beliefs. *Translation and Interpreting* 14(1): 177–197. https://www.transint.org/index.php/transint/article/view/1341/408.
Şahin, M., and S. Gürses. 2019. Would MT kill creativity in literary retranslation?. In *Proceedings of the Qualities of Literary Machine Translation*, 26–34.
Şahin, M., and S. Gürses. 2021. English-Turkish literary translation through human-machine interaction. *Tradumàtica* 19: 171–203.
Seljan, S., I. Dunđer, and M. Pavlovski. 2020. Human quality evaluation of machine-translated poetry. In *Proceedings of the 43rd International Convention on Information, Communication and Electronic Technology (MIPRO)*, 1040–1045. IEEE.
Tezcan, A., J. Daems, and L. Macken. 2019. When a 'sport' is a person and other issues for NMT of novels. In *Proceedings of Machine Translation Summit XVII*, 40–49. European Association for Machine Translation.
Toral, A., and A. Way. 2015a. Machine-assisted translation of literary text: A case study. *Translation Spaces* 4 (2): 240–267.
Toral, A., and A. Way. 2015b. Translating literary text between related languages using SMT. In *Proceedings of the Fourth Workshop on Computational Linguistics for Literature*, 123–132.
Toral, A., M. Wieling, and A. Way. 2018. Post-editing effort of a novel with statistical and neural machine translation. *Frontiers in Digital Humanities* 5 (9): 1–11.
Torres-Simón, E., and A. Pym. 2021. La confianza de los estudiantes de traducción en la traducción automática: ¿demasiado buena para ser verdad? *Revista internacional se lenguas extranjeras* 15: 1–20.
Vieira, L. N. 2020. Automation anxiety and translators. *Translation Studies* 13 (1): 1–21. https://doi.org/10.1080/14781700.2018.1543613.

Voigt, R., and D. Jurafsky. 2012. Towards a literary machine translation: The role of referential cohesion. In *Proceedings of the NAACL-HLT 2012 Workshop on Computational Linguistics for Literature*, 18–25, June. Association for Computational Linguistics.
Webster, R., M. Fonteyne, A. Tezcan, L. Macken, and J. Daems. 2020. Gutenberg goes neural: Comparing features of Dutch human translations with raw neural machine translation outputs in a corpus of English literary classics. *Informatics* 7(3): 32–38.

Yu Hao is Lecturer in Translation Studies at the University of Melbourne in Australia. Her research interests are in translation curriculum development, translation-technology teaching, and international education studies.

Ke Hu is Lecturer in Translation Studies at the University of Melbourne in Australia. His research interests are in language technologies and translation reception research.

Anthony Pym is Distinguished Professor of Translation and Intercultural Studies at the Rovira i Virgili in Tarragona, Spain, and Extra-ordinary Professor at Stellenbosch University, South Africa. His research interests are in sociological approaches to intercultural communication.

Correction to: Cloud Technologies in Media Localisation (Subtitling and Revoicing)

Alejandro Bolaños García-Escribano

Correction to: Chapter "Cloud Technologies in Media Localisation (Subtitling and Revoicing)" in: Y. Peng et al. (eds.) *New Advances in Translation Technology*, New Frontiers in Translation Studies, https://doi.org/10.1007/978-981-97-2958-6_4

In the original version of the book, the following belated corrections have been incorporated: The author name "García-Escribano, A.B" has been changed to "Bolaños García-Escribano, A." in the Frontmatter, Chapter and references. The book has been updated with the changes.

The updated version of this chapter can be found at
https://doi.org/10.1007/978-981-97-2958-6_4

Y. Peng et al. (eds.), *New Advances in Translation Technology*, New Frontiers in Translation Studies, https://doi.org/10.1007/978-981-97-2958-6_14

SPRINGER NATURE

GPSR Compliance

The European Union's (EU) General Product Safety Regulation (GPSR) is a set of rules that requires consumer products to be safe and our obligations to ensure this.

If you have any concerns about our products, you can contact us on ProductSafety@springernature.com

In case Publisher is established outside the EU, the EU authorized representative is:

Springer Nature Customer Service Center GmbH
Europaplatz 3
69115 Heidelberg, Germany

FSC
www.fsc.org
MIX
Papier | Fördert
gute Waldnutzung
FSC® C083411

Kolibri 360 GmbH
Ferdinand-Jühlke-Straße 7
99095 Erfurt, Deutschland
produktsicherheit@kolibri360.de